Against Redemption

World War II: The Global, Human, and Ethical Dimension
G. Kurt Piehler, *series editor*

Against Redemption

Democracy, Memory, and Literature in Post-Fascist Italy

Franco Baldasso

Fordham University Press | New York 2022

Copyright © 2022 Fordham University Press

All rights reserved. No part of this publication may be reproduced, stored in a retrieval system, or transmitted in any form or by any means—electronic, mechanical, photocopy, recording, or any other—except for brief quotations in printed reviews, without the prior permission of the publisher.

Fordham University Press has no responsibility for the persistence or accuracy of URLs for external or third-party Internet websites referred to in this publication and does not guarantee that any content on such websites is, or will remain, accurate or appropriate.

Fordham University Press also publishes its books in a variety of electronic formats. Some content that appears in print may not be available in electronic books.

Visit us online at www.fordhampress.com.

Library of Congress Cataloging-in-Publication Data available online at https://catalog.loc.gov.

Printed in the United States of America

24 23 22   5 4 3 2 1

First edition

Contents

Introduction: Ruins and Debris of a Contested History   1

1. **After Italian Totalitarianism**   27
2. **The Language of Responsibility**   65
3. **Ghosts from a Recent Past**   96
4. **Carlo Levi on the Religion of the State**   140
5. **Curzio Malaparte, a Tragic Modernity**   172

Conclusion: Tearing Down the Monuments   199

Acknowledgments   205
Notes   209
Bibliography   265
Index   295

People think that suffering makes them better, saves their soul, earns them paradise, that it's the necessary condition of happiness. It would suffice to renounce paradise. As I did.

—Alberto Savinio, *New Encyclopedia*

Introduction
Ruins and Debris of a Contested History

One March day the following was found written on a house in Trastevere: "Hang in there, Americans, we're coming to liberate you soon."
—Paolo Monelli, *Rome 1943*

Against Redemption (and Beyond Neorealism)

Elsa Morante recorded Mussolini's death in her diary on May 1, 1945. She was in Rome, observing the excited atmosphere following national Liberation from Nazi and Fascist forces. Mussolini had been killed in Northern Italy by the partisans a few days earlier. The historic news compelled her to write a remarkable entry, a moral portrait of the man who had dominated Italian life for more than twenty years. Morante describes the dictator as the champion of a country and of a people with no sense of the common good:

> All these crimes of Mussolini's were tolerated, even encouraged and applauded. Now, a people that tolerates its leader's crimes becomes an accomplice to these crimes. If it encourages and applauds them, it becomes, worse than an accomplice, an instigator of these crimes. [. . .] Did the majority of the Italian population realize these acts were crimes? Almost always, they realized it, but such is the Italian people that it gives its votes to the *strong* rather than to the *just*; and if it's made to choose between *personal gain* and *duty*, even as it knows what its duty would be, it chooses personal gain.[1]

Morante's focus on the ethical accountability of the Italian people for crimes perpetrated by Fascism is quite at odds with the political narratives and historical interpretations of the following years. These narratives aimed at legitimizing the birth of the new Republic after the ordeal of the war, alleging that Italians preserved a moral stability, despite twenty years of dictatorship—an assessment that found in liberal philosopher Benedetto Croce its most outspoken advocate, even outside of Italy.[2] Neorealist movies and Resistance novels also largely depict the Italian people, particularly the lower classes, as essentially unaffected by Fascist propaganda.[3] Morante goes against the grain, ascribing the considerable support Mussolini and his regime enjoyed to a set of dishonest practices widespread among ordinary Italians. In her arguments, the writer avoids any recourse to cliché, like the supposedly defective "Italian character," which was common among her contemporary commentators as a means to trivialize the national catastrophe and its moral responsibility.[4] On the contrary, she singles out the conscious individual and collective choices that sustained Mussolini and the Fascist regime until the disaster of the war.

Little more than a year later, Morante and her husband, Alberto Moravia, hosted Curzio Malaparte for dinner at their house in Capri. At the time, Malaparte was at the peak of his literary fame: His *Kaputt*, published in 1944 in Naples while the war was still raging, quickly became a best seller across Europe. He wrote indignantly of the views Morante and Moravia expressed on that occasion in a letter to his old friend, Giuseppe Prezzolini:

> At a certain point, I don't know why, it occurred to Moravia to ask me, snickering, if I was sorry Italy had lost the war. Naturally I immediately responded that not only am I sorry Italy lost the war but I'm profoundly saddened it didn't win it. Protests from Moravia and his wife, who cried: "No, it's a good thing that Italy lost the war, it deserved worse, etc., etc."[5]

Malaparte concludes the letter with personal remarks on the state of the country after the military defeat: "I believe, dear Prezzolini, that the only way to react to wretchedness, to defeat, to dishonor, to humiliations, is to feel that one is Italian, to proclaim oneself Italian, etc." His response to Italy's fall was, as he himself states, "my country right or wrong."[6]

The private writings of Morante and Malaparte bear witness to the political and cultural discontent of these years on how to navigate the post-Fascist transition in national history. They sample a larger disagreement with the historical truthfulness of the *narratives of redemption* and of national rebirth ("Secondo Risorgimento") that took shape between the demise of Mussolini's regime in the summer of 1943 and the victory of the Christian Democrats over the Left in the April 18, 1948, general elections. Early postwar narratives of national redemption emerged as a response to the demands of the moment, yet they commanded public discourse and justified political agendas for decades to come.

Introduction: Ruins and Debris of a Contested History | 3

This book distinguishes, analyzes, and theorizes early postwar literary practices as a primary means of communicating intellectual dissent, challenging established categories of cultural analysis of the period, and shedding new light on the role of cultural policies in institutionalizing collective memory. By tracking the heated debates these publications sparked, this study elucidates the range and fluidity of opinions in the years before ideological struggle fossilized into Cold War oppositions and offers a more nuanced comprehension of the passage from Fascism to democracy in Italy.

Whether fostered by the Resistance myth of a new Risorgimento for the country or sanctioned by Benedetto Croce's authoritative reading of the Fascist *ventennio* as a "parenthesis" in Italian history, the idea of a collective redemption prompted interpretations of the recent national past not as one of catastrophe but as one of moral regeneration. "Redenzione" ("redemption"), with its overtly religious or mystical undertones, and the more secular concept of a moral "riscatto" (literally: "ransom") were ubiquitous terms in the 1943–1948 political debate, which appropriated and then normalized language and slogans of the armed insurrection against Fascism and the Nazi invaders. Political redemption and moral regeneration informed collective memory for decades to come, thereby legitimizing the new party system that granted continuity to the Italian state.[7]

The regenerative impact of Neorealism and its imaginary—easily the most influential cultural phenomenon of the period—reinforced a collective sense of a "new beginning," encouraging national reconstruction.[8] While documenting collective war traumas or the structural injustices of Italian society, cinematic gems such as Roberto Rossellini's *Rome Open City* (1945) or Luchino Visconti's *The Earth Trembles* (1948) concurrently paved a clear path to national and personal palingenesis, turning the singular private struggle into a meaningful fragment of the new national epic.[9] Far from achieving the lyrical intensity and complex hermeneutics of Rossellini or Visconti, the literary counterparts to these momentous films expressed, as Charles Leavitt recently put it, "the profound faith in the power of culture to redeem society, a faith that was frequently communicated in Christian terms."[10]

Together with its international outreach, the Neorealist imaginary nurtured a strong sense of collective awareness in the country's cultural and political elites, based on the countless vicissitudes of loss and hardship that Italians shared. The ills of recent history, which affected the lives of every single Italian, became the catalyst for a new perception of national belonging.[11] For early postwar intellectuals, Neorealism also represented a call for cultural renewal, showing and prescribing *new modalities* of intervention, far from the nationalist models of the Fascist regime.[12] In this sense, the oft quoted opening editorial of Elio Vittorini's influential journal *Il Politecnico* aptly exemplifies this larger cultural project: "Will we ever have a culture that knows how to protect man from his sufferings rather than limit itself to consoling him?"[13]

One of the consequences of this project's political soundness was the marginalization of other intellectual stances expressing different, if not opposite, views. Subsequent cultural accounts of the transition preferred to ignore inconvenient experiences like those typified by Morante and Malaparte's excerpts, as they irremediably complicate the frame of national narratives of redemption. Already in 1971, Romano Luperini, from a radical Marxist perspective, characterized the intellectual policies that guaranteed the continuity of the state as "the ideology of reconstruction"—that is, skirting around the unresolved shortcomings of democracy in post-Fascist Italy for the sake of national unity.[14] Two decades later, political journalist Enzo Forcella, who after the 1943 armistice *did not* join the Resistance, critically reexamined his own experience as unassimilable to any redemptive narrative: "It's a matter of months, years, of errors, of doubts, confusion, and uncertainties. What's difficult to accept is the repression, at times the actual erasure, of memory, of these doubts and of these errors. The acquiescence to conformism."[15]

Though its aesthetic dominated the early postwar conversation, Neorealism and the lively exchange inspired by its seminal works do not paint the full picture of the intellectual debate during the post-Fascist transition in Italy. As the excerpts taken from Morante and Malaparte make clear, the sense of a "new beginning" evoked by Neorealist aesthetics or the redemptive narratives of Italian history fell short and could not fully encompass the contradictory and often explosive cultural and social scenario of the time.[16]

Post–Cold War historiography has demonstrated how such a scenario was marked by the institutional and political continuity between the monarchy that supported Fascism and the newborn republic led by the center-right Catholic-oriented coalition.[17] Continuity of the state notwithstanding, private memory and public accounts of the time provide abundant evidence of how these years were also characterized by loss, trauma, and ideological uncertainties after more than twenty years of pervasive totalitarian pedagogy, the enduring effects of war, and of a long dictatorship that set to aggressively modernize the country.[18] In this complex situation, the memory of the Resistance as a second Risorgimento developed *also* as a result of the political needs of the moment. As Rosario Forlenza argued, "There is no doubt that it produced a distorted version of history. It denied public expression to those stories, experiences, and memories that did not fit with the Resistance as popular epic and founding moment for the new national identity."[19]

This study focuses on the heterodox voices that, during the transition, stressed not just the institutional but also the *cultural* continuity between the new democracy and the previous regime. Together with Morante and Malaparte, authors as diverse as Carlo Levi, Alberto Moravia, Umberto Saba, Ennio Flaiano, and Vitaliano Brancati challenged the assumption of Italy's moral regeneration after the break with Fascism. In the early postwar period, coming to terms with this historical continuity implied the haunting problem of Italian responsibility in WWII, the working through of national defeat, as well as the firm disavowal of past cultural and political models. Such past models engendered the definitive shipwreck—not the rebirth—of the national state born with the Risorgimento. According to these authors, only an uncompromising appraisal of the shipwreck could lead to emancipation from Fascism and its cultural models.

After experiencing Italian totalitarianism, the aforementioned authors spelled out from contrasting political positions a radical critique of beliefs like the preeminence of the State and of History over the lives of individuals. These beliefs were crucial principles of the Fascist ideology of Italian national history developed in particular by Giovanni Gentile and Gioacchino Volpe from the idealistic philosophy and historicism that characterized the previous liberal regime and that profoundly influenced early twentieth-century Italian culture.[20] In Fascist and liberal ideologies, these notions assumed the role of unquestionable, metaphysical premises for narratives of national redemption, to the detriment of what Carlo Levi calls in his commentaries the "life-in-relation" of the single person within their community.

The firm rejection of any political finalism—of any political theology—was, for these intellectuals, the starting point for a wealth of compelling inquiries into the debris of prewar ideas and the anxieties of early postwar society. With their writing, they ventured well beyond the strict borders of Italian history into the crisis of European civilization that led up to WWII and the Holocaust. Their works range from Malaparte's critical appraisal of the tragic contrast between the destructive power of modern technology and the fragility of creaturely life;[21] to Moravia's radical humanism and refusal of revolutionary politics; to Brancati's moral inquiry into his own personal responsibility with the regime; to Saba, Flaiano, and Morante's denunciation of how racial and gender biases predated, persisted, and survived the fall of Fascism; to Carlo Levi's envisioning of a new body politic constituted not on exclusion but on inclusion and pluralism.

In this study, I place these better-known writers in dialogue with remarkable but now almost forgotten figures such as Giuseppe Berto, Vittorio Zincone, and Guido Piovene, as well as other intellectuals who, during the transition, critically tackled singular aspects of the discourses of national redemption—from Alberto Savinio to Carlo Emilio Gadda to Primo Levi. As my research shows, the main political and cultural journals of the time, such as *Aretusa, Il Ponte, La Nuova Europa, Mercurio, Società, Italia Libera*, regardless of political affiliations, reviewed and debated these texts; their ideas circulated and were elaborated in original ways. In fact, as Daniela La Penna recently put it, "the postwar periodical press acted as a public performative space where individuals and groups verbalised their distance from the Fascist past and competed for new forms and sources of intellectual and political legitimation."[22]

The disquieting continuity between Fascist ideology and religious propaganda, crucial for the totalitarian project, was at the center of these authors' historical and existential reflections.[23] The nature of their investigations into totalitarianism, ideology, and redemptive readings of history obliged them to take a critical stance against the Communist credo and reexamine the significance of religion and the figure of Christ—an obsessive presence, from Berto to Malaparte to Carlo Levi—in modern society. Interestingly, the rejection of religion as both practice and narrative, and of the meaning of Christ as "Redeemer," goes hand in hand with the reappraisal of his figure as a symbol of victimization and tragic sacrifice—ultimately of scapegoating. These authors' criticism of ideology and religion, as well as their anarchical reading of the figure of Christ, could not but trigger violent opposition from the two new political and cultural forces that dominated postwar Italy, Christian Democracy (DC) and the Italian Communist Party (PCI), as well as from intellectuals aligned with either side.[24]

As writer Corrado Alvaro bitterly meditated in a 1946 article, the legacy of Fascism and the war had to be addressed as a *denial* of the millennial Christian civilization and of its most important achievements:

> Perhaps the most serious thing to happen to today's man has been the destruction of human solidarity; that is, of that concept—perhaps the highest in all of civilization, the greatest achievement of two thousand years of Christianity—by which the wrong of one, tolerated and unseen and not vindicated and not paid for and not redeemed, sooner or later becomes the wrong of all of society.[25]

The crisis denounced by Alvaro was far more radical than the institutional and political struggle for power over the peninsula. For authors such as Moravia, Saba, and Carlo Levi, the recent past had to be relentlessly revisited and reappraised in order to dismantle Fascist ideology. In their works, they signal the conspicuous persistence of totalitarian tenets, not least in what Brancati called "Pure Anti-Fascism."[26] The Fascist ideology of Italian history and its delusions was indeed the principal narrative of redemption to which these writers directed their critical attention. Formal and poetical elaboration, the unremitting search for a plurality of truths in history, and a sense of their literature as *testimony* are all concerns present in their writing in the attempt to break free from Fascist rhetoric and dismiss new redemptive narratives of the early postwar.

The "Political Wrong" of Literature during the Transition

Mussolini's regime grounded its legitimacy on the myths of Italian history, from the Roman Empire to the Renaissance. The totalitarian regime coalesced aggressive nationalism with the liberal secular religion of the fatherland in its ideology of national history. According to Claudio Fogu, Fascist propaganda asserted the absolute immanency and "history-making" quality of its own agency.[27] This conception interpreted the myths of national regeneration of WWI and the March on Rome as its "sacred" historical foundation. The March on Rome meant also the reclamation of the Roman imperial past, of which the regime proclaimed itself historical heir. Fascist rhetoric envisioned present individual sacrifice as an expiation leading to the future redemption of the entire nation from the errors of the past. The myth of Rome and its Empire is the more apparent, though not the only, facet of the historical rhetoric supporting the Italian state until the disaster of WWII.[28]

With the proclaimed goal of refashioning Italy as a world power, Mussolini and his acolytes turned this historicist mentality into reckless fanaticism. Still, a rhetorical mindset *preceded* Fascism.[29] During the transition, historicist self-representations of the country were heralded once again by liberal philosopher Benedetto Croce, reinvigorated by his international moral authority as a long-standing opposer of the regime. These historicist paradigms and rhetorical mindsets would survive in the parties that would later constitute the parliamentarian democracy, albeit profoundly transformed. After WWII, Christian Democrats and Communists both claimed their legitimacy as national forces not only from the founding event of the Resistance against Nazi-Fascism, but also as bearers of transnational narratives. Although utterly divergent in their ends, Catholic and Communist ideologies overcome the present by projecting political and existential fulfillment in the absolute future of Christianity and of the Revolution, respectively. After the establishment of a democratic and constitutional Italy in 1948, Catholic transcendence justified the seizure of power; Communist historical dialectics fostered stark parliamentarian opposition.[30]

Christian or secular, each dominant narrative of the recent past during the early postwar period featured eschatological pretenses. Croce interpreted Fascism as a "parenthesis" or as a "foreign sickness" in an organism that was otherwise healthy and that recuperated its true form through the antibodies gained during the war. With the myth of the "Secondo Risorgimento," anti-Fascist forces celebrated the armed Resistance as the moral rebirth of the nation. In the speeches of their leaders, from Actionist Ferruccio Parri to Monarchist Luigi Einaudi, the Risorgimento's moral legacy turned into a rhetorical call for action.[31] Its appeal also functioned as historical legitimization for the new political forces aiming to ground post-Fascist Italy in the values of the Resistance.[32] In the revealing words of anti-Fascist leader Leone Ginzburg, written shortly before his arrest and murder by the Fascists and published in early 1945, the Risorgimento implies for each Italian "a straightforward choice that precedes any historiographical evaluation. Indifference is not an option."[33]

Encompassing varying positions of the anti-Fascist political spectrum, the "Secondo Risorgimento" narrative thus encouraged many disillusioned young Italians who were willing to pay for their moral *riscatto* to take up arms for the anti-Fascist Resistance.[34] This younger generation was educated in the civic religion of the fatherland under Fascism but was disenchanted after the regime's ethical failures and military setbacks. As Giaime Pintor stressed in his influential 1943 article "The Time of Redemption," this trope epitomized the moral crisis that propelled personal participation within the collective struggle for national redemption, pitting the "new" revolution of his generation against the discredited and now disavowed Fascist revolution.[35]

Finally, Italian Communists, whose brigades were the majority among partisan organizations, perceived the Nazi-Fascist defeat as a confirmation of the Marxist master narrative and the triumph of the Soviet "new man." In the immediate postwar period, the promise of a new leftist society seemed imminent, galvanized by the striking victory of the Red Army on the Eastern Front and the landslide success of Clement Attlee's Labor Party in Great Britain in the 1945 elections.[36] Each of these readings of the recent past projected onto post-Fascist Italy, which had miraculously survived the war and a humiliating defeat, a lineage of progress and regeneration—a collective redemption after the shameful subjugation to Mussolini's regime. As David Ward argued, Catholic and Communist ideologies offered effective "patterns of conversion," able to seamlessly integrate Fascist and liberal ideologies of Italian history into *their* redemptive narratives.[37] More recently, Luca La Rovere pointed out how the debate on the legacy of Fascism in the early postwar mainly focused on how to fold into democracy the so-called Lictorian generation, who grew up during the totalitarian regime and was educated exclusively by Fascist organizations.[38] According to La Rovere, this public exchange considerably complicates the generally held paradigm of a widespread repression of the recent past during the transition, contesting the idea of a clear cultural caesura in 1940s Italy.[39] Once again, Enzo Forcella posed the question with distinctive lucidity. In his diaries he describes how "according to the anti-Fascist historiographical canon, the 'coming-of-age story' of the so-called 'Lictorian generation'" was established in those years along the lines of "the dialectical template of Error-Bewilderment-Redemption. The error of more or less convinced support for Fascism, the bewilderment provoked by the disaster of September 8, and the realization of one's political commitment, with the consequent redemption through participation in the Resistance."[40]

While these "patterns of conversion" sanctioned the new political power, they also obliterated the pioneering texts that nonaligned intellectuals elaborated in those same years on completely different bases. Mediated through fiction or autobiographical accounts, authors such as Saba, Berto, Brancati, and Flaiano represented the vacuum left behind by the demise of the ideology of Italian history that had sustained the state from the Risorgimento to WWII. If the nationalistic (and romantic) idea of Italy was dead, the space was open for alternative interpretations and proposals—not only for new political ideas about the future Italy but also for unconventional narratives about its past.

Italo Calvino famously recalled the early postwar period as characterized by an intense "craving to tell stories." This obsession with telling and retelling, mentioned in the 1964 preface to his 1947 novel *The Path to the Spiders' Nests*, was only partly due to the joy of regained freedom after the dictatorship's repression of discontent and the cruelties of the war.[41] After Fascism and its ideological monopoly of the national past, the truth of Italian history could not be but a plurality of *truths*, as the collective participation in the new democracy made clear. "And the harvest was ubiquitous," confirms Natalia Ginzburg in her 1963 autobiographical novel *Family Lexicon*, "because everyone wanted to take part in it. The result was a fortuitous fusion between the languages of poetry and politics, as they appeared intertwined together."[42]

In this sense, the collective struggle for national liberation was a counterargument to the Fascist ideology of national history. The term "Liberation," observes Giovanni De Luna, denotes a vigorous and even fierce collective agency.[43] By claiming the "history-making" quality of popular participation during the anti-Fascist struggle, the Liberation liquidated the ideology of the regime, which markedly rejected any idea of popular agency. Yet, as the November 1945 showdown of the national coalition government led by Parri demonstrated, the forces that guided the Resistance failed to merge and consolidate the new Italy around the military success against Fascism. That *was* the moment, Alba de Céspedes wrote in the journal *Mercurio*, in which groups of artists and intellectuals "lined up alongside political and military forces against an obvious and universally hated enemy, such that the artist, the intellectual, the politician, the combatant merged into one."[44] Published at the beginning of 1948, de Céspedes's column recalls the Liberation as an extraordinary but unrepeatable existential possibility—testifying at the same time that political disillusionment was already palpable by 1948.

Historian Silvio Lanaro describes the subsequent 1949–1953 period as characterized by the "the putting on ice of the constitution and the repudiation of anti-Fascism as the founding ideology and vehicle of a renewed national identity."[45] With an attentive politics of memory, the parties of the Left then defended (and somehow appropriated) the legacy of the Resistance as the founding myth of *their* Italy.[46] During the transition, experiences that did not fit with the Resistance as popular epic and founding moment for the new national identity were dismissed or belittled: groundbreaking works such as Carlo Emilio Gadda's *Eros and Priapus* (published 1967, but written in 1944–1945) or Primo Levi's *If This Is a Man* (1947) had great difficulty finding a publisher; others, like Carlo Levi's *Christ Stopped at Eboli* (1945) or Morante's *Lies and Sorcery* (1948), though they enjoyed a wide readership, were harshly criticized for their unconventional representations of "revolutionary" subjects, thereby minimizing their cultural value on ideological grounds.[47]

In fact, the 1943–1948 transition does not present a consistent, recognizable, easily framed debate but instead a proliferation, a multiplication of heterodox voices.[48] According to the political philosopher Jacques Rancière, a void of power typically engenders what he calls an "excess of speech":

> Every event, among speakers, is tied to an excess of speech in the specific form of a displacement of the *statement*: an appropriation "outside the truth"

of the speech of the other (of the formulas of sovereignty, of the ancient texts, of the sacred word) that makes it signify differently.[49]

The conditions of this "excess of speech" were produced by the unforeseeable series of events that began with the September 8, 1943, armistice and the discrediting of institutional authorities in Italy. This vacuum of authority opened possibilities for what Rancière called the expression of "the political wrong"—granting the right to speak to subjects that were not considered as such, qua outside of what is consensually held as *the* political.[50] These subjects were chiefly the Italian people themselves, who could exercise the possibility of true participation in the political arena for the first time after the heavily limited freedom and sovereignty granted by the Fascist (and liberal) regime.

The works I examine in this book express the "political wrong" of the transition to democracy in Italy. My analysis restores to us their disruptive political charge in the broader context of the early postwar intellectual debate. Their inventiveness and insight are illuminated by their controversial reception. The case of Carlo Levi's most overtly political book, *The Watch* (1950), is emblematic. The novel received contentious reviews, especially in the press close to the PCI, and aroused fierce discussion when published. Still today, the book and debate are generally overlooked in both literary and intellectual histories.[51] The "political wrong" of *The Watch* was not just the author's portrayal of De Gasperi and Togliatti as equally responsible for the end of the extraordinary season of hope inaugurated by the Liberation, but also the treatment of postwar society's ills as transversal and not ascribable to any single social class. In *The Watch*, individual and collective experiences are unaffected by Marxist ideology. Still, the novel's "political wrong" resides also in its visionary and often oneiric style: while firmly rooted in the observation of Italian postwar reality, it dialogues with modernist and cosmopolitan literary practices. *The Watch* challenges Neorealist poetics, which postulated a simpler, paratactic style supposedly more representative of people's lived experience, by arguing that traumatic experience is inherently resistant to verbalization.[52]

Marginalization within the postwar Italian cultural canon has been the destiny of many publications that expressed the "political wrong" in the passage to post-Fascism. These publications feature not only multilayered and literary self-conscious works such as *The Watch* but also pivotal journals of the period, from Luigi Salvatorelli's *La Nuova Europa* to de Céspedes's *Mercurio*. These journals offered an outlet for nonconformist intellectual and political positions, which had not yet hardened into the Communist vs.

Christian Democrat struggle and the debate internal to each of these parties.[53]

From the cultural criticism of the Liberation's periodicals to experimental novels, all of these works call into question historicist rhetoric. They articulated different truths by *denouncing* policies and procedures of symbolic redemption. At the heart of their anxieties were the "historic imaginary," studied by Fogu, and the rhetorical concept of life that sustained power and the failed policies of the Italian state. Novels such as Flaiano's *A Time to Kill* (1947) and Malaparte's *The Skin* (1949) pinpoint the collective repression and the lack of a radical rift in Italian culture after Fascism. At the same time, daring, if less accessible, literary endeavors like Saba's *Shortcuts and Very Short Stories* (1946) or Carlo Levi's *Fear of Freedom* (written in 1939, but published in 1946) openly challenged historicist rhetoric by deploying contrasting hermeneutic paradigms.[54] The cultural references here are Nietzsche and Freud, or the ethnological findings of the *Collège de sociologie* launched by Georges Bataille and Roger Caillois.[55]

What connected these disparate works was not just the distance of their authors from the Communist Party, which embraced the "Secondo Risorgimento" trope during the transition.[56] All these works outright reject historicism and its teleological readings of Italian history. After already thriving in liberal Italy, historicism inflated Fascist pretensions and survived in the new democratic debate via redemptive narratives. Brancati mordantly captures the issue in his *Roman Diary*, written in the early postwar but published as a volume only posthumously:

> The character of modern rhetoric is not literary, but historicist. Literary rhetoricians are famous for the enormity of their images; modern rhetoricians will remain famous for the enormity of the second term of the comparison in their historical references. Every nationalist, at the end of a skirmish, compares his reign to the Roman Empire; every progressive, at the end of some upheaval or reform, compares his exploits to the Christian revolution.[57]

Contemporary critics, especially among the Communist ranks, were fully aware of how historicism permeated through modern Italian culture and how pervasive Croce's influence was. Overcoming Croce and his historicism meant a repudiation of discursive practices that shaped the formation of most Italian intellectuals. However, after the demise of Fascism, more urgent political agendas took the place of Croce's neo-idealist concept of freedom. Ultimately limited to the ruling class, Croce's freedom now appeared as a philosophical confirmation of the status quo, if not the relic of an old world that had already been subjugated by Mussolini and his cohorts.[58]

The overall question developed in ways that literary critic Giacomo Debenedetti epitomized in a public intervention significantly titled "Likely Autobiography of a Generation" (1949). Speaking on the behalf of a generation that came of age during Fascism and the war, Debenedetti's proposed solution was: "Depart from Croce on the roads laid out by him."[59] Historicism was not just self-referential; it needed to give way to a "new historicism." A few years earlier, another prominent literary critic, Natalino Sapegno, had already clarified this "new historicism." In his influential 1945 article "Marxism, Culture, and Poetry," Sapegno proclaimed Marxism to be the "integral historicism" able to complete and overcome Croce's now defective model.[60] The cultural and critical discourse of the Marxist Left in Italy would then be impregnated with Crocean terminology, from Vittorini's project of cultural renewal in *Il Politecnico* to Ernesto de Martino's ethnological investigation of Southern Italy in pioneering books such as *The Magical World* (1948).[61]

In such an intricate scenario, nonaligned intellectuals publicly took a stand by rejecting historicism and its redemptive narratives altogether. But why did they use *literature* as the main vehicle of their cultural and political discontent? Throughout the life of the Italian state, from Mazzini to Mussolini, national literature was the common ground on which the Italian identity coalesced.[62] Stefano Jossa cogently argues that:

> The political horizon of the literary community is, therefore, tremendous: literature responds to the crisis of history by giving to an Italy that is "fragmented and divided" on the political level a different, cultural type of unity, one founded on the myths and values shared on another level. Thus is created a space of literature, which has for a long time been the site of Italian identity.[63]

However, as Antonio Gramsci denounced in *Prison Notebooks*, first published in the late 1940s, national literature was not a democratic space in Italy—hence his stress on the creation of a national-popular literature.[64] "Gramscians *before Gramsci*," as Luperini bitingly calls them, the critics of PCI-leaning journals such as *Rinascita* or *Società*, as well as Neorealist memoirists like Roberto Battaglia and his *Man and Partisan* (1945), tried to close this traditional gap by theorizing the "poetics of the chronicle" and supporting the populist epic of the Resistance (which we will see in detail in the next section).[65]

On the contrary, the writers I reference here utilized literature *specifically* for the ideological charge it acquired in Italian life. They did not consider literature as merely fiction or as rhetorical discourse with artistic pretensions. Nor did they consider it as simply a cultural institution deeply rooted in Italian society. Despite different agendas and poetics,[66] for writers such as Morante, Moravia, Brancati, Carlo Levi, and Malaparte, literature was an ongoing exercise of critique for the given historical truth by means of the "displacement of the statement" Rancière mentioned. As a matter of fact, these authors recovered an idea of literature that is essentially pre-romantic and pre-national, yet one that is also consistent with the troubled Italian cultural identity.[67] Their accounts do not just defy current ideas of modern(ist) literature; they also return to the core of the humanist tradition for which literature offered *the* ethical paradigm for the field of cultural production.[68]

The voices of this debate on the legacy of the Italian ideology of history cannot be seen merely as "transitional objects." Their problematic reception cannot be justified solely by the ideological pervasiveness of antagonistic narratives of redemption or the global reach of Neorealism.[69] These voices are ascribable to a larger historiographical postwar paradigm that characterized European politics and civilization after 1945. This paradigm positions early postwar Italian culture and society in a broader frame in which, as historian Frank Biess contends, "postwar histories were shaped not just by the external context of the Cold War but also by their preceding wartime histories."[70] In Italy, in the decades that followed, "the uncertainties of the immediate postwar years were forgotten," as Tony Judt put it, primarily because of improvements in living and economic conditions, not unlike what occurred in other Western European countries. Nevertheless, he concludes, "the likelihood that they *would* take a different turn had seemed very real in 1945."[71] The disagreement I retrace in this study bears witness to such possibilities in Italy—and to such uncertainties.

The next section details how two main processes structured the conflict over Italian history in the transition years: the working through of the collective and personal trauma of the national defeat and the ensuing disavowal of past models of life, culture, and politics. Both processes were haunted by the ghosts of totalitarianism and the responsibility of the war.

Admitting the Defeat, Dismissing Past Models

"It was still impossible to tell what country would win the war," claims Galeazzo Ciano in Malaparte's novel *Kaputt* in 1943, and yet "it was clear what countries had already lost it [. . .]. Poland and Italy."[72] As also alluded to by

Malaparte in his letter to Prezzolini, the significance of the military defeat was of fundamental concern to the Italian state, which was born out of the ashes of war and a totalitarian regime. Different interpretations of the defeat echoed across popular opinion but also affected Italian intellectuals and their cultural output. No other issue received more attention than national defeat in the immediate responses to WWII—only to disappear a few years later, overshadowed by new political preoccupations.[73] The question was almost entirely silenced in the country's public discourse after the promulgation of the new constitution on January 1, 1948, and the establishment of the Republic. The victory of the anti-Fascist forces against Fascism and the Nazi occupiers soon became the principal national narrative.[74] If anti-Fascist victory and national military defeat were two sides of the same coin, only the first befitted the selective memory of the newborn democratic state as its legitimizing event.

While the Resistance inspired massive literary, artistic, and filmic production, the vast majority of these accounts were reticent about the military defeat, its responsibility, and its horrors.[75] Countering widespread assumptions, writers like Berto, Brancati, and Malaparte made this burdensome legacy the main theme of their artistic and intellectual inquiry, or, rather, their core poetics. *Admitting the defeat* became the propeller of their writing. They found in literature the appropriate outlet to voice their disagreements with what they felt was an increasingly frustrating public discourse. Their responses take different, at times opposite, poetic, psychological, and political paths. After openly endorsing Fascism, they elaborated the trauma of the defeat in profoundly original ways, arriving at contrasting conclusions.

A melancholic gaze toward the past is the constitutional feature of their writing.[76] Still, it is just the first reaction of a much more articulated response, dissimilar to the collective and individual *cupio dissolvi* that is the real subject of a great many publications and diaries of those troubled years.[77] Reflecting on existential failure after the war, a main character of Piovene's novel *The False Redeemers* (1949) concludes: "I don't always want to live."[78] A case in point is *De Profundis* (1948), a controversial pamphlet by the esteemed jurist Salvatore Satta.[79] In the book, the bleak atmosphere resulting from a supposed "death of the fatherland" clouds the persistence of conservative ideas with apocalyptic tones. Satta employs concepts that informed liberal and then Fascist policies—among them clear anti-Semitic remarks. Pursuing an understanding of the unpredictable events of the national collapse, Satta's *De Profundis* is emblematic for its inability to renounce past models.

Conversely, the writers I reference in my research draw radical conclusions from the national defeat: with their work, they enact a consequential and thought-provoking *dismissal of past models*. Where others mourn the past as ruins, they bitterly observe it as an accumulation of debris.[80] From Malaparte to Saba, this new literature is concerned first of all with the liquidation of the old European civilization, which disgracefully perished with the world conflict. Significantly, their responses often provoked outrage from the early postwar cultural and political establishment, both from conservative and progressive sides.

For authors such as Berto and Brancati, dismissing past models meant also disputing the cultural principles of their education. Their writing recuperates the forms of the traditional novel in order to work through their *individual* responsibility with Fascism. Novels such as Berto's *The Sky Is Red* (1946) and Brancati's *Beautiful Antonio* (1949) explore the moral void left by the dictatorship and traditional Italian institutions—from the Church to the family—that collaborated with Fascism and willingly approved its reactionary myths.[81] Their dramatic rejection of Catholic education and patriarchal sexual roles—in apparent continuity with Fascism—speak volumes to the fallacy of the moral regeneration that the regime change promised to bring to a society still burdened by traditional inequality and condescending practices.

Beginning with Carlo Levi's *Christ Stopped at Eboli*, the works of these writers were tremendously popular in early postwar Italy and achieved considerable recognition beyond national boundaries as well. Malaparte's books were translated into all the main European languages, attaining immense popularity, particularly in Paris. According to contemporary records, he was the only Italian writer able to mirror d'Annunzio's stunning success decades before in the French capital, paving the way for other Italian authors such as Moravia, Vittorini, and Piovene.[82] Bruno Romani, the correspondent for the newspaper *Il Tempo*, significantly reported: "The translation of Malaparte's *Kaputt* meant, for literature, what *Rome, Open City* meant for our cinema."[83]

In addition to Paris—still then the cultural capital of Europe—these books were also successful overseas. In those years, Berto's *The Sky Is Red*, together with the subsequent *The Brigand* (1951), sold about two million copies in the USA and the USSR.[84] In light of this data, it is remarkable that these texts and their authors played such a marginal role in postwar Italian literature and culture. Or rather, how official records, anthologies, and scholarly research about early postwar Italy omitted or just dismissed them without a thorough critical appraisal.[85]

Commenting on history (and memory) formation in the aftermath of historic events, anthropologist Michel-Rolph Trouillot concludes: "Silences are inherent in history because any single event enters history with some of its constituting parts missing."[86] The memory and the formation of a public discourse on the military defeat in Italy—with all its exclusions—has been the focus of a considerable body of scholarly work recently.[87] My research strives to illuminate the moment of interpretative fluidity, in which the intellectuals who addressed the "missing constituting parts" of redemptive narratives of Italian history were still active players in the cultural—and literary—field.

Most of the testimonies of ex-Fascists spared no effort to underplay their personal involvement in the regime by trivializing the Fascist *ventennio* as a whole (e.g., Indro Montanelli, *Here They Do Not Rest*, 1945); or by tracing the personal conversion to the new anti-Fascist agenda as a redemptive journey (e.g., Ruggero Zangrandi's *The Long Journey*, 1948), setting influential standards for the aforementioned "patterns of conversion."[88] This widespread attitude was sustained by a "well-established journalistic-literary tradition [that] contributed to the diffusion of an image of the days that followed the fall of Fascism as the revelation of the substantive extraneousness of the Italians to the regime," as La Rovere puts it.[89] It is no surprise, then, that in a review of Malaparte's *The Skin* published in 1950, Giovanni Spadolini complains about the absence of a "literature of the defeat" in Italy like the one that characterized Germany's defeat in the Great War: "In the great swarm of memorials, of confessions and defenses (useful or useless, stingy or generous), it seemed almost as if our writers were restrained from or afraid of drawing inspiration from collective life in the years of the defeat and invasion."[90]

During the armed Resistance against Nazi and Fascist forces, the stories of the partisan struggles were mushrooming in journals and newspapers in the form of the "chronicle." For its alleged lack of rhetorical embellishment, this genre was then codified by Marxist literary critics in the journal *Società* as the most apt way to represent the heroism as well as the harshness of the Resistance.[91] The genre gave voice and literary authority to a multitude of individual stories that, considered together, could establish the new civil epic of anti-Fascist Italy. The real protagonist of all these stories was the Italian people, and the chronicles had also the merit of echoing a specifically Italian literary tradition, born in the middle ages, in an historical moment when the official doctrine of Communism in Italy was adopting a national agenda.

Philip Cooke affirms the centrality of the Resistance short story for postwar Italian literature.[92] Drawing from a 1949 article by Calvino,[93] he also

18 | Introduction: Ruins and Debris of a Contested History

argues that the partisan short stories stand for a particular case of literature for the masses. Moreover, these stories instituted the rhetorical paradigms that characterized the postwar representation of the period, beginning with the parallel between the Risorgimento and the Resistance, in which the latter was considered a historic completion of the former. Cooke comments:

> There is, in other words, a "carry forward" effect that sees the topoi and language used in that period, for a particular purpose (that of encouraging morale and a sense of group identity), percolating into another period, when the Resistance was effectively over, but other battles were taking place.[94]

The persistence of past historical models profoundly impacted each narrative about a possible collective future. Recent events were interpreted within a framework that had a long cultural tradition. Among the many aspects of this complex milieu, two main trends deeply impacted public and intellectual discourses. First, the memory of the Resistance obliterated the collective consent to Mussolini's regime. The two years of the civil war were characterized by the violent victimization of Italian people: in the aftermath of WWII, this traumatic memory took center stage. As a consequence, Italians' quotidian acceptance of—if not approval or open collaboration with—the crimes perpetrated by the Fascist state over twenty years of rule was relegated to the background. The partisans became a synecdoche for the Italian people as a whole, although they were a small, albeit praiseworthy, minority. Second, as Fogu poignantly observes, a crucial feature of the memorialization-historicization process of this difficult past was that "the replacement of the *biennio* for the *ventennio* in public memory took place in forms that were absorbed and transfigured from Fascist historical culture itself."[95] Once again, at stake here is not only the political and institutional continuity between Fascism and post-Fascism but also the persistence of the rhetorical and literary tradition that was exalted and exacerbated by the Fascist regime. After all, as Guri Schwarz sharply stated,

> The anti-Fascism of the very early republican period was also an instrument of sociocultural stabilization; it was bent to the need to emerge from the war without breaking too sharply with the past and constituted the principal anchor of the political system.[96]

This rhetorical tradition is not an exclusive Italian specialty: "From the beginning of time," writes Léon Blum from his confinement after the collapse of the Third Republic in France, "national calamity has been linked with the idea of sin and error, and with its natural extension: contrition, expiation and redemption."[97] Evoked already by Forcella in his diaries as constituting what he calls "the Bildungsroman of the anti-Fascist canon," these tropes draw heavily from Christian—especially Catholic—practices and institutions. Transferred into the arena of national accomplishments, they set the standard for the collective redemption promised by the ideologies of the modern nation-state. As Alberto Banti and Emilio Gentile have documented,[98] both the birth of the Italian state during the Risorgimento and the Fascist totalitarian regime actively sustained and were backed by a religion of the fatherland whose tropes employ undertones of Christian liturgy. Presented as a revolution, the Secondo Risorgimento trope displayed a rhetorical continuity with recent and more distant pasts.

Signaling rhetorical continuity is not the same as leveling the divergent ideologies of the Italian nation that confronted each other in the 1943–1945 civil war. Fascist ideology was defeated in 1945 after its political collapse on July 25, 1943. Nevertheless, its historicist rhetoric, which envisioned present suffering as an expiation necessary for future redemption from the mistakes of the past, survived in the parties of the newborn parliamentarian democracy. In fact, every war undertaken by the Italian state since the Risorgimento was promoted as redemption for past sins and errors. Leaving aside the propaganda surrounding the two world wars,[99] according to the socialist Giovanni Pascoli, the 1911 Italo-Turkish war was the "triumphant and *redemptive* march" of the new proletarian nation, whereas the 1935 invasion of Ethiopia was repeatedly depicted in Mussolini's speeches as "the *redemptive* war."[100]

The ideology of the State as the vehicle for Italy's and Italians' historical redemption supported the liberal and Fascist regimes through a figural reading of the past as the foreshadowing of the present—another trait with remote origins in Christian hermeneutics. After the war, this ideology yielded to a more personal, almost intimate narrative. As in Zangrandi's widely read memoir, the "long journey through Fascism" to the new secular faith of Communism or to the return to Catholicism evolved into a widespread pattern of conversion. According to La Rovere, this deeply personal yet collective process of atonement developed into the required token necessary to gain access to the new postwar society and its parties—in particular for the younger intellectual generations.[101] The secular redemption advocated by the PCI, a party that presented itself as the heir to the long-lasting Risorgimento tradition, was at odds with the repentance and the return to orthodoxy required by the Christian Democrats. The Catholic ranks followed the lines dictated already in 1937 by Pope Pius XII in the encyclical *Divini*

Redemptoris, in which Communism was proclaimed a "false messianism."[102] Still, both sides retained collective as well as individual features that were not mutually exclusive, as the persistence of a Catholic mindset and traditional social habits in Communist regions showed.[103]

The issue of personal responsibility could be absorbed into a new narrative, especially for those who believed in and actively contributed to the Fascist regime, as well as soldiers who fought and killed for a cause that was now discredited and stigmatized. This narrative enabled traumatized veterans to make sense of what they had experienced during the war, often from the perspective of both the perpetrator *and* the victim. With its neutral connotation, implying something neither negative nor positive, the Italian word "reduce" conveys much more accurately the ambiguity of their moral position than the English term "survivor." These soldiers lived through the war and its violence, yet the designation "reduce" does not indicate whether they were the agents or recipients of violence. It is no surprise, then, that this word appears so often in postwar Italian culture.[104]

For most partisans, the war was not targeted only at the liberation of the national territory from what they deemed as illegitimate occupiers. They also fought for a new social equality against the old elites who supported Fascism for decades. As Claudio Pavone argues in his now classic *A Civil War: A History of the Italian Resistance* (1991), class struggle and revolution were pivotal in a war in which ideology played such a key role.[105] In other words, the anti-Fascist idea of national revolution as collective redemption initially clashed with the Catholic concept of religious restoration through the intimate pattern of "contrition, expiation and redemption." After Fascism and its disastrous war, redemption could only come with a radically renewed society. In this broader perspective, violence also acquired different meanings—and a different accountability. Resistance literature, as Robert Gordon has poignantly argued, was fundamental in shaping this new discourse of violence,

> proposing narratives of "good" partisan violence—a heroic struggle for liberation against overwhelming odds, for the good of the nation (or group or class)—as opposed to the "bad" violence—the violence of pure power and oppression—of the Nazis and Fascists. In more interesting cases, however, writers showed an acute awareness, well before historians opened up this issue, of the moral difficulty of narratives of good violence.[106]

Narratives of "good" violence, often in the form of the Resistance "short story," directly contributed to the formation of a public memory of the period.

However, canonized writers such as Cesare Pavese, Italo Calvino, or, later on, Beppe Fenoglio and Luigi Meneghello resisted univocal and consolatory interpretations of war's violence. In their nuanced accounts, they exposed the personal and collective contradictions of the civil struggle.[107] Moreover, the public discourse regarding the Resistance and the ensuing selective memory sidelined not only the morally justified violence perpetrated by anti-Fascist forces but also the impressive amount of violence and wreckage caused by Allied intervention and occupation of Italian territory. In fact, Allied bombings did not stop after the armistice. The new air warfare aimed at exporting freedom to Fascist countries through the extensive bombings of civilian targets. With a self-indulgent rhetorical abuse, the Allies named the new strategy "wings of democracy." More realistically, historian Leonardo Paggi described it as "openly terroristic behavior."[108]

As Gordon has stressed, a significant number of Italian writers were keenly aware of the moral difficulty of narratives of good violence. This awareness did not avoid the emergence of two main problems characterizing the intellectual production of early postwar Italy—two questions easily transformed into stereotypes in popular discourse. First, a significant consequence of the aforementioned redemptive patterns was the collective victimization of Italians, with the risk of belittling responsibility or even clearing the country's wrongdoing in WWII. The second issue is not at all alien to this collective victimization, engaging some of the nonconformist writers who actively contributed to this kind of literature. By overtly admitting national defeat, Malaparte and Berto gave voice to a discontent that was silenced in conventional Resistance narratives, yet they also occupied a controversial position because of their collaboration with the regime. Their problematic situation resulted in the alleged inability to acknowledge the moral accountability of their act of writing, as they had been responsible *in prima persona* for the construction of a Fascist culture through their intellectual, journalistic, and literary work, often endorsing its imperialist and racist political agenda.

"Every society experiences defeat in its own way," claims Wolfgang Schivelbusch in a comparative study on national responses to military setbacks; "a state of unreality—or dreamland—is invariably the first of these."[109] The collapse of a defeated regime produces a massive psychological strain on the population. The destruction of the regime's symbols by the same people who enthusiastically applauded its achievements in better times is an eloquent sign of this stress, not just of the ephemeral euphoria of regained freedom.[110]

This state of unreality follows the disappearance of the overwhelming presence of the political in every aspect of private and collective life, a characteristic of totalitarian regimes. This existential and historical void cannot but lead to a traumatic break with the past. The resulting trauma is not only a personal catastrophe but also the painful individual participation in a collective bereavement—the loss of a fantasy of omnipotence that characterized the psychological life of individuals and of the masses under the regime. In Freudian terms, this loss is characterized not by the mourning of an external object's deprivation, but with the melancholy resulting from an emptying of the self. This experience corresponds to the impossibility of reflecting one's own narcissism in an external—in this case collective— mirror. Reflecting on the work of mourning in postwar Germany, Eric Santner concludes that

> one fairly common strategy of circumventing this complex layering of mourning tasks (and thereby remaining within the closure of narcissism) was to identify with the victim, to become the one who helplessly and innocently suffered the deceptions and ravages of the fascist utopia as well as the destruction wrought by the allied forces.[111]

In spite of the obvious differences, a parallel can be drawn in the Italian situation, in which the identification with the victim frequently became a substitution for mourning and a defense against historical guilt. The traumatic break from the collapse of Fascism caused a wound so profound in collective imagination and personal experience that, as many commentators signaled, the debate over the nation almost disappeared in the months directly following the end of the war.[112] It was only to reappear when Italian politics converged around positions in line with the new international Cold War opposition before the 1948 general elections.[113] Such a resounding void is distinctively relevant, as it occurred when a shared idea of the nation could finally be negotiated for the first time in more than twenty years, during which the hegemonic power in charge had a monopoly over its meaning.

Literature, once again, strove to fill this void. No writer in Italy denounced the postwar collective symbolic identification with the victim like Carlo Emilio Gadda did. As he writes in *Eros and Priapus*, "The narcissistic lie is, in the course of history, what the dissipation of the individual is in private life. It consists in denying a series of true facts that are not welcome back."[114] Gadda's contentious pamphlet was written in 1944–1945 but was deemed unpublishable at the time. Defying literary genres, political prudence, and (neo)realist poetics, *Eros and Priapus* pursues with unparalleled verbal violence an auto-da-fé of Fascism and of the widespread popular cult of the Duce, which persisted long after his death. To this end, Gadda's writing cannot be but an "act of conscience"—that is, a painful excavation of the individual impulses and collective desire, national conformism, and violent egotism that consigned Italy and Europe to Mussolini and Hitler, and reduced both to a landscape of "dreadful debris" (*paventosa macerie*).[115] Countering any consoling identification with the victim, Gadda claims with another expressionist image that *his own* writing of history is the "poor act of someone who holds a lamp up to the corpse's face, sending cockroaches scurrying out into every direction of the night."[116]

Mussolini's regime placed the supremacy of the Italian nation at the center of its public discourse. Communists and Christian Democrats featured policies that were transnational in their scope but acted with a national agenda. In the early postwar, an open confrontation over the Italian nation was avoided, particularly before the exclusion of the Communist Party from the government in 1947 by the Christian Democrats, up until then allied in the name of the common national cause. With the sanction of the Liberals and the historical justifications formulated by Croce, Italy *before* Fascism became the true expression of the nation, in continuity with a historicist vision that preferred to elide responsibilities and gray zones, for the sake of a supposedly higher national interest—to which the PCI and the authoritative leader Palmiro Togliatti "strategically" adhered, condemning itself to political marginalization.

This complex scenario enriches our understanding of the "political wrong"—as Rancière suggested—of the literary works of Morante, Moravia, Brancati, Berto, Flaiano, Carlo Levi, and Malaparte during the transition to democracy. Together with the other protagonists of these pages, they bear witness to the exceptional intellectual season occasioned in Italy upon the downfall of Mussolini and concluded with the institutionalization of party politics. Their work raised a wealth of questions that postwar narratives of redemption left unanswered. Specific concerns should now be addressed following individual intellectual trajectories or close readings of the most significant publications, as the general plan of my research will display.

Plan of the Work

My examination of each writer's voice in these debates blends intellectual history with analysis of language and rhetorical discourses. I investigate the trajectory of each author through their different literary practices, at times privileging journalistic production over more canonical forms like novels, as in the cases of Moravia and Piovene. This methodology finds confirmation in the range of these writers' works. Their literary production was not meant to be an organic corpus; rather, it was an ongoing experiment with genres and languages, spanning from cultural commentaries to theater, from memoirs to fiction. The plots of their books or short stories often inspired film adaptations. Brancati, Flaiano, and Berto, for instance, wrote several screenplays. The material uncertainty of the time often affected the ephemeral sense of ideas and debates, from book projects to journalistic contributions.

Commenting on the literary achievements of Berto's *The Sky Is Red*, Andrea Zanzotto suggested a crucial dimension for my analysis. Zanzotto points out the distinctive success of the novel's language: "a 'language of transition' that turns out in some way to be self-sufficient, precisely in its transience."[117] According to the poet, only a few works during the transition elaborated a language that, in its "self-sufficiency," could mirror the atmosphere of the period. The attempt to articulate an autonomous language, affected neither by past models nor by any redemptive rhetoric, will then be one of the main focuses of this book. Without indulging in any determinism, the need to devise new literary and rhetorical practices reveals the inherent difficulty to make sense of a troubled and traumatic past.

This multifold approach enables me to enlarge the scope of my investigation, focusing on topics addressed only partially by canonized authors, and with the further possibility of contextualizing their claims through different perspectives. It also allows me to recover the dialogical spontaneity of the political disagreement and of the "excess of speech" characterizing the transition. Lastly, such methodology leads me to conclusions that go beyond the political and poetic development of singular personalities by illuminating the intellectual exchange they had with minor figures—at the same time emphasizing the originality of specific works.

Literary critic Alberto Asor Rosa noted how little discussion there was in Italian anti-Fascist culture on the nature of the totalitarian state.[118] The first chapter of this book challenges this thesis by retracing the contributions that tackled this fundamental issue and situating the Italian case *within* the larger totalitarian paradigm. Allegedly, this assumed lack of discussion was due to a willingness to avoid a direct confrontation with Stalin's USSR, in a period in which many European intellectuals were looking at Soviet Russia as the model for future society, thereby refusing to consider the conspicuous signs of its pitfalls.[119] This might also have been the reason why Italian texts directly addressing this problem were then completely overlooked. Books such as *The Totalitarian State* (1947) by Vittorio Zincone and *The Volga Rises in Europe* (1943) and *Das Kapital* (1949) by Curzio Malaparte are not comparable to the crass anti-Communist polemic à la Montanelli or Longanesi.[120] As intellectuals who fervently adhered to the Fascist totalitarian state, they experienced this political phenomenon from within, and were actively involved in the organization of consensus. Finally, by retrieving the great deal of contributions that Alberto Moravia published in the Liberation press, I retrace the evolution of his thinking on totalitarianism. Between his pamphlet *Hope: Christianity and Communism* (1944) and *Man as An End* (published 1953, but written in 1946), Moravia develops coherent arguments against political utopias by pinpointing the "necessary violence" that revolutionary practices have historically embraced.[121]

The second chapter examines the working through of the past by three former Fascist writers: Giuseppe Berto, Guido Piovene, and Vitaliano Brancati. The common thread tying together their disparate experiences after the war is the literary transfiguration of their previous commitment to Mussolini's regime around the admission of personal responsibility. Through successful novels such as Berto's *The Sky Is Red* and Brancati's *Beautiful Antonio,* or an intense journalistic activity as in the case of Piovene, these writers attempted to work out a new language reflecting the burdensome responsibility of their past choices. Their efforts—at times ill-fated as in the case of Piovene—stand out in the general postwar scenario. Most ex-Fascist intellectuals narrated their past involvement with Fascism as a short-lived moment of perdition before their ideological conversion to the new postwar credos.

The third chapter revolves around the rejection of what philosopher Guido De Ruggiero calls the "fetishism of history," the historical imaginary exacerbated by the Fascist regime that conditioned public discourse even after its fall. Opposition to historicism—heralded by Croce as the teleological progress of freedom—was widespread in the early postwar. Still, only authors who grounded their disagreement on the tragic and traumatic experiences of recent history fleshed out its unequivocal refusal. For them, the rejection of Fascism on a political level could only accompany the refusal of historicism in the cultural realm. Umberto Saba's *Shortcuts and Very Short Stories* was the first volume in Italy to argue for an alternative genealogy of Fascist violence, tracing it back to the nationalist and imperialist myths that constituted bourgeois and liberal culture. The book thus called attention to the civilizational break constituted by the genocidal attack on European Jewry. With her novel *Lies and Sorcery*, Elsa Morante expands Saba's poetic insights into a radical reconsideration of traditional society based on privilege and its bearing on present Italy even beyond Fascism. Traditional gender and racial bias that still haunt the present are at the center of another outstanding novel: Ennio Flaiano's *A Time to Kill*, which harrowingly recollects the ghosts of Italy's colonialism.

The fourth chapter concentrates on Carlo Levi, possibly the most far-reaching in his refusal of past models among anti-Fascist intellectuals. Levi establishes an oppositional polarity with Malaparte: The two develop quite antithetical responses from their common dismissal of the historicist rhetoric inherited from the Fascist and liberal regimes. The chapter examines how Levi elaborated the most consequential critique of the totalitarian state to appear in Italy in those years. Levi's cosmopolitan experiences of Libertarian Judaism, political activity in the socialist-liberal Action Party, and European culture between the two wars conjure up an unpredictable empathy with subaltern and marginal classes in his *Christ Stopped at Eboli*.[122] With stunning poetic intensity, the memoir subverts the stability of the many dichotomies of Western political thought, advocating a new polity based on inclusion, autonomy, and self-government. Furthermore, his other neglected texts *Fear of Freedom* and *The Watch* feature, respectively, as the first critical theory of totalitarianism in Italy and a rebuttal of the models of time, history, and politics that sustained the new party system that took power after the transition.[123]

My investigation concludes with Curzio Malaparte, who programmatically set out to narrate the Italian defeat as an integral component of the general collapse of European civilization. Usually quickly dismissed for his Fascist past, Malaparte was an ingenious and nonconformist intellectual whose outstanding historical sensibility was rivaled only by his narcissism. As Milan Kundera contends, Malaparte invented with his best-known novels *Kaputt* and *The Skin*, "a form that is totally a new thing," able to express the tragic contrast between the destructive power of modern technology and the fragility of creaturely life.[124] With his representational prowess, Malaparte tackled all the main concerns of the discussion on recent Italian history: the rejection of past models, the unrestrained technological violence of the Nazi as well as of the Allied bombings, a critique of the centrality of the State and totalitarianism, the racial agenda of modern power, and the memory of the destruction of European Jewry.

1 After Italian Totalitarianism

The Italian Experience within the Totalitarian Paradigm
In his 1982 essay, influential literary critic Alberto Asor Rosa highlighted how early postwar Italian culture lacked a thorough discussion of totalitarianism:

> In this Italian anti-Fascist and Resistance culture, the importance of antitotalitarian polemic is unexpectedly limited and circumscribed, in a way that is very different than what had happened or was happening in those years in the area of European anti-Fascist culture. [...] On this front there is never an organic refusal of power or the state.[1]

The passage outlines the theoretical limits of the anti-Fascist debate, in a period when the intellectual class that served the regime was almost seamlessly absorbed into the democratic state. Remarkably, the term "totalitarian" was first coined and employed by anti-Fascists in Italy in the early 1920s to denounce Mussolini for his illiberal practices.[2] The Duce replied by reusing the concept of "totalitarian state" as a boastful description of his political ambitions and accomplishments. His notorious aphorism is in this sense quite fitting: "All within the state, nothing outside the state, nothing against the state."[3] For Fascist ideology, the State was the founding principle, the ultimate goal, and the only political reality. The Fascist party itself was, in the late 1930s, absorbed and integrated into the body of the State, unlike the institutional developments in Nazi Germany.[4]

The totalitarian state and its unconstrained monopoly of power and violence were by no means a negligible legacy of Mussolini's dictatorship. Having linked its destiny with Fascism, Italy's state apparatus was widely discredited in the early postwar period, eliciting an extensive popular disaffection to its institutions. The results of this calamitous embrace are still vivid in today's political debate, featuring disagreement, contrastive memories and fostering adversarial perceptions of national belonging.[5] Why, then, did anti-Fascist intellectuals refrain from conducting an extensive analysis of such a burdensome heritage? What about the intellectuals who did not fully identify as anti-Fascist? After all, as Paolo Alatri compellingly wrote in the journal *La Nuova Europa*, just two months after the end of the conflict, Fascism

> died because it hadn't learned how to keep its promises, not because the promises themselves were revealed to be monstrous. It died because it hadn't managed to offer compensation for sacrifices solicited and imposed, not because the sacrifices themselves were discovered to be nefarious and the compensation criminal [. . .]. To this day, the great mass of Italian nationalists would like a politics of "prestige," while they should be thinking only of a mea culpa, which in political terms translates into the radical substitution of the Fascist class for the anti-Fascist one, in the harshest of purges.[6]

As historians Filippo Focardi and Ruth Ben-Ghiat maintain, the totalitarian features of Fascist rule in Italy were already being downplayed in the 1940s. The comparison with Nazi terror and genocidal policies across Europe further aided this minimizing process.[7] The reasons were multifold, since political convenience intertwined with refashioning existing stereotypes by Italians and Allies alike. The stakes were indeed high for both: from Italy's strategic relevance in the new geopolitical configuration, to the necessity of the continuity of the state, to the fear of a Communist takeover—all counterarguments condemning Alatri's firm appeal to political marginality. A new wave of (old) essentialisms about the supposedly "defective" Italian character led to a selective memory, if not an utter reticence, regarding Fascism's active role in the war and related crimes. These clichés depicted Italians as passive victims, prompting a general forgetting of their role as perpetrators. Italian intervention in WWII is still remembered today with a mix of passiveness and insubordination.[8]

Collective memory coalesced around the terrible years of the Italian civil war, foreign occupation of national soil, or painful episodes removed from their original context, such as the disastrous Italian campaign in Russia.[9] Institutional celebrations concentrated on the memory of these traumatic events, obliterating Fascist aggression and occupation of African states, Greece and the Balkans, and Southern France.[10] The Italian racial campaigns that culminated in the 1938 anti-Semitic laws are a shameful case in point.[11] Only recently, prompted in part by the migration (and detention) crises in the Mediterranean of the last decades, public debate in Italy has openly addressed the neglected histories of the diaspora, forced mobility, and colonial violence that feature among the most enduring legacies of Mussolini's regime.[12]

At the time, however, influential and internationally acclaimed anti-Fascist intellectuals such as Benedetto Croce and diplomats such as Carlo Sforza spared no effort in minimizing Italian agency in WWII, especially the popular participation in the regime's imperial campaigns.[13] In public speeches and articles published abroad, such as "The Fascist Germ Still Lives," which appeared in the *New York Times* on November 28, 1943, Croce depicts the totalitarian mentality as inherently alien to Italians, who are intrinsically more "human" than their German counterparts. Fascism, he argued, was a European phenomenon, not exclusively an Italian one. While Nazi barbarity could be traced back to the long history of the German *Sonderweg* ("Special Path"), Fascism in Italy was only a temporary illness. After this bout, Croce concluded, Italians had developed strong antibodies.[14]

Tropes labeling Italians as inherently good began surfacing in books such as Carlo Sforza's *The Real Italians: A Study in European Psychology*. Published in English in the United States in 1942, following its first release in Montreal as *Les Italiens tels qu'ils sont* one year earlier, Sforza's essay aimed to rehabilitate Italians and their country in the eyes of foreign public opinion by countering the Fascist imperial rhetoric of *Romanità*. Interestingly, the clichés displayed in these publications reiterate many aspects of Fascist propaganda, especially the 1920s *Strapaese* ("Super-country") movement or the effort by the ideologues of the regime to spell out the difference between—and the superiority of—Italian totalitarianism and its German analog. In one instance, Sforza argues that "the peculiar genius of Italy is particularist; the opposite of particularism is fascism, which is totalitarian by necessity."[15] These clichés have a long history in Italy and abroad, which cannot be recounted here.[16] Such influential assumptions deeply affected the understanding of Italian involvement in WWII and the Holocaust for decades to come, and can be traced even in books such as Hannah Arendt's *Eichmann in Jerusalem*.[17]

Liberal anti-Fascists did not develop the intellectual tools for a real reconsideration of Italian totalitarianism. As in the cases of Croce and Sforza, they simply declared it alien to the Italian character. A public debate on this issue would have entailed for liberals a thorough reappraisal of the conception of the state at the base of their political views. For decades, the regime's propaganda hailed the 1922 March on Rome as the foundational event of a new era. In reality, Fascism crushed the liberal state in Italy without abruptly breaking with its past traditions but by taking over its institutions one by one and depriving them of any legal and political relevance—beginning with the parliament.

Liberals, however, were hardly representative of the disparate anti-Fascist forces. Among the partisans, for instance, revolutionary culture was widespread—and the major force among the armed resistance were the Communists. Asor Rosa's remark on how anti-Fascist culture avoided addressing the legacy of totalitarianism is still valid today when we consider that a large number of Fascist intellectuals and bureaucrats shifted to Communism. Here, the cult of the State was not at the forefront of the ideological debate. A public debate on totalitarianism would have engendered an implicit critique of the Soviet state, in which Italian Communists placed all their hopes for the future. Galvanized by the victory over Nazism, in which the Soviets bore the heaviest military burden, Stalin's USSR was untouchable to anti-Fascist intellectuals before the onset of the Cold War.[18] Enzo Traverso recalls how few European intellectuals (among them Gaetano Salvemini) denounced Stalinism in the late 1930s in the midst of the Great Terror in the USSR. This position did not change after the temporary disappointment of the Molotov-Ribbentrop Pact. Traverso also reports how, during the conflict, American war propaganda depicted Stalin as the good "oncle Joseph" and how difficult it was for George Orwell to find a publisher in 1941 for his book *Animal Farm*, a biting political satire of Stalin's USSR.[19]

Among the writers who would later embrace the PCI, Alberto Moravia was one of few in the immediate postwar to openly address the issue of the state and its impact on modern life. The principal concerns of his essay *Man as an End* (published in 1953 but written in 1946) pertain much more to moral than to political philosophy.[20] In his book, Moravia criticizes the extreme rationalization and politicization of every aspect of an individual's life, a widespread condition he interprets as a consequence of modernization. In particular, the author focuses on what he calls "instrumental rationality," the modern habitus of perceiving human beings as a means to an end. *Man as an End* firmly rejects the ideological deployments of such habitus, aimed at correcting both individual and collective life, along abstract systems of beliefs.

Moravia's arguments in this essay feature evident political undertones, for he sees the massive implementation of "instrumental rationality" as one of the major characteristics of totalitarian regimes. His *Man as an End* contributes to European thought's return to humanism after the war.[21] Although the essay's anti-Fascist agenda is evident, its main argument implicitly criticizes Communist ideas. This might have been one of the reasons behind the author's decision to delay the publication of the piece, written right after the war, until 1953. In fact, *Man as an End* is better understood in the context of Moravia's other works of the transition years, from his fiction to his hectic collaboration with liberation newspapers and journals. In these neglected pieces, he develops arguments that disavow the myths of social palingenesis that characterize totalitarianism.[22] I will return to Moravia more extensively at the end of this chapter, after my examination of the intellectuals who tackled the role of the state directly in their writing and did not avoid an open confrontation with totalitarianism.

Among them, the most radical is undoubtedly Carlo Levi. His political and literary elaborations of the problem of the state, from *Fear of Freedom* to *The Watch*, constitute an unconventional theory of totalitarianism and a fierce critique of early postwar Italian politics. Levi's intellectual influence during the transition was huge: in the subsequent decades, the rhetorical and political charge of his original position would be conveniently overshadowed by the international success of *Christ Stopped at Eboli*. Levi's polemic against the political use of Italy's past will lead us to new queries, which will be discussed at length in the fourth chapter. For now, it is important to note that Asor Rosa's claim should be at least corrected. While no extensive interpretations of totalitarianism appeared in Italy that could match, for example, the works of the German-Jewish diaspora in New York, valuable texts published in those years approached the problem from alternative points of view, opening the debate to the Italian experience *within* the totalitarian paradigm. In these instances, new and old stereotypes coexist and intermingle with outstanding insights.

Noteworthy analyses of totalitarianism came from intellectuals who knew the mechanisms of the totalitarian state all too well, having worked for years within the apparatus of the Fascist regime. In their postwar writings, they not only condemned the political theology created by Fascism but also crossed into new territory where (most) anti-Fascist intellectuals were not ready, or able, to venture—at least not until USSR's invasion of Hungary in 1956. These former Fascist intellectuals linked totalitarianism with Stalinism: the dismissal of the totalitarian experience under Mussolini grounded and justified their rejection of Communism.

A controversial protagonist in this neglected story is Curzio Malaparte, "Fascism's most formidable writer," as Piero Gobetti called him in the 1920s.[23] Malaparte's postwar skepticism of any narrative of national regeneration was profoundly rooted in his perception of the historical failure of European civilization. Malaparte would develop his unconventional outlook through the polemical depiction of Nazi—and Allied—occupied Europe in *Kaputt* and *The Skin*, examined in the concluding chapter. However, Malaparte's early 1940s articles for *Prospettive*, the journal he directed, and his reports from the Eastern Front, which he collected in a single volume with the significant title *The Volga Rises in Europe* in 1943, display how he articulated an ambivalent autonomy from Fascist culture since the beginning of the war. In fact, Mussolini's regime had barely tolerated his identification as a self-proclaimed "Protestant" Fascist—someone who ambiguously blended intellectual nonconformism and political acquiescence for personal profit.[24] Remarkably, Malaparte's distance turned into a skeptical disavowal of totalitarianism and revolutionary politics during the transition period. His critique of the ideological aspects of Marxist doctrine takes center stage in his play *Das Kapital* (1948), in a moment when popular and intellectual support for Communist parties reached an apex all over Western Europe.

Another little-known contemporary commentator on totalitarianism was the journalist Vittorio Zincone. His essay *The Totalitarian State* (1947) offers a convincing comparative appraisal of totalitarian regimes and the political techniques employed by charismatic leaders such as Lenin, Stalin, Mussolini, and Hitler. Despite their differences, both Malaparte and Zincone spell out in their works how Communism was not the *necessary* solution of the historical impasse following WWII. Admittedly, the two authors' intimate involvement in totalitarianism was far from innocent. In their writings, however, they transform their personal disillusion with Mussolini's regime into a unique hermeneutic instrument. Malaparte and Zincone not only describe the impact of ideology on the body and mind of individuals, but they also explain the internal functioning of totalitarian political projects without downplaying their intrinsic violence.

Anti-Communist slurs were common among conservative or reactionary journalists in the early postwar. Once they conveniently minimized their past collaborations, some of them, like Guglielmo Giannini or Indro Montanelli, strove to foreground their newly acquired ideological independence. In their articles, they piled up populist slogans for a middle class that was wary of a Communist takeover. In this sense, historian Piergiorgio Zunino, pigeonholed Malaparte and Longanesi as "survivors" of the regime.[25] Yet differences between the two authors are profound—especially on an ideological level—and telling.

Despite conspicuous fluctuations, also inspired by Palmiro Togliatti's initial benevolence towards him, Malaparte's rejection of the Marxist teleological interpretation of history had little to do with a stubborn personal adhesion to Fascist ideology or a general contempt for anti-Fascist ideals, as was the case in Longanesi. Giorgio Napolitano, President of the Italian Republic from 2006 to 2015, remembers in a recent interview how Malaparte's

1941 reports from the Eastern Front were received by young Communists like him as a call to arms.[26] Whether or not intended by Malaparte, Napolitano's recollections evidence the ideological fluidity of the period, in which personal disillusionment with Fascism mixed with the confused excitement of a forthcoming change of regime.

Malaparte's and Zincone's critiques resulted from the working through of their autobiographical experience *within* the totalitarian state. Their refusal to embrace Marxism and its political party went hand in hand with another dissent—their resistance to the redemption and forgiveness offered by Catholic politics. This double aversion emerged in their writings once they realized that the sacralization of politics sustaining totalitarian states did not just constitute a political fallacy; it posed a grave threat to the lives of individuals and communities.

Emilio Gentile developed this assessment further in his research on Fascist ideology and politics.[27] The historian argues that the distinctive totalitarian aspects of a modern authoritarian regime such as Italian Fascism were mass mobilization and a conception of politics in which the political entity becomes the source of devotion and cult, organized around a system of beliefs, symbols, and rites. Today, these concepts are considered critical to describe the different, at time contrasting, practices of totalitarian regimes in Europe.[28] Still, Malaparte, Zincone and Moravia insightfully developed similar considerations in the transition years in a highly personal way—through fictional and dialogic representations or journalistic writing with literary ambitions.

Specters of a Revolutionary Past: Curzio Malaparte

Like many intellectuals of the early twentieth century, Curzio Malaparte fully embraced the myth of the palingenetic war and fought in WWI, both in France and on the Italian front. A revolutionary at heart, he then enthusiastically adhered to Fascism, believing Mussolini's movement to be the historic force capable of modernizing Italy and of creating "the new man"—the other nefarious myth of modernist politics.[29] To that end, he also followed with increasing attention the Russian Revolution and the developments of Soviet society. As a correspondent for the daily *La Stampa*, he traveled to Russia in 1929 and successfully published in Paris two essays that analyzed the revolutions in Europe, sacrificing historical accuracy for the sake of his argument: *Technique du coup d'état* (1931) and *Le bonhomme Lénine* (1932). The books were censored in Italy and their author fell from grace, although the real reason behind this fall was his ill-timed criticism of prominent Fascist figures such as Italo Balbo.[30] In the early 1950s, Malaparte would comment: "For the young Italian generations of 1919, Mussolini was their first love, the lover that betrayed them, on the moral (political, social, intellectual, artistic) level, with the old, reactionary generations (the monarchy, the church, big industry, the nobility)."[31]

After the personal shock of his confinement in 1933 for "anti-Fascist activities abroad"—a fact that he would exaggerate after the war—Malaparte kept cynical and ambiguous proximity with the regime and its protagonists. The reasons for this behavior are multifold. On the one hand, the Fascist state was a major source of patronage for intellectuals; on the other, friendship with powerful figures of the regime granted him a mobility and an intellectual liberty otherwise impossible in Italy. This line of conduct was quite common under the dictatorship, particularly for authors who would later constitute the modern canon in Italy, such as Ungaretti, Pirandello, Vittorini, and Gadda.[32] Only in the late 1930s, after his confinement, would Malaparte regain a reasonable degree of freedom as a public intellectual and journalist.

Personal disillusions, including his failure to become a protagonist in Fascist Italy's political debate, prompted him to dismiss any faith in revolutionary politics—a rejection that was confirmed by his witnessing of total war. In his works, he would then pursue a *tragic* understanding of history, thereby challenging postwar redemptive narratives. Nevertheless, the intellectual freedom he regained in the early 1940s as editor of the journal *Prospettive* and war correspondent for *Corriere della Sera* signaled an artistic independence that was rare under Fascism. His ambivalent and calculated detachment from Fascist cultural politics was based more on personal disappointment than on ethical grounds. Yet it sheds light on the regime's ongoing erosion of consent, especially among the intellectual class that was summoned to support its military efforts. As Alatri would clarify in his 1945 article cited above, Fascism in Italy "died because it hadn't learned how to keep its promises, not because the promises themselves were revealed to be monstrous."

Malaparte *theorized* his practice of artistic autonomy from Fascist cultural politics already in 1940—well before the fall of Mussolini. In "Our Sin," an editorial published in 1940 for *Prospettive*, he ambiguously hints at the double feature of his—indeed of modern—writing:

> What counts the most in our literature [. . .] are not the pages written, so to speak, with black ink; it's not the visible writing, but what is legible under the page, everything that is not a precise and perceptible sign [. . .] everything that is written with white ink. We all write with white ink. And what saves

our visible writing is exactly the completely modern awareness of perceiving, under the accepted pages, the thousand others unsaid, foregone, etc.[33]

In this excerpt, Malaparte describes his writing as a self-concealment as much as an exposé, both features coexisting on the same page. Modernist writing is eminently self-reflective and I believe that finding an allusion to Fascist censorship in this passage would be an overinterpretation. Still, through the metaphor of the "white ink," Malaparte argues for the autonomy of literature from politics and propaganda, consistent with his other articles published in the journal.[34] Far from being an act of political opposition, this is an example of Malaparte's poetics. Not a crypto-anti-Fascist agenda but a refusal of moral accountability for the sake of the artistic and intellectual freedom of his writing—a position he would confirm in the following years in *The Skin*.[35]

The idea of art's autonomy from politics supports Malaparte's reports from the Eastern Front during the Axis invasion of Soviet Russia, later collected in *The Volga Rises in Europe*. The book was printed in the winter of 1943—*before* the fall of Mussolini—but did not circulate until the summer. Copies of the first edition were destroyed during an Allied bombing of the printing house in early February. The reprint enjoyed limited circulation in the late summer until the Fascist puppet state of Salò confiscated available copies.[36] Throughout 1943, Malaparte sent fiery letters to his publisher Valentino Bompiani complaining about these repeated delays. Malaparte was wary of censorship but expressed in his letters no doubt that his book would find a large readership in a faltering Fascist Italy. On March 12, he quite unceremoniously pushes Bompiani to hasten the publication: "Don't pass up this opportunity," he writes. "Today everything that's Russian is flying off the shelves."[37] On August 21, after the fall of Mussolini but with the Fascists still in power, Malaparte would be even more explicit: "I wrote that book, *The Volga*, in the pre-Christian period. And it works perfectly in a period like this, in which the triumph of Christianity is at its zenith."[38] In a completely different political scenario, he would go on to reprint the book in 1951, adding details that reinforced his open sympathy for the Red Army, in contrast with his depiction of the Axis forces.[39]

The Volga Rises in Europe constitutes a unique publication in Fascist Italy, as it exposes the contradictions of Mussolini's regime during its downward spiral in an ambiguous manner. The book's most striking feature is Malaparte's refusal to comply with the official propaganda set by the regime, which ordered its reporters to narrate the war against Bolshevism along racial and ideological lines. In the preface to the 1943 edition, he claims:

"The truth is that Bolshevism is a typically European phenomenon. Behind the Doric columns of Piatiletka, behind the colonnade of Gosplan statistics, extends not Asia but another Europe: *the other Europe.*"⁴⁰

Malaparte dismisses here the representation of the war on the Eastern Front as a clash of civilizations, between the "Asian" and "barbaric" Soviet Russia and the "European" and "civilized" (but also "classicizing") Axis Europe. Orientalist clichés and historicist rhetoric supported this robust strand of Fascist propaganda. The Italian press, subjected to the regime's *veline* ("press orders"), and prestigious journalists such as Indro Montanelli and Virgilio Lilli deployed such rhetoric in the very pages of *Corriere della Sera* in which Malaparte published his wartime correspondence. Malaparte himself made ample use of orientalist and racist stereotypes in his previous articles from Greece, former Yugoslavia, and Romania.⁴¹ Still, his reports from the Eastern Front take an unexpected turn once the German Army approaches Soviet territory and a clash with the Red Army becomes imminent. Henceforth, Malaparte's articles unexpectedly focus on the success of the Bolshevik experiment in creating "the Soviet new man." In order to do so, the author had to dismiss trite propaganda—beginning with the cliché depicting Russians as "Asian."⁴²

Malaparte had already criticized the idea that Soviet Russia was extraneous to Europe in his 1932 pamphlet *Le bonhomme Lénine.* Banned in Italy but successfully published in Paris, the pamphlet ridiculed Lenin by depicting the leader of the Bolshevik Revolution as an innocuous and bookish petty-bourgeois. As in *The Volga Rises in Europe,* Soviet Russia and the Marxist intelligentsia are not the only targets of Malaparte's polemics. By representing the hero of the revolution as a familiar figure, Malaparte challenges conservative classes that refused to regard the Bolshevik Revolution as a European phenomenon, preferring to relegate its roots and consequences to a generic and racialized (as conspicuously non-white) "Asia."⁴³

The Volga Rises in Europe narrates the war on the Eastern Front as the decisive stage of European civilization's future. The book lacks any anti-Fascist agenda, but its vivid depiction of the armies battling on the Eastern Front indirectly sheds light on the failures of Mussolini's Italy. At first glance, Malaparte seems to respect the prescriptions of Fascist propaganda. However, his portraits of the people he encountered during the campaign—German soldiers and officials, Ukrainian peasants, Soviet combatants turned prisoners of war—subtly undermine this propaganda, providing information and details that subvert the regime's official instructions. In key passages, Malaparte declares that his book attempts to investigate the "modern world's ethics." According to the author, modern ethics derive from the technical expertise and collective organization of the two colliding armies, which he depicts as functioning like immense, mobile factories. Nonetheless, the efficiency and humanity of the Red Army soldiers clearly contrast with the "abstract" precision of their German counterparts.[44] The "technological sublime" Malaparte employs to narrate the advancing Red Army must have had a bitter taste for the *Corriere della Sera* reader. In a passage such as this,

> Communism's greatest industrial creation is its army. Everything in it, from its weapons to its spirit, is the result of twenty years of industrial organization, of the technical education of qualified workers. The real Soviet social body is the army [. . .] because it is in the army that one can measure the degree of development and industrial progress achieved by Communist society,[45]

the Italian reader could not but compare the accomplishments of Soviet Russia, the proclaimed worst enemy of Fascist Italy, to those of Mussolini's regime. The words Malaparte chooses to describe the Red Army typically echo those of Fascist propaganda. In the same article he writes that Communism in "twenty years," was able to create a "new tough race." Together with the foundation of the empire, the creation of a "new race" was Mussolini's main ambition for Fascist Italy. Thus, it is not by chance that Malaparte emphasizes the centrality of the army in the construction of the Soviet totalitarian state. Without explicit mention of the current Italian situation, he unveils the failure of Italian Fascism as a national endeavor based on the militarization of society. In those very days, the Italian army was collapsing at every front. Only a few months later would the Red Army finally defeat it, sealing the destiny of the regime.

Malaparte underscores how Mussolini's defeat was not only military but also ideological. *The Volga Rises in Europe* reports the epochal fight between Communism and Nazism; in this historic conflict, the ultimate loser is the excluded third party—Italian Fascism. While the war is not over yet, Mussolini's regime, although never explicitly mentioned, certainly cannot represent any real alternative, dwarfed as it is by the military prowess and technological organization of the two main contenders. In Malaparte's writing, the signified clashes with the signifier, the praise turns into criticism. In his own words, the white ink shows what the black ink hides.

In the early 1940s, Malaparte published several essays to expound his literary ideas. These pieces cautiously voice his mounting impatience with Fascist cultural policies. The article "Exquisite Corpses," published in *Prospettive* in 1940, envisages a new literature that rejects aestheticism, which he declares Italy's worst "national ill." On the contrary, he argues that the best works of young Italian writers disclose a common aspiration for a literature beyond formalisms, rhetorically aimed to transcend the limits of artistic projects.[46] Again, Malaparte advocates here for the autonomy of art from politics and reiterates that using an author's biography to judge their literary production is nonsensical.

Considering how committed Malaparte was to influencing politics with his writing, this statement may come as a surprise. In fact, beginning with his early publications in the 1920s, the writer was deeply involved in the regime's propaganda machine as he actively contributed to the creation of a new "Fascist culture." However, his works in the early 1940s take a radically different turn, reflecting his disillusion with the regime and his distance from its cultural policies. By advocating for the autonomy of his art, Malaparte assumes *the role of the witness* to the cruelty and violence that the conflict unleashed. Aware of the *performative* quality of his self-assumed role, he unabashedly intertwines in his narrative firsthand experiences with the stories he gathered on the many fronts of the war. In his accounts, he avoids moral posturing and any nostalgia for a European civilization he himself contributed to dismantling. Europe is, in fact, described as a landscape of rubble. The role of the witness Malaparte assumes had the significant advantage of allowing him to gloss over his past involvement. Yet the author never denies his own belonging to that landscape of rubble to which he bears witness.

Malaparte chose to draw on his long familiarity with totalitarian regimes as material for his new literature, without problematizing his own position as a formerly Fascist ideologue. Still, by concentrating on the disconcerting spectacle of Europe's abasement without any nostalgia for its past, he also avoided writing in bad faith as characterized by authors such as Montanelli or Longanesi, who in their postwar publications preferred to describe the venial sins of the defective national character, thus glossing over Italian crimes and responsibility in the war.[47] Returning to "Exquisite Corpses" and the early 1940s, Malaparte's disturbing awareness surfaces when, in contrast to the coeval "call to arms" of intellectuals in support of the ongoing war and epitomized by Giuseppe Bottai's journal *Primato*, he concludes that

> our own work as writers, in short, is only the detritus of a world formally and morally in ruins, of a literary civilization in decay. [. . .] Let us leave behind (and this is our greatest merit, that which will inspire the respect of future generations) the example of our serene consciousness of that cruelty, which many reproach in our work.[48]

After Italian Totalitarianism | 39

This pivotal passage anticipates the poetics of *Kaputt*, "a cruel book," as Malaparte himself describes it in the introduction.[49] The "cruelty" Malaparte refers to is the intellectual responsibility of representing and elaborating the moral abjection taking place in Europe. In this unprecedented historical context, he argues, every moralistic account sounds false and rhetorical, leaning toward ideological interpretation or sheer propaganda. Additionally, Malaparte affirms his right to literary autonomy in order to distance himself from the cultural "call to arms" that Fascist Minister of National Education Giuseppe Bottai launched with his journal *Primato*, in parallel with the Fascist intervention in the war.

Malaparte's controversial position leaves many questions unanswered, as his proclaimed autonomy oscillates between personal opportunism and bold foresight. Although the blatant propaganda of his *Corriere della Sera* correspondences from Greece in 1940 point to the former, it is also true that he designed and published an issue of *Prospettive* entirely dedicated to French Surrealism only a few months before Italy's entrance in the war against France and Great Britain—untimely as he ever was.[50] In addition, Alberto Moravia—who was banned from publishing for his difficulties with the regime's cultural policies and for his Jewish identity—features in the journal as Malaparte's closest collaborator.[51] In the *Prospettive* article "Moot Points," also published in 1940, Malaparte claims:

> The world, and especially Europe, will be sown with corpses: ideas, feelings, prejudices, philosophies, conceptions of morality, traditions. We will return home just in time to participate in the most marvelous funerals. And if we happen to die, struck by the bullets of Lieutenant Eluard or Captain Breton, we will leave behind no last will and testament.[52]

This passage underlines the aestheticization of struggle and death, a recurrent trope of avant-garde literature and modernist Fascist rhetoric. Still, as suggested by Malaparte himself, to understand this excerpt, we have to "follow the white ink hidden in the page behind the printed words." The literary references are not from autarchic Italy but from two of the most acclaimed Marxist poets of France. After the "funeral" of the old world and its ideas, the regeneration will be on a European scale. Even so, Mussolini's proclaimed "inevitable victory" for Italy is *not* taken for granted—not even on the cultural level.

Malaparte described and even theorized his conduct during the last years of the dictatorship in "Conscientious Objection," a remarkable and contradictory essay written in 1943 after the fall of Mussolini. The essay would have appeared in *Prospettive* had the military occupation of the Italian peninsula not stopped the publication of the journal. It thus remained unpublished until recently.[53] According to Giuseppe Pardini, it was the only writing Malaparte completed during the so-called 45 days of Badoglio. "Conscientious Objection" is best read alongside works such as Czesław Miłosz's *The Captive Mind* or Danilo Kiš's, "Censorship/Self-Censorship," which probe the self-delusion and self-censorship of intellectuals under dictatorship.[54] In the article, Malaparte does not attempt to create a tradition in support of anti-Fascist culture. Instead, he defends the literary achievements of his own generation, which he claims was able to write with a certain degree of freedom in the gloomy atmosphere and suffocating constraints of a police state.

Far from foreshadowing cultural resistance to the regime, Malaparte claimed critical autonomy from totalitarian culture. The idea of his art's autonomy from politics was not only suspect for Fascism but also dangerous for orthodox Marxists, especially after the war. Only a few months later, many Italian intellectuals were outraged when they discovered that the pseudonymous Gianni Strozzi, the author of four columns narrating the liberation of Florence in the late summer of 1944 for the Communist daily *l'Unità*, was actually Curzio Malaparte. The writer was seen as too compromised and publicly exposed with the regime, yet his professed critical autonomy had a major role in the general outcry. For Communists who had fought in the Resistance, a "comrade Malaparte" was morally untenable but also ideologically unreliable.

However, considering how allegiances were shifting in Italy in the tumultuous context of 1944, his pieces for *l'Unità* were not an isolated case. From newly liberated Rome, well-known authors such as Piovene, Moravia, and Savinio, who had previously stated their skepticism and even scorn for Communism, were publishing articles eloquently titled "Intellectuals Are Proletarians," "Hope: Christianity and Communism," and "Europe's Fate," which eyed the reborn Communist party as the political force able to renovate the country.[55] Additionally, Malaparte's reports on the liberation of Florence are not at odds with the declaration of critical autonomy professed in his prewar and wartime articles. In "A Lesson from Florence. Anticipating Reaction," published in *l'Unità* on August 23, 1944, the author claims: "Either anti-Fascism is revolution, or it's only an expedient, political compromise, provisional remedy; it's only a 'deferment.'"[56] His tone here is not dissimilar to the one used twenty years before in his vitriolic pamphlet *Viva Caporetto!*, which attacked the political elite who, during WWI, placed rhetoric and defense of the status quo before the lives of Italian soldiers dying in the trenches.[57] Malaparte's ensuing polemic against anti-Fascist culture is much more consistent with his personal intellectual and literary trajectory than with a supposed fidelity to old Fascist tenets.

"Politically mobile, but not unprincipled," as John Gatt-Rutter described him,[58] Malaparte held varying and often contradictory political beliefs. Yet he remained loyal to his polemical anarchism and to a populist idea of social palingenesis. Malaparte's distance from Fascist cultural politics dates back to the articles of *Prospettive* in the early 1940s and the war correspondence constituting *The Volga Rises in Europe*. In the early postwar period, he would then expand his disavowal of Fascist totalitarianism to a far-reaching critique of Stalinism, which included a denunciation of Marxism in one of his most piercing yet overlooked works—the play *Das Kapital*.[59]

Upon its premiere in Paris in 1948, *Das Kapital* was met with outrage by French leftist intellectuals, who wittingly proclaimed the work "un capital sans interest."[60] Neglected until Maurizio Serra's reappraisal in his recent biography of Malaparte, the work attacks the foundations of both bourgeois and Communist ideologies. The drama takes place in the nineteenth century, in the squalid interiors of a London apartment, with scenes reminiscent more of Dostoevsky's dialogues than of modernist Italian and French theater. *Das Kapital* features a petit bourgeois Karl Marx at the center of the script. Malaparte constructs the play around bourgeois privacy and Soviet cult of personality: By concentrating these two tenets in his main character Marx, the writer condenses two values utterly at odds with each other. As a political exile, Marx is unable to cope with the problems of everyday life: feeding his numerous children, earning a living for his whole family, and keeping up a decent respectability. The hero and forefather of the revolution is represented as an irresponsible father. While his children die of illness one after another, he strenuously works on his philosophical masterpiece for the liberation of mankind, throwing his wife Jenny into despair as she attempts to save their children by any means possible.

By dressing Marx in bourgeois clothes, Malaparte strips the prophet of the proletarian revolution of his mystical aura, at that time widespread even beyond Marxist circles. The writer had deployed a similar rhetorical strategy in the past, as in the mentioned *Le bonhomme Lénine* and its idiosyncratic representation of the Bolshevik leader. Moreover, "Heroes Turned Upside Down" was the anti-rhetorical title of one of Malaparte's earliest political articles, published in 1922 in Gobetti's journal *La Rivoluzione liberale*.[61] *Das Kapital*, however, reaches an utterly different dimension, in which ideological dispute acquires a much more radical—and unexpectedly personal—significance.

The parody of Marx is not the main motif of Malaparte's play. In *Das Kapital*, the king is naked: The spectacle of his nakedness is not at all comic but highly harrowing. Like his beloved ancient Greeks, Malaparte condenses the ideological struggle of his time and compresses it in the very point where its consequences are most devastating—in familial intimacy.[62] The violent encounter between political abstraction and individual everyday life is represented in *Das Kapital* in all its tragic incommensurability. This powerful conflict engenders further confrontations that are inherent to modern revolutionary practices.

At stake here is the clash between the planning of human life by totalitarian regimes and the biological residue common in each single human being—a common residue which resists normativity and biopolitical regulation. As Walter Benjamin wrote only a few years earlier, individual life in its unique contingency does not pertain to ideology but to natural history: "Man is neither a phenomenon nor an effect, but a created being," he concludes.[63] Palingenetic war and the modern myth of a new birth for mankind ultimately scattered individuals, who found a sense of belonging only in their common *creatureliness*. Humans are "created beings": The resilience of creaturely life in all its forms contradicts the revolutionary imposition of a new origin, which postulates the political *correction* of human nature.[64]

Malaparte's post-WWII production strives to portray the unredeemable contrast between creaturely life and modern politics' attempt at violently refashioning human nature. In *Das Kapital*, the writer pushes this contrast into the mind of the protagonist himself, by inventing an extremely effective alter ego to Marx, his secretary named Godson. Although vividly represented, the second character has no real consistency—he could be a ghost, a demon, or simply, Christ. Godson is a Dostoevskian "idiot"; his name is quite explicit in this regard. With his secretary, Marx tests the limits and historical consequences of his ideas. Their rapid dialogues powerfully dramatize the struggle within the philosopher's own conscience, beginning with the question of whether revolutionary violence is necessary. The disagreement between Godson and Marx spells out the contradictions of trying to devise a better society by transcending singular individualities and human suffering. In particular, the problem of evil is brought back to a formulation with biblical undertones: Why the children?

Malaparte clarifies the tragic conflict at the center of the play in an interview for the Italian daily *Il Tempo*. According to the author, "to justice, the ideal furiously pursued by the protagonist, [*Godson*] mysteriously opposes the other [ideal], of charity."[65] This clash between justice and charity showcases the opposition between the new secular society in which God is banned and the religious community. This opposition is based on the recognition that the other is equal before the divine, a realization that entails compassion and respect for human life as founding values. The useless sacrifice of children for the sake of an ideal or future justice is the dramatic apex of the play, as it epitomizes the contradictions of modern attempts to regenerate and "correct" human nature through politics, regardless of violence. Two key passages stage this disagreement:

> Marx: A just man doesn't have the right to judge a guilty man?
> Godson: There are no just men in the world.
> Marx: And so you'd go so far as to say there are no guilty men in the world? [...] There are guilty men, Godson, there are. Everyone who belongs to the class that exploits and oppresses other men is guilty. Every last one needs his head kicked in.
> Godson [*smiling sweetly*]: Even the children?
> Marx: Even the children!
> Godson: [...] What you call "shandemporung" [*sic*], the anger that is born of shame, is a legitimate thing, when one rises up against the oppressors. Nobody can say you're wrong, because you're right, you're right. But nobody has the right to punish the oppressors by striking their children. Only God has this right, Mr. Marx.
> Marx: Let's hurry, then, to punish the oppressors, let's crush them soon, soon! Tomorrow will already be too late.
> [...] Godson [*in a low voice*]: Your children's life is the price you pay for men's freedom. Then ... you are not guilty, Mr. Marx; but ... if the price were not just?
> Marx: It's enough that the cause be just.
> Godson: Yes, it is just ... and ... if it were not ... [...] It's doubt, not faith, that saves men. [...] It's not just about your children, but about all the children on earth. If one day, among all the men the revolution grinds up in its path, you recognized the face of an innocent victim, even just one, what would you do then?
> Marx: I'd continue on my path, Godson!
> Godson: Don't you know that God already asks you, in every moment, to account for every drop of blood that you will shed in the future? Haven't you understood that God is already punishing you, in your children?[66]

Early reviewers of the play commented on the Christian quality of Godson's message, even though the character clearly states that he is Jewish.[67] This is not a minor detail: Malaparte consciously evokes through Godson the recent history of victimization, scapegoating, and violence suffered by the European Jews. Moreover, Godson's Jewish identity widens the scope of Malaparte's message beyond the boundaries of mere religion, or rather, beyond the constraints of Christianity as an institution and a set of practices. As he would fully express in *The Skin*, the Jew for Malaparte is a Christological figure.[68] In one of Godson's monologues, in which the real interlocutor is the audience, the character claims:

> At a certain point in his life, maybe only for a single instant, every man is a Jew ... Every man flees misery and hate. But all those who are persecuted know that only God has the right to judge and punish; only he has the right to strike children, to strike among the innocent also the guilty ... Divine justice does not hesitate to crush an innocent man to punish a guilty one ... [69]

Godson's speeches are ripe with messianic and prophetic undertones—not at all unusual for secular Jewish culture in the first decades of the century.[70] Malaparte's fictional character allegorizes the long history of discrimination against Jews but purposefully avoids historical verisimilitude. The elusive nature of Godson and his characterization as a victim allows Malaparte to make veiled reference to contemporary practices of political violence, omitting at the same time any personal responsibility as a former Fascist. Godson's spectral presence on stage and the religious undertones of his speeches are meant not only to instill doubt in Marx's conscience but also to hint at Stalin's political persecutions in the name of revolutionary justice.[71]

Godson, however, has another, more subtle, function in the economy of *Das Kapital*. As noted by an attentive reviewer such as Salvatore Quasimodo, although Godson is the alter ego of Marx, his speeches are sometimes delirious.[72] He is indeed the incarnation of the *Fool*, representing a long-standing theatrical convention of an outsider speaking an irreverent language within the polyphony of the play. It is not necessary to uncover the Fool's identity but to recognize his voice's ambiguous status, both in and outside the theatrical representation. Godson's truth is tangible, gripping, and contrasts with the abstract reasoning of Marx. Still, his truth is not, or not completely, the same as Malaparte's. The character is not the bearer of the author's viewpoint: "He is ultimately the scenic exteriorization of an intimate part of Marx himself," as the writer himself makes clear.[73]

Malaparte cannot fully endorse the messianic stance of his character, who represents, along with the crucified Jews in *The Skin*, another iteration of the innocent scapegoats of history haunting postwar Europe: limbo-figures, the aborted fetuses of the last pages of *The Skin*, the Goyaesque animal masks of his film *The Forbidden Christ* (1951). All these spectral presences loom over Malaparte's postwar oeuvre in such a way as to recall the bad faith and the muted violence upon which Italy and Europe established a new beginning after WWII. As Kundera pointed out in his essay on the writer, Malaparte understood all too well that "the new European war will play out only on *the battlefield of memory*."[74]

A final aspect of *Das Kapital* deserves closer attention, since it involves Malaparte's personal commitment to revolutionary politics. In 1948, Cold War divisions already kindled political animosity within both Italy and France. Social-democratic discontent notwithstanding, the majority of the Western European Left considered Marx the prophet of human liberation. The philosopher was acclaimed as the founding father of an ideology that seemed to constitute a new intellectual and secular religion, regardless of the second wave of terror raging in the USSR and the horrifying series of show trials in Soviet-occupied Eastern Europe.

By highlighting the paradoxes intrinsic to the Marxist grand narrative, Malaparte acts out two momentous refusals. The more apparent of the two is the rejection of Stalinism and of every totalitarian form of state. What Godson and Marx expose in their animated exchanges are not only the metaphysical and historical fallacies of Marxism but also the unpredictable consequences of such a radical conception of politics. According to Malaparte, Marxism's abstraction is revealed by its refusal to confront its "concrete" analysis with creaturely life. The second refusal is implicitly played out in *Das Kapital* through the reproaches of the Fool and the philosopher's verbal violence. In his theatrical work, Malaparte offers for the first time a rebuttal of his *own* revolutionary past for a public that in 1931 had enthusiastically praised him as theoretician of the revolution with his successful essay, *Technique du coup d'état*. *Das Kapital* marks for Malaparte the end of his revolutionary politics and modernist ideal of a radical restructuring of society that had supported his output for years.

An Untimely Inquiry into Totalitarianism: Vittorio Zincone

The revolutionary myths of social and national palingenesis accompanied Malaparte's youth and intellectual formation, from volunteering in WWI to the March on Rome and to his journalistic inquiries into Soviet Russia. Vittorio Zincone, born in 1911, belonged instead to the generation who grew up under Mussolini's yoke and experienced Fascism as the only political reality. Like many young intellectuals educated in the late 1920s through 1930s, Zincone found in the postwar party system a viable antidote to the collapse of the values of his youth. Unlike the majority of his contemporaries, however, Zincone did not just atone for his past mistakes upon entering the ranks of post-Fascist political organizations. The journalist is best known today for his leading role in the 1950s dailies, such as *Il Resto del Carlino* and *Il Tempo*, and for his tenure in the Lower House of Italian Parliament as a representative of the Partito Liberale Italiano (Italian Liberal Party). Few remember that, in 1947, he intervened in the animated political debate before the April 18, 1948, elections—which sanctioned Christian Democrats' victory over the Left—with the publication of his groundbreaking essay, *The Totalitarian State*. Zincone's analysis of the structures of power and lack of political disagreement within Mussolini's Fascist State resulted in a firm rejection of any form of totalitarianism, including Soviet Communism.

In the late 1930s, Zincone worked as a high-ranking official in the infamous "Ministry of People's Culture," Fascist Italy's Ministry of Propaganda. In this position, he observed firsthand the inner workings of the propaganda machine, the intricacies of totalitarian bureaucracy, and the arbitrary decision-making processes of the Fascist State. A fervent Blackshirt, Zincone belonged to a generation of young intellectuals who had actively supported the regime's revolutionary agenda, only to feel completely betrayed and dispossessed after the war. The de-Fascistization and democratization of this generation was of the utmost importance to postwar political parties—especially the Communists and the Christian Democrats whose ideologies required a large mass base and experienced leaders for their organizations. Whereas intellectuals from the socialist-liberal Action Party called for a radical purge of the Fascist political class, other political formations took a more lenient approach.[75] As exemplified in Elio Vittorini's famous article "Can Youth Be Fascist?," published in 1946 in the journal *Il Politecnico*, Communist cadres were eager to absolve and welcome in their ranks young people who previously served as Blackshirts, particularly in the less blatant cases, and not unlike their Catholic counterparts.[76] Before acceptance into the new party, the repentant young intellectual had to undergo an expiatory "long journey" from Fascism to democratic values. The metaphor of a personal voyage of atonement derives from the evocative title of Ruggero Zangrandi's successful memoir published in 1948, *The Long Journey: My Contribution to the History of a Generation*. Zangrandi's moral crisis with Fascism led him to join anti-Fascist forces and subsequently experience incarceration and deportation. As the title makes clear, his personal story was regarded as emblematic of his whole generation.[77] In his study on the legacy of Fascism, Luca La Rovere has accurately investigated these policies based on specific "patterns of conversion" from Fascist ideology to the new (secular or religious) political credos.[78] In La Rovere's work, the figure of Zincone is reappraised after decades of disregard, together with the value of his pamphlet, *The Totalitarian State*.

Zincone's pamphlet examines the key structural features of the totalitarian state, such as the mass mobilization around a charismatic leader, the submission of individual morality to a collective ethics, the establishment of a revolutionary doctrine of which the political party was the only interpreter, and the consequent treatment of all dissidents as heretics. The major merit of *The Totalitarian State* is its assessment of totalitarianism in psychological and technical terms, *regardless* of ideology. Thereby, Zincone included the Soviet state built by Lenin and Stalin in his comparative analysis of totalitarianism, alongside regimes sustained by extreme nationalist agendas such as Fascist Italy and Nazi Germany. It was this gesture that most likely determined the subsequent neglect of Zincone's work. Through a series of arguments based on his firsthand experience and attentive reading of the major revolutionary texts, Zincone affirms:

> The adoption of the totalitarian method does not depend in any way on the ideological content in a programmatic sense or on the social foundation of the parties that historically have applied it. Parties "of the right" and "of the left," proletarian, bourgeois, and mixed parties, have applied almost identical procedures in the totalitarian conquest of power.[79]

Informed by this unconventional approach, *The Totalitarian State* bestows two remarkable insights that only recent historiography has addressed. Zincone focuses on the overlooked "social tensions" that are intrinsic to the democratic process. Without a legal counterbalance, he argues, such social tensions result in tendencies toward oligarchic power. Therefore, he concludes, "Totalitarianism is not an abnormal and gratuitous phenomenon, but the consequence of a long, spontaneous, organic, and *long-denounced* involution of democracy."[80] Polemical targets here are not only Croce's historicism and his idealist followers but also the Marxist interpretation of the rise of Fascist regimes as the result of an internal crisis within capitalism and power-wielding elites—the interpretation of Fascism as the swan song of the bourgeoisie. By displaying the technical aspects of a totalitarian takeover of power and its repressive policies, Zincone warns that modern liberal democracies are unstable constructions, susceptible of degenerating into oligarchies and new forms of despotism.

The author bases this evaluation on the internal organization of the totalitarian state, whereby political disagreement is suppressed by banning every alternative party, and a "confessional-military party" constitutes the only possible bearer and interpreter of the revolution.[81] Zincone's fundamental point is the intertwining of military and religious organizations within the revolutionary party, in which he sees a disquieting continuity between Fascist and Communist practices and those of the Catholic Church's most efficient propaganda institution—the Society of Jesus. According to Zincone, the interweaving of politics and religion in the modern revolutionary party is the defining concept of the state in its totalitarian form, the outcome of a long political process that is "revolutionary" only in its modern mass rites:

> Party doctrine is represented as state religion and the totalitarian state is considered a theocracy; that is, as a regime where full rights are reserved for the believers in a faith, and the highest power is in the hands of the guardians and interpreters of its orthodoxy.[82]

In the broader international debate, Zincone was not alone in identifying the nexus of politics and religion as the decisive feature of totalitarian states.[83] In the Italian context, however, his idea that totalitarianism *per se*, regardless of ideological underpinnings, is a political project that would inevitably lead to the destitution of individual freedom for the sake of doctrinal orthodoxy was far from widely accepted. Undoubtedly, his anti-Communist agenda plays a prominent role in Zincone's interpretation. As hinted above, *The Totalitarian State* must be contextualized in the harsh political struggle before the democratic elections of 1948. Nevertheless, Zincone's criticism of Communism does not derive from the defense of tradition or the status quo but from his firm rejection of totalitarianism. For the journalist, overcoming Fascism meant refusing the redemptive illusions of mass politics, while accepting disagreement as inherent to democratic participation. Unlike most of his contemporaries, dismissing Fascism *implied* rejecting Communism as well.

Zincone's lucid examination of his own past within the totalitarian paradigm remains unparalleled in the early postwar period among Italian intellectuals. Without resorting to the literary prowess and the provocative stances of Malaparte, the journalist attests to the difficult task of coming to terms with personal involvement in the regime. La Rovere suggests that Zincone's unconventional approach truly participates in the "duty of bearing witness" that many Italian intellectuals deeply sensed in the early postwar era. The historian remarks, however, that "such a reflection could develop free of conditioning and forcing only provided that there is a clear separation, at least at the level of narrative, between personal experience and analysis of the Fascist phenomenon."[84]

This separation was hardly feasible for most formerly Fascist authors. The nexus of Fascist ideology and religious propaganda, crucial for the totalitarian project, was at the center of their historical and existential reflection, as the next chapter will examine. Lack of a public discussion on Italian totalitarianism could effectively facilitate problematic "conversions" to the Communist faith or the idea of a "Christian Democracy."[85] Still, as the artistic and intellectual trajectories of Malaparte and Zincone reveal, the question is ill posed: Not every ex-Fascist replaced one credo with another, and some attempted to operate outside the reassuring umbrella of grand narratives. Malaparte and Zincone are hardly typical cases, yet their critique of totalitarianism showcases the intellectual complexity of postwar transition. Their works witness the intricacies of a historical and political reality—the Fascist totalitarian state—which collective myths of renewal relegated to the past all too quickly.

A neglected 1946 piece written by Zincone for the journal *Mercurio* further illuminates this uneasy passage. Polemically titled "What the Constitution Lacks," the article anticipates the main arguments of his later book, yet it also singles out how ritual and confessional approaches to politics, including a cult of personality and political uses of memory, are intrinsic and not accessory to the totalitarian state.[86] In the age of mass politics, the propaganda machine directed by the state can easily reproduce or create myths of collective redemption anew and associate their cultic power with new charismatic figures:

> A salient feature of the modern type of oligarchical power that studies for the present Italian constitution have not considered at all is [. . .] the cultlike devotion to political men that constitutes one of the indispensable preconditions for the establishment of totalitarian power. The real or presumed "saviors of the fatherland" who, in exchange for deliverance, have asked for absolute power, are myriad [. . .]. Now, confronted with the uneducated masses who have entered into the heart of politics, it is relatively easy to create the myth of "saving of the fatherland," given modern propaganda methods, whose power is absolutely disproportional to the unfortunately very meager progress in independence of individual and collective [. . .] judgment. Thus, modern constitutions should intervene extremely harshly against devotional deformations of politics, like the display and public veneration of images of living men, the dedication of streets and monuments, and in general all the ritual

acts that tend to distance politics from the rigor of reason, transforming it into an act of worship and perpetual enthusiasm.[87]

Zincone suggests that state-directed memory politics coupled with the rhetorical monumentalization of the historical present are characterizing practices of totalitarian states. His conclusions, however, shed disquieting light on modern political projects beyond Fascism. As we have seen, collective myths of national renewal were widespread in early postwar Italy. In the generous attempt to coalesce a new national identity around the values of the Resistance, prominent anti-Fascist intellectuals such as jurist Piero Calamandrei minimized these crucial aspects of totalitarian rule in public speeches and private writings. One of the architects of the Italian Constitution, Calamandrei profusely defended the Italian people to international audiences and sought to establish, through his writings and moral authority, a new national epic based on the martyrs of the Liberation.[88] Still, as in the case of Sforza and Croce, to the disillusioned ears of Zincone, Calamandrei might have sounded like an attempt to turn the clock backward.

After the liberation of Florence in 1944, Calamandrei began preparing a book reflecting on these momentous questions. Although he did not complete and publish his considerations, most likely because of more pressing responsibilities, his assessment of totalitarianism as "fiction" illuminates how distant his interpretation was from that of Zincone. After an analysis of the legal construction of the Fascist state, Calamandrei concludes:

> Fascist totalitarianism is an ad hominem theory, made to measure for a unique genius, in the absence of which the system would lose all meaning and all feasibility. [. . .] Totalitarianism, on close inspection, does not mean anything other than *Mussolinism*. This general theory of the Fascist state has meaning only to the extent that it has that name and that surname.[89]

Calamandrei's judgment of the legal apparatus of the regime is hardly disputable. However, it restricts an understanding of the Fascist state to its legal justification, leaving out the crucial aspects highlighted by Zincone. For Calamandrei, Mussolini's totalitarianism was a fictional name for old despotism.[90]

The limits of Calamandrei's appraisal had crucial political consequences. By allocating all responsibility to the power-wielding Fascist elite and its Duce, this reading also downplays the role of Italians in approving and supporting the regime and its leader.[91] Calamandrei's assessment of Fascist totalitarianism as one of Mussolini's "lies" delayed a thorough understanding of its inner functioning. As Gabriele Pedullà recently claimed, Calamandrei became in postwar Italy "the voice of official memory for the benefit of younger generations: plaque after plaque, monument after monument."[92] His attempt to cement post-Fascist Italy through new monuments and a new civic religion minimized Italian responsibility in WWII.

The success of Calamandrei's politics of memory in the early postwar period sensibly contrasts with the isolated voice of Zincone and his analysis of totalitarianism in light of modernity's social tensions. The monumentalization of the Resistance, however, was only one of the many responses originating from anti-Fascist intellectuals. Understanding Fascism within the frame of modernity was a main preoccupation for many of them, as in the case of Carlo Levi and Alberto Moravia. Personal experiences of discrimination, prison, and exile prompted them to explore ethical and psychological territories that were unknown to the authors examined thus far.

Alberto Moravia: Rejecting of the Revolutionary Myth

What Malaparte and Zincone left unaddressed in their work features instead at the heart of Alberto Moravia's intellectual concerns during the transition: the psychological and personal strain of living under a totalitarian state. Deeply affected by the regime's discrimination before and during the war, Moravia's literary inquiry sprang from an experience of painful alienation from the regime. Fascism's looming shadow over contemporary Italy pushed him to intervene in the political debate with an investigative force unknown to most Italian intellectuals. Moravia never collected or revised the militant interventions he published in the Liberation's press, which addressed Italian Fascism within the broader crisis of European civilization. Not unlike Zincone and Malaparte, Moravia stressed the quasi-religious aspects of this crisis. His reflections, however, pointed to the firm rejection of political fanaticism and of every illiberal solution, including Communism and revolutionary politics.

"I cared for him too, only he was so vain [. . .]. And then, as I explained to you, I cannot be friends with a writer who is not a good writer. Books like *The Skin*, *Kaputt*, are awful."[93] Moravia's judgment of Malaparte leaves no room for interpretation. In fact, both their books and their personalities had very little in common. From the 1930s until July 25, 1943, however, their lives intertwined on several crucial occasions. Malaparte supported the talented younger writer and asked Moravia to collaborate on the many editorial engagements that he himself directed, from the newspaper *La Stampa* to the journal *Prospettive*. Such collaborations were vital for Moravia, who, despite, or perhaps because of, the success of his debut novel *The Time of Indifference* (1929), was harshly ostracized by the regime—first for his supposed anti-Fascism, then for his Jewish origins. As Simone Casini put it, "in racist publications he long represented the quintessential Jewish writer."[94] Moravia's difficult relationship with the regime impacted his writing well beyond the Fascist *ventennio*.[95] Like many other intellectuals of the period, Moravia was obliged to partake in the oppressive work of self-censorship to avoid the state's blackmail and intimidation. On several public occasions, Moravia professed that his books had no political agenda.[96] Yet the bureaucrats in control of culture during the Fascist regime, eager to appease Mussolini's suspicions of the writer, saw Moravia's declared lack of interest in politics as dangerous and immoral.[97] There was no room for political indifference in Fascist Italy. "Intellectualisms," such as Moravia's, were seen as corrupting the healthy body of the state and its people. To be in good standing, writers were obliged to participate in the undertakings of the regime in some way.[98] Censorship and self-censorship forced Moravia to turn personal idiosyncrasies into a state of alienation.

After the war, Moravia enlarged the scope of his writing beyond the critique of the Italian bourgeoisie. In his fiction, he analyzed the legacy and psychological consequences of Fascist political violence, showing how it corrupted minds before affecting bodies, regardless of class divisions. As seen in the male characters of *Woman of Rome* (1947) and *The Conformist* (1951), Fascist political violence not only perverted its supporters; it also degraded anti-Fascist antagonists and simple bystanders. Fascist violence and the author's autobiographical experience are crucial components in his early postwar fiction: brutality inflicted by the totalitarian regime on the psychological level is the point of departure for a multifaceted inquiry into the relationship between power and individuals in modern societies.

These preoccupations are at the center of Moravia's essay *Man as an End*, in which the writer sums up his reflections on modern history's traumatic events. Published in the journal *Nuovi argomenti* in 1953, the essay undertakes a humanist reappraisal of politics and ethics, reversing commonsensical, Machiavellian concepts such as "the ends justify the means" and the idea of "reason of state." With this essay, Moravia aims to subvert the ideological concept of life at the foundation of totalitarian regimes. Modern ideologies, he argues, subordinate individuals to external ends, rendering life itself inhuman—nothing more than a "means" to a political goal. Such ideologies elevate their political goals above humankind, deploying their abstract rationality in a strictly "instrumental" fashion, regardless of its consequences on people and individuals.

In *Man as an End*, Moravia dismisses any political utopia which does not—or indeed refuses to—consider the role of individual and collective suffering in the planning of future societies. The author defines human suffering as "the human residue." He treats suffering as an ontological category, necessary to define human resistance to the "instrumental rationality" of modern ideologies. "Man's suffering—that unchangeable, non-combustible residue," Moravia writes, "derives precisely from a sense of profanation, sacrilege and degradation that only man, among all the creatures, seems in a position to experience."[99] The "sacredness" of each single human being, Moravia continues, is based not just on the individuality and corporeality of suffering, but on the perception that suffering is universal. This radical awareness is not foreign to modern authors such as Franz Kafka and Primo Levi, who more effectively called it "shame."[100] For Moravia, the universality of human suffering constitutes the founding principle of a new humanism that places human beings at the center of ethics, no longer as a means to a political goal but an end per se.

Despite its remarkable insights, *Man as an End* lacks precise, consistent terminology and compelling arguments. Its main thesis, summarized by the title, is that postwar European culture must return to humanism. The main issue with the essay is that Moravia never specifies the object of his inquiry and target of his polemics with stable political terminology, drawing his main terms more from Giacomo Leopardi's poetry than from contemporary philosophical debate. The meanings of crucial words such as "State" and "totalitarianism" are often too vague or blurred together, and the text's rather abstract vocabulary contributes to its opacity. In Moravia's essay, "humanism" remains an umbrella term, too broad to indicate a viable path forward through the many contradictions of modern society, which Fascism and the war only intensified.

Nevertheless, *Man as an End* represents one of the few attempts in Italy to come to terms with totalitarianism immediately after WWII. One passage in particular stands out. It concerns the most challenging legacy of the totalitarian experience—the concentration camp. Moravia argues: "The concentration camp is the most suitable image for representing the static, though apparently frenzied, mechanism of the modern world with its suffering equals life and life equals suffering."[101] The passage anticipates two key aspects of this legacy, which have found adequate attention only decades later: the camp conceived as a characteristically *modern* experience—unthinkable without the technological advancements and the rationalization of modern societies—and human life's resistance to "instrumental rationality."[102] An excerpt from *Man as an End* clarifies both of these seminal tenets:

> The concentration camp, within the concentration camp's limits, is perfectly rational, more so than any factory, any State, or any nation. The famous answer given to an application for provisions: "Buchenwald should be self-sufficient," throws light on this rationality and confirms it.[103]

The passage exposes a profound insight about the camps: Far from being a byproduct, they are consequential to the totalitarian organization of life and intrinsic to its ideology. Moravia stresses how strong the bond is between the institution of concentration camps and the overarching technological features of modern society, underscoring the twisted use of instrumental rationality in totalitarian social planning. In those years, Western culture preferred to describe the great criminals behind Nazism in bestial, devilish tones, while Fascism was depicted in a more farcical manner. Such depictions were targeted at obliterating the popular consensus around Fascist regimes, as well as the disquieting similarities between totalitarian policies and established practices of Western democracies, such as Fordism and colonialism.

As was common in the early postwar, Moravia epitomizes the phenomenon of the concentration camp with Buchenwald, *not* Auschwitz. In the 1940s and early 1950s, it was Buchenwald, a camp mainly targeted at political dissidents, that indexed the Nazi moral abjection in public discourse. This resulted in the downplaying of the racial component of Nazi violence and genocidal practices. The Holocaust's far-reaching implications are not addressed in *Man as an End*, its aim being an existential indictment of modern society and the return to humanist values. Hence the intrinsic ambiguity of this work: Despite radically criticizing rational social planning, the essay never fully grapples with the problem of totalitarianism as such. *Man as an End* prefers, instead, to denounce the "State" as an inhumane political apparatus whose end is mass enslavement and exploitation by a restricted elite.

As mentioned earlier, Moravia's essay was published in 1953. As he declares in the introduction, however, it was written in 1946 in the aftermath of Italy's Liberation and the conclusion of WWII. According to available documents, there is no valid reason to question Moravia's claim.[104] Although it had no direct influence on the debate during the transition period, *Man as an End* should be read as the swan song of a compelling inquiry into the possibilities opened by the collapse of Fascism and closed by the flawed democratic order in charge after the 1948 elections. This was an inquiry that Moravia articulated through an impressive number of articles, most of them addressing political issues, published right after the fall of Mussolini, through the complete liberation of Italy and the crisis of anti-Fascism with the demise of Parri's government in November 1945. As seen at the beginning of this chapter, Moravia would go on to concentrate almost exclusively on his fiction, in which he successfully voiced his major themes through a wealth of different characters. Thanks to the archival research by Marcello Ciocchetti, who retrieved numerous articles of Moravia's early postwar journalistic production, it is now possible to trace the gradual development of his reflections on Italian history and politics during the transition.[105] The writer's reflections on the Liberation papers often took the unexpected literary form of aphorisms. In fact, he planned to collect these aphorisms in a book, significantly titled "Political Diary."[106]

Closely monitored by Fascist police, Moravia never published any openly political articles during Mussolini's dictatorship. However, after the Duce's arrest on July 25, 1943, and during the infamous "45 days" of the Badoglio government, the young writer actively contributed to the anti-Fascist newspaper *Il Popolo di Roma*, directed by Corrado Alvaro. The first two political columns of his career denounce the most blatantly ideological tenets of the Fascist regime, arguing for a radical change. Their titles, "Demagogues and the Crowd" and "Irrationalism and Politics," reflect two major concerns that Moravia would revisit time and again in the following months: the psychological features of mass politics and the necessity of a political practice based on reason. Both tenets are born out of the author's personal reconsideration of Fascist politics and his autobiographical experience. Moravia's articles reflect the general atmosphere of (suspicious) hope for rebirth and freedom that emerged in Rome right after the fall of Mussolini. With the Nazis attentively following the developments of Italian politics while amassing forces outside the city, Moravia proposes a radical revision of national education in order to dismiss authoritarian demagogy: "The political education of the greatest possible number of individuals," he writes, "is the aim that Italy must set for itself today."[107]

With these two articles, Moravia gets at the core of Fascist ideology. They could have cost him his life if he had not managed to escape from Rome during the Nazi occupation following Italy's armistice with the Allies. The writer would resume his reflections on politics only in the spring of the subsequent year, this time in the journals of liberated Italy. In the May/June 1944 issue of the journal *Aretusa*, printed in Naples, Moravia publishes the first of many interventions titled "Political Diary."[108] Each publication contains a series of aphorisms loosely bound to a common theme. They constitute a literary-philosophical personal re-elaboration of the events of the Italian and—to a much lesser extent—European recent past. Although no systematic study has been done on these articles, they are a relevant source for capturing the atmosphere, the contradictions, and the idealism of the transition period. Read together with Moravia's other essays of the same years, "Political Diary" illuminates, in unexpected ways, Moravia's meditation on Italian history.

The installments of "Political Diary" (later published as "Political Notebook") are characterized by disavowals and skepticism, but also wit. Moravia's initial aphorisms revolve around a series of stark, at times uncritical, oppositions, reflecting the outburst of joy after the longed-for Liberation. They are written with the freshness and impulsiveness of a diary. His later contributions evolve, instead, into a much more nuanced questioning of old and new ideological narratives. Unfortunately, the terminology Moravia employs here is once again often hurriedly drawn from literary tradition. The abstract language of these experimental pieces limits the speculative strength of Moravia's ideas, without providing a persuasive set of images.

Despite its limits, "Political Diary" is also the first, albeit fragmentary, attempt to address the political significance of totalitarianism published in Italy, providing arguments for its refusal even beyond Fascism. The author, however, did not return to these articles for a later publication, leaving many remarkable intuitions incomplete. The new political and international configuration after 1948 demanded a different, less skeptical role of public intellectuals. Moravia's aphorisms quickly turned untimely.

The "Political Diary" published in *Aretusa* enthusiastically embraces the Resistance myth of human renewal, while calling into question Crocean and neo-idealist readings of history: "It's not true that everything is freedom and for freedom in the history of the world. Much blood and countless sorrows are the price of men's attachment to their own chains." Neo-idealist readings of history are dismissed through evidence of irrational impulses in the lives of men and of nations. Moravia introduces here a seminal issue into the anti-Fascist political debate. Challenging the myths of Fascism as a "parenthesis" or the Resistance as "the People's War," Moravia addresses the troublesome question of popular consensus in Mussolini's regime, analyzing the appeal of totalitarian rule to individual psychology—a question that would haunt the writer for years to come, taking central stage in his later fiction. In the spring 1944 column, however, his intuition is somewhat pushed to the background by the implicit endorsement of the Communist myth:

> Freedom is nothing other than reason. The reign of reason can appear tyrannical at first, but then by degrees it leads to freedom, that is to say, to life.

The reign of irrational forces begins with tyranny and ends with death. So let us not confuse the two tyrannies.[109]

After limiting the sovereignty of freedom only to a rationally planned society, Moravia *needs* to differentiate "the two tyrannies" to avoid confusion regarding their goals and ultimate outcomes. According to the writer, Communism is based on rational forces, while Fascism is based on irrational ones. The previous passage is telling: It reads as if Moravia is trying to persuade his reader of the eventual good of Communism to first convince his skeptical self. Moravia's successive installments of "Political Diary" will revise this conclusion and reject Communism altogether, but only after an uneasy confrontation with his own beliefs and personal experience. Traces of this confrontation are dispersed throughout his many publications and are now worth following in detail.

Back in Rome after the city's liberation in June 1944, Moravia published the political pamphlet *Hope: Christianity and Communism*.[110] The pamphlet addresses from a psychological and existentialist standpoint the "crisis of civilization" that engulfed European society and led to a catastrophic war. Moravia traces back this crisis to the recent exhaustion of Christianity's historical function.[111] For him, the Christian egalitarian message caused a momentous psychological change in human subjectivity, both on the individual and collective levels. Christianity endowed ancient humankind with hope, a previously unknown modality of existential consciousness, thus transforming ancient subjectivity into a new Christian humanity. As Moravia defines it, "this psychological operation in which man forgets himself—that is, his death—for the benefit of all humanity, we properly call hope."[112] Consequently, because Christianity exhausted its own mission by transforming *all* human beings into Christians (the term has a larger significance than the religious one, delving into Christian egalitarian conception of creaturely life), mankind required in modern times a new prospect of hope.

In *Hope*, Moravia argues that Communism is the heir and continuation of the Christian mission. It is the only repository of a new message of hope for modern women and men—freedom. Yet, what matters to Moravia is not really the content of this new hope as much as its psychological function.[113] Commenting on the projected utopian city of Communism, the writer insists, "What's important is not so much that this city arrive, but that there exist hope for its arrival." Moravia consistently employs religious terminology throughout the pamphlet to reinforce his main thesis of the psychological continuity between Christianity and Communism. His concept of "hope" can be interpreted in secular terms by resorting to what Alain Badiou was to call "*fidelity* to the event."[114] According to Badiou's post-Marxist philosophy, "the event" is what resides outside ontology. The concept of "fidelity to the event" describes the enablement of a decision on the "event" capable not only of making it possible, but also of recasting ontology in a fully new light. Such "fidelity," therefore, expresses the potentiality of a new course.

As Moravia claims, Communist "hope" occurs despite its "pitiless rationality."[115] Again, the writer maintains a certain degree of detachment in his endorsement of Communism, somewhat aware of the possible pitfalls of his own conclusions. It comes as no surprise, then, that contemporary reviewers of Moravia's pamphlet, such as Vittore Branca in the journal *Il Ponte*, spotted his political hesitation and dismissed *Hope* as "a thought adventure, of secondary pursuit for the novelist."[116] Still, Moravia's intellectual, if ultimately skeptical, appraisal of Communism is not a sidetrack in his work. It instead reflects one of the pivotal existential questions that support his narrative—the *impossibility* of any fidelity to "the event." The main characters of his best novels, such as Michele in *The Time of Indifference* and Marcello in *The Conformist*, dramatically embody this lack of faith, this impossibility to any fidelity, which duly turns into a failure to take action. Arguably, it was this very impossibility that upset Mussolini so much while reading *The Time of Indifference*, thereby triggering the regime's hostility and repressive measures against Moravia.

In the subsequent columns of "Political Diary" and in other articles of the period, Moravia questions modernist politics and its myths, criticizing the concept of nation and the acceptance of revolutionary violence. In fact, the author changes his opinion on revolution's psychological effects soon after the release of *Hope*. Already in November 1944, Moravia published a piece significantly titled "Revolution and Pessimism" for the newspaper *Città*. In this article, he advocates for the rejection of revolution as a political practice, claiming that the revolutionary idea is grounded in a negative anthropology:

> It has happened that, above all in the eyes of the masses, the ideologies and the eternal spirit that informs them have been supplanted by the revolutionary act on its own and turned into a fetish. In short, as we have said, the means have obliterated and obfuscated the end.
>
> Now, why do we say that the mythification of the revolution presupposes not optimism, but pessimism? Because the recourse to violence, in particular to violence in the service of the revolutionary idea, is always an act of mistrust

in man, even if suggested and guided by the highest, utopian faith in the ideas that this act would allow to triumph.[117]

In spite of its positive objectives, the modern revolutionary myth is criticized on the basis of the primacy of women and men over politics, of human beings over ideas. With terminology already anticipating *Man as an End*, Moravia rejects the revolutionary myth, contending that the idea of revolution is based on the premise that human beings are not reasonable, "or at least [*reasonable humans*] don't exist in sufficient numbers to allow for a productive discussion." Consistent with the articles published the year before in *Il Popolo di Roma*, Moravia argues for a reformist agenda and the extensive political reeducation on a national level as the most effective ways to foster democracy. The author then associates the negative anthropology supporting revolutionary practice with the vision of mankind in Machiavelli's political thought:

> for revolutionary pessimism, as for Machiavelli, man is nothing but nature and passion, and his improvement depends not on himself, but on the intervention of an external agent. This exteriority of the agent that produces the improvement entails naturally the use of violence and recourse to authority.[118]

Importantly, Gramsci's reflections on the Communist party as the "new prince" would be published only after the end of the war.[119] Unlike Gramsci, Moravia does not underscore the pedagogical and liberating aspects of the revolutionary myth, only the violent and authoritarian ones.

Published when northern Italy was still under Fascist and Nazi control, "Revolution and Pessimism" never explicitly claims *which* myth of the revolution was at stake. In the political laboratory of newly liberated Rome in 1944, the prevalent assumption was that only a Communist revolution would change the future of the country—and redeem its recent past. In this regard, the news of the Red Army triumphantly crushing Hitler's divisions on the Eastern Front supplied the evidence that most intellectuals were looking for. In this context, Moravia's ambivalence is not just a sign of prudence or political uncertainty. His rejection of the revolutionary myth is grounded in personal memory: For Moravia, sweeping away the past would catalyze doctrinal dogmatism, violence, and the limitation of individual freedom. Without explicitly mentioning any communality between Fascist and Communist revolutions, he criticizes the palingenetic and modernist myths of the "new origin" and the "new man," both allegedly forged by revolutionary action. In his later articles, he would concentrate further on the ideological nature of such beliefs and expose how they are bound to end in totalitarian violence.

In 1945, Moravia resumes his "Political Diary" in Luigi Salvatorelli's journal *La Nuova Europa*, deepening the observations he had already anticipated in "Revolution and Pessimism." The writer starts his collaboration with Salvatorelli's journal, politically affiliated with the Action Party, on January 14 with a set of aphorisms that unmistakably condemn nationalism ("We will defend the nation until the last man. Would it not be better to defend men until the last nation?").[120] However, with the second installment of "Political Diary," published on February 11, Moravia takes an explicit stance against the revolutionary myth and its violence. The Communist revolutionary myth is now his *unequivocal* polemical target:

> Revolutionary violence is nothing but a means to make certain ideas prevail. The fact that it has become a myth, or idol, indicates that this means has in fact become an end. Or that the ideas are themselves the means to stabilize and indefinitely prolong precisely that violence.
>
> You talk like this because you're an owner.—And you talk like that because you're a proletarian—And me? You're not a proletarian or an owner, so you have no right to talk.
>
> A bureaucracy that administers ideas rather than money, that fights to preserve ideological rather than financial capital, that wards off distortions, heresies, and deviations rather than wastage and squandering: here is the origin of clerics and clericalism in churches and revolutionary parties.
>
> Why freedom? To free us from authorities, dogmas, theologies. Why revolution? To rediscover dogmas, authority, and theologies.
>
> Property similar to sin. Not having committed it does not suffice, one shouldn't even desire it.[121]

Moravia now considers the continuity between Christianity and Communism, which he discussed in *Hope* as a possibility for individual and collective renewal, a moral, social, and political sclerosis, exemplified by bureaucratization and dogmatic oppositions. He sees the involution of Communist ideology into theology, and of revolution into dogma, as a return to authoritarian practices and a violent repression of discontent. Moravia concludes his piece by describing revolution as "death of philosophy."

On May 20 of his "Political Diary," Moravia presents his skeptical but vigilant rationalism as an alternative to a new wave of fanaticism, which he sees as unleashed by the end of the war: "I've observed that the intolerance of men of faith is directed at reasonable men more than at men of opposing faith."[122] Moravia's piece focuses on how political fanaticism affects the new postwar society, both from nationalist and Communist sides. Openly endorsing a European federalist agenda in line with *La Nuova Europa*'s ideals, the writer will expand his polemics further with his next articles, increasing his journalistic collaborations with a wealth of different papers. In a column for *Libera stampa*, published on April 11 and titled "Nazism and the Nation," Moravia addresses the legacy of nationalism in Italy beyond Fascism and reactionary movements. The writer singles out a nationalist agenda in Communists and partisans themselves, at the time still fighting for the freedom of the country:

> But the deep sources of [*the partisans*'] struggle were nevertheless always their attachment to the nation and their will to ensure its survival. That is, to preserve it and bring it back with all the attributes and deficiencies that had declared its crisis [. . .]. The Communists who were such universalists at the end of the First World War today concede a great deal to this popular nationalism; in the expectation, probably, of making use of it later for their more general ends.[123]

In the same newspaper on June 5, barely a month after the end of the conflict, Moravia deals another blow to the reassuring rhetoric of Liberation as national redemption from past ills. "This Postwar Period" again addresses fanaticism, describing intolerance not just as a remnant of Fascist ideology but as the dominant habit of a generation of young Italians raised and educated under totalitarian rule. For Moravia, the persistence of an intolerant mindset is the most burdensome legacy of totalitarianism and the civil war in Italy, akin to practices fueled by a religious mentality:

> All those who were born and lived under totalitarian regimes, either because very early they felt the need to fight them and were unable to not fight them with their own weapons, or because they were morally dominated by them, have a strong unconscious inclination to intolerance. Which we can today certainly define as religious in nature; that is, as not limited to marginal or temporary questions (liberal societies, too, have their little intolerances) but

assaulting the very foundations of humanity. [...] With their reactionary struggle, the Fascists initiated a war of religions. Today, with the shooting war over, this war continues.[124]

A few days later, Moravia resumes the aphoristic writing typical of "Political Diary" to approach what he deems the seminal questions of postwar reconstruction. In the weekly *La città libera*, the writer envisions the possibility of a federalist Europe able to overcome nationalisms ("On Europe," June 14, 1945) and also investigates the problem of the masses ("On Masses," July 19, 1945). Here, too, Moravia interprets the question in terms of a "religious" problem caused by Italians' total lack of political culture. Criticizing what he calls the "easy mysticism of public life," the writer concludes with another piercing accusation of Communist utopia:

> Some seem to think that the perfect democracy or self-government of the masses can be obtained only when work has become a nervous tic, morality a muscular reflex, thought a lapsus. Those people don't realize that freedom achieved at this price would no longer have any value for men reduced to automatons.[125]

The longing for individual freedom that pervaded *Hope* has disappeared. Political utopias are discredited as a new form of obscurantism, limiting personal liberties and degenerating into contempt for the individual. In modern revolutionary myths, he concludes, the individual is dismissed for the sake of collective fallacies—another expression of anti-humanism.

The political debate of these months reached its peak in Italy as the government presided by partisan leader Ferruccio Parri was unsuccessfully attempting to enhance a reformist agenda through policies of national unity. Although Parri's government was supported by an anti-Fascist national coalition, the Action Party he represented was devoid of a real popular base. As I will detail in Chapter 3, the collapse of Parri's Action Party and dreams of radical renewal based on the values of the Resistance would catalyze the internal debate along international Cold War lines, leaving behind intellectual hopes for truly democratic participation. Moravia intervened in this broader debate by pointing to the instability of the political situation, stressing how possibilities for cultural and political intervention in the public sphere were increasingly narrowing. Remarkably, his articles also questioned the shared memory of dictatorship alongside the redemptive narrative that was taking place in those very months and that Parri himself endorsed in his speeches.[126]

After the overtly anti-Communist article titled "On Masses," Moravia publishes two additional series of aphorisms in *La città libera*, under the new title "Political Notebook." In the last two series, Moravia's style has changed. The author loosens the semantic concentration that characterized his previous "Political Diary." His writing is now more articulated, his points more gripping. The new pieces tackle dictatorship and its heritage, and Moravia's voice is now closer to that of isolated figures such as anti-Fascist exile Gaetano Salvemini, who openly addressed the problem of Italy's responsibility in the war ("we need to stop it, then, with this lie that Italy isn't responsible," Salvemini writes in a 1946 letter to Ernesto Rossi and Leo Valiani).[127]

In these last two contributions, Moravia tackles the thorny question of the widespread popular consent to Mussolini's regime. After the September 6 installment dedicated to dictatorship, the "Political Notebook" published five days later features a harsh indictment of the Italian people. Moravia contends that Italians endorsed and actively participated in Fascist policies, a participation that Fascism organized as *regimentation of the masses*. Unreservedly, Moravia holds Italians responsible for the criminal acts of Fascism and for the country's intervention in WWII. To underscore their enthusiastic participation in the regime and its crimes, the writer bitingly employs the same sexual language used by theoreticians of mass-psychology—and by Mussolini himself:

> Dictatorship as lust knows no limits. And as with lust, it happens that the dictator, in his desire to subjugate, to mortify, to defile, finds a people eager to be subjugated, mortified, defiled. As always, to do certain things well, it takes two.[128]

Contrary to Mussolini, however, Moravia avoids gender-based tropes or hackneyed essentialisms such as the supposedly defective Italian character. According to the writer, the Italian people's responsibility for Fascist crimes and overwhelming consent to the totalitarian state haunt the newborn democracy. In fact, tendencies to invest political credos with religious auras still persist.

The experimental proses of "Political Diary" would be subsequently removed from Moravia's intellectual body of work—probably for their outspoken anti-Communism. Still, the author's rejection of the Communist myths of redemption is consistent with his indictment of totalitarianism and his analysis of the psychological negotiations between the Fascist state and its subjects. Moravia identifies the legacy of totalitarian consensus in postwar Italy in the appalling lack of democratic education that characterizes Italian society. In words that echo the fierce accusation Elsa Morante spelled out in her diary after the death of Mussolini, Moravia describes the Italian people as the guilty accomplices who escaped their due punishment:

> The people that has [*sic*] killed the dictator proclaims to finally feel free. Like the criminal who considers himself innocent because he has destroyed the knife, the revolver, the cudgel he used to carry out the misdeed.[129]

2 The Language of Responsibility

Italian Fascism, a Personal Failure

This chapter addresses the question of admitting personal responsibility for Fascism—especially by intellectuals who would make this acknowledgement the fundamental subject of their writing. Berto, Piovene, and Brancati felt stranded amid postwar ideological oppositions, uneasy about their place in a heavily politicized cultural establishment, unable to conveniently forget their haunting Fascist past. In their literary endeavors, these authors not only had to recount the distressing trauma of a personal failure, but they also had to invent a new language capable of disposing of Fascism's rhetoric and its intoxicating myths.

Coming to terms with personal responsibility for national defeat takes center stage in a highly unconventional article published in 1953 by novelist Giuseppe Berto. In the piece, Berto harshly accuses the majority of Italian people of *refusing* to openly face up to Fascism. The writer states that most Italians at first supported Mussolini's regime and its imperialist agenda only to conveniently free themselves of any responsibility once the war was lost:

> For the first time in our history we had assumed a leading role, and we failed spectacularly. And now, rather than identify the causes of such a failure in our misguided ambitions and in our inability to carry out a task that clearly was not ours, we insist on blaming a few individuals, as if in that time we had not even participated in the events in which we were in fact good or bad actors. It's too easy to say: they tricked us. We needed to have it in us not to be tricked. And it's even more dishonest to say: they didn't trick us but they forced us, and we cleverly waited for the day when the whole castle of rhetorical ridiculousness would come crashing down. We needed to have it in us to rebel against ridiculous things that lead to ruin. Instead we did nothing, idling in the face of our greatest defeat.[1]

Berto here promotes a radical approach that was uncommon in the wake of the war. Indeed, his working through the national defeat begins with admitting personal, existential failure. In the quoted excerpt, he carefully avoids referring to social classes or ideological readings. Instead, he addresses his readers with a stark "us," implying a disturbing communal agency in the events of WWII and the twenty years of Fascist rule in Italy. The trauma of national defeat experienced as a personal failure will haunt Berto's writing as the main *unredeemable* event throughout the postwar transition.

A veteran of Italy's lost war with a painful history of imprisonment, Berto narrates in his first novel, *The Sky Is Red* (1947), the struggles of a helpless group of orphans during the Allied bombings. The novel was an unexpected success, both at home and abroad. It was the highest-selling post-Liberation Italian book after Carlo Levi's *Christ Stopped at Eboli*.[2] Like other prominent early postwar writers with similar backgrounds, from novelist Vasco Pratolini to poet Vittorio Sereni, Berto figures as a fitting example of the "lost generation" that grew up under Fascism in the GUF organizations (the student wing of the Fascist Party) and fought in the national army. After the conflict, the lost generation's "conversion" was a point of contention between the two main political forces of Communists and Christian Democrats.

One of the early reviews of *The Sky Is Red* is revealing in this regard. Literary critic Giancarlo Vigorelli writes in the weekly *Oggi* of 1947 that the book has the value of a "generational testimony," adding that Berto's writing stands out for being "disconnected from today's usual mythologies."[3] Like Berto, Sereni, and Pratolini, Vigorelli was born in 1913. With his successful novels *Family Chronicle* (1947) and *A Tale of Two Poor Lovers* (1947), Pratolini became the champion of "social realism" in Italy. Sereni, through haunting lyrics in *Algerian Diary* (1947), recalled his war experience and his two-year imprisonment as a POW in Africa under French rule to widespread critical and political acclaim.[4] Berto, instead, defied all cultural and political affiliations, becoming a great outsider in postwar Italian literary circles. In what sense, then, could *The Sky Is Red* represent a whole generation and avoid the "usual mythologies" of the period?

Such mythologies hinted at the "patterns of conversion" of the late 1940s, represented by the language of political redemption in books such as Elio Vittorini's *Men and Not Men* (1945) and the hegemonic return to humanism promoted across Europe by influential and *engagé* intellectuals à la Jean-Paul Sartre. In his 1996 polemical essay *The Death of the Fatherland*, historian Ernesto Galli della Loggia insists that the early postwar period's best cultural representations, far from reflecting popular participation in the Resistance, instead pinpoint the country's lack of moral regeneration. According to Galli della Loggia, this is major evidence of the failure of anti-Fascist forces to ground postwar Italy in a shared idea of the nation:

> The image of Italy in the immediate postwar years presented to us by the films of neorealism (starting with the pitiless *Bicycle Thieves*), as well as by the novels that testify to—albeit sometimes from very different points of view—the many realities of the peninsula (I'm thinking of Fenoglio's stories, Berto's *The Sky Is Red*, or Malaparte's *The Skin*), is really not the image of a country as theater of some form of moral regeneration.[5]

A main objection that can be leveled at Galli della Loggia's thesis helps us understand the exceptionality of Berto's novel in the broader Italian scenario and the question of individual responsibility of Fascism. The "death of the fatherland," lamented by the historian, encompasses only *one* idea of the nation. Given the regime's disastrous performance during the war and its impotence toward Allied bombings, the nationalist understanding of the nation, which was older than Fascism itself, disintegrated well before September 8, 1943.[6]

Berto witnesses the downfall of this ideological narrative, the nationalist secular religion of the fatherland which Mussolini and his cohorts imposed on Italians for twenty years. From the first sentence of his article, Berto focuses on the one trait of Fascist propaganda that most gratified Italian supporters, from the petite bourgeoisie who grew up reading the nationalist literature of Carducci and d'Annunzio to the hegemonic elites who dreamed of economic expansion through the further occupation of North Africa and the Mediterranean.[7] He bitterly parodies the belief in a destiny of global domination that was paramount in Mussolini's rhetoric and found its justification through the ideology of Italian national history as the basis for Fascist ambitions. The lost war and Mussolini's capitulation triggered the traumatic abandonment of this belief. For Berto and his generation, the Fascist state's failure constituted the betrayal of their youth's ideals, the doctrine learned in school and rehearsed day after day in the Fascist organizations for the education of young Italians.[8] The end of the regime laid bare how hollow the myths that informed their upbringing were. As Moravia remarked in an essay on the Italian bourgeoisie, published only a few years earlier:

> The military catastrophe destroyed above all that part of Fascism that more or less directly drew on ideals or pseudo-ideals of distant cultural origin. The

defeat definitively consigned to the past D'Annunzio and Gentile, Nietzschean heroism and Barresian nationalism, the ideas of the Roman Empire and the ethical state.⁹

The military defeat ensured that the idea of the country as an imperial power came to an abrupt—and humiliating—conclusion. Moravia spells out how the nationalist idea was profoundly rooted in Italian society even *before* Fascism. Mussolini's regime exacerbated it to an unpredictable and irresponsible level, with tragic consequences for the whole country. The military defeat showcased how nationalist ideology tragically contrasted with historical reality and how the classes which supported Fascism lacked any sense of responsibility. As journalist and filmmaker Mario Soldati bitterly remarked only a few days after the national catastrophe of September 8, 1943:

> In these twenty years all of us Italians, with a small number of glorious exceptions, were, actively or passively, Fascist, and hence we deserved such an end. There is in this, however, a heartrending injustice, that the best of us are today the worst affected, that is to say, our soldiers.[10]

Historical facts *do* count in Moravia's and Soldati's readings of the recent past. Their recognition of responsibilities does not aim at a general absolution or collective atonement but rather at making the appropriate distinctions that such a complex and harrowing situation fully deserves—beginning with the intellectual myths that the war proved false.

In particular, the ethical responsibility of writing became a critical question in the post-Fascist literary debate. As we have seen, authors such as Malaparte and Berto offered radically opposite responses to this issue. Both refuted the widespread postwar politicization of art that, on the score of Sartre and Gramsci, would refashion the intellectual models of the 1930s all over Europe. Malaparte overtly—and conveniently—claimed that art could not follow any political agenda. Berto created instead an unstable yet fascinating language that voiced the uncertainties and the sense of "worldlessness" (*Weltlösigkeit*) experienced by young Italians who grew up in the totalitarian state. He and his peers were now individuals without a perceived community, as they witnessed the demise of their values during total war and regime change. In a column published in October 1945 for *La Nuova Europa*, Bonaventura Tecchi, an influential voice of those years, approached this issue differently—one more representative of the prevailing tone of the debate. In an article significantly titled "The Advantages of the Defeat," Tecchi addresses both politicians and writers promoting their possible role as "educators" in the general moral renewal of the country:

> If writers [...] today glimpse "a new kind of responsibility," if they convince themselves, as appears to be happening, that writing involves a serious social and moral responsibility, while yet remaining faithfully attached to the unshakeable grounds of their art [...]; it would be one of the advantages—and perhaps not one of the smallest—of the defeat.[11]

Despite Tecchi's compelling words, it is not clear how writers could acquire this new moral role *because* of the defeat. The active participation of writers and artists in the political arena, particularly in the suggested role of educators, was hardly a novelty. One has only to think of the pivotal role they played in totalitarian regimes, working for the propaganda machine. The extensive contributions of Italian intellectuals to the journal *Primato*, one of Minister of National Education Giuseppe Bottai's principal projects in the last years of the regime, is a case in point.[12] The late 1940s and the early 1950s saw the gradual publication of Antonio Gramsci's *Prison Notebooks* under the supervision of PCI leader Palmiro Togliatti. Gramsci's ideas regarding the new Communist party, from the role of culture in the party's prospective hegemony to the theorization of the "organic" intellectual, circulated broadly and became widespread, although with significant distortions.[13] New in Tecchi's reflections, however, were the sense of freedom from external constraints and the refreshing possibility of a truly democratic participation that many felt during the transition—especially before the 1948 general elections when political engagement ossified into irreducible Cold War oppositions.[14]

As seen in the previous chapter, a large number of intellectuals who actively collaborated with Mussolini's dictatorship were welcomed into the cadres of the PCI or the DC. Many of them had worked for the regime until the very end—in some cases up to the early summer of 1943—before turning into fervent Communists or advocates of Christian humanitarianism.[15] In their studies on Italian intellectuals in the 1940s, Sandro Gerbi and Mirella Serri show that many applauded racial and anti-Semitic Fascist campaigns with enthusiastic articles or subscribed to blatant lies about the justifications for Italian military efforts. This questionable ethical territory can hardly be assimilated to Berto's romantic delusions and religious crisis. After the war and ensuing reconstruction of the country, the issue raised by Tecchi regarding the responsibility of writers in the democratic education of post-Fascist Italy became an urgent question, particularly after the acknowledgment of how endemic intellectual bad faith had been in the last years of the regime.

Bad faith in all its variety is the main focus of Guido Piovene, a relevant literary figure of the post-Fascist transition but seldom remembered today. Piovene was an accomplished journalist and successful writer who zealously, if perhaps insincerely, supported the regime. In the early postwar, he made moral and intellectual duplicity the subject of an unceasing self-analysis through his journalistic activity and the characters of his novels. Unlike Berto, however, Piovene did not find an adequate transitional language with which to conduct a critical reappraisal of his past. Instead, his writing displays the persistence of Fascist rhetoric and worldview. Despite the author's efforts to break free from the many ghosts of his past, Fascist aesthetics profoundly structures his discourse and testifies to its conspicuous survival in the aftermath of the regime's downfall.

This chapter ends with Vitaliano Brancati, who assumed in his writing full responsibility for his Fascist past and made it the paradigm for a moral inquiry into postwar Italian society. "In my twenties," he confesses in an autobiographical account, "I was Fascist to the bone. I find no extenuating circumstance for this."[16] Author of the stunning *Roman Diary*, posthumously published in 1961, and of the satirical yet desperate novel *Beautiful Antonio* (1949), Brancati develops his melancholic gaze on his unredeemable youth through an unbending examination of tropes, clichés, and intoxicating ideas that characterized Fascism and continued to suffocate the regained freedom after its demise. With a unique talent for humor, Brancati signals the presence of Fascist tenets behind conciliatory facades of postwar politics and bourgeois conversation. His criticism of imperialism, cult of personality, and Fascist virility is unrivaled by any other Italian author. In his highly diversified literary and journalistic writing, Brancati reflects on the nonnegotiable individuality of guilt and the intrinsic violence hidden behind the alluring conformism of Fascist and nationalist discourses.

Berto, Piovene, and Brancati represent different, conflicting aspects of the Fascist intelligentsia that survived the death of the nationalist credo. Their works express a collective experience not separable from a personal struggle. Their writing also attests to the painful postwar adaptation to a world of values that radically diverged from the ones of their youth. As Vittorio Sereni suggested in "Notes from a Dream," the *poéme en prose* that appropriately concludes his *Algerian Diary*, "Only now do I truly understand that it's over, that the war is lost. How many regrets will (others') youth bring us from now on."[17] Accepting democratic values implies a radical critique of the fallacies and myths of the nationalist culture these authors grew up believing. The language and motifs of their early postwar publications are revealing in this regard: Their avowal of individual responsibility with the regime translated into distinctively personal literary practices that stand out in the transition's cultural scenario.

National Defeat as Religious Crisis: Giuseppe Berto

Giuseppe Berto remained an outsider from Italian cultural and academic establishment for his entire life: He was both frustrated and complacent with his position as a nonconformist author. Berto's troubled biography and marginality in modern Italian literature are instrumental to his unique contribution to the question of moral responsibility. In the novels *The Sky Is Red* (1947) and *The Works of God* (1948), the writer portrays the impossibility of a return to religion after the shattering breakthrough of the war, resulting in a radical nihilism.[18] Berto's personal investigation is an unorthodox strand within the heavily politicized scenario of postwar Italian culture. His intuition of the Italian defeat in WWII as a *religious* problem, first of all for the common people, merits more investigation.

Reckless, idealistic, and ambitious, the young Berto was reared in a small provincial town in the Veneto region. Profoundly loyal to national ideals but in search of adventure, he participated as a volunteer soldier both in Ethiopia and later in North Africa with a spirit closer to Stendhal's Julian Sorel than to the Roman heroes prescribed by Fascist propaganda. Berto returned from the colonial war well-decorated, yet his second military campaign was a shocking and humiliating personal disaster. He was captured by the Allies in Tunisia after the collapse of the Italian Army in 1943 and sent to Texas, where he spent thirty months in Hereford, a concentration camp for POWs. In this isolation, with little news of the war still raging in Europe, he wrote his first novel titled *The Sky Is Red*, which enjoyed huge success in Italy and abroad when it was published in 1947, landing him a spot as a screenwriter at Cinecittà. Berto's subsequent books also gained success abroad and the warm praise of influential international writers such as Ernest Hemingway.[19] Still, he stubbornly stuck to the position of thorny outsider, eager to publicly take up the most problematic issues that nobody wanted to discuss in Italy during the years of the economic boom—such as the fate of Italian soldiers who, like him, fought for the wrong cause and suffered defeat, deprivation, and internment.

As in the case of many of the authors whom I examine in this book, it is impossible to sever Berto's biography from his narrative production, for the profound sense of historical testimony and personal confession that permeates all of his writing. The acute sense of abandonment and existential void of an entire generation after the defeat—which Vigorelli appropriately singled out in the referenced review of *The Sky Is Red*—in his work assumes the value of personal bewilderment. Berto would courageously admit this tremendous existential impasse in *The War of a Black Shirt*, the fictionalized diary of his experience in Africa published in 1955, whose uneasy composition troubled him for many years before publication.[20] In the preface of the book, he concludes:

> I publish this book not for those who were Blackshirts, but for others, perhaps for those who were their adversaries and enemies, because I would like them to recognize in my soldiers a human substance common to all soldiers and all armies. In order for the war to be truly forgiven.[21]

A scandal when it appeared in the 1950s, *The War of a Black Shirt* anticipated themes that only forty years later could be addressed properly. Berto's fictional diary hints at an unbearable sense of guilt, which would be fully spelled out only after a long period of personal depression and the completion of his major literary achievement, the 1964 novel *Incubus*. In "An Unintentional Approach" (1965), a compelling and often witty essay in which he comments on his own literary production, the writer claims:

> Berto's sense of guilt appears in two ways that we will try to examine separately, even if they are conterminous and oftentimes confused: the sense of guilt that as a man he feels generally for the war's cruelties, and the sense of guilt that as an Italian and a Fascist he feels for having contributed to the war's onset.[22]

In the essay, Berto offers a ruthless examination of his early novels, speaking of himself always in the third person. By distancing from his former self, the author expresses how troubled his relation with writing is and how writing helped him cope with personal and often shameful traumatic experiences linked with the war and his alignment with Fascism. Literary self-analysis is the opportunity for unfolding a harrowing tangle of sorrow, isolation, and inexpiable guilt:

> In the collective blamelessness Berto wanted to hide his own guilt. To his guilt as a man, Berto added his guilt as an Italian, or rather, as an "Italian who had worn the black shirt" [...]. Berto provoked in his characters, still blaming the "universal evil," an obfuscation of the faculty of judgment and understanding,

and ultimately of communication, such that the poor devils are reduced to being even poorer devils.[23]

These later reflections illuminate, retrospectively, the inner tensions of Berto's early novels. Similar to Piovene, the 1960s feature a major change in his narrative, embracing personal memories in the form of a thorough reappraisal of the past. His essay "An Unintentional Approach," however, reveals how, *already* in the late 1940s, Berto's fiction addressed his generation's crisis as based on personal responsibility with Fascism, beginning with his novel *The Sky Is Red*. Unlike his overtly autobiographical books of the 1960s, Berto's novel is not biased by later considerations and postwar experiences. It uniquely documents the existential void and lack of models for young Italians who, after the fall of Mussolini, could not embrace the post-Fascist "patterns of conversion." In a little-known 1961 essay, poet Andrea Zanzotto signaled how outstanding *The Sky Is Red* was among early postwar Italian fiction:

> What makes this work effective? Alongside few others from those years, it represents the unpredictable success of a "language of transition" that proves self-sufficient, in some manner, precisely in its transience: a mirror of the necessary transience of the "après le déluge" atmosphere, postbellum in the most restricted sense, limited approximately to between '45 and '50.[24]

Zanzotto underscores how the novel's language uniquely mirrors the exceptional atmosphere of the postwar transition. My point here is that language and rhetorical strategies of Berto's book are informed by a groundbreaking and highly idiosyncratic intuition—the perception of the historical defeat of the Italian nation as a religious crisis.

The Sky Is Red begins as a traditional, almost nineteenth-century, realist novel: with the description of the beauty of the countryside and the lazy life of an unnamed town in the Veneto region, easily recognizable as Treviso. The introduction of the characters immediately challenges this image. From the railway station, Berto follows the streets of the town to its most miserable neighborhood, focusing on the poverty and petty lives of prostitutes and thieves. Still, what makes the novel stand out is not the focus on this hidden world, a *topos* of European Romantic literature, from Schiller to Victor Hugo, but the way the town's underworld is completely wiped out by the unpredictable historical events of the war. Aerial bombings destroy lives, achievements, and bodies of the population with unforeseeable violence, not dissimilar to the eruption of the plague in a long literary tradition, from Boccaccio to Manzoni. Indeed, *The Sky Is Red* is the best instance in Italian culture of what W. G. Sebald called *Luftkriegsliteratur*—the literature recounting the trauma of aerial warfare and bombings on the civil population.[25] The function of the first chapters is now clear: The traditional world of yesterday—a world that was at any rate *not innocent*—is crushed forever. After the bombings, the town is not merely a series of ruins, where, despite the wreckage, signs of the next reconstruction and the return of a previous order can be discerned, but a monstrous and irregular accumulation of debris. A visual correspondence can be found in the city of Berlin portrayed by Roberto Rossellini in his film *Germany, Year Zero*, released two years later. Characters of the novel, such as the young stranded protagonist and the old, former Fascist schoolteacher, make *The Sky Is Red* an antecedent and an allegedly hidden source for the script and the visual impact of the film.[26]

The protagonist Daniele is a bourgeois teenager raised in a seminary. He has lost his parents in the bombings and finds a new family of sorts in a group of desperate young survivors living in the remnants of a brothel in the miserable neighborhood described above. The other characters are Tullio, a generous young thief of Communist persuasion; his girlfriend Carla, who works as a prostitute; the younger Giulia, whom Daniele loves and who eventually dies of tuberculosis; and Maria, an autistic child who joined the group and is totally dependent on Giulia's care.

After its release, *The Sky Is Red* was immediately associated with Neorealism. A closer look, however, reveals how Berto assembles an array of Romantic literature clichés in his novel—from the *Bildungsroman* of the young Daniele to the generosity of the thief Tullio, from the deep compassion of the prostitute Carla to the typical medley of love, illness, and death present in Giulia. As literary critic Giorgio Barberi Squarotti poignantly claimed, the novel is

> the radical alternative to neorealism, where there are indeed many elements of the Romantic tradition, and ample use is made of wayward boys, ruins of cities, thieves, and prostitutes, but all in service of a faithful reflection of reality that leaves characters and situations as documents of society and history, and certainly does not see any message behind them.[27]

Page after page, differences with contemporary fiction become increasingly pronounced. Berto's novel is allegoric, not realistic. Historical events are just a pretext to stage the fall of any ideal of a regenerated society—paramount to Fascist national rhetoric, especially for the youth. "The facts of *The Sky Is*

Red," Berto writes in 1963, "were invented nearly out of whole cloth: in the novel there is no sign of the Resistance, and the novel concludes in the autumn of 1944."[28] Besides Resistance and Liberation, partisans and reconstruction are also not present in the book. In fact, no northern Italian town or city ever experienced the total collapse of institutions and of the fabric of daily life as the book portrays, not even during the grimmest phases of foreign occupation. As Donald Heiney rightfully contends, the novel "is therefore less a history of actual events than a document of Berto's emotions toward the war as it seems to him in the prison camp in Texas."[29]

Recent readings of the novel agree that the young protagonists of the novel attempt the constitution of a utopic community governed by solidarity against a condition of "universal evil," but they ultimately fail. Unlike romantic tragedy or orthodox Resistance narratives, there is no redemption for any of the characters: Tullio is killed during a fight between his gang and American soldiers, Giulia dies of tuberculosis, and Carla remains a prostitute. The protagonist Daniele, bewildered by Giulia's death, sets out to leave. He takes a freight train without knowing its destination. In the highly evocative concluding pages of the novel, he finally decides his fate. While the train is running, Daniele strips himself of all his clothes and throws them outside—for the benefit of anyone who could pick them up. After cutting every residual bond with his life, he prepares for a sacrifice with explicit Christological undertones: "And now he felt a great coldness, because he had stripped himself naked for love of other men. Like Jesus and other saints too, but he did not quite remember now who it was."[30] Daniele commits suicide, imitating Christ's passion and atonement. Yet his imitation is only formal: His sacrifice will not change the life of anyone and remains an obscure, almost solipsistic act.[31] Daniele's suicide is a parody of Christ's sacrifice, almost a blasphemy. The novel ends with musings on men's expectations after the war and a lyrical depiction of the change of seasons in the land outside the town.

Berto's proposed title for his novel was originally "The Lost People," echoing a well-known verse from Dante's *Divine Comedy*. The publisher of the book, Leo Longanesi, changed it to the more captivating *The Sky Is Red*, after promising the young writer that the new title would be chosen from the Holy Scriptures, as Berto expressly requested. The other title proposed by the author, "The Sins of God," was downright refuted by the publisher but showcases an apparent continuity of intents.[32] This continuity is confirmed by the other work of fiction Berto wrote while in Hereford, the novella *The Works of God*. Published in Italy in 1948, after the success of the first novel, the story features the shattering of a traditional patriarchal family of farmers in Northern Italy because of the outbreak of the war. Usually overlooked by commentators, *The Works of God* partakes in the same creative tension of the previous novel. The juxtaposition of the two works sheds a clearer light on each one and elicits an overall interpretation of Berto's early work as an outstanding response to the national defeat.

Although the narrator of *The Works of God* is impersonal, the novella is told from the point of view of the characters, who grasp very little—if anything—of the historical facts that so harshly impact their lives. Berto's poor Mangano family faces the collapse of traditional ties, echoing Giovanni Verga's classic nineteenth-century novel *The House by the Medlar Tree*—a book that was a main reference for Neorealist filmmakers, but not so much for Fascist culture.[33] Unlike Verga's story, however, the family lacks a strong male figure. Survival is granted thanks to the courage and the resolution of the women, particularly of the daughter-in-law la Rossa. Moreover, unlike Padron 'Ntoni in *The House by the Medlar Tree*, the old patriarch Mangano does not just represent a traditional society that has lost contact with reality; he is also completely unreliable, despised by la Rossa for being useless and always drunk, pitied by his wife—simply called "mother" in the novella—and their daughter Effa. The allegory is (all too) overt: Old Mangano embodies the traditional peasant society facing the unknown threat of total war. This society has lost not only its historical function, but also every hint of dignity. Whereas the approaching front forces la Rossa and the mother to organize a hurried getaway from the farm, old Mangano drinks and babbles on about his experience as a soldier during WWI—only to later be blown up with his pig by stepping on a land mine during the forced march at night.

Many remarkable themes are represented in the figure of Mangano. The biblical tone of the narrative and the chiaroscuro of the characters distance the novella from realist fiction. Similar to *The Sky Is Red*, Berto's writing style forges an allegorical shadow around the story and its protagonists. Still, the main feature of Mangano is his babbling. He cannot articulate an adequate judgment on unforeseen events—babbling is his sole language. The only words he can pronounce with full intention are his curses against God, in which he expels his violence and frustration. Only another character in the story openly summons God—the mother, who begs her family to pray together with her. The story ends with the mother continually repeating how impossible it is to understand and make sense of what just occurred.

With bitter irony in "An Unintentional Approach," Berto explains the meaning of the title: "*The Works of God* is a blasphemous title. No one, however, will dispute that blasphemy expresses, albeit in a completely perverse way, a religious sentiment."[34] Berto's first two books not only describe how the war demolished the old world, but they furthermore represent blasphemy. Berto's characters desperately accuse an absent God of betrayal. This indictment is poignantly acted out through the parody of Christ's sacrifice in *The Sky Is Red* (it is very difficult to imagine a more unorthodox *imitatio Christi* than a suicide) and through the pity sons and daughters feel toward their father's curses and their mother's prayers in *The Works of God*. Again, the trauma of the war is thus portrayed as the most profound kind of religious crisis.

However, which is the religion at stake here? Despite the title, there is no trace of traditional Catholicism in *The Works of God*, whereas priests and their worldview are quickly dismissed in *The Sky Is Red*. Priests' knowledge is an empty cage for Daniele. The reported last thoughts of the protagonist reveal a complete detachment from traditional religion and the biting irony of the author: "Like Jesus and other saints too, *but he did not quite remember now who it was.*"[35] Modern war renders characters such as Daniele, or Effa, rootless, although they still reside in the land of their birth and where they spent their entire lives. The two move in their respective stories as if in a sort of exile, the environment around them nothing but piles of debris rising skyward and extraneous to their lives.

Since these unrecognizable places used to be their homes, Daniele and Effa are effectively *weltlos* ("without a world"): Their gazes attest nothing but melancholic loss.[36] Exiled in their own home, they have no choice but to leave it for another place. Their fates are only superficially dissimilar to those of the characters that decide to remain and carry on, such as Carla in the first novel or the mother and la Rossa in the novella. The *weltlos* condition of Berto's characters probably hints at the existential experience and the inner tensions of the inmate in the POW camp. Timelessness and displacement are the condition, the *Weltlösigkeit*, of individuals within the camp, in which the state of exception becomes the norm and others hold the reins of their very existence—and for a considerable period of time. Remarkably, Berto would write, in the next few years, gripping stories that elaborate on his prewar experience in Ethiopia, in which the self-induced exile becomes an almost ontological category.[37] It is now time to weave together the many threads of my reading of *The Sky Is Red* by returning to its concluding scenes.

As mentioned previously, recent comments have showcased the allegorical quality of the novel, especially in its final pages. This interpretation, however, isolates Daniele's suicide from the overall narrative, avoiding coming to terms with the two fundamental passages that bracket this event. Before setting out to depart, Daniele pays a visit to the people he knows.

Among them is a peculiar character, the "old man," a schoolmaster who was introduced to him by Tullio. The old man was formerly a fervent Fascist, and his presence is, at the same time, consoling and disquieting. Anchored in his past, like the mother in *The Works of God*, he is clearly unable to cope with the present and is consciously waiting for his own death. Nevertheless, he tries to find words of hope for the young Daniele:

> "Great strength is needed to go on living, because it's not only you and I who are desolate; everyone is in the same position as we are, alone and desolate, and no one can give us any help. This is one of the fruits of the war, that people should feel so alone and so desolate and should find no support in anyone." [. . .]
> Daniele said nothing during the long pause that followed.
> "You mustn't give way to despair," said the old man.
> "I don't give way to despair," said Daniele. "I'm just in a complete muddle."
> "Then you must wait for the passing of time," said the old man. "And try to believe in something. You'll see that everything will straighten out."[38]

Despite his benevolent intentions, the old man has no real grasp of what oppresses Daniele. For both characters, the loss of their community and its values caused by the war is the source of all evils. Still, for the old man the war is a fatal, metaphysical accident. He keeps on interpreting the reality unfolding before his very eyes as a matter of "believing"—still abiding by Fascist rhetoric and code of honor. Not only does the old schoolmaster fail to provide a convincing explanation for what happened, but he also remains stuck to a model of beliefs and behavior that Daniele finds now useless, if not downright inauthentic:

> For a little while he went on thinking about the old man, and he almost laughed within himself. The old man had meant to encourage him, and yet he had merely said things that had no meaning for either of them, things in which neither of them believed. Tullio might have said things like that, and have spoken of the great day when good would come upon the earth for all men. But then Tullio was not one who had abandoned all hope. And yet it was he who had died rather than anyone else.[39]

The confusion Daniele witnesses reflects a lack of models for the "lost generation" who grew up under the regime. In the novel, after the refusal of the Catholic option through the rebuttal of the priests' knowledge and the dismissal of Fascist ideals as inauthentic, the Communist solution embodied by Tullio is debunked by reality, despite its romantic generosity. Daniele cannot but repeat the gestures of the only model he barely remembers—a creaturely Christ outside institutions. His formal sacrifice, an involuntary parody of Christ's self-immolation, resounds with Berto's bitter irony in the existential vacuum left by the defeat. In any event, instead of indulging his fictional character, Berto enlarges the scope of his story with a direct intervention no commentator has adequately explained. History returns to center stage as Daniele's allegory dissolves:

> Gradually they came to understand. It was no longer a war that had to be endured, it was a war that had been lost. In spite of all that was said, it must be recognized that it was a lost war. And they had been left alone to bear the burden of defeat, a burden too great for an impoverished people, in a land devastated and disabled by war. Nor was it possible to foresee when the burden of the defeat would be lightened.[40]

After this final comment, the defeat of Daniele is no longer an allegory of the human condition in the exceptional and heinous circumstances of total war. It is instead an instance, a synecdoche of the moral defeat of an entire people—the *Italian* people—who believed and followed a "God that failed" and is now condemned to mourn the loss of any guidance, indeed of any narrative. Each truly romantic novel is a religious feat: The conclusion of *The Sky Is Red* is a disarming exercise in nihilism and mourning for the loss of the secular religion of the nation.

As Zanzotto signaled, few works captured the Zeitgeist of this transitional moment as Berto's novel. A main component of *The Sky Is Red*'s "transitional language" is Berto's piercing irony—absent in the more overtly allegorical *The Works of God*. While allowing the employment of a pathetic register in many passages of the novel, this irony points to the many momentous consequences of the *religious* defeat of Fascist Italy. A comparison with the failed attempt of a different "transitional language" can properly illuminate this point.

Poet and Marxist critic Franco Fortini published his only novel, *Christmas Agony*, in 1948.[41] The book narrates the impossibility for a war veteran to find a place in postwar society. The metaphor of illness accompanies the protagonist Giovanni throughout the novel, and his eventual death comes as no surprise as the character is unable to cope with the trauma of the war. Despite the interesting chapters describing Giovanni's experience as an occupying soldier, allegedly in the Balkans (the text is purposely vague in this regard), the novel's cultural references overwhelm the story itself. Aesthetic models such as Thomas Mann's *Death in Venice* prove utterly inadequate to capture the reality of the transition: "I am not afraid of death, but of corruption," claims Fortini's protagonist. "It's not death that frightens me, but decay," Fortini writes. "And if there is guilt in me, I want to be able to atone for it, I want to be able to pay for it; and then to wake up."[42] Compared to the untimeliness of *The Sky Is Red*, Fortini's novel reads as all too current—it is an existentialist novel *written in Italian*.

Christmas Agony, however, points to a relevant theme that is developed not only in *The Sky Is Red* and indirectly in *The Works of God* but also in Berto's stories of the same years: the decline of the myth of the war experience as one of the foundations of European civilization. In this regard, the distance between the two authors is telling. For the protagonist of Fortini's novel, the war experience is unspeakable. Still, the main problem for WWII veterans is not just their inability to report the war experience, as was the case in the Great War when "men returned from the battlefield grown silent—not richer, but poorer in communicable experience," as Walter Benjamin, among others, argued already in the 1930s.[43] WWII veterans now strive to find an attentive audience eager to listen and believe their tale. This piercing concern was indeed widespread: not only for Holocaust survivors such as Primo Levi, who masterfully addresses this issue in *If This Is a Man*, but also for a playwright like Eduardo De Filippo. In his popular comedy *Naples Get Rich*, first staged in 1945, De Filippo presents another veteran who, upon returning to Naples after the war, finds his familial world turned upside down.[44] Yet the main shock is not material but moral: No one wants to listen to his tales. *Naples Get Rich* reverses the ancient Western tradition of the *miles gloriosus*, a literary trope first utilized in the writings of Homer, Plautus, and Tibullus. For centuries, this trope featured a soldier returning from war and finding pleasure in recounting—or just boasting—his adventures to his community.

This founding experience is wiped out in Berto's stories. According to historian James J. Sheehan, the decline of the myth of the soldier is a consequence of WWII traceable all over Europe.[45] In Berto's narrative, however, this decline is accompanied by the explicit rejection of another classical and then romantic trope, which found a novel codification in Fascist militarist rhetoric—the so-called beautiful death, which, from Homer's *Iliad* onward, elevates the fallen warrior to the state of glory.[46] The romantic and then Fascist myth of the heroic death is explicitly dismissed in one of Berto's stories about his experience in Ethiopia. Very few writers in the 1940s, not only in Italy but all over Europe, amplify and link rejection of the war to an equally strong rebuttal of colonial conquest, as Berto did with his stories.

The Language of Responsibility | 81

The disillusioned protagonist of the short story "Eucalyptuses Will Grow" claims:

> There was nothing he particularly desired, except to do something great, maybe. But even allowing that he died a hero, here they would have buried him under a pile of rocks, and in his country they would come to know about it only much later, practically in secret, since it was no good for it to be known that a black-skinned people was shooting at whites because it didn't know what to make of paved roads and the Hymn of the Balilla [. . .]. Such a death was not exactly a great thing.[47]

    The impossibility of recounting the experience of the war was a common feature of European literature since WWI, as reported by Benjamin.[48] Berto articulates this theme in an unexpected fashion in *The Sky Is Red*. The author anticipates a debate that would be crucial in the decades to come: the inability of existing categories and worldviews to comprehend the crimes perpetrated during the total war. After the war, testimonies from Nazi concentration camps would prove the inadequacy of traditional notions such as anti-Semitism to fully grasp the extent of the Nazis' assault on humanity, attesting to the totalitarian attempt at "the transformation of human nature itself," as Arendt put it.[49] Yet, at the center of Berto's novel are the effects of bombings and warfare on the Italian population, not specifically Nazi crimes—of which the writer had almost certainly little knowledge while writing his novel.

    The unprecedented scale of WWII's violence was impelled by aberrant ideologies which mobilized entire nations to promote their totalitarian goals. It was also based on the escalation of uncontrolled technological prowess applied to the war machine for the destruction of the enemy's entire body politic, blurring any distinction between combatants and civilian population. The traumatic experience of modern warfare shatters the foundations of society itself, as its pervasive violence impacts the whole population. The constant presence of death is a threat and a shocking daily reality for everyone, not just for soldiers.

    In *The Works of God*, the mother's desperate words signal how the civilian population had no means to make sense of the destruction provoked by total war, let alone comprehend its scale. *The Sky Is Red* develops this issue even more radically. Among the members of the utopian community at the heart of the novel, the autistic girl Maria stands out. According to Michel David, the only commentator who noted her presence, Maria "is a new character in Italian fiction, and her irrecoverable psychology is depicted with a felicitously instinctive hand."[50] She is the true testimony of the defeat, her inability to speak a consequence of her inability to articulate her thought. Her total lack of sympathy for the tragedies of the other characters, her meaningless gaze, and her own body testify to the inhumanity engendered by the war. Berto invented Maria's character during the thirty months of his imprisonment in the Hereford camp.[51] Although the two experiences of survival are radically different, Maria is similar to another babbling child of WWII, the two-year-old Hurbinek in Primo Levi's *The Truce*, who was born in Auschwitz.

The Persistence of Fascist Rhetoric: Guido Piovene

Unlike Berto, Guido Piovene was always on the "right side" of history during his literary career. He was a spectacular case of shifting from Fascist to Communist ranks after the catastrophe of the regime. Relentless self-analysis and intellectual "bad faith" are indeed the leading themes of Piovene's tormented literature, along with the ambition to redeem personal and historical failures through art and literature. Remarkably, his wide-ranging writing during the transition displays how he was unable to fully come to terms with his Fascist past. In fact, Fascist rhetoric and language continued to profoundly shape Piovene's intellectual and moral agenda.

Born to countryside Venetian nobility, Piovene became a respected journalist in the 1930s, mainly for his work for *Corriere della Sera*, in which he distinguished himself by reviewing art and literature with sophisticated subtlety. He also had praise for anti-Semitic legislation.[52] When his novels were translated into French after the war, an article on Italian novelists published in 1948 for the daily *L'Aurore* bitingly noted:

> M. Guido Piovene, que se distingua dans la guerre d'Espagne par ses cris de haine contre les rèpublicains et le long du règne mussolinien par ses applaudissements au régime, fait aujourd'hui figure de grand résistant salué avec respect par les éléments de gauche.[53]

Piovene's journalistic production dramatically changes after September 8, 1943. A refugee in Rome, like many other intellectuals trying to escape the Nazi invasion, he became the author of Resistance articles in which he passionately endorsed the Communist Party.[54] In the fall of 1944, he thus remembered in the journal *Mercurio*, directed by Alba de Céspedes, the momentous days of Nazi occupation of the city:

> In those months I learned what is the essence of fellowship among men, usually so difficult for us men of letters. I experienced the highest joy that

can touch a man, that of finding himself among men of every kind, including the most unfamiliar, and feeling in solidarity with all of them. I also felt the birth of writer in me, because I saw disappear, as if by the grace of destiny, every literary and bourgeois falsity. Finally, I had evidence for the first time that I was not a complete coward. I'm not saying I have courage; I know courageous men, and they're different.[55]

This piece stands out among Piovene's writing of the 1940s, autobiographical prose and fiction alike. The highly cerebral quality of his writing yields here to a confession that has the features of a personal, longed-for liberation. As Franco Cordelli recently wrote of him, "In the language of emotionality, his terms are truth and lie and, between them, redemption, or better, redeemer, redeemers."[56] For his peculiar intellectual and literary prowess, Piovene is not fully representative of the political "redemption" that involved so many of his peers—turning from the wrong to the right side of history at the proper moment. Along with his avowal of the PCI—his friends would mockingly call him "the red count"—in those years, Piovene attempted a sophisticated dissection of the motifs, justifications, lies, and self-deception that characterized his adherence to Fascism, or rather, the haunting stain of the lack of any revolt to Mussolini's yoke.

The two tortured novels Piovene published after the war, meaningfully titled *Pity against Pity* (1946) and *The False Redeemers* (1949), focus indeed on failure and self-deception. Not particularly relevant from an artistic point of view, they feature endless self-analysis through demanding dialogues in which the main characters try to hide the petty motivations behind their acts.[57] His best novelistic production appeared after the 1960s, when books such as *The Furies* (1963) and *The Cold Stars* (1970) would find more convincing modalities to reflect and represent the analysis of his self-deception, and the ensuing duplicity that characterized his youth under Fascism.

The profound nihilism of his transition novels features a haunting continuity with his earlier production, such as *The Letters of a Novice* (1941) and *The Black Gazette* (1943). The analysis of bad faith is pivotal, especially for his first novel. *The Letters of a Novice* thus begins: "The characters in this novel, while all different from one another, have one point in common: they are all repulsed by deep self-knowledge."[58] In newly liberated Rome, Piovene would endow his self-deceptive characters, which together conjure up an ambiguous portrayal of their author, with the definition of this malaise, so common among Italian intellectuals. On November 11, 1944, he wrote for the paper *Città*: "Bad faith is exposed when a fantastic movement attempts to disguise itself as a logical conviction. Bad faith is revealed when a partial, fickle, fortuitous sympathy becomes in a flash total adherence."⁵⁹ In light of his recent "conversion" to Communism, these words reveal a tormented trajectory that is better illuminated by his further articles. Just a few days later, Piovene added in the same paper:

> There are men, especially among intellectuals, who cultivate in themselves a lack of clarity, with the same care with which true thinkers cultivate the precision of thought. Their secret aim is utilitarian. That lack of clarity allows them to follow fashions, to always surrender to the current [. . .]. The "revolutions" are never in "this" revolution. Always "further on," always in the future. Or else they are in "this" revolution, but they are also in the next one. And when a revolution goes badly, they move on to the next one.⁶⁰

Piovene's post-Liberation articles share similar preoccupations with the novels he published before and after the war. In the economy of his narrative, external reality counts very little. It is but a mere opportunity to stage internal struggles. At stake here is the typical conflict characterizing many intellectual antiheroes of modernist literature, from Pirandello to Musil: the impossibility of taking sides, thanks to the moral relativism of modern times. In Piovene's fiction, this relativism becomes not only torturing sickness, but also convenient acquiescence with power. The writer would clarify this point in a column on the relations between literature and politics published right after the Liberation. The article, however, reads like a rebuttal not only of Fascist, but also of Communist conceptions of propaganda art:

> To the politician who asks him to use his books to promote [*propagandare*] democracy, dictatorship, war, peace, and so on, the artist could with equal right respond: "No, you instead seek to favor the rise of a society suited to the spread of symbolist or hermetic poetry, etc. The politicking artist is as absurd as the aesthete politician."⁶¹

In Benjaminian terms, Piovene rejects both the politicization of art and the aestheticization of politics. According to the writer, both the two options are conducive to what he sees as the only "degenerate art," the one in which its author does not radically compromise himself: "I don't at all believe that art helps, as a poet said, 'to sweeten life'; I believe, if anything, that it helps to embitter it: this must accordingly lead us to compromise ourselves in the most radical way."⁶²

In light of these affirmations, one would expect a thorough and painful reappraisal of past errors, a pitiless self-examination, perhaps through the ironic medium of fiction and language, which can create a barrier between the raw facts of life and their representation. Piovene's novels of the late 1940s do not follow this path. It is not difficult to confuse the characters speaking in *Pity against Pity* and *The False Redeemers* with one another. Their voices form a continuous self-accusation without even getting close to the radicalism Piovene argued for in the essays expounding his poetics. The author himself is aware of this literary failure when in *Pity against Pity*, by far more interesting than *The False Redeemers*, one character admits:

> The greater the need to dissimulate, the more urgently we confess. Such a confession derives always from pity and from the need to hide ourselves: it is a defeated lie; we are sincere because we are desperate liars. The person who has received a dishonoring insult speaks of it to render it acceptable. The invert makes a public display of his illness. We demand to be loved for our illness and our cowardice, because we reveal ourselves in them. [. . .] Confession is always false; telling the truth and telling a falsehood are equally deceitful.[63]

Through the words of his character, Piovene exposes the reasons behind his writing without even mentioning any agency, responsibility, or accountability for what he wrote. The lies about his past turn more blatant the more the confession proceeds. Moreover, Piovene trades a moral failure, his personal compromise with Fascism, a determined historical contingency, for a *literary* failure. His stress on the impossibility of a true confession can easily be traced to a modern skeptical tradition which, from Vittorio Alfieri to Italo Svevo (only to remain within national borders), was already critically welcomed and codified.[64] After all, the self-absolution of his historical compromise with Fascist power is overtly stated in one of the concluding passages of *Pity against Pity*: "We are in a world in which it is never possible to know whose fault it is."[65]

Going back to the dichotomy between politicization of art and aestheticization of politics, Piovene refuses both in order to save precisely the metaphysical quality that Benjamin signals as lost in modern art—the work of art's *aura*. Piovene's nihilism is indeed incomplete: If the literariness of his failure is acknowledged, the failure of his human experience, of his compromise with power, is redeemed. His represented failure is now part of an accomplished literary tradition, a recurring rhetorical trope. When he explains the title of his novel by affirming "Pity against pity: the dreadful complicity between victim and assassin," there is no hint of in-depth psychological or historical analysis, but only literary conformism.[66] Piovene's novelistic articulations of his compromises with Fascism are a prime instance of what Bersani called "redemptive aesthetics," in which "*the corrective virtue of works of art depends on a misreading of art as philosophy.*" Bersani adds that such aesthetics and the related cultural elaborations might be thought of as "the creation of what Nietzsche called the theoretical man [. . .], the man who attributes to thought the power to 'correct' existence."[67]

The ambition to correct existence with art is a main feature of Fascist rhetoric, from d'Annunzio to Marinetti to Mussolini. In his writings of the transition years, Piovene still relies on such aesthetics, intellectual subtleties regardless. An evident example is in the passage referenced above: To explain his moral illness, he calls into play homosexuality as an example of sick deviance from the norm. In its anxiety for total control, for full politicization of life, Fascism multiplied taxonomies, labels, archives, and bureaucracy—from its internal organization to the prescriptive regulations of customs to the racial laws.

A similar anxiety is to be found not only in Piovene's novels but also in his articles in newly freed Rome. In the paper *Città* in December 1944, Piovene runs a column significantly called "Characters," in which he endeavors to examine different human types. The column features a series of deviances that, according to its author, characterize postwar society. The real problem here is that there is no hint of humor in Piovene's attempt, but there is a serious, at times lyrical, analysis of deviances—in line with the sanitizing practices obsessively repeated under the regime. The list of characters under scrutiny is eloquent: "the person who kills himself out of fear," "the homosexual," "the immoralist," "the self-righteous," and so forth.[68]

Despite Piovene's claims, advocation for a Fascist-style aestheticization of politics and a rhetorical, elitist concept of life redeemed by literature pervade his writing in the second half of the 1940s. As a last instance, an article published by Piovene in 1947, titled "The Church," showcases not only an evident proximity with Fascist rhetoric, but also the disturbing presence of Mussolini's speeches through a refashioning of the Duce's favorite tropes and anxieties. Speaking of Italians, Piovene claims:

> This people must still truly suffer, conscientiously and with risk, if it wants to enter history, from which it has excluded itself. Its suffering has been superfluous, and in the end not even true, since it has been aimed not at entering history, but at escaping it. Now, the single goal of every people is to participate in history; that is, to obey God: the choice before it is not to live or to die, but to live in or out of history.[69]

As opposed to Berto, Piovene did not find an adequate transitional language. His writing displays instead the persistence of a Fascist worldview, despite his disavowal of the regime's aesthetics and rhetoric.

Individual Responsibility Is Not Negotiable: Vitaliano Brancati

A radical reappraisal of the Fascist past, through fictional and autobiographical writing, is at the center of the work of the last Italian author examined in this chapter. Vitaliano Brancati is best remembered today for his novel *Beautiful Antonio* (1949), which became a popular film directed by Mauro Bolognini, starring Marcello Mastroianni and Claudia Cardinale. In the novel, Brancati harshly parodies provincial Sicily's morals and sexual customs, tackling a most infamous Italian vice—machismo. The writer focuses on what he calls "gallismo," the peculiar Sicilian variant of machismo, particularly relevant during the 1930s–1940s.[70] Few remember today that, behind their exhilarating *vis comica* and the witty criticism of Italian society, Brancati's novel and his other works of the period constitute one of the most personal and painfully self-aware reconsiderations of individual and collective subjugation to the false myths of Fascism.

By parodying Fascism's vulgarity and hypersexualized masculinity, Brancati's *Beautiful Antonio* tackles a crucial historical aspect of Italian society. The novel narrates the vitalism and cult of virility typical of Italian Fascism as profoundly rooted in the narrow-mindedness and pettiness of traditional Sicilian (read: Italian) society much earlier than Mussolini's takeover. Bolognini's movie, shot in 1960 after the death of the writer, anesthetizes the subversive charge of the book. The film's story is staged after the war, avoiding political references, whereas its ultimately redemptive ending—conspicuously straying from the original novel—transforms a highly corrosive bourgeois drama into a self-indulgent, though entertaining and at times disquieting, *commedia erotica*.[71] The cinematic adaptation of the novel is revealing: It showcases once again how in the 1950s and 1960s the political and civil charge typical of the literary production during the transition was lost—or conveniently overlooked.[72]

Brancati's outstanding intellectual and journalistic production, however, documents the possibility of a different path through the historical contradictions of early postwar Italian society. In this regard, a polemical prose piece published in 1946 and titled "Instinct and Intuition" eloquently illustrates the uniqueness of Brancati's approach:

> In my twenties I was Fascist down to the very roots of my hair. I can find no extenuating circumstance for this: I was attracted by the worst elements of

Fascism, and in my case I can't call on the excuses rightfully belonging to a bourgeois conservative tyrannized by the words Nation, Ancestry, Order, Quiet life, Family, etc. Out of I don't know what miserable tendency lurking deep in my nature, and which still today makes me sleep with one eye open, like the caretaker of a house recently visited by thieves, in my twenties I was sincerely ashamed of every lofty, noble quality, and I aspired to humiliate and debase myself with the same directness, longing, and vehemence with which one dreams of the opposite.[73]

Taken from the short collection *The Fascists Grow Old* (1946), "Instinct and Intuition" testifies to a radical shift from the other writers analyzed in this chapter. In the very title, Brancati addresses two intoxicating words of Fascist propaganda. He discloses their appeal to younger generations, who were hungry to participate in the political adventures promised by Fascist ideology. "Instinct" and "intuition" are recurrent words of the cultural-philosophical debate of the early twentieth century, easily associated with thinkers such as Nietzsche, Bergson, Sorel, and Gentile. They are in implicit opposition to traditional terms such as "Order," "Comfortable Life," and "Family," which explain the simultaneous success of Fascism with Italian conservative classes.

For Brancati, all these umbrella terms may help one approach the general problem of Fascism, but they are not an excuse for the *personal* excitement and fascination with Fascist ideas. This fascination with the regime and its hollow ideals is the starting point of Brancati's inquiry. Moreover, the Sicilian author pursues such an investigation without the reassurance of the kinds of alternative political or religious narratives he enjoyed in his youth: "I considered Fascism a religion [. . .] I considered Fascist Italy a temple [. . .] I experienced the joy of a herd animal: to be in agreement with millions of people."[74]

According to Leonardo Sciascia, one of Brancati's most attentive readers, the Sicilian writer stands out for "his surrender to guilt, his confession of it and tormenting of himself about it."[75] Brancati is not interested in surveying collective guilt, but in analyzing how each individual abdicated to the regime personal responsibility and moral judgment—beginning with himself. After the disasters of Fascism and total war, he elicits a radical examination of the perverse meaning of words and ideas that were uncritically employed to the detriment of life and freedom. In his highly diversified writing, which ranges from diary to aphorisms, and from theater to fiction, Brancati reflects on the intrinsic violence hidden behind key tropes of the Fascist discourse and the regime's obsession with monumental history. The author refuses the abstract vagueness of these tropes, which cover up the general and profound lack of self- and historical awareness. He signals their disquieting persistence in the conformism of postwar society, in the bigotry of what he calls "Pure anti-Fascism," and in the polarization of Italian life alongside the new overarching ideologies.[76]

Brancati's writing is a true act of resistance to new (and old) conformism. His prose is concrete, precise, purposely anti-rhetorical, and eager to detect in a word, a conversation, or a joke the persistence of old clichés and unresolved social tensions or political constraints leading to a new obscurantism. After the hard-won freedom from tyranny, Brancati strives to spell out that tolerance, freedom, and the integrity of a person are nonnegotiable values in any society—thence his profound skepticism of Communist and Catholic ideologies. Such values can be granted only through the ongoing practice of reason and irony, for he knows all too well that "the pleasure of falling back into an old sin is sweeter than any redemption."[77]

From his columns for *Il Tempo* and *Corriere della Sera* to his brilliant *Roman Diary* to his more celebrated fiction, Brancati's writing never wavers from a radical acknowledgment: Any revisiting of the "journey to the end of the night" represented by Fascism and the war must begin with the admission of personal responsibility. As Sciascia observes, Brancati "felt that the responsibility of Fascism was on his shoulders."[78] Defying the postwar trend of moralizing about Italians' supposed "national character," Brancati starts his reflections on Fascism from self-analysis and the memory of his own conduct: "And if to describe the stupidity of '33–'43 means for me to describe my own stupidity? Am I allowed to speak ill of myself, or have I become sacred to the Fatherland by the fact that in that period I was burdened with national flaws?"[79]

This witty remark highlights the distance between Brancati and his contemporaries, especially intellectuals who were also former Fascists. As we have seen, Piovene's shift from Fascism to Communism corresponded to a different stress on similar terms of the political discourse: from the wrong to the right side of history. For Piovene, the main danger for postwar Italy was *going outside history*, reverting to its historical weaknesses under the complacent protection of the Catholic Church. The alternative answer was, of course, *understanding* the true path of history and therefore endorsing the PCI. Brancati's reply defies such binary oppositions between Communism and Catholicism. In his 1947 article "The Capital," the writer sketches a passionate political discussion. Faced with the question of which side to take in the debate, he answers: "Well, I make no decision!" His interlocutor then concludes, as it were a terrible curse: "So you will remain outside of history!"[80]

The article provides evidence of Brancati's distinctive approach, countering early postwar political discourse. To the implicit question of his column—what does it mean to "remain outside of history"?—Brancati responds with reminders of the hollowness of ideological oppositions based on *metaphysical* concepts of history and of overarching rhetorical concepts that dramatically affected his life under Fascism and that of millions. Despite his deep, at times uncritical, respect for Croce as the philosopher of freedom, the writer describes historicism as a momentous fallacy. Or rather, he describes the effects of historicism on people, speeches, and policies:

> The character of modern rhetoric is not literary, but historicist. Every nationalist, at the end of a skirmish, compares his reign to the Roman Empire; every progressive, at the end of some upheaval or reform, compares his exploits to the Christian revolution.[81]

Brancati does not indulge in conceptual demonstrations about the historical misconstruction that lies at the base of Fascist ideology as well as vulgar Marxism. He instead voices his criticism through ironic observations, which cannot hide a profound melancholy for the general loss of innocence, a radical pessimism akin to that of his beloved nineteenth-century poet Giacomo Leopardi:

> Everyone wants to know "where the world is going" in order to follow diligently behind it. No one suspects that the world could be wrong; no one asks happiness to go in the opposite direction. Who has ever said: "Everyone thinks about it like this, so the truth must be found somewhere else"?[82]

Still, Brancati is neither an apolitical intellectual nor a *qualunquista*. He dedicated numerous articles to examining the social discontent and the hostility to politics at the roots of Sicilian separatism, or of the "Fronte dell'uomo qualunque" ("Common Man's Front"), the ephemeral populist movement launched by Guglielmo Giannini. To interlocutors remarking on his "nineteenth-century nostalgia," he replies with an anti-historicist program based on secularism and his acute sense of profound estrangement. In an article explicitly named "I do not love my age," in which he characterizes his times as "a century in which almost everyone is a conformist, but the most conformist of all are the revolutionaries," Brancati traces the leading features of his literature. His accounts "all consist in writing up a material that is so repellent according to the norms and style of an early nineteenth-century narrator; that is to say, of a gentleman, of a generous heart, of a truthful mind."[83] Aware of the risks of abstraction and reactionary moralism intrinsic to any such literary operation, Brancati merges in his prose the point of view of an early nineteenth-century narrator with that of a skeptical *philosophe* of the previous century.

The result is a melancholic gaze resisting traditional standards of confession and absolution. To this end, Brancati questions the main assumptions of modernist literature by problematizing the title of Proust's masterpiece. In the article "Can we waste again the time we have already lost?," the author asserts that his writing is not instrumental to regain lost time.[84] *His* time spent under the delusions and the idols of Fascism is lost forever. One of the principal characters of *Beautiful Antonio*, anti-Fascist Edoardo, after the end of the civil war and with the victory of his side, sorrowfully comments on the death of Mussolini: "That man has pocketed our youth."[85] Brancati's writing warns against wasting the present with new delusions and similar mistakes. In this way, his self-analysis conspicuously takes leave of the traditional self-scrutiny that is based on the rhetorical repetition of "spiritual exercises." As historian Fabio Cusin contended in those same years, traditional "spiritual exercises" were of no value to process personal responsibility for Fascism, since they are geared toward gaining absolution, while remaining alien to thorough introspection.[86]

WWII brought new interest in a genre—the diary—that had until then held relatively few attractions for Italian intellectuals. From Ada Gobetti to Elio Vittorini, from Piero Calamandrei to Mario Soldati, memorable diaries narrating or reflecting on those troublesome years appeared during or after the transition. The internal point of view of a diary reveals not just opinions and reactions of the author to historical events; it often showcases their awareness that writing implies a certain degree of responsibility—sometimes even beyond explicit intentions. In this regard, Brancati's observations in his *Roman Diary* about his old-time friend Leo Longanesi's *Let's Talk about the Elephant: Fragments of a Diary* are telling. Published in 1947 and probably heavily reworked after the conflict and the downfall of Mussolini, *Let's Talk about the Elephant* documents the persistence of an unrelenting Fascist mentality camouflaged by cynicism and *sprezzatura*.[87] "Longanesi," Brancati comments, "tells us nothing about his sins as an Italian: he makes of them neither an object of remorse, nor the stuff of caricature. He confesses the sins of others. (I believe that this is the flaw in all our diaries)."[88]

Here, as elsewhere, Brancati is painfully conscious of the moral accountability of writing in order to break away from Fascism and its mentality. As an author who is not *strictu sensu* political, Brancati is nevertheless fully aware of the political and liberating force literature may acquire. This is one of the reasons behind his stark defense of the freedom of art from political prescriptions and his adamant opposition to ideologically oriented literature. A hilarious passage from *Roman Diary* is illuminating in this regard:

> In the name of the Fatherland, of the Race, of Justice, no ignoramus would hesitate to climb up on a chair and proclaim:
> 1. The artist must represent our time.
> 2. The artist must not grasp or represent this or that aspect of our time, but the essential.
> 3. The one who'll tell you what the essential is, is me.[89]

The target of Brancati's polemic is not only the art of the regime and its remnants but also socialist realism and the poetics of the chronicle as supported by Marxist intellectuals and their journals. Dismissive of Sartre and his existentialism, the Sicilian writer also skeptically regards Gramsci's concept of the "organic" intellectual and his influential notion of the lack of national-popular literature in Italy. Although he pays sincere tribute to Gramsci's intelligence and courage, Brancati mordantly observes that the philosopher's assertion of what writers *should feel* in producing a truly national-popular literature opened the door to a return to the dictates of Fascism's "Ministry of People's Culture."[90]

Brancati is also on guard against the historical monumentalization of anti-Fascism, in which he sees continuities with Fascist fanaticism as well as offenses to historical truth and the memory of people who rebelled against oppression. Speaking about the "true heroes" who never endorsed Fascism, he bitterly concludes:

> The reverence we owe them doesn't allow us to apply to them a pathetic lie, which they wouldn't know what to make of anyway: the effects of their work, between '25 and '43, was nil. Italians preferred a well-fed party official, someone who vaulted over obstacles and broke in girls, to a musty socialist in prison.[91]

Fascist rule and the war are sources of constant inquiry for the Sicilian writer, particularly for their impact on the contradictory years of the transition. Some of his remarks call to mind Malaparte's comments in *The Skin*: "We must be merciful toward those victors who, for their undeniable virtues, certainly deserve the consensus of victory, but not the disgusting flaws of 'the strongest!'"[92] There are many intellectual points of contact between these two authors, completely opposite otherwise for their personalities and literary styles. These points are: the rebuke of the new postwar redemptive narratives, the struggle for the freedom and the autonomy of art from political control, the radical affirmation of the failure of revolutionary politics, and the appraisal of Fascism as a regime of mass mobilization. The last acknowledgment guided Brancati and Malaparte to a stark opposition to Communism—each in his own unique way.

Between Brancati and Malaparte there is, however, a fundamental difference, which determines a constitutional opposition between their work. At the foundation of Brancati's writing lies a self-analysis lacking in Malaparte—an absence that haunts the latter's entire postwar production. Biographical and historical experiences intermingle in their books as the principal subject of their inquiry. Both in autobiographical and fictive form, their narratives rework the unsustainable burden of Fascism, national defeat, and the war. As mentioned above, for the Sicilian writer, no examination, no approach to recent history was possible without first admitting personal responsibility for the catastrophe, not only as an individual but also as an *intellectual*. Admitting that individual guilt is nonnegotiable is already a momentous achievement in a Europe torn apart by mass ideologies and collective *Schuldfragen* (questions of guilt). Perhaps Brancati's nostalgic idealization of Western civilization before what he perceived as the present decadence sharpened his self-indictment. His and his generation's intellectual guilt lay in conscious intoxication, in the lack of resistance to pseudo-values.[93] Hence Brancati's paradoxical praise of the so-called ivory tower, as was named the intellectual choice of not taking part in the political arena. The ivory tower was the true *bête noire* of Fascist propaganda, which violently repressed any hint of indifference or lack of enthusiasm for the regime's achievements.

It is no coincidence that in Brancati's *Beautiful Antonio*, all the characters struggle and die for pseudo-values. Few works of literature represent vulgarity with such delicate, ironic decency: The reader is moved to pity the novel's characters. In this sense, Brancati is the worthy heir to Flaubert. The main focus of the novel is the protagonist's sexual impotence, already a crushing blow to the edifice of Fascist virility. In provincial Sicily, this personal problem is a tremendous social stigma, not only for the protagonist Antonio but also for his family and circle of friends. All the characters live, act, and make decisions for themselves and for others governed only by egoism, social prejudices, and superficial assumptions. The overall plot would be farcical if the history of those years, Fascism, and the war did not reveal the senseless tragedy of all those wasted lives. The radical self-analysis of the Fascist past that is behind *Beautiful Antonio* allows Brancati one last criticism. In the already mentioned 1946 article titled "Can we waste again the time we have already lost?," the Sicilian author expands on an issue that would be taken up again in the novel through the words of the protagonists:

> One pines for "good old '35" and "good old '36" as if the ships that set off at the time to "conquer the Empire" were not already the ghosts of ships, thanks to the fatal political error that, invisible to most people, highly visible to the few, lurked in the seemingly, provisionally successful action that pushed them through the Suez Canal, like flies in the nostrils of a sleeping dog, and one forgets that a citizen forced to salute in a certain way, to mutter the truth like a servant in the kitchen, to cry out with an exultation he doesn't feel, in short a man compelled to lie, receives no compensation from a great fleet that, a hundred kilometers from him, roams the sea in his name and in the name of all those compelled to lie like him and together with him.[94]

It is hard to find a similar indictment of Italian imperialism in 1946, and not just among former Fascist writers. Brancati decries the fallacy of imperialist dreams and explicitly links imperialist agendas with repressive policies at home. Imperialism and internal repression would express their worst in the practices of occupation during WWII. The author, however, does not mention capitalism or class struggle in this unambiguous link. The mutual alliance of Fascism and imperialism is not dismissed through Marxist interpretations, typical of those years, but through the acknowledgment of the common fallacies behind both: Despite national delusions, politics of power are not aimed to enhance individual freedom or civilization, at home or abroad. For Brancati, there is no disavowal of Fascism without a consequent disavowal of imperialism.

In the last pages of *Beautiful Antonio*, when the shame of the protagonist's impotence becomes public knowledge and the social stigma sticks to his entire family, Antonio's father, the fiery Alfio Magnano, displays his bitterness publicly. The old man accuses everyone nearby of stupidity and shallowness, particularly for abiding a regime that, in his delirious yet lucid cries, would have brought everyone to the catastrophe of war. Magnano concludes his speech with a gloomy prophecy with racist overtones: "It will end with savages, blacks, yellow men, cannibals with rings in their noses and feathers in their hair all coming right here!"[95] Alfio Magnano then dies during an aerial bombing, right before the Allies occupy Sicily and the city of Catania, where Antonio and the rest of his family live. At the sight of multinational armies entering the city, the bigot mother of the protagonist thus addresses his son: "'Antonio, did you hear?' she said in the thin little voice that had been hers ever since the death of her husband. 'Your poor father must have been spoken with angels. The streets of Catania are full of savages!'"[96]

This brilliant comic scene is extremely telling. Alfio Magnano's indictment of Fascism ends with a curse, addressing God as responsible for his son's shame. Although of a different class and cultural level, Alfio resembles another old man who finishes his life cursing an absent God—Berto's peasant patriarch of his *The Works of God*. Both characters are tragicomic figures, blind to the reality unfolding before their eyes because of their pride based on social delusions. The peasant and the bourgeois represent a world that preceded Fascism: They both engender its mentality with their arrogance and hollowness. As an irrational and unjust system of power, Fascism is consequential to a bigoted, antidemocratic, and patriarchal society totally unable to question its own assumptions. This traditional society survived Fascism and still operates in the postwar. A further groundbreaking recognition runs throughout Brancati's novel. In the ironic representation of Antonio's parents' narrow-mindedness, the Sicilian writer voices a radical conclusion: Fascism's cult of *Romanità*, of virility and male sexual prowess, its aberrant racial policies, and its dogmatic mindset are not just side effects of Mussolini's policies; they are at the core of an ideology deeply rooted in Italy. According to Brancati, recognizing these truths is the only effective way to question Fascism and the recent imperialist Italian past.

This momentous recognition will be at the center of the next chapter and will be examined as profoundly intertwined with the myths of modernity that received a decisive blow with the grim reality of WWII. The intellectual trajectories of Italian authors who engaged with national defeat and defied the official narratives of party politics would take different, even opposite, paths after the transitional years. "But here," concludes Brancati at the end of his self-analysis, "begins for me an entirely different story, one that, not doing me the dishonor that the first one does, should not be told."[97]

3

Ghosts from a Recent Past

Against Historicism

On November 24, 1945, the magnificent main room of the Biblioteca Angelica in Rome hosted the inaugural address of one of the oldest and most prestigious Italian cultural institutions, the Accademia dell'Arcadia. Given the circumstances, no better guest could have been chosen for the keynote address than liberal and neo-idealist philosopher Benedetto Croce, who delivered a speech titled "Arcadia and Eighteenth-Century Poetry" on that occasion. In line with the attending acolytes of the Accademia, he adopted a pastoral nickname for the event—Eudoro Dianeo—preserving the academy's centuries-old classicist tradition.[1] Nor could a better date have been selected for the exclusive cultural circle to state its formal and symbolic continuity with pre-Fascist Italy. On that very day the first postwar government, led by the partisan leader Ferruccio Parri, was obliged to resign as liberal and conservative forces withdrew support for his coalition.

Parri's government was born out of the armed Resistance and included all the anti-Fascist forces which defeated Mussolini, from monarchists to Communists. For many intellectuals, especially from the socialist-liberal Action Party, Parri's resignation signaled the end of a collective ideal of national renewal. Parri's demise corresponded to the institutional and *cultural* victory of Italy's state apparatus, presided over by conservatives, over the clear rupture with the past that Resistance fighters longed for.[2]

In the eyes of Italian and international observers, institutional continuity was granted by the unquestionable moral authority of Croce. A little less than two years earlier, in a much more consequential speech than that at the Accademia dell'Arcadia, the Neapolitan philosopher had famously proclaimed that Fascism was to be considered a "parenthesis" in the existence of Italy and Europe, a country and a civilization that rediscovered their historical mission through the war's sacrifice.[3] With Parri's resignation, traditional forces appeared to have regained control of Rome and its variegated culture. Institutional continuity was reestablished after the short but eventful season in which Italian intellectuals flocked to the capital to celebrate freedom and build the future of the country together. One consequence of their disillusionment was a shift of political allegiance: Many of them radicalized and joined the ranks of the Communist Party.[4]

Despite this season's bitter end, the memory of the frantic months that followed Rome's liberation on June 4, 1944, lingered for the next few years. In early 1945, when Northern Italy was still under the yoke of Hitler and Mussolini, the mood in the newly freed capital was entirely different. Remarkable journals such as *Mercurio*, directed by Alba de Céspedes; *La Nuova Europa*, by Luigi Salvatorelli; and *Città*, founded by Paola Masino, together with many other protagonists of these pages, such as Piovene and Moravia, were launched in this euphoric atmosphere.[5]

These outlets best express the early postwar Zeitgeist, the political proliferation of voices, and the post-Liberation "excess of speech," which, after the downfall of Parri, faded with the Christian Democrats' victory in the April 18, 1948, general elections. *La Nuova Europa*, for instance, fervently contributed to this unique season. Aligned with the Action Party, the journal published not only dissenting and unorthodox political views but also literary experiments with a specific goal—creating a new culture for Italy as a first step toward the recreation of a European community beyond national divides and imperialist agendas. The political and the literary, indeed, intertwined in texts that defied stable or traditional classifications. A principal polemical target of these innovative texts was, once again, Croce, whose aesthetics prescribed not just a division but a set hierarchy between culture and politics, with the former conceived as a higher spiritual activity than the latter.

Such an unparalleled season was also indelibly linked to mounting international tensions and, in the case of *La Nuova Europa*, to the fortune of the Action Party, which collapsed in 1947 soon after Parri's government. Moravia's "Political Diary," which he mostly published in Salvatorelli's journal, exemplified such cultural experiments, contributing to a genuinely multidisciplinary exchange. During those frenetic months, philosopher Guido De Ruggiero's essays "against historicism," published in *La Nuova Europa* (1945), historian Fabio Cusin's polemical *Antihistory of Italy* (1948, but its groundwork was laid during Italy's civil war), and avant-garde artist Alberto Savinio's articles collected in *Europe's Fate* (1945) all called for a cultural renewal after Fascist *and* liberal Italy. Despite obvious differences, these authors' proposals for a "new culture" are characterized by the recognition that rejecting Fascism on a political level necessitates disavowing historicism—and Croce—in the cultural realm.

In the same pages of *La Nuova Europa*, where Moravia offered his reflections on current politics, another author was publishing short, groundbreaking texts, which attempted to establish a cultural and ethical autonomy from Italy's recent past—including liberal Italy and its neo-idealism. Between February and July 1945, poet Umberto Saba published six series of "Shortcuts" in the journal: unconventional concise prose pieces that only partially fit the definition of aphorisms. Some "Shortcuts" address real people, as in a dialogue; others are brief moral fables. Political contention was only one of "Shortcuts"'s topics, which ranged from national history and European literature to personal anecdotal memories and reflections on racism and anti-Semitism. The following year, Saba collected his experimental prose in a volume titled *Shortcuts and Very Short Stories*.

Saba's *Shortcuts* was highly praised by the press, but in the effervescent atmosphere of the Liberation, its piercing humor and disquieting images seemed untimely.[6] Through the colloquial tone of an amicable conversation, Saba ruthlessly pointed out the contradictions of the postwar political and social scenario. The poet not only denounced the negative legacy of historicism for the country; he also offered an alternative genealogy of Fascist violence in defiance of Croce's historicist progress of freedom and Marxist interpretations. For Saba, Fascist violence derived from the nationalist and imperial myths that constituted bourgeois and liberal culture. Through a poetic language grounded on everyday life's experience, he singled out one by one the ghosts of the recent past that continued to haunt postwar Italy and post-Fascist Europe.

Saba's *Shortcuts* coped with questions in the postwar period that were at the time conspicuously silenced, such as the inherent racism of Italian society and the epoch-making significance of the Nazi *and* Fascist destruction of European Jewry. Saba's book partakes in the broader cultural opposition to historicism that developed after the Liberation. Like him, De Ruggiero, Cusin, and Savinio articulated their discontent by looking at intellectual sources that were alternatives to Croce's neo-idealism, such as Freud and Nietzsche. After surveying such cultural opposition and its visions for a future Italy, this chapter will examine how Saba's *Shortcuts* elaborated a poetic language in which individual life is not subservient to political ideology, in which life is instead accepted *in all its forms*, including traumatic experience. *Shortcuts* and Saba's last poetry urge for a post–WWII *new grammar of life*, which defies the redemptive narratives of postwar Italy.

Saba's powerful address to the country's repressed memory was not isolated. With her novel *Lies and Sorcery* (1948), Morante would expand Saba's intuitions to a radical reconsideration of traditional society and its bearing on present Italy, even beyond Fascism. In her novel, Morante investigates the social fantasies that haunt modern Italy and its redemptive narratives. The secularized protagonists of *Lies and Sorcery* pursue an illusory individual redemption that is bereft of collective emancipation because they cannot escape their obsessive attachment to *privilege*—expressively based on social and gender discrimination.

The theme of ghosts from the past haunting the present—illuminating persistent gender and *racial* bias—features prominently in another outstanding novel that appeared in those years: Ennio Flaiano's *A Time to Kill*, published in 1947.[7] The novel centers on the violence perpetrated by Italians on Ethiopians and their land during colonial occupation. It also highlights how the chronic self-delusions that popular culture and mass propaganda favored nationally—such as Mussolini's imperial rhetoric or the racial superiority of the Fascist "new man"—left evident traces in the general postwar forgetting.

Together with Saba's *Shortcuts*, the debut novels of Flaiano and Morante openly confront postwar Italy's repressed memory, from colonial wars to gender and social exclusion. Their respective works constituted an intellectually sound and aesthetically complex counterargument to Croce's consoling narrative of Fascism as a "parenthesis" in modern Italian history. The historicist concept of "freedom" faded from view in the wake of Fascism's principal legacy: Italians' lack of a democratic education and their attachment to privilege.

History from the Point of View of the Victims

Many are the polemical targets of Saba's *Shortcuts*, but the principal one, from the very first page, is Benedetto Croce. The third "Shortcut" reads:

> LAST CROCE In a house where one person hangs himself, where others kill each other, where some prostitute themselves, and some are dying painfully of hunger, where still others are destined for jail or the madhouse, a door opens, and you can see an old woman playing the spinet. Playing it very well.[8]

With precise brushstrokes, Saba paints Croce as a "spinet player," a modern pied piper surrounded by the unembellished reality of early postwar Italy. The poet's demeaning representation of the conservative champion of neo-idealist historicism and his role in early postwar Italy can be better understood in the context of the broader cultural battle that *La Nuova Europa* was leveling against Croce in those months. Around the same time Saba published his first "Shortcuts" series in the journal, philosopher Guido De Ruggiero published a thorough rebuttal of Croce's historicism. During most of the *ventennio*, De Ruggiero followed Croce as the moral leader of the opposition to Fascism. In 1925, he was one of the few intellectuals who signed Croce's "Manifesto of Anti-Fascist Intellectuals." Despite the profound respect he professed for the Neapolitan philosopher, De Ruggiero's political views changed and radicalized over time. In 1942, he was among the founders of the Action Party. Three years later, he wrote a series of articles for *La Nuova Europa* in which political disagreement became philosophical discontent. In his column "Beyond Historicism," published on January 28, 1945, De Ruggiero underscores the continuity between historicism and Fascism in what he calls the "fetishism" of history:

> The adoration of history is the form, albeit the highest form, of fetishism, consisting in the cult of the creature in place of that of the creator. [. . .] We do not have an unconditional adoration for history. We know, yes, that it is the only field where human activity is explained; but we also see that this field is full of errors, injustices, madness. The principle of a rationality of the real rings in our ear like mockery; that of the necessity of the occurrence like an empty logical (or tautological) formula that conceals the contingency of events, too often entrusted to the blindness and folly of men; that of the guiding freedom of history, like the consecration of a vain and unthinking impulse.[9]

De Ruggiero's philosophical discontent with historicism, then, brought about a larger dissatisfaction with Croce's historiography. Prompted by the regained freedom of expression after two decades of Fascist rule, De Ruggiero advocated for a history written from the point of view of the victims. In the article "The Crocean Phase," he claims: "It seemed to us that the victims, appointing themselves vindicators of principles that surpassed their time, have placed into the conscience of the world the foundations for a future recognition, and thus the need for a new history."[10]

De Ruggiero's objective in writing his articles "against historicism" was more ambitious than just pinpointing the philosophical aporias of Croce's system. His most pressing concern was to underline the necessity of reforming schools and education in Italy, as they were grounded in historicist concepts that impinged on critical thinking and action. His was an utter refusal of the "parenthesis" trope: It was now urgent to rewrite Italy's modern history from the point of view of "today's tragic experiences."[11] Outside conservative ranks, and especially in Communist circles, the aversion to Croce's historicism was widespread. Yet only Actionists overtly linked historicism to Fascism.[12] That Fascism's obsession with history had its roots in liberal Italy was indisputable in Marxist circles. It proved much more controversial to critically highlight the Hegelian influence on Marx—as De Ruggiero openly did in his pieces.[13]

The task of rewriting the country's modern history from the point of view of its recent "tragic experiences" was taken up in those same years by Fabio Cusin, a lesser-known but radical historian who had relevant experience in common with Saba. Like Saba, Cusin was born in Trieste and was also half Jewish. Moreover, he had a prominent interest in psychoanalysis (and, unlike Saba, in sociology). Croce notoriously discredited both disciplines, but their approaches would deeply affect Cusin's most significant work, *Antihistory of Italy*, published in 1948.[14] Like Saba, Cusin was an outsider with sympathies for the Action Party. Yet his unique intellectual trajectory sheds light on the greater aversion to Croce's historiography.[15]

Cusin's *Antihistory of Italy* is based on the unequivocal link between historicism and Fascism. As he claims in the introduction: "The experience of the present, understood as rebellion against unbearable oppression, has imposed a revision of the past that becomes a real coming to terms with history as traditionally understood."[16] For Cusin, opposition to historicism is grounded in recent history's traumas, beginning with the total war against Fascism, which he recognizes as an ideology *legitimized* by a historicist mindset: "It was the predominant historicism that suggested to the leaders the idea of the revolutionary and definitive character of their work and established the concept that the new movement constituted a period of its own."[17]

Cusin implicitly connects his revolt against idealistic historiography to Piero Gobetti's famous definition of Fascism as an "autobiography of the nation," signaling how democracy and "real" liberalism were compromised *even before* Mussolini and his cohorts took power. With remarkable prescience, Cusin concludes his book's reprimand by attacking Allied propaganda and anti-Fascist culture, arguing that both Allied and anti-Fascist forces avoided distinguishing the differences between Nazism and Fascism. Thus, he contends, they paved the way for a simplistic and Manichean reading of the recent past, offering an unrealistic and ultimately absolving view of the Italian contribution to WWII and the European crisis. It was in those years that the consoling myth of "Italiani brava gente" ("Italians as inherently good people")—which portrayed Italians as fundamentally compassionate and humane despite their association with Fascism—spread.[18]

Saba's aversion to Croce needs to be situated in this broader philosophical and historiographical scenario. It is no coincidence that Cusin's *Antihistory of Italy*, which the author outspokenly named a "renewed attempt to revolt against tradition," was not just a polemical text but, quite literally, *an alternative history of Italian literature.*[19] To dismantle the idea of culture that Croce spearheaded, Cusin launched a critical revision of the locus where Italian identity coalesced: national literature, from Dante to Francesco De Sanctis, whose influential *History of Italian Literature* (1870) was conceived as a monument *aere perennius* to the Italian nation. For both Cusin and Saba, Croce embodies the specter of an oppressive past, of an institutionalized culture that would once again strangle the free flow of new life and ideas by privileging academic fetishes of past glories. As in Saba's memorable image, the old-fashioned "spinet" Croce plays beautifully among the national debris *is not a piano.*

Both Cusin's *Antihistory* and Saba's *Shortcuts* overtly reject the moral monumentality that the Neapolitan philosopher represented. Croce embodied rigorous anti-Fascism, as De Ruggiero acknowledged in his articles, but to radical intellectuals looking for change, he championed tradition, the immobility and paternalism of the ruling class, and even a deliberate hostility to modernity. For younger generations, he represented the old redemptive paradigm that privileged stability and continuity over revolution and thorough reforms. Marxist intellectuals, too, attacked the philosopher as the symbol of the ghosts of Italy's past. They were prompted by PCI's leader Palmiro Togliatti, who "studiously organized a cultural programme that revolved around the release of Antonio Gramsci's unpublished writings," thus paving the way for what Daniela La Penna called "the erosion of Benedetto Croce's influence over the intellectual field."[20]

Saba, however, concludes his *Shortcuts* by offering a counter-model for the advocated new culture that is utterly at odds with idealism and historical materialism. His last shortcut is also the shortest: "GENEALOGY OF SHORTCUTS Freud—Nietzsche."[21] By pointing out the impact of the two thinkers on his own *Weltanschauung*, Saba suggests a clear alternative to Croce (and, to a minor extent, Marx). Needless to say, Freud and Nietzsche were the two figures who contributed the most to dismantling idealist and historicist culture in Europe.

In the newly liberated Italian capital, Saba's poetic formulations and alternative cultural references significantly strayed from the overtly ideological "patterns of conversion" that developed around the new political forces. As mentioned earlier, however, Saba was not alone in resisting Croce *and* the new orthodoxies. Alberto Savinio—another unclassifiable author who ambivalently crossed paths with Fascism but whose works Fascism eventually banned—addressed the question of Croce and his historicism with singular clarity.[22] In his manifold writings of those years, Savinio strove to illuminate different angles of the broader issue of postwar cultural renewal. With a series of articles that appeared after the Liberation, Savinio challenged hegemonic historicism with unpredictable yet crisp arguments. Croce had based his interpretation of European history on the revelation of freedom, on freedom as a matter of (national) emancipation. In a piece titled "Restless Adolescents," Savinio asks: "But how can we talk about freedom as long as we lack the 'psychological' condition of freedom and man hasn't acquired an awareness that the forces he obeys are of his own invention?"[23] The author demands a change of cultural paradigm beginning with a personal, *psychological* emancipation from the ghosts of religion, ideology, and metaphysics.

Remarkably, Savinio describes the post-Fascist change of cultural paradigm as a new "Copernican revolution."[24] The writer envisions the struggles of postwar Italy and Europe as akin to the opposition between the old Ptolemaic world—which places humanity at the center of creation—and the infinite and multicentered cosmos envisaged by Copernicus, in which mankind is but an accident. "Theocratic" totalitarian states such as Mussolini's Italy and Hitler's Germany, he contends, still partake in a Ptolemaic vision; they resist a Copernican understanding of a world without set limits and hierarchies—a democratic, if not a *socialist* new world.[25] Swiftly imbuing aesthetic terms with political connotations, Savinio employs analogies from the art world to reinforce his argument and explain Fascism's failures. *Pompier*, for instance, is a derogatory term that modernist artists used to reject traditional painters who focused exclusively on historical and academic subjects in their works. He concludes that

> In politics, the pompier thinks that a great political endeavor can only be pursued on the model of the Roman Empire. And Hitler, who is the greatest pompier to have appeared so far on the face of the earth, to our detriment, dreamed of recreating in his own way the Roman Empire, though without explicitly declaring as much.... It is an outdated—and unrealizable—way. *It is a way that still draws on the Ptolemaic mindset.*[26]

Savinio collected the political articles he wrote after the arrest of Mussolini in the volume *Europe's Fate*, published in 1945. In these pieces, he criticizes Fascist rhetoric, historicism, and *pompierismo* as if they were different facets of the same problem. The rejection of Fascism on a political level parallels the disavowal of historicism in the cultural realm. The volume envisages a united Europe and urges for the overcoming of the "national" idea—a legacy of nineteenth-century liberalism that the author claims has ceased to be productive. According to Savinio, dismissing nationalism for a new polity beyond the nation-state is analogous to shifting from a Ptolemaic to a Copernican paradigm. The last piece of the collection, which gives the title to the entire book, pushes the famous call of Marx and Engels's *Manifesto of the Communist Party* further. He writes: "'Partisans across Europe, unite!,' meaning by 'partisans' and 'partisanism' the genuine element of Europe that works according to its own impulse, and not to the orders or inspiration of others."[27] For Savinio, the "idea of the social community" is the only authentic drive that can bring about the desired unification of Europe; it constitutes both the concept *and* the action able to replace the nineteenth century's "liberal idea."

Interestingly, in the preparatory papers of the book, which are preserved at the Archivio Vieusseux in Florence, Savinio initially wrote "Communist idea," which he then corrected with a pen to "idea of the social community."[28] This shift speaks volumes about the uncertainty of the period. Today, Savinio's dalliance with Communism seems even more unlikely than the quirkiest of his metaphysical paintings. But in the final months of the war, when the fight against Nazis and Fascists reached the peak in Northern Italy, Savinio launched a unique book series in which he reprinted classic texts of utopian literature, from Lucian of Samosata to Tommaso Campanella's *The City of the Sun* and Thomas More's *Utopia*. Savinio intended this series to be his contribution to the spiritual reconstruction of Italian society. In his introduction to More, however, praise for the British author's distinctive *typology* of utopia elicits criticism of Marxism. In More's utopia, Savinio argues, "The sense of *communist* has yet to be subjected to that 'contraction' to solely economic factors to which it will later be subjected by Karl Marx."[29]

For Savinio, revolution is unthinkable if based solely on economic and historical processes. The model for intellectual inquiry here is Nietzsche and his anti-historicist *On the Genealogy of Morals*, the pioneering investigation into the linguistic genealogies that forged Western morality.[30] Savinio deems Nietzsche's epistemology decidedly more relevant for understanding the present than ideological and economical superstructures. The main target of Savinio's polemic is the concept of civilization intended as linear progress and dialectical development at the core of Croce's concept of freedom and of vulgar Marxism. Savinio concludes the aforementioned article "Restless Adolescents" by spelling out the limits of such ideas of freedom: "Let the revolution come in Italy, but a revolution that produces profound and durable results that free not only the bodies but also the minds of Italians."[31]

All the reviews of Savinio's *Europe's Fate* focused on its final passage about the importance of the "idea of the social community," praising or dismissing the book altogether according to the political affiliation of the reviewer, either socialist or liberal.[32] Though typically silent regarding the juridical and institutional reorganization of the continent, *Europe's Fate*'s relevance lies in Savinio's attempt to envision the intellectual principles that should inform the construction of a new Europe born from the ashes of totalitarian regimes. To that end, the text explicitly rejects historicism as the philosophical foundation of postwar education and cultural reconstruction. The key reference here is another anti-historicist pamphlet by Nietzsche, the seminal *On the Uses and Disadvantages of History for Life*. It is no coincidence that De Ruggiero, too, references Nietzsche's influential pamphlet widely in his articles for *La Nuova Europa*.[33]

The call for new intellectual models against historicism is also discernible in Saba's most outspoken attack on Croce, his 1946 article "Poetry, Philosophy, Psychoanalysis." The Neapolitan philosopher notoriously disavowed Freud's studies as irrelevant for art and poetry, essentially confirming the Fascist and Catholic cultural ban of psychoanalysis on moral grounds. Saba passionately replies that

> *it's not enough to have read Freud* or other psychoanalysts to understand something of psychoanalysis, and of its importance that goes beyond (far beyond what Croce thinks) therapeutics and a subsidiary mode of psychological investigation. [. . .] What Freud brings to light—*without searching for it*—is simply the new world.[34]

By attacking Croce's dismissal of Freud, the poet singles out how useless, if not harmful, Hegel and Kant were for what he emphatically calls the "new world," instead tracing an alternative intellectual genealogy for postwar culture: "Copernicus—Darwin—Freud."[35] His proposed genealogy welcomed the achievements of modern science and declared the obsolescence of the old humanist paradigm. Saba's outlook was distinctively unconventional in a historical moment in which the return to the "human" was entreated all over Europe as a response to Fascism, both in good and bad faith.[36]

Saba's defense of psychoanalysis acquires, then, an unexpected political undertone, echoing Savinio's reference to Copernicus and his conclusion on revolutionary politics. According to the poet, when contrasted to Freud's revolution, "even a great political and social revolution—such as, for ex., the Russian Revolution—is only a revolution *on the surface*."[37] Backed by the intellectual revolutions of Nietzsche and Freud, Savinio and Saba not only debunk historicism, but they also single out the pitfalls of vulgar Marxism as springing from historicist ideologemes.

Literary critic Walter Pedullà wrote of Savinio that "this seemed to him the only useful constructive activity: reveal the 'fabrication.'"[38] This is, in my opinion, *precisely why* texts such as Savinio's *Europe's Fate* and Saba's *Shortcuts* were considered so problematic in postwar Italian culture and have been somehow ostracized for decades: Although they do not contest Marxism in principle, they disagree that Marxist philosophy offers the only possible path to emancipation. *Europe's Fate* and *Shortcuts* enact a cultural battle that is constituted by an apparent *pars destruens* ("reveal the fabrication") but also—and perhaps more importantly—an exceptional *pars construens*. The two books are concerned with offering life the occasion to unfold in all directions, for they are lyrically open to the limitless possibilities of the real. *Europe's Fate* and *Shortcuts* depict vast spaces and are suspicious of boundaries, borders, and constraints of every sort. Right or wrong, they convey on every page the vivifying atmosphere of the Liberation, as they propose ideas not just for the coming democracy in Italy, but for Europe and all its peoples.

In a later article about the relationship between Voltaire and Friedrich II of Prussia, Savinio depicts homosexuality as a supreme form of awareness.[39] The author's open acceptance of homosexuality, however, is only nominally linked to sexual orientation. Savinio thinks of homosexuality in intellectual terms, as a higher state of "indifference," in which the notion of gender dissolves because difference *no longer constitutes a problem*. Savinio's very personal utopia, referred to as "hermaphroditism," is reminiscent of Plato's *Symposium* but also of a long-standing anti-classical tradition from ancient to modern times.[40] This was a brave move, for it calls into question the religious—and not only Catholic—cult of the family, but also because his utopic "hermaphroditism" elicits an alternative typology of freedom.[41] Savinio conceives of freedom no longer as a consequence of national accomplishments or historical redemption. Instead, he links it to emancipation from the burden of past ideas: "The tragedy of the world," he writes in 1944, "comes from the fact that the world is cluttered with things that have lost all meaning, but believe they possess it still."[42]

Among the ideas that still "clutter" our present are discrimination and repression based on racial and sexual bias. Savinio concludes his cheerful eulogy of Voltaire and Friedrich's relationship with a truly groundbreaking statement, which remarkably will return almost verbatim in Primo Levi's reflections on anti-Semitism thirty years later in his book *The Periodic Table*: "I propose this hypothesis," Savinio concludes, "only the state of impurity is fertile."[43]

Savinio's and Saba's insights from the postwar transition remain unparalleled in early postwar Italy. The two authors experienced literature as a Nietzschean "gay science," as able to cast disquieting shadows on the present and future. Saba and Savinio privilege the search for truth over rhetoric, ideology, and redemptive narratives.[44] Their preoccupations seemed misplaced when published, typically at odds with what Saba called the "blood and tears" paradigm of Resistance narratives. Following Nietzsche's lead, these two authors professed a critical history in stark opposition to the monumental and antiquarian history of Fascist and liberal regimes.

Still, their critical history "against historicism" left a conspicuous mark on postwar Italian literature—anticipating later pivotal developments. A recuperation of Savinio would become possible only when a new wave of avant-garde intellectuals in the 1960s would fully appreciate his linguistic paradoxes and *ante-litteram* deconstruction, as well as his subtleties à la Voltaire.[45] Saba's intellectual influence would instead flourish immediately. "I had Rome and happiness./One I enjoyed openly and the other/I kept quiet out of superstition," he wrote in "Gratitude," a poem recalling the outstanding year he spent in the capital after its liberation.[46] The elderly poet lived this unexpected season of gaiety and literary productivity as an utter surprise after the terrible years of anti-Semitic discrimination and subsequent hiding in Florence, where the psychological strain of persecution almost led him to commit suicide. Unlike Malaparte and Savinio, whose "imperfect" Italian identity (Malaparte's father was German, Savinio grew up in Greece) played a role in their "compensatory" fervid nationalism and support of Fascism, Saba's Jewish identity represented an internal rift, impossible to reconcile.

Saba's ghosts became all too real after the 1938 promulgation of racial laws and even more so after the 1943 Nazi occupation of Northern Italy. Discrimination and persecution threw him into the condition described by Arendt as *Weltlosigkeit*, the "absence of world" experienced by someone whose diversity set them apart from the human race altogether. Saba expresses this harrowing personal condition in a letter to his daughter, Linuccia, written in 1944:

> I began to feel bad, to foresee bad things a week or more before the Germans attacked Belgium and Garfagnana. I *felt* that things weren't going well: and I've already waited, to say nothing of before, all '38, '39, '40, '41, '42, '43, '44. Don't you think it's too much for an old and exhausted man like me? [. . .] I alone understood that Nazism and Fascism were a cancer, which wasn't

operated in time and against which there is no longer a cure. But it's not about this. It's about how everyone can live with this cancer; and I can't. I suffer too much. I don't have a moment of peace. I'm not telling you the images that come at me one after the other, without allowing me a moment's rest.[47]

Shortcuts was born from this overwhelming experience. Traumatic history is probably the best counterargument to historicism. Untainted by false ideas of progress and the degenerations of nationalism, the poet's "new culture" would confront ghosts from the past that the fall of Fascism did not keep at bay. As Elsa Morante concluded in a remarkable piece she wrote on Saba only a few months before his death in 1957, "Like the protagonists of myths, fables, and mysteries, every poet must go through the trial of reality and anguish, until the clarity of the word frees him, and frees the world, too, of his unreal monsters."[48]

Many dissident intellectuals in Italy attacked Croce in the early postwar with criticisms that linked historicism to Fascist ideology, from philosopher De Ruggiero to historian Cusin to avant-garde artist and writer Savinio. In the same years, Marxist circles strategically absorbed Croce's tropes into their own discourse by elaborating what literary critic Natalino Sapegno called an "integral historicism."[49] Saba's specific influence lies in elaborating a poetic language in which life is not corrected by ideology, but it fully embraces history's traumatic experience. With *Shortcuts*, he was also among the first in Europe to grasp and signal the *civilizational break* that occurred during WWII with the Nazi genocidal attack on European Jewry.

Umberto Saba: In the Shadow of the Camps

Dear Mr. Primo Levi,

I don't know whether you will like being told by me that your book *If This Is a Man* is more than a beautiful book, it's an inevitable book. Someone had to write it: fate decreed that this someone be you.

Thus begins the letter Saba sent to Primo Levi on November 3, 1948. It expresses the congratulations of an old and famous poet to a promising young writer on his first book. After a closer look, however, Saba's letter reveals something more consequential: his passionate endorsement of the cultural project that *If This Is a Man* stands for. "If it were within my power," he continues, "I would make it a mandatory school textbook."[50]

Saba concludes his letter by commenting on Italy's dire situation after Christian Democrats' victory in the April 18, 1948, general elections. His disappointment was shared well beyond leftist intellectual circles. Saba argues that internal and international politics justify his paranoid fear of a complete takeover of Italian life by the Catholic Church. Despite the grim scenario, he highlights how Levi's work is destined to outlive such disillusionment. "I have the impression that the book can also live beyond the crisis," he finally writes in his letter.

Saba's remark was truly unorthodox at a time when Italian culture—especially literature—was striving to celebrate the Resistance as the new national epic. Resistance narratives focused on the sacrifice of the countless women and men, often of humble origins and with no political preparation, who resisted and fought back against Nazi and Fascist forces.[51] In contrast, Levi's devastating testimony of Auschwitz had no uplifting models to offer. *If This Is a Man* stresses how the wounds of WWII—and not just for Italians or European Jews—could and would not heal. Remarkably, Saba describes the epic hagiography of the Resistance as "a culture of crisis" while seeing in Levi's work the possibility of cultural renewal. Saba's discontent is targeted not only at conservative forces but also at the redemptive narratives that early postwar leftist culture produced.

In a book on Jewish autobiography from the Bible to Philip Roth, Elena Loewenthal proposes to consider Saba among the "salmon-poets, poets who go in the opposite direction of logic: that of life, of memories, of literary conformism." Loewenthal maintains that every time Saba claims in his letters "I am dying," he means "Do you see how I'm alive?"[52] Similarly, in his exchange with the young Levi, the book that nobody wanted to read—or to publish, since Einaudi notoriously rejected *If This Is a Man* months earlier—becomes the one that will mark an entire era, well beyond the time of its publishing.

Despite favorable reviews, Levi's *If This Is a Man* received scant reception during the transition.[53] Unlike his contemporaries, however, Saba showed prescient insight and profound empathy by immediately understanding the book's timeless value and promptly ascribing it to what he names the "new world." As he repeats several times in his *Shortcuts*, the "new culture" he advocates for will arise only after the end of the current crisis, which he describes as not having ended with the war, despite having begun in 1914.

Levi's *If This Is a Man* and Saba's *Shortcuts* share a fundamental acknowledgment: that what happened within the barbed wire fences of Nazi concentration camps would change the self-representation of mankind and deeply affect every subsequent analysis of civilization and history.[54] When Saba writes that his "Shortcuts" are all "in some ways, survivors of Maidanek,"[55] he points to the same bewildering insight that supports Levi's account of his own internment at Auschwitz: The experience of these two camps is the unavoidable starting point for every attempt at cultural renewal. The two books—and not just their authors—are indeed *reduci* (loosely translated as "survivors") of the series of events that led to the planned extermination of European Jewry, which, only later, would be designated as the Holocaust. Such a recognition, and the idea that tomorrow's culture will necessarily have to take *all this* into account to rebuild civilization and community, would dominate their lives and memory.[56]

Moreover, both Saba and Levi share another recognition that anticipates the historical and philosophical debates of later decades: What happened in Majdanek and Auschwitz did not only affect Jewish people (or other minorities, including political prisoners). It would also bring about a reappraisal of Western civilization as a whole.[57] "Maidanek," writes Saba at the end of a "shortcut" on the current political debate, "cannot be expiated"—it is not *redeemable*.[58] One year later, in 1947, Georges Bataille arrived at a similar conclusion when he insightfully noted: "Like the pyramids or the Acropolis, Auschwitz is the deed, the sign of man. By now, the image of man is inseparable from that of a gas chamber."[59]

When *Shortcuts* was published, the Nazi's genocidal attack on European Jewry did not even have a name. In his book, Saba chooses the word "Maidanek" to index the complex historical event that we associate today with the terms "Holocaust" or "Shoah." The news of the small concentration camp south of Lublin, liberated by the Soviets in 1944, captured Saba's imagination as the *revealing* event of WWII. Majdanek was the first camp freed by the Allies: When the news of its horrors reached liberated Italy, the public impact was huge.[60]

For Saba, it was also a historic epiphany. In his prose, the news of "Maidanek" (I will use here Saba's spelling) immediately acquired the radical epistemological value of an unredeemable rupture in Western civilization. Here Saba anticipates historian Dan Diner, who would aptly characterize the Holocaust as *Zivilisationsbruch*, "civilizational break," decades later.[61] In the following months, even grimmer news of other camps reached Italy, illuminating the existence and organization of what David Rousset called in his own memoir "l'univers concentrationnaire."[62] Saba's poetic imagination, however, lingered on the small Polish camp south of Lublin, privileging the shock value of its first appearance. To paraphrase Pirandello's famous image in his novel *The Late Mattia Pascal*, it was a sudden rift in the papier-mâché sky of centuries-old humanistic convictions. Saba perceived that the cultural and epistemological crisis anticipated by Pirandello was hardly over: In "Maidanek," he found a proper name to indicate its unpredictable degeneration.[63]

"Maidanek" is indeed the conceptual and poetic center of *Shortcuts*. Like a black hole, the book's composition gravitates around the camp's disquieting presence. Saba repeats the name of the Polish camp time and again in crucial positions of his short texts as if it were a rhyme he cannot avoid. In Saba's prose, "Maidanek" has polysemic functions: The place is a metonymy for a concentration or extermination camp. Yet, as a signifier, it also *names* the historical process that we refer to today with the word "Holocaust." Even beyond *Shortcuts*, "Maidanek" recurs in published works and private correspondence. Its image evokes the various meanings that "Buchenwald" and then "Auschwitz" would subsequently acquire in Western cultural debate.[64]

According to Saba, "Maidanek" is the outcome of a civilization born out of an oppressive religious mindset, an institutional education based on castrating morals as well as the false illusions of forced modernization.[65] Even his lambasting of Croce and historicist culture finds in "Maidanek" its ultimate justification. In a controversial shortcut that he eventually decided not to publish because, as he confesses in a letter, "I don't want to end up lynched," Saba portrays himself thus: "I am, in ascending order, the anti-Mussolini, the anti-Croce, the anti-S.S. The three Blessed Men [*Benedetti*] who have cursed Italy."[66] Besides the pun that combines the Pope (the "Santissimo") and Nazi SS ("Schutzstaffel") as the ultimate evil, it is disconcerting that Croce figures as a worse problem for Italy than Mussolini himself.

Saba's prose wittingly defies simple explanations: His hyperbolic language demands an ironic interpretation—his "shortcuts" are similar to a Freudian "joke" or, more precisely, to a *Witz*.[67] In approaching his unpublished shortcut, we should then reverse the eccentric trio's sequence and start from the end—with the Pope as the worst "curse" for the country, Croce as nothing but a byproduct of religious and reactionary obscurantism, and Mussolini as its latest ominous consequence. This is an eloquent way of spelling out the continuity between the liberal and Fascist regimes and underscoring the dogmatic tenets of their respective ideologies.

Saba's biting caricature of Croce and the shock value represented by "Maidanek" loom large over the entire book. The early shortcuts in which these images first appear set the tone for his reflections about the imminent postwar political and social restoration—embodied by Croce—in contrast with the daunting new questions that "Maidanek" and the war posed. For Saba, the historical reality of the camps urges for a radical rethinking of civilization, beginning with its anthropological and cultural foundations.[68] Utterly devoid of messianic undertones, *Shortcuts* hastens the coming of the "new world." In the intention of its author, the book represents the first step toward a new culture "after Maidanek," one able to bear its historical weight, as he implicitly—and polemically—suggests in the first two shortcuts.

Like the opening stanzas of classical epic poems, *Shortcuts* begins by outlining its matter and style. The first two shortcuts, titled "SHORTCUTS' HANDWRITING" and "SHORTCUTS," respectively, unveil how the book's formal aspects influence its rhizomatic content. Shortcut number 1 enumerates the visual and graphic, almost material, characteristics of the book, beginning with the one that most accurately defines its composition: "They are full of parentheses."[69] The second piece, after providing a by-the-book definition of "shortcut," ends instead with an ambivalent tone: Shortcuts, the poet suggests, "can make you nostalgic for long, flat, paved, provincial roads."

Despite mentioning only formal aspects, the two short texts sketch the principal features of the "new culture." Parenthesis, complexity, and ellipsis call into question the illusions of ideology, of a narrative that encompasses the totality of the real, one-way streets that are ultimately *provincial*, narrow-minded, and parochial. The idea of a widespread "nostalgia" for large and straight "provincial roads" introduces the reader to the shortcut named "LAST CROCE," featuring Saba's spiteful caricature of the philosopher as a spinet player. One of Italy's "curses," together with the Pope and Mussolini, Croce and his restored postwar authority hinder the new culture Saba desires. For the poet, Croce's reassuring, recognizable, paternalist figure stands for the persistence of a spectral past still haunting the present after Fascism's alleged "parenthesis."

Saba's *Shortcuts* instead features *multiple* parentheses. The book's convoluted syntax resists reductive ideological schemes and attests to the contradictions of the early postwar period. Dialectics and heteroglossia are not at stake here. Like modern physics, Saba's shortcuts accept the indeterminacy principle as an epistemological limit. For Saba, Croce is instead stuck in Newtonian mechanics. In this sense, their respective use of the parenthesis trope could not be more different—or more polemical. Saba responds to Croce's notorious reading of the Fascist *ventennio* as a "unique" historical parenthesis by claiming not only that the "roads" of liberal idealism are provincial, but that the book he himself is writing—and with it, the desired new culture—is "full of parentheses." Saba's parentheses do not stand for separation, but for addition, insertion, inclusion—of doubts, of multiple and coexisting possibilities, of episodes signaling the "returns of the repressed." Ultimately, they draw attention to "genealogical" proliferation and shifting of meaning—to name the anti-idealist epistemological approaches of Freud and Nietzsche, respectively.

Countering Croce's teleological history of freedom, Saba sketches a highly personal epistemology, both unsystematic and undialectical, as he reflects on modern history in the symbolic shadow of "Maidanek." Drawing from Nietzsche's anti-metaphysical approach and Freud's psychoanalysis, Saba attempts a *poetic* comprehension of the events of recent history:

> AFTER NAPOLEON each of us is a little better, if only because Napoleon once lived. After Maidaneck . . . [70]

Ellipses usually nurture ambiguity. In this case, in Shortcut number 5, they instead underscore the importance of the message. In Saba's poetic understanding of history, the conspicuous omission demands the active participation of the reader—dialogue substitutes dialectics. Napoleon embodied the sentimental myth and the heroic mythology of nineteenth-century idealistic-liberal civilization. His persona championed the Zeitgeist and values of Romantic Europe, which were later transmitted to the *fin de siècle* entrepreneurial bourgeoisie. Italy's liberal bourgeoisie inherited these values in the early twentieth century. Saba implies that, being intoxicated with neo-idealist and historicist culture, Italy's bourgeoisie *believed* and thus followed Mussolini. The evidence, the "fact" of "Maidanek," however, not only showcases how the bad faith of a liberal civilization turned into a conservative and reactionary class, but also how European civilization as a whole, and not just its bourgeoisie, is profoundly tied to Fascism and extermination camps.

Throughout *Shortcuts*, Saba is keenly aware of how difficult his anti-historicist project—his suggested "new culture"—was to accept in early postwar Italy. Shortcut number 49 is, in this sense, quite explicit:

> DEAR READER, don't let the sometimes paradoxical, sometimes even playful (?) appearance of (some) of these SHORTCUTS fool you. They were created out of more than ten years of experience of life, art, and sorrow.
>
> They are, more than anything else, in some ways, survivors of Maidanek.[71]

This shortcut features a disquieting imbalance between the casual atmosphere of friendly exchange Saba evokes and the sudden rupture of meaning the inclusion of "Maidanek" provokes. In particular, the term "SHORTCUTS" here is emblematic. It refers not only to the book Saba is writing but to the concept of a book devised to include the ghosts from the recent past and resist, at the same time, consoling narratives. In a letter to his daughter, Linuccia, Saba claims: "I've reviewed the latest proofs of *Shortcuts*. It's more than a beautiful book, it's the book of the twentieth century, as *Candide* was the book that summed up the eighteenth century. Few, very few, will understand it. But the work is vital . . . as your poor father was."[72]

Saba emphatically envisions his *Shortcuts* as the book that sums up the twentieth century. To achieve that goal, he has but one possibility—his book has to be a *survivor* of "Maidanek."[73] *Shortcuts* fully contributes to the early postwar intellectual frenzy: The "new culture" would create a new audience by experimenting not just with forms but also with morals and ideas. A few weeks after the publication of *Shortcuts*, Saba fondly recalls the vivifying atmosphere surrounding the book's birth to the literary critic Giuseppe De Robertis:

> Shortcuts that, on top of everything else, are TRUE TO THE LETTER, are a work of love. There was so much goodness and so much love in my soul when, in 1945, I wrote them in Rome (and think about what a frightening trial I was just coming out of . . .) [. . .] One could not be more "inspired," one could not be more "cheerful," than I was then. Think about how much, and with at least an appearance of justice, I could have been "wicked." But my comprehension of life had arrived then at the point that I managed to enclose even Maidanek in a circle of goodness . . . [74]

"Enclosing Maidanek in a circle of goodness." Saba's powerful yet elusive image requires unpacking. According to the poet, such a circle stands for two different but intermingled issues: an advancement of universal knowledge and a personal exorcism. For Saba, the required deeper historical understanding is also a valid contribution designed to keep his own personal ghosts at bay. As he implicitly suggests in the letter, the poet barely escaped anti-Semitic persecution only a few months earlier. Still, Saba's image is emblematic of poetry's cognitive power: In Shortcut number 88 he unabashedly declares that the praise he would like to receive is "He cried and *understood* for everyone."[75] To the distortions of postwar redemptive narratives, Saba opposes his personal, fragile, and *maternal* predisposition to "understand" everyone and everything—including the horrors of war and totalitarianism.

In Saba's poetic lexicon, this unique comprehension is named "amore." What he calls his own "goodness" when facing "Maidanek" is neither a political nor a moral response to the crimes perpetrated by Fascism during WWII. Rather, it is an uncompromising search for truth, with the awareness that any attempt at a deeper understanding does not expiate past and present sufferings. Saba's own weakness, his anxiety of being persecuted, allowed him to see in the perpetrator flesh, impulses, and drives that are *his own*, that he recognizes in himself and in the society that nurtured him. Saba is crossing psychic territories here that are beyond questions of forgiving or forgetting—to him, insufficient or unviable responses. At stake is not whether the perpetrators belong to humankind anymore, like in Vittorini's novel *Men and Not Men* published the previous year, but rather how the biopolitical practices and techniques have become "the sign of man," to paraphrase Bataille in his assessment of extermination camps.

Saba never blurs the difference between victims and perpetrators. Nor does he resort to consoling conclusions. His is the perspective of the "civilizational break," similar to the one that propels Robert Antelme to recognize in his perpetrators the same biological *species* to which victims belong.[76] His principal argument is that a civilization based on ideologies that dismiss the life of every single individual for a supposed higher good is constantly at risk of degenerating into "Maidanek." Whether religious or ideological, life's sacrifice cannot redeem the ills of history. The Romantic myth of self-immolation for the fatherland, for instance, had already received a fatal blow in the trenches and technological slaughter of WWI, even before it was appropriated by Fascist propaganda. Saba spells this concept out in Shortcut number 43: "Well, what was the fundamental reason for the acceptance of fascism in Italy—and everywhere else—if not a mistaken attempt by the bourgeoisie to create a new life for themselves, to *rejuvenate* themselves?"[77] Saba's nostalgia for Romantic patriotism (see his reference to Napoleon) does not stop him from realizing that radicalized "noble" ideas of sacrifice can conceal xenophobia. Between idealism and totalitarian states, there is much more continuity than rupture.

Saba's *Shortcuts* paves the way for a criticism of political theologies, signaling how the cult of the fatherland has become idolatry and dogma. This also explains why the book is so critical of the two political forces that will influence postwar Italy. Saba openly fears an Italian republic lead by the Christian Democrats, whom he considers a party that would preclude any radical change. His letters, in this regard, leave no room for speculation. On June 7, 1946, he writes to his daughter, Linuccia: "Fascism had turned Italy into a carcass, and on carcasses descend ravens. What's happened is just what, with such anguish, I foresaw: a Catholic republic is far worse than an apolitical monarchy."[78] On March 1, 1948, he went even further in his letter to Vittorio Sereni: "The priests have this baleful aspect, that they are the (largely faithless) champions of a morality for little children, that they impede the formation of a new morality."[79]

"Conservative moralism" is also the reason for Saba's polemics against the Communist Party. The poet spells out his aversion in one of the many shortcuts of those years that he preferred not to make public, but that he disseminated in his letters:

> COMMUNISM was for many young people (between twenty and thirty years old) the way to normalize themselves. To become—in their turn—conservatives, and—in the strict sense of the word—moralists. At any rate—one way or another—they had to get there.[80]

Critics have mostly avoided Saba's frequent anti-Communist remarks.[81] Yet these comments are key to understanding his cultural agenda, the envisaged "new world" that had little in common with political utopias. In this regard, Shortcut number 87 is a case in point. Addressed to Mario Spinella, a Marxist intellectual that Saba frequently visited while in Rome, the shortcut is also the last in which the image of "Maidanek" appears in the book:

> MARIO SPINELLA [...] What he had to tell me was that neither he nor his friends (young Communists) knew what to make of SHORTCUTS. They are—he explained—small, felicitous items, born of happiness. (Perhaps, what he meant was of the liberation.) THE CAMP OF THE JEWS by Giacomo Debenedetti, that was great. Blood and tears came through in that.
>
> Perhaps Spinella was right. Maidanek cannot be expiated.[82]

Giacomo Debenedetti is the literary critic who authored *16 October 1943*, the moving chronicle of the Nazi round-up of the Jewish ghetto in Rome. The text enjoyed a vast circulation: Published for the journal *Mercurio* in December 1944, Jean-Paul Sartre soon translated it into French for his journal *Les Temps Modernes*. As Robert Gordon highlighted, "*16 October 1943* in particular was crucial as a model for the early postwar decades, in its reportage and chronicle, linked like several deportation testimonies to the neorealist moment."[83] Aside from this highly influential account, Debenedetti published in those months two other relevant pieces addressing the question of Italian Jews under Fascism: "Eight Jews," which narrated a controversial case during the trial of the Fosse Ardeatine massacre, and "The Camp of the Jews," a review of Jacques Bernard's *Le camp de la mort lente*, published in *La Nuova Europa* on April 1, 1945.

In his letters, Saba affectionately addresses Debenedetti as "Giacomino." Debenedetti was the literary critic that the poet felt closest to, and not just because of their shared Jewish identity. Debenedetti wrote illuminating essays on Saba that underscored the ethical function of his poetry.[84] And yet Saba felt that the critic's praises were one-sided, as they highlighted the consolatory charge of Saba's poetry and overlooked its cognitive power.

Saba's poetic imagination, which is vividly present throughout his *Shortcuts*, is also an active willingness to *comprehend life* in every possible determination. In the letter to De Robertis, cited previously, Saba unabashedly calls *Shortcuts* "a morally good book" ("un libro buono"), concluding: "Think about how much, and with at least an appearance of justice, I could have been 'wicked.'"[85] The reference here is not just to his experience as a survivor of anti-Semitic persecution, but to the literature of "chronicles," as advocated in Marxist circles. Saba deems *this* literature the product of a "culture of crisis." In Shortcut number 87, such a culture is embodied by the orthodox Marxist Mario Spinella. The young intellectual does not expect literature to voice different opinions but rather to narrate the Resistance's epic—including the "Jewish question"—in terms of *blood and tears*. Saba judges the culture that Spinella exemplifies as profoundly "moralist," unable to grasp the radical meaning of "Maidanek" and of the inexpiable caesura it entails. For Saba, young orthodox Marxists like Spinella privilege Debenedetti's "The Camp of the Jews" and "Eight Jews" to his *Shortcuts* because indignation and resentment cannot yield to understanding.

In an article on the complex relationship between Saba and Debenedetti, historian Alberto Cavaglion notes how the poet reacts with a certain dismay to the literary critic's interventions on "the Jewish question." After Debenedetti's remarkable achievement of *16 October 1943*, Saba notes how the critic increasingly aligns his reflections with Resistance rhetoric and the populist epic of the Communist Party. Saba does not downplay the historical significance of the Resistance—his "Teatro degli artigianelli" remains one of its most inspired lyrics—but he is concerned about its fossilization into monumental gestures.[86] Cavaglion concludes that "not a small part of *Shortcuts* will represent in fact a kind of countermelody against any narrative founded on tears and blood."[87] To Saba, the poetics of the chronicle, what Gordon ultimately calls the "neorealist moment," is but an updated version of old historicism.

The atmosphere of a liberated Rome prompted Saba to explore new possibilities of speculative inquiry. After the brief but intense creative season of *Shortcuts*, he would never again attempt a literary experiment that was overtly political. Still, his opposition to consoling readings of recent history maintained an ethical charge that key authors of postwar Italy such as Carlo Levi, Pasolini, and Morante would further develop.[88] For them, Saba became an unexpected intellectual model: In a season of *engagé* authors and "organic intellectuals," he shied away from moral authorities derived from the political arena and let his poetry speak for itself. Remarkably, he would remain loyal, at times even uncritically, to the moral authorities that he recognized first and foremost as *intellectual* authorities, such as Freud and Nietzsche.

Saba would develop his reflections on Jewish identity and the Holocaust's long shadow well beyond the postwar transition. He was aware that his reflections—see, in particular, his posthumous novel *Ernesto* (published 1975, but written in 1953)—would be misrepresented in the highly polarized atmosphere of Cold War Italy. Aggravated by neuroses and mental breakdowns, Saba's last years were integral to his fascinating biography, so lacking in external events and so wonderfully full of life and unanticipated confessions. In a 1949 letter to Edoardo Weiss, who was responsible for the introduction of psychoanalysis in Italy and a key figure in Saba's self-scrutiny, the old poet confided all his consternation for his fate and that of his country:

> Today I am once again reduced to silence (as I was during Fascism); I can neither collaborate with the priests, nor put my name down beside certain others [...]. I am thus—literally—unemployed; and I would have so many things to say ... But they are things that no one wants to hear, that no one would even publish.[89]

Shortcuts and Open Wounds: Ennio Flaiano

"I went on. I knew that one has to accept shortcuts without discussion."[90] Thus begins the adventure at the center of Ennio Flaiano's novel, *A Time to Kill*, when the protagonist, a lieutenant of the Italian army during the 1935–1936 invasion of Ethiopia, decides to leave behind his unusable truck after an accident. He elects to take a shortcut through unknown territories to return to the military camp. "The Short Cut" was indeed one of the working titles Flaiano considered for the book, and shortcuts recur at many crucial points of his narrative.[91] In *A Time to Kill*, shortcuts are not just paths into the impervious African landscape. They also stand for a kind of knowledge cemented by practice and experience, resistant to complete verbalization, opaque to Westernization. In the novel's final version, "The Short Cut" would be the title of the first chapter in which the lieutenant's self-regard and carefree attitude dissolve after his encounter with Mariam, a young Ethiopian who was washing herself by a river, alone and naked.

For the lieutenant, Mariam is an epiphany of sorts in the dry and unwelcoming foreign landscape. He has indeed lost his sense of direction: The fortuitous encounter, narrated from the viewpoint of the pursuer, becomes, for the Italian official, an opportunity for an unexpected sexual escapade. The lieutenant forces the young woman to have sex with him. Even here, there is little verbalization between the two, who then spend the night together until a wild beast threatens them. In an act of self-defense, the protagonist shoots many bullets in the darkness and the animal flees. One of the bullets, though, accidentally hits and lethally wounds Mariam.

After a clumsy attempt to save the young girl, the protagonist decides to end her agony with one last shot. Only after trying to hide any trace of Mariam's dead body does the lieutenant find his way back to the military camp: "I had found the short cut again," he recounts.[92] Mariam's burial is a patent attempt at symbolically canceling her, her rape, and her killing from his memory. The whole incident has an allegorical resonance that will loom large in the rest of the story. The protagonist's crimes and his attempt to erase them from memory speak volumes about Italy's ill-fated imperialism, its violence and moral corruption, and its voluntary repression in postwar collective memory.[93]

The first chapter, titled "The Short Cut," ends here. The rest of the novel features the downward spiral of the protagonist, an ordinary man who is intelligent enough to understand, through the adventures narrated in the novel, his own mediocrity. After killing Mariam, he tries to escape his sense of guilt—but also the shame of recognizing his own baseness—by attempting, by all means, to return home to Italy to his fiancée. Tellingly, he remembers his Italian partner as a person "who threw herself into the water without taking off her clothes" to mark the civilizational distance between her and Mariam.[94] For the lieutenant, returning to Italy means also appeasing his conscience of crimes he cannot fully process: "Once I had buried the corpse," he repeats to himself, "I had done my duty toward the others and now I must continue to do it in silence. The woman did not count, only my guilt toward the others," because after all, "Africa is the sink of iniquities and one goes there to stir up one's conscience."[95] To that end, however, he will commit further and unnecessary crimes, driven by no real reason but his mere survival. The lieutenant's escape is complicated by his mounting paranoia that Mariam gave him more than sexual pleasure: A growing sore in his hand could be a sign of leprosy, which would confine him to isolation and the total loss of his life "before Africa," to which he now wishes to return.

Published, like Berto's *The Sky Is Red*, by Leo Longanesi in 1947, *A Time to Kill* won the first edition of the Strega Prize and has become—especially in the last decades—the literary text on Italian colonialism par excellence. The novel was Flaiano's first and greatest literary success, though he is more often celebrated today for his work as a screenwriter and his close collaboration with Federico Fellini on films such as *La dolce vita* and *8½*.[96] When published in 1947, however, *A Time to Kill* did not appear as reminiscent of a past that was conveniently forgotten: Reviewers highlighted approvingly how it denounced the folly and arbitrariness of Italian colonialism in Africa, referring implicitly to Mussolini's invasion of Ethiopia.[97]

What contemporary commentators did not point out is that Italian colonialism had profound roots well beyond the Fascist past and had been legitimized by a historicist cultural production that predated and arguably facilitated Mussolini's imperial dreams.[98] What is more, some reviewers praised the novel's critical depiction of colonialism because "Africa contaminates all white men who set foot on its land. It seduces them with its pulsating warm blood, it enthralls them with its secret embrace, like Mariam did in the hollow of the rock, with the passing lieutenant; it inserts its ills into their brain and their blood."[99] Comments such as these by Giovanni Ansaldo, who signed this review under the pseudonym Stefano Frati, were not rare. Instead of focusing on the complexity of Flaiano's unresolved novel, they expressed an ambiguous deprecation of Italian imperialism.[100] Only a few years later, for instance, on the occasion of the novel's reprint in 1954, Gino Nogara would concentrate on "the beautiful Ethiopian Mariam, whom we do not hesitate to describe as one of the most vivid and original female creations of Italian fiction since the last war."[101] An interesting remark, especially since she barely speaks in the novel.

The aforementioned reviews of the book reject Italian imperialism, not because of its injustice but because *Africa is immoral*—although it still tickles male desire. The sexualization and feminization of Africa are typical clichés of the colonialist and orientalist discourses of the period, and occasionally Flaiano's narrative employs such stereotypes as well.[102] Mariam's character is molded precisely on these premises, as aptly signaled by Roberta Orlandini: "The narrator moves on a higher but no less dehumanizing plane: with his retrospective reflection he transforms her into an archetype, into a

Mother Earth, into an essence of Africa itself, thus stripping her of her own contemporary reality."[103]

Although Flaiano entertained the cultural stereotypes of his time, he highlighted with *A Time to Kill* a moral problem that few commentators noted when the novel first appeared. Among them was Umberto de Federicis, who in *l'Avanti!* stresses how the book provides "the image of an entire generation that abandoned itself to an ugly adventure that dragged it from one cowardly act to another solely out of fear of the reckoning."[104] Flaiano's novel details the moral crisis of a common man who, like many of his contemporaries during the *ventennio*, conveniently avoided true self-reflection. Yet the diversity of the colonial setting, its sexual promiscuity, the harsh African landscape, and the encounter with its many peoples force him to confront who he really is. Circumstances and characters, though they appear casual, are active agents in the plot. They reveal the protagonist to himself in the precise moment when coming to terms with this trauma is no longer deferrable.

A Time to Kill thus illuminates the emerging space between colonial rhetoric and individual consciousness.[105] According to cultural historian Derek Duncan, "this 'gap' is not the empty place of blank contradiction, but rather the space in which narratives of cultural intelligibility are produced and subjectivities formed."[106] In fact, the word "Fascism" and its imperial rhetoric are not even mentioned in *A Time to Kill*. Through his novel, Flaiano articulates a personal, almost intimate criticism of Fascist imperialism; his difficult rejection of colonialism reads much more convincingly because it is less outspoken, less *monumental* than the disavowals we find in the book's early reviews.

Like many orientalist texts, *A Time to Kill* is less about the colonized than about the colonizer, who projects onto a generic exotic other desires and anxieties that are his own. Among the vast production reveling in this imaginary, the novel stands out precisely because of Flaiano's lucid awareness of the fetishistic drives behind such a conventional exotic imaginary. The novel features a first-person narrator who recounts his misadventures during Italy's occupation of Ethiopia. The story is told with a significant temporal distance: The protagonist's reckless actions in East Africa are in tension with his bitter reflections at the time of writing. As the lieutenant retrieves the story from his memory, he both judges his former self and tries to make sense of his past experiences. The two perspectives are artfully intertwined, at times in the same sentence: "Why did I not understand these people?"—he wonders—"They were poor creatures, grown old in a country from which there was no way out; they were great walkers; great experts on short cuts; maybe wise but ancient and uncultured."[107] The "shortcuts" theme returns again here, now explicitly referring to the knowledge of the colonized. We read in this sentence that the narrator accepts what his former self mistakenly doubted: indigenous people's different epistemological approach, the autonomy of their knowledge, irreducible to Western gaze and values.

Throughout *A Time to Kill*, Flaiano deploys orientalist and exoticist narratives as outlets of national self-delusion. His story reveals the skeletons in the closet of the new Italian Republic, such as the widespread consensus for Mussolini's "African Empire," which in 1947 was still a fresh experience and shared memory for many Italians.[108] Remnants of this consensus surface in the cited reviews of the novel. Yet the book also shows how this self-delusion was collective and based on a cultural discourse that, once again, predates and gestured toward Fascism and its historicist aesthetics.

Flaiano himself fought as a sublieutenant in the Second Italo-Ethiopian War from 1935 to 1936. Some relevant documents from that time and articles written in the early postwar period pin down how the conflict between character and narrator, between the reckless actions of the first and the bitter reflections of the second, can be traced back to firsthand traumatic experiences and later considerations on the part of the author. In his private diary titled "Aethiopia. Notes for a Popular Song," which Flaiano writes during the military campaign, he testifies to the atrocities committed by the Italian army against the civilian population and notes down remarks on Orientalism that resonate with his later reflections.[109] Referring to a soldier who had just arrived from Italy, Flaiano comments: "He was dreaming of a conventional Africa, with tall palm trees, bananas, dancing women, a mix of Turkey, India, Morocco, that ideal land of Paramount films called the Orient, providing so much inspiration for small orchestra pieces."[110] Besides the amusing pun about orientalist geography, the key to interpreting this passage lies in another private document of the same period, which allows us to understand how *that* soldier, like many young Italians who went to Africa with confused ideas of Fascist palingenesis only to find widespread prostitution, was probably himself. In a letter sent from Axum on April 11, 1936, to his close friend Orfeo Tamburi, Flaiano confesses:

> I can no longer imagine myself as a "new man," so much do I desire the ease of a calm and ordered life. Given the possibility of possessing all the desirable women of the region, I realized that all the *matrimonial* thoughts that had

assailed me in the preceding months, all the feminine nostalgia, collapsed like burst balloons.[111]

Only after WWII is Flaiano able to fully process his own personal failure in the broader context of that of his nation. Orientalism as a popular discourse, supported here by the visual impact of the burgeoning cinema industry, reinforces an inauthentic historicist culture that "manufactured consent"—and legitimized the Fascist wars of aggression in the eyes of the broader public.[112] Flaiano articulates all these insights in an important article published on October 15, 1945, in which he reflects on a recent public screening of Giovanni Pastrone's *Cabiria*. The successful pre-WWI epic silent film is famously set during the war between Rome and Carthage and boasted the collaboration of Gabriele d'Annunzio:

> Someone had the suspicion that the adventure of 1940 had already begun with that long-ago film, so abundant with Punic Wars, mare nostrum, and vindication? It really must be said: this public of ours that frequents cinemas does not know how to do anything but laugh. And about the same things that it had admired and defended as citizens [. . .]. In any case, *Cabiria* is from 1914. A year after Scipio Africanus founded *Il Popolo d'Italia* in Milan.

Oscillating between pity and sarcasm, Flaiano's article is significantly titled "The Great Forerunners."[113] *A Time to Kill* can be seen as the mise-en-scène of many of its considerations. Just as in the novel, the issue of guilt and expiation is central to this piece. The author comments on the audience's reaction to the film and hopes that the general outburst of laughter, "when a Dannunzian intertitle attributes to the powerful warrior the most ingenuous expression of imperialistic pride," could have a positive meaning. That is, people have digested their sense of guilt for the consent to Mussolini's regime. Two years later, this hope has disappeared: In *A Time to Kill*, the specter of past crimes—the killing of Mariam and the atrocities committed by Italians in Africa—haunts the protagonist's consciousness throughout the novel. The malady of his soul becomes physically visible and tangible in the open wound of his right hand.

In the last part of the book, the lieutenant finds shelter in a village whose inhabitants have all been killed, except for one. The only survivor is the old Johannes, who fought alongside the Italian army as an askari and remained in the empty village to bury all his companions. "That was his strength," the lieutenant observes, "the strength to stay with his dead and to live his last days with them. He did not take it upon himself as a penance in order to merit paradise, but for the sake of remaining in good company."[114] The relationship between the two, however, is tense, especially because the Italian official treats Johannes as a subaltern. The old askari does not hide his impatience for the unwelcome guest, and when he picks a fight, the lieutenant realizes that Johannes is Mariam's father. The unexpected revelation changes their relationship: It is Johannes who heals the lieutenant's open wound, the "piaga" on his right hand, with appropriate medicines. The protagonist then finally returns to the Italian camp to turn himself in to the military police, only to find out that no one has denounced him: His crimes will remain in his memory alone.

The word "piaga" has many meanings in Italian: "sore," "open wound," and "plague" are the most common, but it is also colloquially used as a metaphor for an "annoying person" and, more broadly, for an "endemic problem." Historian Angelo Del Boca reports how Fascism's racist propaganda used this specific term to describe mixed grown children in East Africa's Italian colonies.[115] In the concluding pages of the novel, the protagonist tells his story to a trusted sublieutenant, a skeptical and ironic character, arguably the closest in the novel to Flaiano's point of view.[116] The sublieutenant previously distinguished himself with his wittiness in his exchange with other Italian officials who denigrated the indigenous civilization. In contrast with a higher-ranking official, who scorned Ethiopians for having not built any roads, the sublieutenant comments that, in spite of this, they have their own "shortcuts."[117] In the lively conversation that concludes the novel, the lieutenant and sublieutenant discuss the meaning of "piaghe."[118] Their reasoning echoes the remark about "shortcuts" with which the protagonist's adventures began: "'Well then, the sores [*piaghe*] cannot be discussed, they must be accepted.' And because I smiled the second lieutenant said that we could even try a rational explanation, but in ten years' time. 'No,' I said quickly, 'let's accept them without discussion.'"[119]

As in Fellini's movies, the novel's resolution brings no certainties, no real change—and no redemption for any of the characters. Shortcuts are emblematic of a different kind of knowledge, one which the colonial campaign sought to master without recognizing its autonomy. Since shortcuts and what they stand for cannot be forgotten, they have become open wounds. Yet, accepting and divulging the wounds of uncharted experience is the first step in processing collective and private self-delusions. Flaiano's *A Time to Kill* gestures toward integrating the memory of the crimes committed into personal and national history, from colonialism to

Fascism. That is, learning to live with all these ghosts without blatantly lying, first of all, to oneself.

On Living among Ghosts: Elsa Morante

Flaiano's *A Time to Kill* was written in a few months in 1947 and published in the summer of the same year under Longanesi's supervision. The last novel I will examine in this chapter had, instead, a much more complicated birth. The story of its manuscript deserves to be recounted here, for it sheds light on the tortuous experiences endured by intellectuals who flocked to Rome after its liberation. We already met Elsa Morante in the Introduction when we mentioned her private notes on Mussolini's death in May 1945, which pinpointed Italians' long complicity with the Duce's crimes. Two years earlier, during the general escape from Italian cities before the Nazi occupation that would take place after September 8, 1943, Morante and her husband Moravia were able to leave Rome, where they lived, just before the takeover.[120] The couple then found shelter in the small village of Fondi, in the Ciociaria, a poor region south of the capital that would become, in the following months, the theater of heinous crimes against civilians.[121] Before leaving Rome, however, Morante left the manuscript of her first novel, provisionally titled *Life of My Grandmother*, in the hands of their friend Carlo Lodovico Bragaglia. The couple returned to the capital in May 1944, and Morante would retrieve her manuscript, only to rework it assiduously over the next two years. Once completed, the voluminous novel would be published in June 1948 by Einaudi with the title *Lies and Sorcery*.[122]

Two months later, the novel won the prestigious Viareggio Prize, thanks to the sponsorship of Giacomo Debenedetti, but it divided the reviewers, who had difficulty locating it in the literary trends of the period.[123] In the next few years, however, influential intellectuals would unequivocally assert the book's literary excellence—beginning with György Lukàcs, who in 1961 hailed *Lies and Sorcery* as the best modern Italian novel.[124] Lukàcs also detailed the reasons behind his enthusiasm for Morante's book in private correspondence: The book constituted for him "a monumental parable on the ethics of man today."[125] Decades later Natalia Ginzburg, working as an editor for Einaudi when the novel was proposed, fondly remembered the huge impact the manuscript had on her after a first reading:

> I read *Lies and Sorcery* in one go and I loved it immensely: however, I can't say that I clearly understood at the time its importance and greatness. [. . .]

> For me it was an extraordinary adventure to discover, among those chapter titles that seemed nineteenth-century to me, our own age and cities, with the same piercing and painful intensity as our own daily existence.[126]

Among postwar European literature, *Lies and Sorcery* stands out for its resistance to labels, both today and in 1948.[127] Morante's first novel, however, actively contributed to the rebellion against historicism that characterized the transition. *Lies and Sorcery* profoundly erodes the assumed certainties of early postwar Italy by narrating how status and power shape social fantasies. The book stresses how the *individual* redemption sought by each character, who tragically pursue their private ghosts and prefer to believe in the fictions they themselves invented, is bereft of any real intent of *collective* emancipation. The characters' self-inflicted deceptions and their repeated redemptive discourses crafted in religious terms reveal an obsession with privilege that permeated traditional society in Italy—especially in the South—and that the recent modernization left untouched. The novel exposes how privilege structured and disciplined individual desire well before the advent of Fascism in ways that persist after its demise. This fixation on privilege features a predominant gender bias, showing once again a problematic persistence deliberately ignored by early postwar political discourse.

Morante's novel and its language are jarringly radical, bewildering progressive and conservative readers alike. The characterization of some of the novel's male figures, such as Francesco De Salvi and especially his father, Nicola Monaco, resonates strongly with the piercing remarks on Mussolini that Morante noted in her diary upon his death. Indeed, her remarks on the Duce were sketched as she was writing the novel and focused on how Italians eagerly collaborated with the grand delusional narrative Mussolini created around his persona.

In *Lies and Sorcery*, Morante imaginatively deploys the intertwined languages of romance and neurosis to express the contradictions of her time, one torn between old privileges and modernization. The novel exposes the social, psychological, and political burdens of a society that preferred to believe in the ghosts of its past privilege rather than face the existential questions posed by secularization. To the critics lamenting *Lies and Sorcery*'s distance from collective history and epoch-making facts—ultimately its resistance to Neorealism—Morante responded by describing her personal experience as a *tragic* encounter with reality:

> For everyone, the passage from fantasy to awareness (from youth to maturity) amounts to a tragic and fundamental experience. For me such an experience

was represented and anticipated by the war: that's where, prematurely and with ruinous violence, I encountered maturity. I said all this in my novel *Lies and Sorcery*, even though the novel does not talk about the war at all.[128]

Morante's novel begins with a young woman, Elisa, who sets out to write her own family saga in the hope of healing from her maladies. For weeks after her adoptive mother Rosaria passed away, Elisa is unable to leave her room in the Rome apartment where they lived together for fifteen years. Elisa's parents died when she was ten, and Rosaria took care of her as they moved to Rome from the Sicilian city of her childhood. Elisa recounts the story of three generations of her family in order to heal from what she calls the hereditary disease that ruined their lives: the folly of believing in a fabricated reality to overcome the shame of their modest condition.[129] In her narrative, she evokes her ancestors' voices as if she were conjuring their spirits, helped by childhood recollections that ambiguously but systematically blur the difference between memory and fiction. Nevertheless, the ghosts of her childhood exact an unbearable toll: "Having convinced me that they were consoling, celebrating, and redeeming me after liberating me from a disturbing reality, my characters insisted that I deny reality entirely and replace it with their shadowy world."[130]

For Elisa, storytelling is supposed to bring about understanding and possibly resolution. Understanding should then lead to healing—like in Freud's psychoanalysis. Still, there is a complex type of irony at play in the novel, as it involves an anthropological judgment on the failed secularization of the society narrated by Elisa. This irony can accurately be characterized as *tragic*, for it exposes the irreconcilable conflicts within the Southern Italian society that the book zealously portrays. In Morante's novel, such tensions come to a head inside the family, the institution that is supposed to grant social stability and continuity in tradition.[131]

The tragic irony between the imagined family saga and the petty story of her parents negates the possibility of healing for Elisa—and with it the literary or even mnestic redemption of her family. Anxiety and psychological strain accompany the reader in this marvelously written fairy tale that is anything but fair. Elisa alerts the reader of her difficulty in establishing an objective distance between her protagonists and their imagined flowery un-reality, which decomposes before our eyes: "In my memory I transformed their middle-class drama into the stuff of legend. And, as will happen to a people without a history, that legend glorified me."[132] This unresolved conflict condemns the young woman to neurotic repetition and the favoring of fabricated reality, as if it were her true memory. Elisa's story is, in fact, the repetition of the *Familenroman*, the "neurotic's family romance" described by Freud. It is the pathological correction of the parents' life story to compensate for one's frustrated desires. On "family romance" Freud concludes:

> If we examine in detail the commonest of these imaginative romances, the replacement of both parents or of the father alone by grander people, we find that these new and aristocratic parents are equipped with attributes that are derived entirely from real recollections of the actual and humble ones.[133]

Additionally, the novel is crowded with Catholic rituals and processions, imposing baroque churches, and popular superstitions. Except for Elisa, not a single character shows any sign of spirituality, for they believe only in their radical egotism. Similar to Morante's moral portrait of Mussolini, a "Catholic without believing in God," her characters are dazzled by "the prestige of certain words: History, Church, Family, People, Fatherland, etc., but ignore the substance of things."[134] Institutional religion features in the novel as a seal of social and economic privilege. Essential in Catholic theology, the concept of redemption from original sin affects multiple aspects of Elisa's story, but it constantly intertwines with status and power. In this novel, characters understand the sacred and the relationship with the divine as a *do ut des*, an individual negotiation with higher forces (strictly speaking, concepts such as "fatherland" or "people" are not present in the book).

Religious terminology and practices are ubiquitous in *Lies and Sorcery*, even in the discourses of male characters who *all* proclaim themselves nonbelievers (though some of them conveniently abide by Catholic laws and rituals). Terms such as "riscatto" or "redenzione" pepper Elisa's narrative throughout, from her personal considerations to her "family romance." Despite having a more genuine relationship with the divine than all the other characters, she ostensibly employs such terms out of a religious context, usually in her metanarrative reflections and in her appeals to the reader. Elisa's appeals attempt to recuperate a more sincere, intimate communication—perhaps the common language that was never spoken in her own family. Overall, the redemptive trope so common in the early postwar public discourse in Italy recurs time and again in the novel, but importantly, it is deployed only in the first person. Morante exposes the genealogy of this trope, going back to its religious roots. Yet she presents the secularized protagonists of her novel as deprived of a sincere relationship with the divine. They are all equally unable to free themselves from traditional institutions and rituals which have become inauthentic.

The spiritual void of Morante's characters is the reason why the novel is much more than a palinode of literary escapism, as critics hurriedly read it when first published.[135] Elisa's story exceeds the declared sublimation of personal experience through "imaginative romances," which she admittedly considers "my redemption from the disquieting reality."[136] In fact, *Lies and Sorcery* combines highly stylized language and plot with uncanny historical precision. In a seminal essay, Cesare Garboli shows how the book is set in the historical period known as *la belle époque*, the years between the end of the nineteenth century and the outbreak of WWI. Remarkably, Morante's characterization of the period resists trite cultural clichés, though such clichés profoundly affect the lives of her characters.[137] *Lies and Sorcery* can thus be better described as a fictional investigation into the societal underpinnings of a larger *political* malaise—that is, the collective illusion of fulfilling frustrated social desires by acquiring privilege that is only nominal. With their eyes fixed on privilege, her characters pursue an individual redemption that is bereft of personal or collective emancipation. As Sharon Wood acutely points out, Morante's book focuses on "the moral and intellectual squalor of the petite bourgeoisie—the very class that decades later was to provide a bedrock of support for Fascism."[138]

Returning to *Lies and Sorcery*'s plot will help us illustrate this point. In the initial pages of the novel, Elisa explains her decision to exhume her relatives' memory through writing to redeem their failures. The family saga begins with her grandmother Cesira, a petit bourgeois schoolteacher with ambitions of climbing the social ladder by marrying the elderly Teodosio Massia di Corullo, a formerly licentious but ultimately romantic nobleman who dissipated his patrimony. The unlikely fruit of their loveless marriage is the elusive, ruthless, and fascinating Anna. She squandered her life in the presumptuous defense of her noble status, refusing to come to terms with the miserable material conditions of her existence and jealously safeguarding her nominal privilege. Anna's disturbing demeanor ultimately causes her mental illness and her family's social alienation.

Anna's daughter, Elisa, adores her, but her love is unreciprocated. At the beginning of the novel, Elisa confesses her inability to condemn her mother, as well as the other "characters" of her "family romance." This uneasy mother-daughter nexus informs the narrator's complex psychology.[139] Elisa's unrestrained love for her mother sets the tone of her narrative, yet it resonates with the political undertones that delineate the novel's moral geography:

> My heart might be compared to those of ancient rulers who had different laws for commoners and for the nobility, the latter being mostly unassailable,

exempt not only from punishment, but even from guilt. And the same actions that were deemed crimes among the humble people, were considered right and good among the elite.[140]

Anna is the real protagonist of *Lies and Sorcery*. And not just because of Elisa's adoration: At the center of the plot is Anna's morbid fixation on her adolescent love, her elegant, vain, manipulative cousin, Edoardo Cerentano. He is the only *male* child of local noble landowners and related to Anna—his austere and bigoted mother, Concetta, is Teodosio's sister. Edoardo's cat-like figure dominates the story, beginning with the second part of the novel, which tells the tale of the adolescent yet psychologically daunting love affair between him and Anna. The differing social statuses of the two lovers is the real propeller of their mutual desire. Their reciprocal attraction is fueled by social anxieties that verge on fetishism. Anna's stubborn haughtiness toward the people close to her contrasts with her complete subjugation to Edoardo (and his family): "In her state of utter subjugation to her Cousin, Anna would have thought it madness to even think of objecting to those parties she was excluded from. The prerogative of his magnificent birthright, this only made him more precious in her eyes." By the same token, "an overabundance of pleasure caused Edoardo to stray from his sense of social superiority, but not so far as to make him consider denying this difference between them. On the contrary, he yearned for Anna to mentally absorb her lowliness to the point where he would be able to actually see her tremble in his presence and become utterly submissive to him."[141]

When Anna realizes the limited role she plays in the life of her fetishized idol, Edoardo, she does not rebel against the blatant disparity of their relationship. Rather, she builds a new kind of "family romance." Edoardo's fanciful speeches about his supposed destiny of marvelous adventures excite her imagination. Anna resigns herself to his eventual departure but finds a way to sublimate her frustrated desire. She would have his child: "This child would, of course, be a son, and she would name him Edoardo."[142] Their twisted romance forms the apex of the novel. Its haunting memory, however, will profoundly affect all the characters revolving around Anna. Edoardo refuses to have a child with Anna: His response betrays not just his misogyny, but also how love is nothing but a narcissistic mirror for him ("You astonish me. These are things that only men are supposed to know, not women, at least not until they are married [. . .]. Who has taught you all these things?" he sarcastically replies). At this point, Elisa pauses her tale and spells out the real trauma that is behind her malaise and that of all the women in her family:

> At this juncture, please permit the writer of this story the observation that fate passed up a felicitous opportunity that day. If Edoardo had acquiesced to Anna's wish, perhaps Elisa, yours truly, would never have existed. Instead, in place of the skinny, bitter, black-haired girl, a healthy, golden boy named Edoardo would have been born and he certainly would have earned Anna's love, a love that poor Elisa never knew.[143]

The whole novel is a repetition of this trauma and sheds a disquieting light on traditional Italian society's gender biases. Morante critically stresses how women solidify their subjugation by conceiving of motherhood primarily as a redemption from femininity, improperly treated as their own original guilt. To the women of *Lies and Sorcery*, motherhood means, first and foremost, *giving birth to a male child*. To all but the narrator, Elisa: She implicitly senses how this perceived guilt of being born a woman fuels her own neurosis. Conversely, the possibility of giving birth to a male child compensates for Anna's frustrated narcissism and spurs her willful subjugation to Edoardo.

This convention has profound roots in Catholic practices and the twisted interpretation of Christian mysticism that is typical of the traditional ruling classes depicted in the novel, for they understand religion as an instrument of power and symbol of their privilege. All this is openly proclaimed by Edoardo's mother, Concetta—a formidable champion of bigotry, self-righteousness, and privilege—in her staggering addresses to her son:

> When I became pregnant with you, I was sure that this time it was a boy since God had promised this to me during The Elevation in church. [. . .] How many times I prayed to Him saying: "Lord, listen to my voice. What little beauty there is in my body, take it from me and give it to my son. What does it matter to me if I become ugly? I am already married and the mother of a family."[144]

In the economy of the novel, Concetta's presence is pivotal: She is the outspoken voice of an atavistic mentality that was anything but over in Italy in 1948. Her sacrifice for her son, which is staged during a public procession later in the story, is utterly self-serving. With the approval of the local clergy, her public act of penitence for Edoardo's benefit becomes a theatrical performance in which the city and its people are transformed into *her* stage and *her* spectators. The aim of Concetta's public display of contrition for her son is to establish, once again, her unabashed privilege. A few pages later, Concetta's inner thoughts plainly attest to the nexus between religion, privilege, and motherhood: "The blessed being that was her son, the privileges he was born to, the envy of other mothers, these things were the clear results of a God-given law sanctioning pridefulness in the favorites as well as their contempt for others."[145]

Concetta and Anna form one of the basic polarities of the novel. The eventual superimposition of their respective idolatry for Edoardo will signal the end of Elisa's story. But for now, the young Anna has only strong, adversarial feelings toward her aunt: "No previous rival had provoked in her the hatred and envy she now felt for Donna Concetta. [. . .] Concetta was blessed for having given birth to Edoardo." Anna's jealousy is motivated by Concetta's right to possess the object of her own desire: As Edoardo's mother, she is the only woman who can indisputably "tell everyone *he is mine*."[146] Giving birth to a "healthy, golden boy called Edoardo" thus becomes the fulfillment of her most repressed desire. Anna loves the *blonde* and noble cousin Edoardo as she mirrors him in her persona and her unfulfilled narcissistic needs. In the impossibility of *being* him, she then wants to have him as a lover (there is an exceptional scene in which the two exchange their clothes and enjoy their self-love by admiring the face and the body of the other; their reciprocal *jouissance* is concluded by Edoardo's remark that "in some countries kings and emperors were allowed to marry only their sisters, a union that otherwise for the populace was a crime, but for them was a sacred law and privilege").[147] Furthermore, with the impossibility of having Edoardo as a lover, Anna then wants to *possess* him as her own child. Sharon Wood's comment on the novel is enlightening here as well:

> the perennial myth of delighted motherhood, peddled by male and female novelists alike, is demolished in the person of Anna, whose attitude to Elisa, adoring daughter of the dark-haired Francesco rather than the blonde beloved Edoardo, is at best one of indifference and at worst one of unfeeling cruelty.[148]

Wood stresses how *Lies and Sorcery* critically debunks the romanticized image of motherhood perpetuated by literary tradition.[149] Her remark also introduces Francesco, the last protagonist of the ménage à trois at the center of the book (which will involve Elisa's adoptive mother Rosaria too). But before focusing on Rosaria and Francesco, let us return to Edoardo and his final speech to Anna prior to physically disappearing from her life. His speech has almost a prophetic quality and consecrates Anna as the priestess of his memory, with all its ambiguities. The memory of Edoardo looms over all the other characters after he vanishes from sight in the remainder of the novel.

Edoardo's flagrant lie in his farewell to Anna will perversely become the ultimate truth of the novel: "It isn't true that I came to say good-bye to you, I came to ask you to be my wife," he claims. His final words dispel any doubt about his intentions:

> "Furthermore," he added, "don't have any illusions that by marrying me you will be happy. After we're married, I will wander off as I please, on visits, to parties, on trips around the world. But you will have to wait for me, shut up at home. [. . .] I also don't want you to remain beautiful because your beauty will then be my cross to bear. A wife shouldn't be beautiful. She should be a saint and nothing else."[150]

Edoardo's farewell to Anna bleakly illuminates the condition of women in traditional Southern Italian society, in terms that profoundly corrode the narratives of collective emancipation of those years.[151] His speech needs, however, an adequate introduction and contextualization.

In the years of the economic boom, celebrated Italian movies from Mario Monicelli's *Big Deal on Madonna Street* (1958) to Pietro Germi's *Divorce, Italian Style* (1961) showcased with subtle irony the persistence of an atavistic mindset regarding women, especially in Sicily (the case of Giuseppe Tomasi di Lampedusa's 1958 novel *The Leopard* is more complex but also part of the equation). As we have seen in the previous chapter, Vitaliano Brancati narrated in his novel *Beautiful Antonio* (1949) how Sicilian *gallismo* (the regional version of machismo) and gender stereotypes heavily affected the lives of individuals, fostered the acceptance of a Fascist mentality, and laid the groundwork for blind faith in the Fascist ethos. Finally, it is worth repeating how in the colonialist imaginary that Flaiano exposed, in *A Time to Kill*, the naked bodies of African women markedly contrasted with the covered body of the Italian fiancée, "who threw herself into the water without taking off her clothes," pitting erotic desire—and imperial conquest—against respectability and social stability.[152]

Such traditional social structures of subjugation based on heterosexual male desire are repeated by Edoardo in his final encounter with Anna. The young, manipulative nobleman is too cultured and refined to take the path of local "gallismo," and too assured of his traditional privilege to believe in any political affiliation. He instinctively rejects any form of coercion in his dealings with Anna: There is no need for it. Like the angel in Dante's

Purgatory who writes the seven "P" letters on the pilgrim's forehead, a reminder of the seven sins ("peccata") for which he must atone, Edoardo bestows upon Anna the rule for her redemption through repentance and expiation: She will spend the rest of her life in absolute devotion to his memory, a task that is both "lie" and "sorcery."

Morante exposes here not just the lie of giving birth to a male child as redemption from femininity, but the coercive spell that the word "wife" constitutes in traditional Southern Italian societies. After this speech, Edoardo vanishes from Anna's life to start a second, more enduring existence in her memory. She will live out the rest of her life fulfilling her promise to a ghost. Edoardo's fetishized ghost will haunt and deeply affect the existence of most of the other protagonists—including Elisa, who has literally never met him *in person*.

The following parts of the novel radicalize Morante's critique of traditional Italian society and its social fantasies showing how privilege and gender bias persist in modern Italy. Redemptive narratives that were so far relegated to the religious and personal sphere now become the common language of superstition and ideological self-deception. The other two protagonists of the story aptly illuminate this point: Francesco De Salvi, a young student with revolutionary pretensions of universal equality and freedom, whom Edoardo loves and eventually pushes into the arms of Anna on a whim, and Rosaria, a colorful and generous sex worker, who Francesco—to demonstrate his disdain for social conventions—wants to marry in order to redeem her from her sins. Before disappearing because of a deadly illness, Edoardo will provoke Francesco's breakup with Rosaria by currying her favor with jewels and money. Edoardo is maliciously pleased to show Francesco that his dreams of social palingenesis are based on personal frustration with his humble social origins (which he constantly lies about despite his revolutionary aspiration).

The pattern of contrition, expiation, and redemption from an original sin—be it on moral grounds or as part of a grander plan of social palingenesis—drives the reciprocal desires of Francesco and Rosaria as well. The centuries-old theological elaboration of the Catholic concept of redemption wanes here: In the novel, Christian conversion is emptied of any higher religious significance. Rosaria's and Francesco's ideas of redemption, though divergent, signal how they both live in a world where secularism is an incomplete work in progress. Superstition survives when religious ethos fades. The vastness of their illusions totally absorbs them; their grand ideals color the spontaneous and inoffensive narcissism of their youth. When Rosaria tells her co-workers that she cannot join them anymore ("The man she loved, a great gentleman, a saint, wished it so. He had freed her from her sinful ways and shown her the path to Paradise with his passionate and wise words," she says), it is because "the fear of sin, the desire for redemption were such terrible and fascinating things."[153] When Francesco subsequently falls in love with an indifferent Anna, he will find justification for his abrupt change of heart and his unexpected lack of loyalty by drawing on the same illusory narrative of redemption: "By uniting himself permanently with Rosaria he was going to defy the world, but instead with Anna, wouldn't she be able to help him redeem it?"[154]

Francesco thus marries an impoverished Anna. Soon after, the birth of Elisa—dark-haired and dark-skinned like her father—becomes a mark of inferiority for the prideful mother. Elisa's birth pushes Anna to despise her husband even more, as he is guilty of not being noble and *blonde* like Edoardo. Once the news of Edoardo's death reaches her, she falls into a delirious downward spiral. In her derangement, Anna unequivocally refuses her husband's love—and that of her daughter—in order to maintain a perverse belated loyalty to her adolescent romance. After all these years, she is still determined to carry out the task that Edoardo assigned her in his farewell. In an extremely disturbing passage, Anna admits she cheated on Francesco, without telling her husband that her lover is but a ghost, sadistically causing his utter desperation. Anna is not alone in this folly. Every week, she meets her aunt Concetta, who has also lost her sanity after her idolized son passed away. Once rivals, the two women now share a common raison d'être: the stubborn and pathological denial of Edoardo's death. To inflate each other's neurotic self-delusion, they spend hours fetishizing over the objects and pictures of his life in the dark rooms of the Cerentano palace. Nevertheless, the real purpose of their meetings is even more disconcerting: The two women avidly read the letters that Edoardo supposedly sent to Anna from his travels. In fact, these letters are written by Anna herself during her delirious nights, when her husband is out working. The two women prefer to believe in their fabricated lies.

Anna's delusions and her hallucinatory, perverse loyalty to Edoardo are reinforced by Elisa's storytelling. At the time of the recollected events, Elisa was still a child lacking the skill to separate ghosts from reality, unable to judge her beloved mother objectively. The novel ends when Francesco's accidental death aggravates Anna's delirium. Her agonizing demise marks the conclusion of Elisa's "family romance." Before the final resolution, however, Rosaria returns after many years to the unnamed Sicilian city where the story takes place in search of Francesco. When Rosaria casually meets him taking a stroll with his daughter, her mixed feelings betray her mentality. She tells Francesco: "'Is this one of your daughters?' My father explained to her that I was his *only* daughter and she, bemoaning this fact, exclaimed: 'A girl! Only one girl! If only she were a boy! Why don't you,' she added, 'have a handsome boy so that Rosaria can be his godmother!'" Still, it would be Rosaria who would take care of the orphan Elisa after both her parents passed away, calling her "Franceschina" as a sign of affection.[155]

Lies and Sorcery's plot is visibly reminiscent of nineteenth-century feuilleton and popular literature. Yet its conventionality is uniquely vivified by modern anxieties inspired by Freud and Kafka, a choice totally at odds with the cultural trends of the early postwar period.[156] The novel is a fantastic and disquieting pastiche, able to reveal the contradictions of contemporary Italy and its profound roots in the supposedly immobile past of traditional society. Its most attentive critics concentrated on the novelty of Elisa's language and storytelling style, distinctively effective in the depiction of the characters' *modern* alienation.[157]

Among the many reviews *Lies and Sorcery* received, Italo Calvino underscores how social privilege structures the relationships among characters. He points out how "in this poem of frivolity and aspiration to privilege one hears an echo of the class resentment to which this privilege gives birth."[158] In another article, published in 1949, after the book's more influential reviews had already appeared, Goffredo Bellonci insists instead on how the novel purposely defies the then widespread return to realism: "Elsa Morante could have written a provincial, social novel, establishing the setting, naming and describing the city, making the characters creatures of history and the news in a real time, measurable with a clock. Instead she set about doing the opposite."[159] Finally, in an essay reflecting on the novel decades after its publication, Carlo Sgorlon and his wife, Edda, note how the relationships among characters in Morante's novel—love and romance included—feature a possessive and almost "feudal" quality:

> In the ahistorical world of her narrative, democracy does not exist, neither as a historical structure, nor as a mindset. There is no equality or justice, but on the contrary, supreme inequality and blatant injustice. The unhealthy dream of social uplift of the characters in *Lies and Sorcery* is dictated not just by a tangle of prejudices but by the desire to pass from plebian to patrician rank.[160]

Sympathetic comments of this kind have not always been the norm, as they single out the ways in which the novel describes how social privilege structures relationships, affecting even the time and space of the characters' lives. As Edda and Carlo Sgorlon signaled, Morante narrates a world in which "democracy does not exist"—not even as a mindset. But the world depicted in *Lies and Sorcery* did not exist eons ago, and it is neither fantastic nor tainted by Mussolini's or Hitler's cohorts. Historically, it is the time that just predates Fascism, as both Garboli and more recently Wood highlighted. In Italy, the Belle Époque was named *the liberal age*. It was the period in which practices of coercion and social exclusion that would later define Fascism were seeded in an attempt to create a modern political substitute for structures of privilege that had been previously legitimized by religion. Saba hinted at this fundamental insight when he stressed the link between the Pope, Croce, and Mussolini in the shortcut we have examined above.

The liberal age is the backdrop of Anna's and Francesco's long walks hand in hand with Elisa, in which cafés, gramophones, postal trains, and public gardens share the cityscape with horse-drawn chariots, palaces of local nobility, and baroque cathedrals of the clergy. It is the urban setting of a partially secularized society. This is the context in which the discourses of privilege and utopian palingenesis of our two protagonists will become more radical, but also neglect their toll on creaturely life (Elisa claims that only with Rosaria was she able to feel like "a natural and accepted part of all creation").[161] This was possible only when the subjects of such discourses—the petite bourgeoisie to which both Anna and Francesco belong despite their delusions—forgot their original frustrated desire and fully believed in their illusory "family romance," which, in hindsight, we can now call nationalism and imperialism.[162] It is thus no coincidence that this age is the same historical period Croce exalted in his speeches as representing "the *true* Italy": the liberal age—Belle Époque in Europe—still unstained according to the idealist philosopher by the *foreign disease* of Fascism.

Edda and Carlo Sgorlon are right when they claim that democracy does not exist in Morante's novel, but their crucial point needs to be unfolded further. Although undemocratic, it is incorrect to claim that the reality she depicts in her book is ahistorical, as they do. *Lies and Sorcery*'s time is not to be measured with watches, as Bellonci insightfully noted. Its time is not simply that of the chronicle or traditional historical novels because *Lies and Sorcery* resists historicism firsthand.[163] Like Saba's *Shortcuts*, Morante's work draws a different geography in which chronological time, the time of centralized history of both Croce and Mussolini (whose own personal "family romance" dates back to the Roman Empire), is continuously defied by the dense, nonlinear temporalities of its characters. In the space of Morante's novel, different temporalities coexist. Through Elisa's storytelling, for instance, the novel encompasses the different temporalities of women without the presumption of establishing or assigning definitive roles for their existence, their social fantasies, or even their ghosts.

There is one last remarkable motif in *Lies and Sorcery* that radicalizes the anti-historicist discontent examined in this chapter. (The coexistence of different temporalities in early postwar Italy will also be at the center of Carlo Levi's work, as the next chapter will detail.) There are sections of Morante's novel that foreground how social fantasies and personal desires can turn into dystopia. They reveal a psychological space between repression and collective denegation that very few people in Italy were eager to cross at the time—primarily literary critics.[164]

Toward the end of her story, Elisa summarizes the content of the letters Anna writes to herself, which she offers to Concetta, pretending they were sent by Edoardo from his travels abroad. When talking about these letters, Elisa dismisses the point of view of the ten-year-old child—previously employed as a shield for her own involvement in her parents' delusions—and assumes a more distanced tone. She has indeed kept these letters for years in her room in Rosaria's home in Rome. The letters are not a product of Elisa's fantasy; they are *a document*. But as a document, they are evidence of the story that Elisa only partially tells: not the story of her family romance, but that of her mother's pathological fixation. Because of the pity she feels for her mother—and for herself—, Elisa decides to integrate this precious document into her story but only to a limited degree. Given the ordinary, if not pedestrian, style in which the letters are written, she prefers to select and summarize their content. In his missives, the imagined Edoardo promises Anna eternal love, refers to people and places he has visited, and anticipates their life together once he returns from his travels. This idyllic picture is complicated by the outstanding details of this seemingly conventional romantic frame. Elisa observes that:

> Although, as we have seen, the cities visited were located on widely diverse latitudes, they all resembled each other quite closely, and one could even say that it was actually just one metropolis spread over the entire globe, or, in other words, over the part of the globe we might identify as "Abroad." It's useless for us to dwell on the implausible details of this mysterious Babylon. [. . .]
>
> The supreme form of government there was most certainly (even if the writer doesn't particularly specify this) the absolute monarchy. [. . .] Unfortunately, it does not appear from the letters that these crown-wearing friends of the traveler's were as sweet and kind to their subjects as they were to him. On the contrary, their exploits, which were lauded and boasted about by the fake

cousin, would convert even the most ardent monarchists to republicans if they were to learn of them. For the traveler and his various royals, it would seem that the most delightful privilege of their power was profanation and injustice, the honor of a sovereign measured by the number of his victims. Now, the saddest thing of all was that the fake traveler, who'd declared himself Anna's fiancé, boasted of participating in the same kinds of heinous sovereign exercises as his royal hosts and in which, according to his letters, he took great pleasure and joy.[165]

The imagined Edoardo then writes Anna about the place where they would live together. It is not just a house, but a royal palace:

> one could say that the gloomy Germanic melancholy created it so Southern jealousy would choose it as its dwelling. (. . .) The building's chief quality, the Cousin fervently boasted, was that it was surrounded by a *closed* wall with no way in or out, and therefore no means of communication with the outside world. Not even the natural light from the sky would be able to penetrate down into the palace.[166]

At this point Elisa interrupts her report and, for the first time, she comments on the unsettling nightmare depicted by her mother: "All of this, however, gave rise to a suspicion that instead of a beloved bride, the letter writer wanted a kind of priestess whose only job was to worship her husband's many attributes." Elisa then spells out the twisted drives that inform Anna's behavior: "One would have said that being imprisoned, interrogated, spied upon, and persecuted didn't cause her to be angry or distressed in the least, but rather gave her pleasure."[167]

No critic at the time of publication commented on this superb piece of visionary writing. Morante's novel opens here a real can of worms in a country tainted by Fascism, which resolutely wanted to forget the years of consent and the joy felt by many at being relieved of any responsibility—freedom included. Morante touches upon this disquieting intuition, compiling extraordinary pages in which memory and dystopia interfere with the experienced reality that the reader just left behind, and which is afraid to remember, perhaps afraid of discovering an unexpected nostalgia. These last pages feature among the most compelling ever written on totalitarianism, as they portray a totalitarian state not as it actually happened in history, but as it might reside in our deepest unspeakable desires.

4   Carlo Levi on the Religion of the State

The Radical Humanism of a Brilliant Expatriate

Carlo Levi's memoir *Christ Stopped at Eboli* (1945) is the most extensive criticism of the modern state to appear in Italy during the post-Fascist transition. The book finely recollects Levi's forced confinement in Southern Italy's remote Lucania region for anti-Fascist activity. For Levi, recounting his daily exchange with the local peasant community and his acquaintance with the atavistic structures of subjugation he found in Lucania becomes an opportunity to challenge the Western political tradition based on the centrality of the state. In contrast to the concept of the polity historically elaborated by this tradition, Levi argues that the peasantry of Lucania represents a community model based on inclusion, not exclusion.

    This chapter retraces Levi's intellectual trajectory during the transition by assessing *Christ Stopped at Eboli* in the context of his early postwar production, from his essay *Fear of Freedom* to the novel *The Watch*. These two lesser-known yet outstanding texts pursue an unconventional theory of totalitarianism and a bold reappraisal of the Italian state born out of a new party system.[1] Moreover, Levi had a prominent role in the anti-Fascist press and Action Party's newspapers, during and after the war. He was the editor of *La Nazione del popolo* in Florence from the liberation of the city in 1944 to August 1945, then of *L'Italia libera* in Rome until the demise of the party in February 1946. His books and prolific journalistic activity constitute an eclectic yet consistent corpus. Read in its entirety, this corpus develops a distinctively antiauthoritarian critique of modern politics and its redemptive narratives.

    Early reviewers interpreted *Christ Stopped at Eboli* as a "poetic survey" of the living conditions of Southern Italy.[2] Thereby, they separated the book from Levi's political experience and minimized its polemical force. In the very first lines, the author famously introduces the peasant community of Lucania as "outside History and the State," implicitly undermining historicist tropes such as "Secondo Risorgimento" for Italy. Unlike his contemporaries, Levi does not lament the absence of institutional intervention in the peasant communities as the principal factor for their destitute conditions.[3] For him, the urgent problem is instead the ceaseless interference of "History and the State" *in* the autonomy and self-government of peasant communities.

In Levi's memoir, History and the State are embodied by the distant power of Rome and by its local functionaries. As David Ward remarked, Levi's refusal of past models placed him among the most radical of the Action Party's political thinkers. His envisioned moral regeneration of the country was based on the ideas of autonomy and self-government that Italians experimented with during Liberation.[4] Although Levi is often labeled as the author of just one book,[5] his early postwar production further elaborated the criticism of modern politics he began with *Christ Stopped at Eboli*—that is, the reliance of the modern centralized state on politics of exclusion. His subsequent books explore philosophical and cultural traditions that could extend the debate over Italian history beyond Marxist dialectics and the country's self-assigned exceptionality in the European context. In this chapter, I will develop this interpretation following the question of political redemption as it appears in Levi's heterogeneous production, drawing from sources as disparate as French post-surrealist sociology to central-European Jewish culture.

The polemical target of *Christ Stopped at Eboli* is centralization and the lack of popular participation in the Italian state since the Risorgimento. Contemporary commentators refused to acknowledge the fundamental message of Levi's memoir: the marginalization of the Southern popular classes represents the larger failure of the national state as a community. From such a perspective, every narrative of redemption based on the centrality of the State perpetuates this underlying inequality. Commenting on Levi's works, Giovanni De Luna convincingly argued:

> The proper assessment of our inability to be normal can actually become an analytical category, suggesting a cognitive path capable of situating [our inability's] roots precisely in the copresence of various identities, the conflictual relationships among which have been the specific manner in which this country has elected to grow and mature over the course of the short century since national unification [. . .]. The fact is that the conflict itself represents the richest interpretive category for defining a national identity in dynamic terms.[6]

Levi's analysis challenges the redemptive narratives of both the PCI and the DC, whose main concern in the early postwar period was reestablishing the national state's authority. Since party politics heavily influenced literary circles in Italy, the critical threat posed by Levi's political books contributed to the *literary* rejection of his work. On this subject, the private considerations on Levi by Cesare Pavese, the most highly acclaimed writer of his generation, shed quite a revealing light. In his diary entry dated March 22, 1947, Pavese reflects on the epistemic value of modern storytelling. At the center of his musings, however, is not only modernist poetics, but also the international acclaim that his fellow anti-Fascist Levi received for *Christ Stopped at Eboli*:

> The man who tells it now is not the one who "knew human nature," and discovered profoundly significant psychological truths, but one who deals with reality en bloc, whose harsh experiences give rhythm, cadences, embellishments to his story. Hemingway has violent death; Levi, prison; Conrad, the mysteries of the Southern Seas; Joyce, the stereoscope of word-sensations; Proust, the impossibility of seizing fleeting moments; Kafka, the cipher of absurdity; Mann, the mythical reassessment of facts. I apologize for having included Levi.[7]

Pavese's entry is a reflection on experience and writing, yet the passage is carefully crafted to disparage Levi, whose memoir was a literary blockbuster of early postwar Italy. Levi was confined in Lucania in 1935, after he fell victim to the OVRA operation that dismantled the anti-Fascist "Giustizia e Libertà" ("Justice and Freedom") organization in Turin, to which both he and Pavese belonged. Giustizia e Libertà was a liberal and socialist organization based in Paris. The goal of the Fascist secret police was to crush its biggest branch in Italy, jailing or confining its most active intellectuals. Two years later, Mussolini's agents would notoriously assassinate the leaders of this clandestine movement, Carlo and Nello Rosselli, who were exiles in the French capital and close friends of Levi.

Because of this OVRA operation, Pavese was also convicted and exiled to a remote village of Southern Italy, Brancaleone Calabro. Still, his novel *The Prison* (1949), which stems from his personal experience of confinement, had little of the poetic and political persuasiveness of Levi's memoir. As Luisa Mangoni remarked, "In most cases, in the internal exile's experience, attention—all of life—is oriented toward the 'after.'"[8] This was not the case for Levi's book: His warm recollection of life in Agliano and Grassano, the two towns in Lucania where he spent his confinement, is unique among the literature of Fascist confinement. In *Christ Stopped at Eboli*, Levi articulated a highly intellectual yet passionate poetic depiction of his encounter with the local peasantry, engendering a new wave of political and ethnological attention to Italy's South and its peoples, from anthropologist Ernesto De Martino to historian Fernand Braudel, both of whom openly acknowledged Levi's substantial influence on their work. As Mangoni concludes, "'free from his own time,' immersed in the facts, Levi could feel like a contemporary of the peasants, of their world outside time." Unlike the confinement of fellow anti-Fascists exiled by Mussolini to remote lands, the encounter with the peasant communities of Lucania was a revolutionary experience for Levi. Bitterness toward Levi's literary success aside, why, then, did Pavese, a writer who was acutely aware of his audience even when writing his private diary, make such a spiteful remark?

One answer may lie in politics and the animosity between the Communists and the Action Party to which Levi adhered. As a number of testimonies confirm, Levi had a difficult relationship with Communist intellectuals. Reviews of his books published in the late 1940s and the early 1950s, in forums such as *Società*, *Belfagor*, and *l'Unità*, engage in personal attacks on the writer, contesting his literary talent and political proposals. Carlo Muscetta, Marxist literary critic and influential editor of Einaudi, took issue with Levi's protagonist role: "The descent of Carlo Levi, painter and doctor, wizard and writer, is depicted in his own book as an epiphany, as the advent and revelation of a divinity to be worshipped."[9] The journalist Gianfranco Piazzesi claimed, "It seems to us that Levi is not the most suitable person to understand and interpret the needs of that population."[10] Finally, Ranuccio Bianchi Bandinelli, the renowned antiquarian who guided Hitler among the ruins of Imperial Rome in his official 1938 visit before becoming a Communist after the war, began his review of Levi's *The Watch* thus: "Rarely has an artistic limit in a literary work seemed to us so tied to and conditioned by the limits of the man who wrote it."[11]

The bad blood between Communists and the Giustizia e Libertà movement had already started in the 1930s with the virulent controversy between Palmiro Togliatti and Carlo Rosselli. The libertarian and socialist agenda of Rosselli's movement harshly criticized the Stalinist (and statist) turn that Togliatti and the PCI fully endorsed and did not abandon until the Russian dictator's death. After the assassination of the Rosselli brothers, Levi and the newly born Action Party—founded in secret in 1942 and which included prominent anti-Fascists such as Piero Calamandrei, Leone Ginzburg, Altiero Spinelli, Luigi Salvatorelli, Vittorio Foà, and Emilio Lussu—continued Giustizia e Libertà's fight under the military leadership of Ferruccio Parri.[12]

Whether it sprang from ideological disagreement or other factors, personal antagonism toward Levi was widespread and is now well documented—as in the case of Pavese.[13] Ideological and personal hostility, however, do not fully explain the acrimony most Communist intellectuals had toward Levi's books, one that even today profoundly affects a thorough understanding of his oeuvre.[14] Since the international praise and artistic quality of *Christ Stopped at Eboli* could hardly be disregarded, Levi's complex memoir was reduced by critics to its most obvious aspects, important but by no means univocal to the economy of the book: the heartfelt description of the miserable conditions of Southern peasants and the "ethnological" focus on subaltern culture. In fact, keenly aware of the interest aroused by the book, Muscetta himself planned a series of *à la Levi* poetic reportages about the Italian South for Einaudi publishing, with the intent of further profiting from the success of the book.[15] Although Muscetta's project never materialized, the isolation of the Southern question within the complex texture of Levi's book engendered the dismissal of the text's political charge.[16]

Personal attacks by Communist intellectuals against Levi went beyond the ideological conflict with the Action Party. This party voiced the possibility of a third way for Italy, specifically *within the Left*, but it collapsed in 1947 because of its lack of popular support, sharp internal discontent, and disregard for the broader international situation rapidly polarizing around the two Cold War superpowers. Levi's literary success and the critical charge of his works, however, survived the collapse of his party, for they signaled the lack of pluralism and dramatic involution of political debate within the same Left.

Nemo propheta in patria: The controversy around *Christ Stopped at Eboli* has to be framed within the larger political climate of the early postwar, with its intense discussion about national renovation. Levi's memoir was published in June 1945 when the national coalition government led by Parri was still in power. As acknowledged by Levi himself, the momentous experience of armed Resistance and self-government led by local "Liberation Committees" animated the political debate, as well as the plans and hopes for change. Furthermore, Levi wrote his memoir in 1944 in Florence as the city was being liberated, a process in which he played a significant role.[17] In *The Watch*, he would intensely recall that unique collective experience, which he constantly refers to in all his writings:

> It was at the end of August, 1945. I'd come straight from Florence, carrying my traveling bag in my hand. A few hours before I'd left behind that town where everyone still lived in the stimulating atmosphere of the Resistance and one didn't believe there was a difference between politicians and ordinary people; where everyone did what he did naturally, in a world independent

and without closed compartments, in the factories, on the job or on the local committee of liberation.¹⁸

Levi's joyful fresco of Florence after the Liberation contrasts with *Christ Stopped at Eboli*'s famous incipit, in which he paints Lucania with bleak, sorrowful strokes. Levi's memoir bears witness to the hopelessly harsh existence of Lucania's peasants and their subjugation to the "distant" power of "History" and the "State." For the peasants, these two terms are no more than abstract concepts irreducible to their everyday lives. State and History are designations of faraway forces that have always excluded them from political agency. The peasants' continual marginality might seem antithetical to the anarchic and optimistic atmosphere of liberated Florence: "But to this shadowy land, that knows neither sin nor redemption from sin, where evil is not moral but is only the pain residing forever in earthly things, Christ did not come," the author adds.¹⁹

Already on the first page, Levi introduces the image that informs his whole book and that would become proverbial in postwar Italy: Christ, the Redeemer, and his revolutionary news never reached the villages of Southern Italy. In Levi's text, the redemption offered by the "good tidings" of Christianity is not only religious, but also political. The foremost target of his polemic is not the Catholic Church, but modern secular religions, from Fascism to Liberalism to Communism—all with capital letters. According to Levi, with their theocratic idolatry of the State, these ideologies were incapable of thinking through and building a polity in which the peasantry could actively participate and regard it as their own. In other words, secular religions of the State failed to create a real *Gemeinschaft* ("community"), preferring instead to focus on a hierarchically governed and regulated *Gesellschaft* ("society").

Levi's bold ideas were met with stark opposition from both Liberals and Communists, who accused him of individualism and aestheticism.²⁰ Even positive reviews of *Christ Stopped at Eboli* display indignation at the living conditions of the Southern peasantry depicted by Levi, but only a partial understanding of his ideas. On February 2, 1946, Actionist Corrado Tumiati highly praised the book in the journal *Il Ponte*, concluding that "Christian civilization [. . .] has not redeemed the peasants."²¹ Two weeks later, in *La gazzetta del mezzogiorno*, socialist Tommaso Fiore stressed how the salvation of Southern peasants could not be belated: "It is necessary to redeem them, then, economically and morally, on pain of our own condemnation."²² In an article titled "Magical and Desolate Lucania," renowned literary critic Vittore

Branca pointed to emigration to the US and the myth of America as the only possible hope for Southern peasantry.[23]

All these elements are present and eloquently deployed in *Christ Stopped at Eboli*. The inadequacy of religious institutions, the responsibility of politics in economic (and moral) stagnation, and the inevitable outcome of emigration evidence how the nationalization of Southern popular classes failed. These observations coalesce in an accusation not only of Fascism but also of the policies implemented by the Italian state since unification. All of these comments, however, isolate single, if critical, concerns from Levi's text, hinting at a possible solution to the problem of Southern peasantry from *above*. The major polemical target of his book—centralization and the total lack of popular participation in the polity—goes largely unmentioned.

In fact, Levi provides explicit suggestions for addressing the question of the South in the last chapter of his memoir. Avoiding economic analysis or class dialectics, the author enlarges the scope of the question from political to ontological concerns, subverting traditional categories of social analysis and blurring the boundaries of political, historical, and philosophical discourses:

> The State, I said, cannot solve the problem of the South, because the problem which we call by this name is none other than the problem of the State itself [...]. We must make ourselves capable of inventing a new form of government, neither Fascist, nor Communist, nor even Liberal, for all three of these are forms of the religion of the State. We must rebuild the foundations of our concept of the State with the concept of the individual, which is its basis. For the juridical and abstract concept of the individual we must substitute a new concept, more expressive of reality, one that will do away with the now unbridgeable gulf between the individual and the State. The individual is not a separate unit, but a link, a meeting place of relationships of every kind. This concept of relationship, without which the individual has no life, is at the same time the basis of the State. [...] It is the only path which will lead us out of the vicious circle of Fascism and anti-Fascism. The name of this way out is autonomy. The State can only be a group of autonomies, an organic federation.[24]

This analysis builds on concepts of autonomy and federalism that were central to the libertarian and socialist analysis of the Giustizia e Libertà movement since the 1930s. The Action Party inherited and developed these ideas as guiding principles of its radical agenda. Transforming the country into a federalist state was a recurring goal for many reformists since the Risorgimento. From nineteenth century political thinker Carlo Cattaneo to the anti-Fascist "Rivoluzione Liberale" group gathered around Piero Gobetti and his newspaper, liberal intellectuals focused on federalism as the most appropriate political system for the country. On many occasions, Levi declared an intellectual and personal debt to his close friend Gobetti, who died in 1926 after a violent attack by a Fascist mob.[25]

Autonomy is a key concept in Levi's diagnosis, first elaborated by Gobetti and then enriched with a socialist component in the self-government model of autonomous communities by Carlo Rosselli.[26] Already in 1932, Levi published the article "The Concept of Autonomy in the Program of G.L." in *Quaderni di Giustizia e Libertà*, written together with Leone Ginzburg, who would perish in a Fascist prison in 1944. Contesting Fascist primacy of politics over life, Levi and Ginzburg argued, "Autonomy is the understanding of the human being as a place for all relationships."[27] Through their radical humanism, they also insisted that society was neither the result of a contract nor the outcome of history or class dialectics. Rather, it was based on a "continuous circulation of living blood." According to the two authors, establishing autonomous institutions would also diminish the role of politics in society, relegating it to a mere "technique." Referring to the Italian state, Levi and Ginzburg conclude, "We will truly be able to speak of unity only when local independent organisms have emerged and flourished. Centralization corresponds to totalitarianism: and just as the latter is the enemy of freedom, so is the former of national unity."[28]

Levi and Ginzburg's programmatic refusal to outline the "coming community" before its actual realization draws from their rejection of past political models—utopian literature included. By criticizing the concept of the political as an inherited set of practices, they also reject liberal and Fascist concepts of history, as well as historical and class dialectics. As David Ward remarked, emerging from the pages of Levi's writing "is an analysis of the origins of Fascism that goes well beyond that put forward by any other Action Party intellectual."[29] In a 1947 article titled "The Cities," Levi expands on these tenets, displaying a profound continuity with his prewar reflections and, likewise, a profound trust in democratic pluralism:

> For the first time in its post-unification history, Italy has naturally (not by choice or according to a program) detached itself from the past, emancipated itself: it is no longer, or no longer only, a "fatherland." We shall have new architecture and new cities if this detachment is capable of being creative, if

this adult life is free, if citizens and peasants can both recognize themselves in the new state: we will cease to be Arcadian and Futurist academy members if we can figure out how to build an autonomous and modern democracy.[30]

Remarkably, Levi presents Italy's emancipation from its past as an epiphenomenon of the war. He does not describe this emancipation with the epic tones of a historic collective struggle, but as a spontaneous and creative reaction to an objective external reality, with no overarching narrative to encompass all of its singular events. For Levi, democracy is a matter of collective *and* personal emancipation, of acquiring freedom through individual autonomy.

Among the many reviews of Levi's work cited here, Eugenio Montale's article on *Christ Stopped at Eboli* stands out for stressing the pivotal role of subjectivity in the book. The piece was published on the same day as Tumiati's review, and it draws attention specifically to the last chapter of Levi's memoir:

> Carlo Levi inserts here his theory of the other civilization, of the peasant civilization [. . .]. It would be out of place to analyze how much is utopian, how much is feasible, in such ideas (ideas that have, what's more, been much debated in recent years). What's important for us is just to point out that the book bears these ideas without suffering, in fact it demands them as a necessary clarification: a sign of a total identification with his material on the part of someone who could one day seem like a brilliant expatriate, irretrievably distant from his roots . . . [31]

Montale concentrates on two crucial features overlooked by other commentators. First, in Levi's text, there is no discontinuity between his testimonial narrative and the deliberative, political conclusion of the book—arguably a rare case in modern literature. Second, by shifting the attention from Levi's recollection of his confinement in Southern Italy to the writing subject, Levi himself, Montale emphasizes the unexpected relationship between Levi's life as a cosmopolitan expatriate and his exile in Lucania.

Montale's praise of the book focuses on Levi's "total identification" with Lucania's peasants and their unique world, despite the author's sophisticated uprootedness. His admiration is pivotal to understanding how radical Levi's literary elaboration of his experience in Lucania was, which fascinated an international audience and outraged Italian *literati*. In fact, Levi's "total identification" with the peasants of Agliano and Grassano *was not at odds with* the cosmopolitan roots of his thought and his own identity. Rather, his identification was consistent with concepts of time, history, and redemption that critically countered the ideas of progress guiding current teleological narratives of history—from Croce to vulgar Marxism. In a certain sense, Levi found these alternative concepts within *his own* difference: through his contact, allegedly during his years in exile, with what Michael Löwy called "the multidirectional unity" of the cultural encounter between "libertarian romanticism and Jewish messianism."[32]

Autonomy and Anarchic Resistance: From *Fear of Freedom* to *Christ Stopped at Eboli*

The key to opening these doors lies in *Fear of Freedom*, the extraordinary essay that Levi published in 1946.[33] The text was composed during his exile in France in 1939. The grim and oppressive atmosphere of the *drôle de guerre* before the Nazi invasion looms large in these pages and affected its writing. *Fear of Freedom* offers a bold and eclectic countertheory of power and the state, the first comprehensive interpretation of totalitarianism to appear in Italy.

The book's eight chapters examine totalitarianism's success in the context of the present crisis in Europe. By blending philosophy, ethnology, and psychoanalysis, it offers an ambitious genealogy of modern authoritarian regimes. According to Levi, the "idolatry" of the political at the core of Fascist and Nazi ideologies has emerged through the transformation of the *sacred*, a process with a long lineage in the transformation of sovereign power. The sacred "ambiguously" resides between the undefined unconscious state common to every human being and the necessary individuation each individual represents. For Levi, this transformation corresponds to the passage from the sacred to the *religious*. The sacred is a source of freedom and art as well as the origin of the terror that individuation brings about in every human being—a terror that Levi names "fear of freedom." To avoid the burden of responsibility and the corollary fear that this freedom entails, individuals prefer to "relegate" their freedom to an external party, which would then govern the sacred and transform it into the "religious." "Religion is relegation," Levi states.[34] To avoid the "unbearable" ambiguity of the sacred, individuals prefer to "become mass" and relinquish their freedom for the sake of an external religious law, which would grant them relief from ontological fear. The task of every religious entity is then to transform the sacred into the "sacrificial." Levi thereby introduces his theory of the scapegoat as necessary and consubstantial to "divine" monarchy as well as to twentieth-century totalitarian states, anticipating relevant tenets of later thinkers such as René Girard and Giorgio Agamben.[35]

The following excerpt from *Fear of Freedom* illuminates Levi's heterodox blending of different traditions and disciplines on the same page, from Jewish messianism to Christian *apokatastasis*, from Vico to Jung:[36]

> There can be neither freedom nor justice as long as the law resides outside things in divine estrangement.
>
> But the coming of Christ is also a myth, like the sin of Adam: and in reality fall and redemption are eternal and ever present. Redemption cannot happen once and forever, any more than sin occurred once and for all the beginning of time. A ceaseless fall and a ceaseless renascence make up history: and when liberation becomes religion, then liberation is useless. "For if righteousness is through the law, then Christ is dead in vain," says Paul.[37]

To interpret this passage, it is necessary to return to the political theory Levi had developed as a member of the anti-Fascist "Giustizia e Libertà" group—and, in particular, to the aforementioned article he wrote with Leone Ginzburg, "The Concept of Autonomy in the Program of G.L." In this article, the two authors discuss "autonomy" as the "affirmation of moral values in politics." From this standpoint,

> Politics is not always so essential an activity (governmental politics, at least); it can truly be *delegated*, when, for the coexistence of autonomous institutions, it no longer represents more than a technique, a matter of business management. [. . .] One frees oneself from politics through politics. In Italy, instead, disinterest is the incapacity of self-governance. Thus every politics, today, is an affirmation of autonomy.[38]

According to Levi and Ginzburg, "autonomous institutions" commence from "a concert of forces whose various purposes cooperate toward an end, the latter more in common the more the former are particular. Alliance, therefore, not concentration." The polemical target of this article is the Fascist totalitarian state. Still, the political alternative that the two authors propose is based not on predefined social groups or political entities but on individuals and their moral integrity.[39] Remarkably, Ginzburg and Levi conclude that individuals, in their affirmation of autonomy, can *free themselves* from politics by *delegating* it to the self-governed institutions created to safeguard individual autonomy. Concentrations of power can thus be avoided by envisioning politics through the lenses of the "individual" and their "alliances."

In *Christ Stopped at Eboli*, Levi would hone this idea with the new concept of "individual-in-relation." Unlike in totalitarian mass politics, here the individual is autonomous but not isolated. In this new concept of the individual, the writer perceives the possible denial of any "relegation" to religious powers to an external law that—as he writes in *Fear of Freedom*—is "outside things, in divine estrangement."⁴⁰ The two terms that Levi uses for his political theory, "delegation" and "relegation," are thus in paradigmatic opposition. The first affirms what the second denies—the autonomy of each individual.

Levi's concept of autonomy discloses a radical immanentism, pointing to "religious" relegation as a source of injustice and enslavement in the social arena. Since history and progress are not necessarily related, Levi demands a total dismissal of redemptive (religious) narratives. Hence, the writer argues for the necessity of a new "juridical and abstract concept of the individual [. . .] that will do away with the now unbridgeable gulf between the individual and the State," as he affirms in *Christ Stopped at Eboli*, and that "will lead us out of the vicious circle of Fascism and anti-Fascism."⁴¹ Levi concludes that the Resistance has opened the way to such a new concept by experimenting new possible forms of communal living, which envisaged social life beyond the inherited dogma of the nation-state.

Fear of Freedom received almost exclusively negative reviews in Italy when published in 1946. A young Italo Calvino, for instance, dismissed it as reactionary in *l'Unità*, stigmatizing its "aestheticism" and its "mystical-barbaric irrationalist culture."⁴² Marxist critics lamented the lack of any economic dimension in Levi's analysis of totalitarianism.⁴³ Literary critic Giancarlo Vigorelli was the only one to direct attention to the cultural matrix of Levi's text. According to Vigorelli, since "every Jew, as everyone knows, always takes inspiration from the Bible," Levi's book reads as "a game alternating between messianism and rationalism." All things considered, "since Carlo Levi doesn't know how to do without an entire typically Jewish culturalism (à la Martin Buber), no idea becomes persuaded or persuasive."⁴⁴

Vigorelli's derogatory tone illustrates the disquieting persistence of anti-Semitism in early postwar culture.⁴⁵ For him, *Fear of Freedom* is not convincing because its author cannot *renounce* his own cultural roots. The critic points to the richness of Levi's sources as somewhat alien to Italian culture. The difficulty of accepting Levi's syncretic operation within the canon of Italian literature, apparent in Vigorelli's comments, showcases a hostility that precedes and would impact the reception of Levi's heterodox political ideas. The critic's scorn for modern Jewish culture, however, points to a possible reason why Levi's corpus was largely disregarded by his contemporaries—their utter ignorance on the subject. Vigorelli's references to the "game alternating between messianism and rationalism" and Martin

Buber are indeed crucial for a thorough reappraisal of Levi's originality within the Italian context.

Levi himself hinted at this underlying aspect of his work in the preface that he included when *Fear of Freedom* was published in 1946. As he claims there, the book was written during his exile in France in 1939. Unlike his previous confinement in Lucania, Levi was not only banned from his country for political reasons, but he was also stripped of full citizenship on account of being a Jew. Levi shared this experience with a number of Jewish intellectuals escaping totalitarian regimes, from Ernst Bloch to Walter Benjamin. At stake here is not whether Levi ever met Benjamin or read Bloch, but how the critical concepts developed in those years by German-speaking Jewish philosophers allow for a more nuanced—and transnational—understanding of his work.

"Seul à bord de la guerre," as an inspired French critic put it, Levi was stranded in a small town in Normandy when he wrote *Fear of Freedom*, without access to interlocutors or necessary texts.[46] Still, *Fear of Freedom* explicitly references the Bible as its fundamental model. When Levi's book first appeared, only Vigorelli focused on the author's debt to the Bible, disparagingly connecting Levi's cultural approach to other modern Jewish authors.[47] What Vigorelli failed to recognize, however, was that, in Levi, aesthetics and politics are organically intertwined: The biblical reference is essential for his rejection of propaganda and religious art. In *Fear of Freedom*, Levi reflects on the political connotations of these two terms, especially after their abuse in Fascist regimes. In his view, religious art and propaganda tend to overlap. Levi often deploys them as synonyms, but he crucially separates propaganda from religious art when the latter holds a mythological value—namely, when religious art is able to create myths. The Bible is the case in point here: "Art may be considered as a *mythology*," Levi claims. "Strictly speaking, there is no religious art [. . .]. The Bible itself, as the mythology of the Hebrew people, is nothing but a work of art."[48]

Levi situates *Fear of Freedom* in the Bible's wake: Stripped of its transcendence and theological signification, the sacred text of Judaism and Christianity is considered a work of art, able to bring myths into existence. As the "mythology" of Jewish people, the Bible constitutes a creative model for his writing style. Additionally, Levi's skepticism toward religion does not preclude his syncretism with other traditions, such as Saint Paul's "Letter to the Romans" or the classic, then Christian, trope of the *descensio ad inferos*.[49]

A column published in the same year for *La Nazione del popolo* helps to elucidate this point and signals how the concept of messianic redemption was certainly present in Levi's musings on contemporary history. The article is titled "Notes on *The Great Dictator*," and it is a review of Charlie Chaplin's acclaimed movie, which appeared on Italian screens only after the demise of Fascism. Levi interprets the identities of the two main characters—the dictator Hinkel (a transparent parody of the Führer) and the modest Jewish barber, both played by Chaplin—as a reference to the "messianic liberation of the world."[50] He argues that "Charlie's vision is a messianic vision, that of an eternal Jewish myth, which has no need nor possibility of realizing itself in history: it is, for each, a personal story of sin and redemption."[51]

Levi introduces here a motif that is seminal to understanding how the thrust toward reality in his work is inextricable from a utopian dimension. Although utopia and history, as well as history and redemption, are mutually exclusive, they can coexist in *personal* history and individual time. This is why, Levi adds, the encounters between "the Jew and the Junker" (the German gentleman) in Chaplin's film "occur, as is natural, *only in heaven*," or in "Hell, which is an inverted Heaven, in the Concentration Camp." With the following conclusion, Levi implicitly aligns his own work with this Jewish tradition: "These fundamental themes free the incident from any particular determination, from any character of 'historical context,' to make of it a sort of sacred drama, which oscillates Judaically between maximum abstraction and maximum concreteness."[52]

Fear of Freedom, however, is not just a sketch of Levi's aesthetics; it is also a genealogical interpretation of the modern state and its power. According to Vittorio Giacopini, Levi's essay sets forth "an extraordinary (counter) theory of politics as self-mutilation, suicide in installments, systematic amputation of human potential and social occasions."[53] For Levi, the historical forces responsible for the conversion of the sacred into the religious are external to the individual and are presently incarnated by the "religion of the State." Similar to the ways in which religious institutions maintained their divine power since prehistory, modern totalitarian states must convert the sacred into the "sacrificial"—and with it, find a "scapegoat." Levi claims:

> The religion of the state requires, in sacrificial form, the renouncement, surrender and death of something human. Without self-mutilation man cannot make a god out of his own capacity for human relations [. . .]. On the individual level, the necessary sacrifice is to renounce autonomy.[54]

Levi indicates the widespread surrender of individual autonomy to the religion of the State as the source of the current crisis. His critique targets not only modern totalitarianisms but also liberal concepts of the state and their respective ideologies of history, of the past, or of progress—from Croce's idealism to vulgar Marxism. Before explicating his theory in the contemporary body politic, Levi grounds it in the individual, consistent with his professed radical humanism. The self-mutilation Levi mentioned above is not just a metaphor. It is a real surrender of the individual body to the divine in order to be safe from the "fear of freedom." Sublimated in the mass politics of modern times, this self-mutilation finds an ancestral root in tribal rites.[55]

Most commentators highlight Oswald Spengler's and José Ortega y Gasset's influence on Levi's arguments, overlooking the critical impact that French sociology and anthropology had on the development of the writer's leading ideas.[56] Levi's concept of the sacred originates in modern sociological studies on religion, by then a flourishing field of research that spanned from Émile Durkheim to Roger Caillois (*Man and the Sacred*, 1939). Caillois's study is a bold yet unsystematic investigation of the sacred in human societies, based on the assumption of the constituent *ambiguity* of the sacred— according to Agamben, a remarkable "mythologem" of modern thought, from William Robertson Smith and his *Lectures on the Religion of the Semites* (1889) to the "trivialization of religious experience" in early twentieth-century bourgeois society.[57]

Fear of Freedom builds up his conceptual edifice on this established scholarly tradition—from Smith to Caillois. The influence of the French sociologist, however, is especially critical for Levi's idea of politics as self-mutilation, the basis of his subsequent theory of the necessary (violent, sacrificial) exclusion of a part of society for the existence of the religious State. In *Man and the Sacred*, Caillois discusses the ritual self-mutilation in tribal societies: "The defilement of death can reach them next and cause them to perish. Often, they save themselves from death by mutilating their bodies, generally by cutting off a finger. Thus, the part is sacrificed in order to save the whole."[58]

In Caillois's description of ritual self-mutilation, Levi found an unsettling continuity with his current political situation. Tribal religious practices performed on the physical body could represent a first instance of the same biopolitical procedure perpetrated by modern State on the body politic. Levi concludes: "On the social level, the necessary sacrifice must be the mutilation of a part of society. A group, a class, a nation must be forcibly driven out, treated as enemies, turned into strangers, so that they may become the god's witnesses and victims."[59]

No other thinker in Italy during this period pointed out the constituent *necessity* of racism and a politics of exclusion from citizenship for a (totalitarian) state to thrive. To my knowledge, outside of Italy, the only interpretation of Fascism in this vein was Arendt's view on racism in *The Origins of Totalitarianism*.[60] In the typical emphatic tone of *Fear of Freedom*, which at times obscures the radicalness of its ideas, Levi argues: "Who therefore, as a consecrated victim, shall bear upon his shoulders the divinity of the state? Who shall support the state without being a part of it? Evidently the strangers [who] seem to be a divine quality [. . .], sacred things, to be sacrificed."[61]

Levi plainly exposes *Fear of Freedom*'s main political thesis in a column titled "Racism and Idolatry of the State," published in 1944 for *La Nazione del popolo*:

> The racial policies were not a random incident, and their present collapse has overwhelmed not only those persecuted, but the entire life of our country. Since racism is the very basis of Nazism, one of its necessary moments, one of its synonyms; and we would never be able to consider ourselves free from the shadow of Fascism until we have swept out of our souls and our customs even the merest memory of racial discrimination. The problem involves our entire civilization, and it must not, today, be hushed up, nor reduced to a simple question of justice and vindication.[62]

Undoubtedly, Levi's personal history of imprisonment, exile, and expropriation of property, first as a political dissident and then as a Jew, contributed to this tremendous political insight.[63] Such a perceptive understanding of Fascism informs his representation not only of Jews, but also of all subalterns excluded by the State and its History, as Levi capitalizes both words in the incipit of *Christ Stopped at Eboli*. Levi's anarchic fusion of different cultural traditions profoundly affects his approach to Lucania's peasantry. It informs what Montale acutely called his "total identification with his material." In his denigratory review, Vigorelli pointed out the roots of Levi's unique identification with the peasant communities. They are to be found in early twentieth-century Jewish utopian libertarianism, which is deeply imbued with religious flair and often akin to the writing of *Fear of Freedom* by means of their common biblical model.

"This concept of relation, outside of which the individual does not exist, is the same one that defines the State," Levi writes in *Christ Stopped at Eboli*. Pivotal concepts of Giustizia e Libertà, such as autonomy, federation, and the reorganization of the polity around human relations, are influenced by Gobetti's earlier reflections, but they also echo the thought of Martin Buber and his "social utopia."[64] According to Buber, "social utopia seeks above all to replace the state with society."[65] This entails not only political, "external" change, "but also an 'internal' transformation of human life through the communitarian restructuring of human relations." Buber's social utopia is based on the mystical revival of traditional Jewish communities of Eastern Europe. Yet his social thought transcends Romantic nostalgia and articulates the new society through "the rebirth (not the return) of the organic commune, under the form of a decentralized federation of small communities."

Remarkably, the idea of the rebirth of the primeval community (pre-capitalistic but also against the state) is common to most Jewish political thinkers of the early twentieth century, from anarchist Gustav Landauer to the young György Lukács. In his pioneering study, Michael Löwy showed that the many ideological directions of these thinkers, from Anarchism to Marxism to Zionism, share a common thrust toward revolutionary libertarianism that is not free of religious and messianic undertones.[66]

In such a variegated scenario, society's transformative new birth is not conceived in terms of progress, but rather as the establishment of a new modern community which retains the relational quality of primeval communities. Such a concept—*Tikkun* in Hebrew—encompasses both redemption and restoration. According to the eminent scholar of Jewish mysticism Gershom Scholem, "the *Tikkun* is both the restitution of an original state and the establishment of an entirely new world."[67] To better focus the significance of this idea of redemption, heterodox Marxist Ernst Bloch coupled it with the Christian theological concept of *Restitutio ad Integrum*, a restoration to original condition before the fall from grace.[68]

Not unlike the aforementioned German Jewish thinkers, Levi's "anarchy without anarchism"—as Giacopini calls it—is based on a marked distrust of progress.[69] His *Fear of Freedom* does not offer any positive readings of history, refusing historical materialism and its concept of time. Still, the idea of *Tikkun* and Jewish social libertarianism profoundly influenced Levi's elaborations, from the concept of autonomy to self-government to federation. Raised in the positivist, secular culture of bourgeois Turin, Levi considered himself an assimilated Jew and allegedly shared very little of the religious mysticism of these thinkers. For the *Ostjuden*, the Eastern European Jews, close traditions such as Chassidism and the *shtetlekh*, the small towns they inhabited all over Eastern Europe, were living instances affecting their social utopia, as was explicitly the case with Buber. Still, the assimilated Levi experienced firsthand an unparalleled "social utopia" in Lucania's peasant communities.

Bolstered by this identification, Levi found in the intellectual tradition of Jewish libertarianism, along with Vico's fundamental idea of cyclical history, nonlinear ideas of history and time, as well as the denial of progress.[70] Liberalism, Communism, and Fascism ultimately rested on *bad* conceptions of redemption, which obliterated the individual in favor of the State. Against the modern "idolatry" of the State, Levi recuperates a concept of history that is primarily one of *catastrophes*, reconnecting with the core of Jewish messianism.[71] As he commented on Chaplin's *The Great Dictator*, messianic vision is, "for each, a personal story of sin and redemption." Hence, the catastrophe of WWII represents for Italy the historical opportunity to break free from its past, the individual and collective reckoning through which Italians can rebuild the country according to new relations, a new law, and a new sense of community, as Levi repeats on countless occasions.[72] In this regard, *Christ Stopped at Eboli* does not just denounce the miserable conditions of Southern peasantry and demonstrate how the centralist State failed to create a national community. The book cannot be reduced to an exposition of Levi's autonomist theses through a moving autobiographical account either. Levi's memoir encompasses all these seminal motives. Yet his profound "empathy" originates from the acknowledgment that the world he discovered during his confinement—Lucania's peasant community—was the *existing* alternative to the chronic crisis of the Western *Weltanschauung*.

David Ward remarked that Levi's vision is an "implicit rejection of the first world's claim to be historically more advanced than the third."[73] What is more, in his close contact with the peasant communities of Agliano and Grassano, Levi may have felt that his "double nature" of Italian *and* Jew was not at stake and not a potential matter of exclusion. In the peasant community, no self-mutilation seemed needed, whereas "that land of mine where I can no longer set foot, [. . .] those in power, in their fear of all that is sacred, seem to have discovered that I too have a dual nature and am, like my dog, half baron and half lion."[74]

What even his fellow Actionists Tumiati and Fiore did not entirely grasp in their praise of *Christ Stopped at Eboli* is that, for Levi, redemption is paradoxically *not necessary* for the Southern peasantry but is of vital importance for "Don Luigino" and his kin—the other protagonists of the book. In Levi's memoir, Don Luigino epitomizes the *notabili*, the parasitical layer of traditional Southern Italian society mainly composed of unproductive petit bourgeois. Don Luigino and his kin claim their power from atavistic privilege. Their only activity is the exploitation of the local peasantry on behalf of metropolitan—or religious—power. The economic and social redemption envisaged by the Italian Left for Southern peasantry could not be the solution, for the problem resides instead in the accumulation of power by this parasitical class on behalf of the centralized State. In fact, Don Luigino and his kin shirk any responsibility to their subalterns, implementing, instead, a politics of marginalization and exclusion. In this regard, no redemption is possible for Lucania's peasants because they are *already* redeemed. For them, messianic time "has no need nor possibility of realizing itself in history" because it has *always* been there. As Levi clearly states in the first page of his book, "to this shadowy land, that knows neither sin nor redemption from sin, where evil is not moral but is only the pain residing forever in earthly things, Christ did not come."[75]

Consistent with the theory deployed in *Fear of Freedom*, the trope of the descent of Christ does not stand just for Christian (or historical) redemption. It also epitomizes the passage from the sacred to the religious, which brings about questions of morality and metaphysics—and with them subjection, politics of exclusion, and marginalization. The peasant community of Lucania is "outside History and the State," but not because these two institutions do not interfere with it. In fact, the continual intervention of History and the State, embodied in the book by the distant religious power of Rome and by its local administrator Don Luigino, *is* the problem. The exclusion of peasants from the "religious" power of History and the State represents for Levi a positive possibility, fertile ground on which to create autonomy and self-government.

Levi describes the nature of human relations within the peasant community as open, free, and tragic. He writes: "Here anything is possible, [. . .] and there is no definite boundary line between the world of human beings and that of animals or even monsters."[76] The peasantry's human relations are an implicit criticism, the alternative model to the sovereignty of modern nation-states. Levi adds that peasants are always historically defeated but never totally crushed. Unlike the religious power of the State, their community is a model based on inclusion, not on exclusion. Thereby, the largest social phenomenon of Southern Italy, the massive emigration directed especially to the USA, is not the only possibility for the economic emancipation of Southern peasants. It is instead an act of resistance to the State's sovereignty, an escape from its control. It is an erasure of its borders. The peasants' world is before and after the nation and the state; its existence is, by definition, transnational. In their criticism of Braudel's *The Mediterranean and the Mediterranean World in the Age of Philip II*, which in its conclusion quotes Levi's memoir in almost nostalgic tones, historians Peregrine Horden and Nicholas Purcell understood this all too well:

> On, as it were, the margins of his account, Levi includes precisely [. . .] the prime ingredients in the normal variability and connectivity of Mediterranean

microregions: fluctuating relations between pastoralism and agriculture; the manipulative state with its taxes and symbols; the mobility of people both voluntary and compulsory.[77]

If the peasantry *is* the model for anti-State resistance, redemption is required not for the peasants but for the Southern petite bourgeoisie. Levi's biting sarcasm and lack of piety toward Don Luigino and the other parasitical local "notabili" of Agliano and Grassano reveal how these representatives of a distant power, fiercely opposing any autonomy and full participation of the people in self-government, are the main obstacle to a real solution of the Southern question. If any redemption is wanted, it is for their social class, which Levi depicts as decaying both morally and physically, with strong expressionist strokes. In an article published in 1946 and explicitly titled "Don Luigino Won Over to Democracy," Levi addresses this problem as one of the principal issues for the renovation of the whole country: "The redemption of this middle class must not be left untried [. . .]. 'Don Luigino Won Over to Democracy' can truly be one point of a state program that sets out to resolve the southern question."[78]

Without a doubt, Levi's vision of Southern peasantry is often partial or reified, biased by *his own* utopian libertarianism. As Mario Alicata stresses in a famous article, "One ought to be wary of postulating the existence of a *unified* cultural world under the generic name 'cultural world' of the peasants or, worse, of southern 'peasant society.'"[79] As every work of memory, *Christ Stopped at Eboli* is a selection—conscious or not—of Levi's experiences in Lucania, influenced by previous and subsequent experiences in the life of its author. In fact, Levi never claimed any scientific objectivity for his book. Instead, he employed literature and poetry, not just as critical tools to air his disagreement, but for their intrinsic political charge to create "a new system of identification" through the art of writing, as Rancière suggested.[80]

Ultimately, Levi's indictment of Fascism via Lucania's peasants was a piercing critique of any established ideology of the State—and of History—to the detriment of individual freedom. Italian academic culture, particularly its Marxist vein, reduced Levi's work to a "poetic survey" of the South, isolating its anthropological components and systematically disavowing its wide-ranging connections to European culture. The *political* reasons for this rejection are clear: Levi's text unsettles the guiding principle of early postwar party politics—the restored continuity of the centralist state. The violent polemic against his persona—which at times includes anti-Semitic undercurrents—corresponds to the threat that the intellectual energy and poetic persuasiveness of his book posed to the new cultural and political establishment. In the days of the struggle to free Italy, Levi consciously wrote the only possible mythology of modern times, the one that he personally witnessed—that of Gagliano's peasantry and their Resistance to the religion of the State. This mythology is utterly at odds with the chronological, empty time of modernity and uncritical progress, the *bad* redemption that Levi would represent and thoroughly analyze through the symbol of the watch in his next book.

Not all people exist in the same Now: *The Watch*

In the preparatory papers of his last philosophical work, *On the Concept of History*, Walter Benjamin made a surprising remark on Marx and his idea of revolution: "Marx says that revolutions are the locomotive of world history. But perhaps it is quite otherwise. Perhaps revolutions are an attempt by the passengers on this train—namely, the human race—to activate the emergency brake."[81] In the 1940s, and until at least 1956, most European Marxist intellectuals—from Sartre to Lukács—would have downright dismissed Benjamin's comment as reactionary. This is why Benjamin's remark proves particularly poignant as I begin the last part of my investigation of a writer who went against the grain such as Carlo Levi. Benjamin's disavowal of progress is especially appropriate to introduce Levi's controversial novel *The Watch* (1950), which was considered the literary work that sanctioned the end of the transition from Fascism to democracy in Italy.

Benjamin's *On the Concept of History* was published in 1947 in the French journal *Les Temps Modernes*. While his preparatory papers were not public knowledge at that time, his critique of vulgar Marxism is relevant here for many reasons. Not only would Levi have endorsed it—as the disavowal of progress and historical dialectic deployed in *Christ Stopped at Eboli* attests. He would also have agreed with the primacy Benjamin gives the "passengers" over the "locomotive," stressing how humankind has agency over time and history. Agamben argued that while modern political philosophy concentrated on the elaboration of a concept of history, it also avoided working out a corresponding concept of time. Historical materialism, he concludes, is no exception:

> Because of this omission, it has been unwittingly compelled to have recourse to a concept of time dominant in Western culture for centuries, and so to harbour, side by side, a revolutionary concept of history and a traditional experience of time. The vulgar representation of time as a precise and homogenous *continuum* has thus diluted the Marxist concept of history: it has

become the hidden breach through which ideology has crept into the citadel of historical materialism.[82]

This aporia is at the center of Benjamin's preoccupations in *On the Concept of History*. Benjamin's theses thus elaborated a concept of "messianic" time—as outlined in the previous section—that resisted the empty, linear, teleological time of progress and capitalism, as well as of vulgar Marxism. Benjamin devises a time of possibilities, "open at any moment to the unforeseeable interruption of the new." As Löwy commented, "The 'messianic arrest' is a rupture in history, but not the end of history."[83] Revolutions, therefore, appear as the activation of an emergency brake, when the passengers halt the course of history and progress, and retrieve or create anew their own concept of temporality. Revolutions are not the end of history.

Starting with its title, the denial of empty, teleological time is at the center of Levi's *The Watch*. The novel opens with Levi's lyrical description of the night hovering over Rome. As a Vichian historical cycle, this identical atmosphere returns at the close of the book. What is usually considered a symbol of chronological time, exactitude, or modernity—namely, the watch—is physically lost in the book's first pages. The story begins with the symbolic, and then real, loss of the gold watch that Levi's father gave to him as he was dying. Levi accidentally damages the watch upon his arrival in Rome. Any attempt to repair the watch fails and he ultimately loses it forever while meandering through the city. Damage and loss, however, are preceded by the detailed account of a disquieting dream. In literature, dreams are much less ambiguous than in real life: In the dream that opens the book, Levi foresees the disappearance of his watch and faces a tribunal court of which Croce, "the Virgil of Naples: honor, light, lord and master, teacher of my contemporaries,"[84] is president. The court debates the ownership of the gold watch—that is missing in the dream—and Croce eventually assigns Levi ownership.

In the novel, the damaged and missing gold watch is quickly stripped of objective connotations to assume the protagonist's subjective reality, Levi's private history and personal time. Allegorically, the story of the gold watch has a correlative in the narrative itself, which features the loss of a linear, objective time. *The Watch* follows Levi's meanderings in the city, through eventful and seemingly insignificant encounters, digressions, and flashbacks. Time explodes in the novel in a myriad of misleading fragments as Levi's gold watch also breaks. Only at the end of the book, when Levi receives a similar watch from his Uncle Luca after his death—a new paternal figure, possibly more influential than Levi's natural father—does a new time begin for the protagonist. In the personal life of the character, a new cycle starts after the consequential death of the uncle-mentor.

The watch's symbolic meaning changes as the novel progresses, from personal to historical and back again. In medieval *quêtes*, the knight personifying a certain virtue leaves the castle in search of an adventure to prove his worth. Only through such an adventure, through the acquisition of a specific experience, does the knight *become* the specific virtue he already embodies.[85] Conversely, in Ludovico Ariosto's chivalric poem *Orlando Furioso*, knights and maids, kings and scoundrels, all risk their lives and those of others for the satisfaction of their personal instincts and desires—of which they are often not even aware. In *The Watch*, Levi explicitly alludes to the figures of Don Quixote and Sancho as references for the descriptions of his own characters.[86] Although Cervantes condensed the contradictions of Ariosto's numerous characters in the two protagonists of *Don Quixote*, the incredible number of encounters and appearances in Levi's narration recalls the *entrelacement* of chivalric romances. The richness of human relations is outstanding in *The Watch*, especially when we consider that the plot encompasses only three days in the life of its protagonist. Levi's novel is characterized by an inexhaustible openness to the other and a sense of marveling at the limitless possibilities of human life.

As *Orlando Furioso* criticizes medieval finalisms, Levi's novel denies not just *Bildungsroman* but modernism as a whole. Grand narratives are debunked, collective dreams of historic renewal fall apart, and still, the main character is able to achieve a full return to his origins. This palingenesis sparks the beginning of a new cycle in Levi's life through a close experience of death. The author illustrates a heterodox idea of temporality by juxtaposing seemingly irreconcilable elements: the time of politics and of people's everyday life in Milan, Rome, and Naples; the highly intellectual speculations among the editors of the newspaper Levi directs and his harrowing visit to the poorest neighborhood of Rome, Garbatella; the memory of the revolution in Florence where "everyone still lived in the stimulating atmosphere of the Resistance and one didn't believe there was a difference between politicians and ordinary people," and the intrigues of power in the Roman *palazzi*.[87]

Levi's unconventional temporality can best be described by what Ernst Bloch called "nonsynchronism" (*Ungleichzeitigkeit*). The German philosopher argued, "Not all people exist in the same Now. [. . .] Times older than the present continue to effect older strata [. . .] they do not emerge in a hidden way as previously but rather, they contradict the Now in a very peculiar way, awry, from the rear."[88] Although Bloch employed this concept to interpret the electoral success of Hitler in industrialized Germany, Levi's anarchic assemblage of different temporalities is a profound criticism of accepted social narratives, showcasing the inner contradictions of any overarching historical assessment and multiplying the voices in the political arena. In a key passage of the novel, Levi cries out: "What chance was there to resolve the crisis that was much more than a change of government, involving as it did events with no intercommunication, and times diverse and incomprehensible to one another?"[89] At a formal level, the nonsynchronism of time in *The Watch* and its paratactic development displaces the personal time of the protagonist from center stage, thus denying a typical feature of modernist novels. Levi privileges instead the expanded time of the individual-in-relation through conversations, encounters, and large social frescoes consistent with the new concept of individual "meeting place of relationships of every kind," as advocated in *Christ Stopped at Eboli*. Unlike literary Neorealism, Levi's novel defies any idea of art as a chronicle of reality.

Often quoted by historians but mostly avoided by literary critics, *The Watch* is also a political novel: It is Levi's idiosyncratic account of the downfall of the Parri government in 1945. The author interprets this demise as the definitive failure to create a new Italy based on the values of the Resistance, the spontaneous "Liberation Committees," and ultimately, the concepts of autonomy and socialist self-government that sustained Levi's political action. *The Watch* witnesses the restoration of the state in continuity with its past, and the grim close of an extraordinary season of hope for change launched by Liberation. The novel is both within and outside the bounds of my research, for its nostalgic retrospect of the political and existential experience prompted by Liberation is already haunted by the new season of the so-called particracy ("partitocrazia") in Italy. The beginning of a new cycle in Levi's life with the end of his political engagement that characterized the 1930s and the 1940s corresponds to a new cycle for the country after the end of the transition.

All these motives coalesce in the critique of any unifying temporality as a system of power and regulation of life. The conclusion of the Parri government, the personal confession of existential crisis and rebirth, the collective epic of the Italian people, and finally the allegorical *quête* for reestablishing "human" time through the acquisition of a new watch resist univocal assessments of time in religious and ideological narratives. Levi's discontent is not only based on the historical defeat of revolutionary against conservative forces in the country. The dazzling variety of postwar Italian life—able to reject the burden of the past—clashes with the political maneuvering of the party system, which inherited and preserved the liberal and Fascist state. *The Watch*'s comprehensive approach recalls *Fear of Freedom*, in which aesthetics, philosophy, religion, and history intertwine in a single discourse.

In this regard, from the very first page, *The Watch* is a novel of Rome, of the nonsynchronism of its multiple pasts coexisting in the present. It is the epic of Rome's vivid and picaresque people living *en plein air*. They resist the stagnant air of the Palazzo, in which fossilized politicians and bureaucrats, still living in an indefinite past temporality, regained control of the country after the brief experience of the Liberation. Yet Rome is not the novel's only center: The new temporalities born out of the war are represented in *The Watch* as a multitude of "homelands." As Levi himself clarifies in a 1947 article, "The city was no longer the *fatherland*, the immutable, divine land of the fathers, but something that was made and was changed day by day, unbound from history, detached from the father, adult and alone."[90] The novel features not only different, contrastive, nonsynchronous times but different places: Turin, Florence, Milan, and Naples.

Pursuing a new assessment of temporality, *The Watch* disavows old geographies. Levi portrays Florence and Milan, for example, through the extraordinary temporality of what Benjamin called *Jetztzeit*, the "Now-time" of the revolution, when people defeated Fascism and decided their own autonomy. The "Now-time" of Florence and Milan resists the old hierarchical structure of the polity that Rome's past(s) embodies, demanding the reconstruction of social and political relations on a federative basis. Moreover, the "Now-time" of Florence and Milan elicits a criticism of the temporality and human geography that Rome represented for past and present regimes: centralization, the empire, and the idea of *Romanità*.

In a column in the Roman newspaper *Il Tempo* published on August 30, 1943, during the first Badoglio government, Alberto Savinio wrote that only intelligence could

> warn against the bad advice of imitation, protect from the idiotic suggestions of poorly written, poorly read, and poorly interpreted history. It is only intelligence that can show the absurdity of a repetition of the war of Rome against Carthage (as of any other repetition). It is only intelligence that can show the "physical" impossibility of a reconstruction of the Roman Empire and the "cinematic" nonsense of a *Romanità* imitated in its external forms.[91]

The article, significantly titled "Defense of Intelligence," advocates for a return to critical thinking after the violent suppression of disagreement that Fascism established throughout its reign. Savinio's focus on the "disadvantages for life" of what Nietzsche would call "monumental history" is a definitive critique of the politics of history "in the age of its mechanical reproduction" that Mussolini's regime fostered. Savinio denounces "repetition" as dangerous in social and political interactions, as a sign of the persistence of a "Ptolemaic mindset" unable to understand the restless flowing of life. "Repetition" as a social and political practice is rejected for its nefarious effects on the present—especially when used to justify arbitrary political decisions.

The dangerous repetition of past models is a major theme in Levi's *The Watch*. The writer artfully depicts these detrimental aspects through a number of minor characters across social classes. From the petit bourgeois hosts of his apartment—a parasitical couple fancying themselves an artist and the unrecognized daughter of Spanish nobles—to the politicians and bureaucrats exhilarated by Parri's demise and eager for the return of the old order, the repetition of past models is the chronic disease spreading throughout the novel. Still, this "spiritual illness" is distinctively contagious in Rome, a city where, according to Northern partisans who flocked there after Liberation to continue their struggle, "the wine is insincere" and "words unstick from their content."[92]

The polemic against Rome and its parasitical role in the country is a long-lasting motif in modern Italy, at least since its unification. On an intellectual level, Rome has always been the principal target of the discourse on national renewal and the polemic regarding the defective national character—from the Risorgimento to Futurism and avant-garde Florentine culture before WWI, to Mussolini's early speeches before his ascent to power.[93] In this regard, Savinio's column is also a remarkable departure from this anti-Rome tradition. His criticism of political repetition of past models is on par with his dismissal of the ideologies of history that sustained liberal and Fascist Italy—from Mazzini's myth of the "Third Rome" to the concept of *Romanità* that was at the center of Fascist ideology.[94]

From the nationalist Enrico Corradini to Mussolini, *Romanità* rested on an idealized set of values that ancient Rome supposedly represented and that the new Italy would restore.[95] Positions on the topic vary conspicuously— Giovanni Papini's attack on the capital city during his Futurist tenure was colored with anarchic parochialism, whereas Giuseppe Bottai's claim that Rome was "simultaneously the target and the goal; it was the reviled city and the coveted city; it was the city against which one had to fight and the city for which one fought," is redolent with late-Romantic undertones.[96] As Emilio Gentile remarked, "The celebration of Rome was the great passion of the men of letters of the Third Italy." The Fascist myth of *Romanità* was therefore "modernistically interpreted as a myth of action for the future."[97]

Savinio affirms the inconsistency of this myth and the negative consequences of its persistence. In democratic Italy, national parties such as DC and PCI would reinterpret the myth of Rome for their own ends, overlaying pre-Fascist anti-Rome rhetoric with new missions of civilization.[98] With *The Watch*, Levi continues the controversy launched by Savinio in a new form. The perspective is no longer that of the skeptical cosmopolitan tradition embodied by Savinio in the wake of Voltaire, Stendhal, and Nietzsche. Since *Christ Stopped at Eboli*, the agents of the protest against Rome are the peasants: "The State, whatever form it might take, meant 'the fellows in Rome.' 'Everyone knows,' they said, 'that the fellows in Rome don't want us to live like human beings.'"[99] In *The Watch*, peasants are joined in their discontent by the humiliated partisans and their biting comments on the political turnover after the fall of the Parri government:

> This was, to be sure, the common opinion among all Italians [. . .]. Rome signified all the negative aspects of a world that was false and had failed [. . .]. All one's own ills and the ills of others were expressed in that name, and in hating it all men were brothers.[100]

Writing history from the point of view of the defeated is an ambitious and risky task, specifically when the voices of the subaltern are interpreted through the author's own language. *The Watch*, however, is not a historical but a fictional and subjective account of the eventful days of the demise of Parri's government, recounted as Levi *processed* them in his memory.

Levi shifts from focusing on the intellectual discourse against *Romanità* to popular discontent toward the capital as the center of a distant and unjust power. Like the peasantry in *Christ Stopped at Eboli*, the creative diversity of Rome's people *resists* the old temporality restored by party politics. With profound empathy, Levi opts for the portrayal of, as Nicola Carducci defined it, "the immediate sense of an extreme fullness of life," which characterizes the inhabitants of Rome in their everyday life, without indulging in neoromantic delusions. These lives are irreducible to normative ideas and univocal temporalities, such as the *Romanità* dreamed by Mussolini, which epitomized a monumental replication of the past. The simultaneous presence of different times, represented by Levi through the novel's variegated voices, refuses the exclusive control of temporality—and thus, of the myth of Rome—claimed by Fascism over Italian people. As Richard Bosworth claims: "Well before he fell on 25 July 1943 and was killed on 28 April 1945, Mussolini had lost control of the past, simultaneously surrendering his, his regime's and his ideology's present and future."[101] Yet Levi's critique of the monumental past's repetition is also at the base of his dismissal of Croce and postwar liberal politics based on the continuity of the state.

Far from replicating pre-Fascist clichés of Italy's capital, Levi complicates the frame of reference by displaying how different temporalities intermingle in the city's "life-in-relation." This vision defies the Fascist claim of exclusive control over the city's past, which ultimately translated to a hegemonic mastery of its present. The writer aims instead to debunk the myth of Rome and reveal how its stereotypes contributed to obscuring any clear evaluation. Levi concludes:

> it had nothing to do with Rome or no Rome, since it was in Rome that the battle must be fought. To free ourselves from old accumulated trash and parasitical habits we must not go back to municipal longings, but fight against the sovereignty of the state, of all states, work for European federation, and so forth.[102]

When writing *The Watch*, Levi's far-reaching project had already been surpassed by new political developments, which affirmed the continuity of the state through the new hegemony of Christian Democracy. However, the principles of the Action Party, although defeated during Italy's transition, still influenced the construction of a larger European federation. Fellow Actionist Altiero Spinelli's *Ventotene Manifesto* is one of the cornerstones of the current European Community.[103] In this context, Levi's *The Watch* stands out for its heterodox richness of voices and temporalities—a richness that Marxist critics hurriedly dismissed as *qualunquismo* ("political apathy") upon its publication.

Literary critic Carlo Muscetta, who figures in the book as the character Moneta, wrote a review of the book full of scorn and insight. His slating of the book discloses the radicalness of Levi's literary operation. The Marxist critic argues:

> This crowd of juxtaposed individuals, without history, this enormous social breakdown, artificially recreated in a picaresque paradise is, if you will, the legend of the Resistance as it dies in political apathy ("qualunquismo"). And it took an Actionist to write it. The dubious Muse allowed the author of *The Skin*, who attempted something similar, only to root around, rear end aloft, among the garbage of literary journalism.[104]

Muscetta points out the aspect of Levi's novel that was considered utterly unacceptable—and truly dangerous—to Communist ideology. Instead of an Italian society harmoniously following the laws of historical materialism on its path to emancipation, Levi portrays an Italy with no class consciousness, a country socially crumbled and defeated by its own "fear of freedom." There is no proletariat and no bourgeoisie in *The Watch*, or rather, proletarians and the bourgeois are present as single individuals, in their creativity and autonomy or in their hollow repetition of false models. They are not *representative of their own class*. Levi's controversial distinction between "Contadini" ("peasants") and "Luigini" (from Levi's own character Don Luigino, discussed above), probably the book's most famous passage, polemically targets historical materialism.

In the novel, after Parri's last press conference as Italy's Prime Minister, the character Levi takes a long walk with two old friends, Andrea and Carmine.[105] Together, they discuss the recent Action Party defeat. Andrea proposes an alternative history of Italy, taking a cue from Levi's *Christ Stopped at Eboli*: Italian history can be read as a struggle between the "Contadini" and the "Luigini," the only two "real" parties into which the country is divided. Andrea contends that the "Contadini" are not just peasants from the South or the North, but also blue-collar workers "educated in the creative rhythm of the factory" and "that small part of the bourgeoisie who are energetic and up-to-date, who still survive in our country" that can "build up a factory." "Contadini" are the "rich landowners [. . .] who know how to carry on reclamation projects and restore the abandoned and degenerated land." Together with artisans, physicians, scientists, and women, "all the people who make things, create them, love them and are content with them are Contadini." Andrea represents the anti-Fascist Leo Valiani, but in the novel, the character clearly voices the author's ideas, while the Levi character is portrayed as listening with curiosity. Andrea argues that the "Luigini" are instead

> the ones who submit and command, love and hate the hierarchy, and serve and reign. They're the bureaucratic mob, employees of the state and the banks, model clerks, the military, the magistrates, lawyers, the police, college graduates, errand boys, students and parasites [. . .]. Then there are the industrialists and businessman who keep going on the multimillions of the state, and also the workers who stand by them and the landowners and peasants of the same sort. All these are Luigini.[106]

This opposition is provocative, yet it rethinks society through open, flexible categories that do not demand any overarching finalism. Levi's polarity does not encompass any organic theory of politics or Italian history but is empirical enough to dismantle fossilized narratives. Far from being "political apathy," as Muscetta dismissed it, this reading of the present (and past) sociopolitical situation of the country places the individual and its agency at the center of what is held as *the* political. This understanding also takes into account how the main paradigms that inform politics can be mystified—leftist categories in particular. Levi's critique is not an irresponsible attack on politics, *per se*, but an accusation of the parasitical structures of power that grew *around* Italian politics, and that stripped words and ideas of their content. "The truth," Andrea concludes, "is that the formation of our party system is luiginal, the techniques of our party battles and the structure of our state are luiginal, so that if a peasant movement wants to survive, it must find a new form and organism of its own."[107]

The "enormous social breakdown" of "juxtaposed individuals, without history" signaled by Muscetta are unacceptable ideas for postwar Marxism. Yet they stubbornly question any account of the Resistance as a teleological history of self-consciousness and definitive emancipation. Different temporalities coexist in postwar Italy. Liberalism and orthodox Marxism proved unable to understand the possibilities of time, which Levi depicted in his novel and in which he firmly believed.[108] The consequences of this understanding are also relevant in the formal, compositional aspects of the novel. In one of the many heated debates between two of the novel's characters, Casorin and Moneta—the first representing the writer Manlio Cancogni and the latter, as anticipated, Muscetta himself—Levi attempts a reappraisal of storytelling by showcasing how any narrative (the novelistic in particular) is unable to encompass the totality of the real. Through the words of Casorin, Levi dismantles any argument for socialist realism in literature and implicitly introduces a critical category that would have a significant impact on subsequent literary and social studies—historical, and therefore personal, trauma. Casorin argues:

> The individual is there; there are the masses, but there are no human relationships. Take any man, alone and barren, and divide him into different plots, make an object of him, complicate him by events, close him up in a first and an afterward, and then tell his story if you can. You still don't get out of the abstract. What sort of novel do you want after Auschwitz and Buchenwald?[109]

Of course, Levi is not advocating here for "traumatic realism."[110] He is instead stressing the discontinuous, qualitative, nonlinear regimes of time that traumatic events bring about. What happened in the Nazi camps are "black holes" in history that changed Western civilization's self-perception, including the humanistic tradition at its basis. Prior to Theodor Adorno's reflections on Auschwitz, which would appear in 1951, Levi anticipates the enormous impact of the Holocaust in all fields of human life.[111] Levi unveils the delusional aspects of teleological narratives, which ultimately reduce the limitless richness of any individual and their traumatic history to "one colored tile of a mosaic that has been designed in advance, one function in an abstract game."[112]

With his article, Muscetta probably intended to respond to the many challenging points raised in *The Watch* that involved him personally. In his review, he signaled the novel's affinity with another recently published controversial book, *The Skin*—a literary judgment that was meant to disparage Levi's work as a whole. Muscetta indicates the "enormous social breakdown" as one of the weaknesses of *The Watch*, one that reveals an unpredictable correspondence with Malaparte's *The Skin*, published the previous year. Both novels, through the different personalities of their respective authors, established counterarguments to the narratives of national redemption. They also challenged the "legend of the Resistance," as Muscetta put it, which developed in those very years. Although Levi and Malaparte showcased the fallacies of this legend from antithetical political perspectives, they both questioned its frame of reference and gave voice to the people excluded from its narrative, concentrating on the politically unspeakable that only literature could voice.

The relationship between Levi and Malaparte began in 1932 with an article in which the anti-Fascist Levi firmly attacked "Fascism's most formidable writer," as their mutual friend Gobetti called Malaparte.[113] An echo of this hostility and the reputation Malaparte held in leftist circles can be found in a letter from Giulio Einaudi to Levi before the publication of *The Watch*: "This book should be launched as the anti-Malaparte; that is, it constitutes the antivenom for readers of *The Skin* (without explicitly stating as much, as Curzio doesn't deserve such an honor)."[114] Indeed, the two novels speak to each other from opposite political sides. They both display a profound, if distinct, impatience toward the cultural and ideological involution that followed the end of the transition with the political victory of the Christian Democrats in April of 1948.

On opposite sides of the political spectrum, Levi and Malaparte enjoyed the spectacular success of their books in the 1940s, and both endured the hostility of the Italian cultural establishment. In fact, the polemical charge of their writing, together with the cosmopolitan reach of their experiences, alienated a cultural establishment that—after the proliferation of voices between 1943 and 1948—crystallized around an ideological debate in which both authors could not find a comfortable footing. Their respective postwar cinematic projects follow similar lines. Films such as Malaparte's *The Forbidden Christ* or Duilio Colletti's *The Earth Cries Out* (1948), for which Levi co-wrote the screenplay and which recounts the exasperating question of Jewish refugees in Southern Italy after the war, feature a keen attention to national issues that were at the time silenced.[115] These films tell the inconvenient stories of Italian POWs' homecomings and of European Jews who survived the Holocaust only to find themselves with no place to return to after the war. Like their authors, these tragic stories could not find a stable place or a real solution within the redemptive paradigms offered by the national parties that occupied the post-transition political debate. In a certain sense, what Actionist and then Socialist senator Manlio Rossi-Doria—who was the inspiration for the character Carmine in *The Watch*—wrote more than forty years after the publication of Levi's novel is also relevant for other protagonists of my book:

> There is no doubt, in fact, that the chorus of negative reviews or pitiless pans with which *The Watch* was received did not spring from artistic or literary considerations, but rather from the inconvenience, irritation, and intolerability of the message contained in the book [. . .]. I am also perplexed when I think about the relative, even if illusory, ease with which Carlo Levi accepted the work's failure, and I wonder if this wasn't perceived as an act of closure or almost, I would dare to say, of liberation from the most intense and impassioned period of his life.[116]

5   Curzio Malaparte, a Tragic Modernity

Testimony to a World in Decomposition

Curzio Malaparte's conspicuous and obtrusive *persona* has often obscured his literary talent. His major works, the novels *Kaputt* and *The Skin*, bracket the post-Fascist transition and its debate. Malaparte's two books, in which he artfully interlaces firsthand experience with fictional accounts, constitute a ruthless inquiry into the collapse of European civilization. In his WWII novels, Malaparte defies ideological and ethical normativity by polemically assuming *the role of the witness*, thus testifying the end of an era in which he tried to play the part of a protagonist with varying degrees of success. In *Kaputt* and *The Skin*, Malaparte inscribes his own experiences into the whirlwind of twentieth-century history and the Italian experience into a broader framework. His prose captures the Zeitgeist of the transition through its representation of a tragic reality that resists any redemptive interpretation.

Milan Kundera hinted at this interpretation in his collection of critical essays titled *Encounter*, in which he celebrates *The Skin* as a landmark in the history of the novel: "The new Europe as emerged from WWII is caught by *The Skin* in complete authenticity, that is to say, caught by a gaze that has not yet been revised (or censored) by later considerations and that therefore shows it gleaming with the newness of its instant birth."[1] The Czech author paves the way for understanding the *historical* significance of Malaparte's work by placing it in the postwar European transition. Building on his conclusion, I will further argue that *Kaputt* and *The Skin* signal the tremendous epistemological shift that occurred in the West during the first half of the twentieth century and culminated with WWII. The two books disavow early postwar assessments of history by openly acknowledging that technological warfare has supplanted humanistic values. They also portray how creaturely life—in the sense described in the first chapter—dramatically withstands any totalitarian attempts to correct human existence through politics.[2]

Malaparte's novels interpret the collapse of the Italian nation during WWII as an instance of the majestic downfall of European civilization. They tackle two seemingly opposite sides of the same story: *Kaputt* narrates the events of Nazi-occupied Europe, whereas *The Skin* follows the Allied liberation of the peninsula. With ambivalent complacency, Malaparte raises in both books questions of violence, historical agency, and the national defeat's legacy that postwar Italian society and politics would have rather left unaddressed or conveniently forgotten. Systematically minimized in his home country, Malaparte's uncompromising depiction of human abjection and resilience during WWII had a considerable impact on both sides of the Atlantic, leaving a transnational legacy still today only partially explored.[3]

In postwar Italy, progressive intellectuals preferred to consider Malaparte the defective by-product of a successful, long-standing but ambiguously disparaged national tradition of *literati*,[4] in which "the exemplariness of the biography is of much greater interest than the meaning of the works," as Stefano Jossa described it.[5] More recent critics dismissed his output as a voyeuristic and unruly spectacularization of the war's horrors.[6] Others judged his writing as nothing more than a manic attempt to swallow up historical reality for the sake of his unrestrained narcissism.[7] His novels have also been lambasted for allegedly equating the different moral positions of perpetrators and victims.[8] Malaparte's books are judged in light of his political opportunism. One of his contemporaries, Giancarlo Vigorelli, has instead observed: "If he was an opportunist, he knew how to be, like few others, untimely [. . .]. He may have got up to all sorts of things, but he almost always paid for it personally, losing out more than once."[9] In more recent studies, such as Maurizio Serra's *Malaparte: Lives and Legends* (2012), and *Cahier Malaparte* (2018), edited by Maria Pia de Paulis, the focus on the moral judgment of his persona has given way to a more complex—and compelling—reappraisal of his work.[10] His postwar skepticism of narratives of national regeneration was indeed deeply rooted in his perception of the historical failure of Europe.

"My generation's error," Malaparte writes in 1952 near the end of his intellectual career, "had been to believe in men, in the possibility of men's redemption."[11] In his WWII novels, the author unveils modernity's delusions with two complex motifs: the Christological allegory of sacrifice, and the perception of the break between human imagination and technological progress in terms of potential destructiveness. Both of these distinguishing themes highlight what Serra described as the main preoccupation of Malaparte's post-Fascist narrative: "to once again accuse historical belonging of assassinating natural belonging."[12]

To this end, Malaparte's formal investigation is equally outstanding. He explores both traditional *and* modernist vocabularies of violence, scapegoating, and sacrifice but profoundly transforms them to expose the unredeemable quality of modern historical delusions: from the myth of palingenetic war to Fascist, as well as Communist, attempts to "correct" life with ideology.[13] In the same vein, Malaparte's approach to literature contrasts with another modern attempt to ideologically "correct" human existence—aestheticism, in which art substitutes ideology as the redemption of history and life.

In his study *The Culture of Redemption*, Leo Bersani illustrates the pitfalls of such an ideology of art, which underscores "the limitless bad faith of a society that looks to art for its salvation."[14] This conception was nevertheless widespread in Crocean or late-romantic aesthetics, by then prevalent among Italian critics. By privileging art over life, or collapsing the two, as in Gabriele d'Annunzio's kitsch commodification of his own "inimitable living," neo-idealist and Dannunzian aesthetics redeem life—and politics—through art.[15] Despite d'Annunzio's influence in his writing, Malaparte refuses this aesthetic when he declares: "It's from decadent poetry, luxurious poetry, that fascisms are born. Hitler from the aestheticizing decadent poetry of Stefan George. Mussolini from the decadence of d'Annunzio's poetry. Petain from the *merde parfumée* of Barrès."[16] Such a conclusion, written in the early 1950s, attests to the author's assiduous, first-person confrontation with the main historical and artistic events of the century. Malaparte's distaste for aestheticism and monumental history, however, is not a consequence of the national defeat, for it dates back to his early literary successes.[17]

In the 1920s, Malaparte was a fervent advocate of the Fascist revolution. Although his unorthodox views repeatedly caused him problems within the party's hierarchy, his books and political commentaries brought him impressive public recognition—and literary fame well beyond Italy. *Viva Caporetto!* (1921) and *Technique du coup d'état* (1931) feature heretical counternarratives of WWI and the Russian Revolution, respectively. The two texts intertwine firsthand testimony and fictive accounts of momentous speeches and dialogues, such as the one between Lenin and Trotsky before the revolutionary takeover of Saint Petersburg. In a 1932 review of *Technique du coup d'état*, Leone Ginzburg underscored Malaparte's penchant for "arranging historical facts according to the convenience of his own ideological demonstrations."[18] In fact, his narrative style betrays the influence of classical sources, for which history was the foremost *literary* genre. Malaparte, however, scornfully rejects the antiquarian and monumental history that was widespread in Fascist Italy and had a long tradition since the Risorgimento. His dismissal of historical rhetoric in *Technique du coup d'état* is consistent with his disavowal of decadent aesthetics:

> Since the beginning of the Nineteenth Century Europe has been used to judging men and events in Italy as the products of a very ancient philosophy and style of life. To a great extent the history of modern Italy is interpreted in this manner by reason of the natural disposition of the Italians towards rhetoric, towards an eloquent and literary manner of expression.[19]

Malaparte's impatience with the limits of Fascist cultural politics—while it does not imply a political disagreement with the regime and its Duce—develops alongside his increasingly international interests of the late 1930s. As the regime waned, Malaparte's cosmopolitan interests took center stage. His modernist journal *Prospettive*, in which he published translations of Éluard, García Lorca, Joyce, and Heidegger, is a telling example and has only recently attracted the attention of scholars.[20] In the first chapter, we analyzed how Malaparte fleshed out in *Prospettive* noteworthy ideas concerning the autonomy of his own writing from politics. It is in this context that Malaparte elaborates his concept of "the cruelty of literature," which characterized his literary reflections of the late 1930s and would sustain his WWII novels.

As Kundera has pointed out, with *Kaputt* and *The Skin*, Malaparte invented "a form that is totally a new thing and that belongs to him alone."[21] In the two books, Malaparte paints an astonishing fresco of the failure of European civilization, the world to which he completely adhered, enthusiastically participated in, and eventually dismissed. Unlike many of his "fellow travelers," intellectuals, and artists who experienced the tumultuous first half of the century, Malaparte met the downfall of his Europe after WWII with a creative, almost excited response. The melancholy found in certain pages of *Kaputt* is more a gesture of reemploying Proust as a "ready-made" than a nostalgic homage to a lost civilization and to its most elegant voice.

When asked in 1947 to describe Italy "after the flood" of WWII, Massimo Bontempelli—who in the early 1920s launched the modernist journal *"900"* with Malaparte—had no choice but to cast a melancholic gaze toward the past: "It seems, today, that with 1914 an entire world ended. We believed, with true faith, that we were preserving its seed in more than one experiment between the wars. But those were solitary illusions [. . .]. By July 1914, the world of pure interests was already over."[22] Bontempelli concludes—rather unconvincingly—in a patriotic tone: "The worst disaster, for men and for countries, is the one that most brings shame; and Italy is today among all nations the one with the least to be ashamed of." Malaparte's response to the war's devastating experience was quite the opposite. In "Story of a

Manuscript," which introduces *Kaputt*, he explains: "*Kaputt* is a cruel book. Its cruelty is the most extraordinary spectacle that I have witnessed in the debacle of Europe in the war years."[23] According to the author, the German word "kaputt" is the real protagonist of the novel, as it adequately conveys "the sense of what we are, of what Europe is—a pile of rubble. But I prefer this *Kaputt* Europe to the Europe of yesterday—and of twenty or thirty years ago. I prefer starting anew, rather than accepting everything as if it were an immutable heritage."[24]

Kaputt's poetics expand on Malaparte's reflections on war and modern literature at the center of his 1942 essay, "Exquisite Corpses." As mentioned in the first chapter, with his "untroubled recognition of literature's cruelty," Malaparte acknowledges that before catastrophes of meaning, history, and ideologies, the task of the modern writer is to *bear witness*.[25] In this passage from his comprehensive biography, Serra paves the way for a nuanced understanding of Malaparte's writing vis-à-vis the war and its atrocities:

> His refusal to denounce and to be indignant led some to accuse the author of indifference, if not docility. But that would, in fact, be asking him to be a different man than he was; or worse, it means overlooking his behavior, which consists in getting mired in the war, calmly splashing around in it, experiencing it far and wide, but *without* waging it and *without* taking a position on it, because he wants only to recount it. Why weigh down this catalogue of infamies with rhetorical hymns to virtue? His task is to make us share that hallucinatory atmosphere, communicating to the reader the tactile, auditory, olfactory, sensory, but *never* sensuous impression of a world in decomposition.[26]

In the aftermath of the war, Malaparte never fully confronted his past as a former ideologue of Fascism, most likely dissatisfied with the new values of postwar Europe.[27] Nevertheless, his adherence to *witnessed* reality is what makes his writing stand out from other accounts of the period, even when this reality is consciously deformed in a (post-)surrealist gesture.[28]

In the early postwar period, in the wake of the vast success of Sartre in France and Gramsci's theories regarding the organic intellectual, Malaparte's statement about art's autonomy from politics seemed like a provocation. The cruelty of his literature allowed ample margin for fictionalization and exhibited close connections to pioneering artistic movements in Europe, from German *Neue Sachlichkeit* to French Surrealism.[29] Malaparte's testimony to this time of catastrophe represented an alternative to the realist poetics prescribed in Marxist circles.

Malaparte's declared autonomy has critical implications for his presentation of the total war. The piercing questions he raises in *Kaputt* and *The Skin* challenge narratives interpreting Europe's derangement as part of higher plan—from Croce to vulgar Marxism. His profound skepticism is based on the personal shock he experienced on the war's many fronts and his direct observations of the different totalitarianisms involved in the struggle. Malaparte defies attempts to rectify the recent past through selective memory, exploring with his writing the new ethical questions posed by totalitarianism and war. The protagonist of Malaparte's play *Du côté de chez Proust* (1948) summarizes the author's intentions when he explains that: "La question me hante de savoir pourquoi et comment les sociétés pourrissent. [. . .] Car c'est là la clé de l'énigme. C'est là tout le sens de mon oeuvre d'écrivain."[30]

At times, Malaparte overindulges in the aesthetic quality of his findings or in his self-representation as the reluctant witness of war atrocities. His self-fashioning as a witness was not pursued innocently, as it conveniently leaves out his past commitment to Fascism. Despite many unresolved aporias, Malaparte's testimonial fiction uniquely explores the disastrous encounter between modern industrialization and biopolitical power in Nazi warfare and genocidal policies throughout occupied Europe. The author also addresses the issue of Allied responsibility in the war, questioning the use of violence on civilian targets. After *Kaputt*'s gloomy depiction of Nazi-occupied Europe, *The Skin* is one of the few examples in European literature which narrates the Allied bombings of Axis civilians. Malaparte portrays the Allies' employment of technological power against civilian targets in tones that defy military or political justifications.

Reviewers such as Giovanni Spadolini and Guy Tosi promptly recognized the testimonial function of Malaparte's narrative.[31] Still, his ambivalent use of fiction and testimony requires in-depth clarification. In the last decades, the literary debate on testimony reached its apex after the publication of Giorgio Agamben's influential book *Remnants of Auschwitz: The Archive and the Witness* (1998).[32] The fundamental question of Agamben's study is how the figure of the *Muselmann* resists normative approaches to biopolitical inquiry. In Auschwitz, the prisoners referred to other inmates who had lost the capacity to react to external stimuli and were reduced to mere biological survival as *Muselmänner*. In their eyes, the *Muselmänner* had to be avoided, as they were destined to certain death. Primo Levi famously describes them as the "non-men who march and labor in silence, the divine spark dead within them, already too empty to truly suffer."[33] According to Agamben, the *Muselmann* embodies an unprecedented ontological possibility, attesting to the "regression" that human life experienced in Nazi camps. Building on Holocaust testimonial literature, Agamben institutes a no-man's-land between life and death, in which language fails to be meaningfully articulated. He calls this zone "testimony," significantly setting forth the possibility of a new theory of literature or of discourse. Shifting the framework from a discourse of ontology to one of rhetorical strategies actuated within juridical discourse, Jacques Derrida notes instead that testimony has with fiction "a common source": "If the testimonial is by law irreducible to the fictional, there is no testimony that does not structurally imply in itself the possibility of fiction, simulacra, dissimulation, lie, perjury—that is to say, the possibility of literature." Considering testimony first of all as "an act," Derrida focuses on its iterability: It is in the space created by this iterability "where literature insinuates."[34]

Among Malaparte's early commentators, the critic Tosi insightfully hinted at this direction in his review of the 1946 French translation of *Kaputt*: "Malaparte appartient à cette race d'écrivains, qu'on n'imagine que debout, pour qui la littérature n'est pas un exercice bureaucratique mais un témoignage. Un témoignage—et non seulement un document."[35] Tosi not only elevates testimony to the rank of art *for* its fictiveness, but he also explains how the subjective agency of testimony is its distinctive aesthetic quality. As Serra suggested, Malaparte aims to present the sensorial experience of "a world in decomposition" before our very eyes.

Malaparte's testimonial fiction starkly contrasts with the Neorealist poetics of the chronicle. According to Lucia Re, the prescriptive realism of this poetics compelled writers "to eliminate any alteration that may have deformed the event in the excited memory of the witness."[36] Malaparte is well aware of the inherent contradiction of these aesthetics, as were other authors of the same period, such as Italo Calvino, despite their radically different agendas.[37] Calvino's Resistance novel *The Path to the Spiders' Nests* (1947) is closer to picaresque storytelling or to Ippolito Nievo's *Confessions of an Italian*—a nineteenth-century classic—than to socialist realism. As Furio Jesi writes in his critique of prescriptive social realism, "Among literary documents there is no autobiography that is exclusively moral or exclusively mythical. The simultaneous presence of temptation and vision determines a reciprocal conditioning of the acts that are based on one or the other."[38]

For Malaparte, testing the reader's limits by showcasing the fictiveness of his testimony might have seemed like a much more viable solution than camouflaging a clear political agenda with a supposed regained innocence. His literary solution was artistically productive, personally advantageous, and far from ingenuous. His past adherence to Fascism was thus not at the center of his books, yet it was present throughout his narrative as a contextual circumstance.[39]

Malaparte reiterated his aesthetic principles in his subsequent novel, *The Skin*, with the much-quoted episode of the couscous lunch with French officers in the Ciociaria region, right before Rome's liberation. During the meal, one officer mocks Malaparte, echoing the harsh criticism the writer received from many French intellectual circles:

> "I should like to know," said Pierre Lyautey, turning to me with an urbanely ironical air, "how much truth there is in all that you relate in *Kaputt*."
>
> "It's of no importance," said Jack, "whether what Malaparte relates is true or false. That isn't the question. The question is whether or not his work is art."
>
> "I would not wish to be discourteous to Malaparte, for he is my guest," said General Guillaume. "But I think that in *Kaputt* he is pulling his readers' legs."[40]

In the novel, Malaparte's reply illustrates his aesthetic beliefs—made plain in this quotation by the character Jack. The ensuing lengthy and bombastic digression, which ends with a macabre joke, has the primary goal of fooling his detractors. On a metatextual level, however, Malaparte openly exposes his readers to the fictionality of his writing, demanding complicity and applause. As in classic rhetoric, the *enargheia* (literally, "vividness in presentation") of his storytelling recreates reality before the very eyes of the listeners, who are entrapped in Malaparte's illusory net of words. It is then up to the reader to approve of Malaparte's verbal artistry and therefore accept the role of accomplice to his fictions, as done simply by reading his book.

By exposing his craft and calling for the reader's complicity, Malaparte aims to relieve his writing—and himself—of any ethical responsibility. By dissolving any distinction between testimony and fiction and representing the two as a *performance*, Malaparte avoids the ethical paradox Derrida signals as a productive possibility and a warning for testimonial discourse. "Literature," writes Derrida, "insinuates here" for the constituent iterability of testimony—for its performativity. The step from the modernist utopia of the autonomy of art and literature to propaganda art and the aestheticization of politics is short—a step Malaparte knew all too well. His anarchic gesture is a continuation, not a rupture, with Fascist politics and aesthetics. It also hints at the controversial nexus between revolution and the cult of force, both conspicuously present in modernist aesthetics.

However, despite, or rather *because* of, the many contradictions his writing embodies, Malaparte's refusal of all available postwar redemptive narratives stands out even more distinctly among WWII literature. He resorts to a kind of narrative—the testimonial—in which the only coherence of the scattered stories and narrated facts is given by the presence of the voice saying: "I was there." *Kaputt* is the perfect example of this type of narrative in which the true protagonist, as the author claims, is not a character or a historical fact but the multifarious meaning of a word: *kaputt*.

Creaturely Life and Technological Warfare: *Kaputt*

Malaparte crafts his novel *Kaputt* around a series of conversations he participated in while working as a correspondent in WWII's main theaters. During these occasions, he encounters the war's protagonists and their respective entourages: from the Nazi *Generalgoverneur* of Poland Hans Frank to the Fascist Minister of Foreign Affairs Galeazzo Ciano, from the young Jewish girls forced to prostitute themselves in a brothel for German officials in Ukraine to the animated discussions in Finland with European ambassadors. *Kaputt*'s skillfully embroidered structure allows Malaparte to wander all over Nazi-occupied Europe and accompany the reader to see the atrocities, as well as to spot the contradictions, weaknesses, and arrogance of the winners of today—who the author knows will be the losers of tomorrow. The structure of the book is paratactic: Malaparte accords equal dignity to the stories of Swedish aristocrats and Ukrainian peasants. His principal message—the collapse of European civilization—emerges as a sum of its multiple stories and innumerable voices. *Kaputt* is a multi-centered novel, yet its narrative unity is provided by the testimonial persona, Malaparte himself.

As Primo Levi, the most articulate witness of modern European literature, understood all too well, testimonial literature is anti-modernist.[41] Testimonial literature stands in opposition to avant-garde action. It is not a break with a preceding tradition but a quest to recuperate genealogical *predecessors* to provide authority and rhetorical evidence to the new, unheard-of narrative.[42] It is "archaeological" research in the sense given by Michel Foucault: a disclosure of the archive. In *Kaputt*, Malaparte faces the downfall and scattering of the European "common home" that he contributed to dismantling with his Fascist revolutionary pretensions. His archaeological research is oriented toward the defining moments, the archetypes (*Urbilder*) of Western culture. In fact, only these archetypes can fully account for the denouement of modern Europe's most consequential myth since the French Revolution—the myth of palingenetic war, which the Nazi turned into a kitsch spectacle of total destruction.[43]

Under the aerial bombings of Belgrade, in the Romanian pogrom of Iași, the Warsaw ghetto, and the Finnish tundra, Malaparte's narrative avoids any metaphysical escapism by focusing on the technological and biopolitical aspects of war and totalitarian power. In doing so, he anticipates what will be the great paradigmatic change of the postwar era. Attention will shift from the figure of the soldier, as occurred in the aftermath of WWI, to that of the victim. The victim is considered first in its corporeality, in its creaturely life, in its existence as a suffering animal. Most of the victims of *Kaputt* are animals: horses, mice, dogs, birds, reindeer, and flies. The novel's sections are indeed named after them, yet animals are more than just emblems of the human condition in Nazi-occupied Europe. For Malaparte, they are subjects of history on their own. The frozen horses on Lake Ladoga, the dogs exterminated by the Nazis in Ukraine, or the salmon engaged in an unequal fight with an armed German official in Finland are all the agents of stories expressing human aberration and *hybris*. The Nazi assault on humanity is first and foremost a crime against nature.

There is a sense of blasphemy in these episodes, like the rupture of an arcane covenant that is nevertheless inherent to all living beings. Nazi crimes against nature violently clash with the "religious" recognition of life's sacredness, the communal belonging of all beings to life. Effaced by Nazi crimes, this sacredness is immanent in biological life for Malaparte. Furthermore, he names this original understanding of life "Christian," privileging the creaturely aspects of the Christian message over the theological-political weight of its historical institutions. When the author recounts his dream of a crucified horse in Golgotha to the Swedish Prince Eugenio in the first part of the book, it is not the artfully crafted comments of the noble host which stand out, but the horse's post-surrealist image. Developing some of the possible interpretations of this image, Malaparte associates "the sacrifice of the Horse-Christ" with the ideological denial and political annihilation of bare life wrought by Europe on its own body politic. Remarkably, the author concludes: "All that is noble, gentle and pure in Europe is dying. The horse is our homeland."[44]

Kaputt is replete with appalling images in which totalitarian power attempts to suppress bare life and reduce humanity to its political and ideological existence. Yet, in his disconcerting fresco of WWII, Malaparte neither condemns technology as the ultimate reason for humanity's fall from grace nor indulges in supernatural or ideological escapism. In his war correspondence from the Eastern Front, his admiration for the military and technological power of the German and Soviet armies remains unaffected. In his private diary, he enthusiastically comments on the spectacle of aerial bombings on the Gulf of Salerno with an ambivalent "bellissimo."[45] However, unlike Marinetti or Jünger, his appreciation for modern technological warfare is never detached from a profound awareness of the fragility of the human condition, as experienced firsthand by soldiers on the battlefield. Many descriptions of the Nazi and the Red armies colliding on the Eastern Front betray Malaparte's excitement for modern warfare's technological power. Nevertheless, in his WWII novels, this excitement for technology, typical of Fascist modernism, yields to unusual attention to the bodies of the dead—men and animals alike.

With *Kaputt*, Malaparte describes what philosopher Günther Anders would, a few years later, call "Promethean shame" (*prometheische Scham*) in his tormented inquiry into modernity. According to Anders, the second industrial revolution determines the historical separation between what man can imagine and what technology can produce. The divorce between representation (*Vorstellung*) and production (*Herstellung*) is total, and the two terms become more and more irreconcilable. Promethean shame is therefore the humiliation humans feel when facing the perfection and power of their own technological creations. The increasing distance between representation and production entails a devastating ethical consequence: human incapacity to think and comprehend the destructive power of technological achievements in its totality. Anders concludes his analysis by asserting that technology has become the first subject of history, hence the "obsolescence of man," which is also the title of his major work.[46]

In his *Secret Journal*, written during the war years, Malaparte meditates: "The intermediary between us and God, between man and God, is the animal."[47] If the divorce between representation and production is at the core of the collapse of values in European civilization since WWI, the effects of this rift will not be clear when studied solely on human bodies. Human bodies are already affected by this breakdown, for they are both agent and target of this unintelligible destructive capacity. The separation can be read (and portrayed) only on the bodies that testify to the *before* of this catastrophe and are still untouched by it—animal bodies.

The suicide of Europe is thus consequential to the biopolitical utopia of sacrificing the constitutive animality present in human beings. According to Malaparte, this animal side is the residual common ground of our existence. Disposing of this animal constituency is tantamount to rejecting our humanity and its most basic sense of belonging. In *The Skin*, Malaparte further develops this argument, finding in human skin a powerful symbol of this biological, pre-political affinity. This same theme is also the core motif behind his film *The Forbidden Christ*, in which the modern tragedy is represented by the impossible encounter between Christian eschatology and unredeemable human history. In the film, this theme finds a haunting visual double in the horrifying display of butchered animals.[48] Malaparte's further intuition is that in the post-humanistic world where technology is the subject of history, no ethical discourse can exclude creaturely life from consideration.

Nowhere in *Kaputt* does the divorce between imagination and the destructive capacity of technology become more apparent than in the description of aerial bombings.[49] Malaparte expounds this separation in "The Haywire Rifle," the concluding chapter of the section "The Dogs." The writer chronicles the bombing of Belgrade in 1941 when German armies invaded Yugoslavia. The bombing is told from the point of view of Spin, the Italian ambassador Mameli's dog, which is unable to cope with this destructive power coming from the sky. Spin reacts by utterly refusing this new world, characterized as a sudden break with the past. The dog's subsequent withdrawal from the world could almost be described as a Freudian melancholy.

Malaparte recounts the dog's reaction to the aerial bombing thus: "The world had collapsed; something dreadful, something supernatural might have happened; Spin couldn't figure out. [. . .] No human or natural law existed anymore. The world had collapsed."[50] Poignantly, the opposition here is not between nature and civilization. Spin is a hunter dog and Malaparte describes how Spin loves the sound of his master's rifle when hunting. Spin considers the rifle's roar the perfect completion of his own world, in which the dog is on the side of the powerful hunter, free to run in the woods after the prey.

With the story of Spin, Malaparte introduces a pathetic element into the shocking description of Belgrade's destruction, referring also to the ferocious plunder and violence that followed the aerial bombing. Similar to other episodes in the novel, the story echoes and corrects a previous piece written during the war for *Corriere della Sera*. On April 27, 1941, Malaparte published an article titled "The Hour That Sealed the Fate of Belgrade," the last of a series of columns narrating the Nazi takeover of the Serbian capital. In line with official propaganda, the original piece is aimed at showcasing the technological perfection of the German war machine, in contrast with the racial disorder of the Balkan city, a confusion finally terminated by the Axis intervention. Even on that occasion, the story of "Spino, the dog that was afraid" vitalizes the narration.[51]

It is no coincidence that the dog, which becomes a protagonist in *Kaputt*, has his name changed from the Italian "Spino" to the anglicized Spin. First, placing the dog in the foreground allows Malaparte to stress the effects of technological warfare on the natural landscape, criticizing the apparent message of his own propaganda piece. Second, Malaparte significantly veers from his *Corriere della Sera* article, describing Spin as "a good English dog, purebred, Arian in the best sense of the word: In his veins ran not even a drop of colored blood; he was a good English dog raised in the best kennel in Sussex."[52]

Malaparte's biting irony is twofold here. With this portrayal of Spin, he dismisses warfare as the noble prerogative of the elites, a conception that was the basis of nationalist propaganda across Europe and of colonial rule beyond the European continent. For the "educated" British dog, "gunshots were a part of nature, a traditional element of the world, of its world. Without gunshots, what would life be?" However, faced with the massive killing capacity of aerial bombing, "pure breed" and assumed racial primacy do not count for much. Additionally, the piece is a subtle polemic against the assumed moral superiority of the liberators, a remark that the writer will further articulate in *The Skin*. In fact, Malaparte is also alluding to the catastrophic experience of Italians in 1944, the daily devastation caused by unremitting Allied bombing. It is the so-called strategy of the "wings of democracy," which annihilated Axis forces and crushed their populations.

In a recent study, historian Leonardo Paggi described Allied aerial campaigns as openly terroristic, making clear that after the infamous September 8, 1943, armistice, "the aerial offensive, far from stopping, will become increasingly intense and widespread, no longer attributable, in the same way as with the Nazi massacres, to a rational calculus of means and ends."[53] The destruction produced by aerial bombings has been addressed for the German case by W. G. Sebald's well-known essay, *On the Natural History of Destruction*. In the piece, the author lamented the lack of a *Luftkriegsliteratur* in postwar German culture, that is, a literature narrating the material and moral ruins caused by aerial warfare. According to Sebald, literature failed to recount such a crucial experience, thus excluding its memory from the German reshaping of public identity after Nazism. He portrayed this absence as a case in which German literature renounced its supposed critical role in the national public sphere:

> There was a tacit agreement, equally binding on everyone, that the true story of the material and moral ruin in which the country found itself was not to be described [. . .]. The darkest aspects of the final act of destruction, as experienced by the great majority of the German population, remained a kind of taboo like a shameful family secret, a secret that perhaps could not even be privately acknowledged.[54]

Sebald's argument applies to the Italian case, but with a crucial difference. As Paggi points out, in postwar Italy the problem was not the lack of a shared memory of the aerial bombings but a historically accurate memory: "The bombardments, notwithstanding the extremely high price in terms of human lives that they entailed, will be rigorously expunged from the republican memory, which is defined entirely around Nazi-Fascist violence."[55] Together with other examples of Allied violence in Italy, such as the mass rapes in Southern Lazio by the French Army led by General Guillaume,[56] the destruction of Italian cities and the ensuing wreckage are either silenced or associated with Nazi violence, whose coterminous devastation of the country and retaliation against the Italian population escalated in the last years of the conflict. As Paggi observes, the "wings of democracy" policy deliberately ignored the values that anti-Fascism set at the core of its political agenda, marking the end of Europe's central position in the world.

"I prefer starting anew, rather than accepting everything as if it were an immutable heritage," Malaparte writes in *Kaputt*'s introduction.[57] The book assumes the end of Europe's centrality as a given, as a historical fact. Nevertheless, the story of Spin represents a relevant example of the *Luftkriegsliteratur* that Sebald lamented as lacking in German culture after WWII. Aerial bombings are, instead, a constant presence in postwar Italian literature and cinema. In my second chapter, I examined Berto's *The Sky Is Red* and Piovene's *Pity against Pity*, two novels that use the bombings of Italian cities as the background for their plots. The cultural production on this theme is considerable, and Allied bombings surface in Resistance novels such as Beppe Fenoglio's *Johnny the Partisan*.[58]

In *The Skin*, aerial bombings recur continuously in the many stories told by the Neapolitans about the devastation of their city. Malaparte, however, develops the groundbreaking theme of the massive violence provoked by the "wings of democracy" well beyond national borders. The annihilation of German cities found an iconic representation in Roberto Rossellini's *Germany, Year Zero* (1948). In *The Skin*'s chapter "The Rose of Flesh," Malaparte provides a detailed and horrifying description of the effects of white phosphorus bombing on the population of Hamburg, with explicit references to Dante's *Inferno*.[59]

Dogs intervene in the hell of Hamburg to rescue their owners whose skin is burnt after the white phosphorus bombing. In the economy of Malaparte's fiction, animals are a metonymy for what is purest in mankind. In his secular view, they explicitly embody Christian sacrifice. In *Kaputt*, animals do not only provide the emblematic titles of each section; they vividly participate in the narrative as victims and heroes, scapegoats and martyrs. Indeed, the novel epitomizes the baroque liturgy of Christ's passion, repeated in each of its sections in the guise of a specific emblematic animal figure. Animals acquire a Christological function and share their destiny with the human victims of the biopolitical war.

Kaputt introduces the fundamental characteristics of a theme—Christological sacrifice in a world without redemption—that would find full articulation in *The Skin*. Still, Malaparte provides a remarkable conclusion in the earlier novel for an unsettling topic that will haunt his later writings: the issue of political theology embodied by the modern State. Modernist myths of the new man and of revolutionary politics, both on the Fascist and Communist sides, are debunked by the war. In *Kaputt*, however, political theology survives the collapse of European civilization, as the chapter "Summer Night" expounds.

In the isolation of the Finnish summer, in which the sun never sets and sheds its pale light over timeless evenings leading to no night, Malaparte recounts meetings and discussions of European diplomats gathered not far away from besieged Leningrad. Through the spectral northern lights, the suspended atmosphere of these conversations appears more a disquieting parody of Thomas Mann's *The Magic Mountain* than the fine rituals of European cosmopolitan society. After an exchange about the wonders of Turkish tapestry, the discussion shifts to the relation between modern politics and God:

> "But this is horrible!" exclaimed Countess Mannerheim. "How can anyone conceive of the idea of killing God?"
>
> "The entire modern world is trying to kill God," said Agah Aksel. "God's very existence is in peril in the modern consciousness [. . .]. The murder of God is in the air; it is an element of modern civilization."
>
> "The modern state," said Costantinide, "deludes itself into thinking that it can protect God's life simply with police measures."
>
> "It's not only God's life. The modern state deludes itself that it can protect its own existence," said de Foxà. "Take Spain as an example. The only way to turn out Franco is to kill God, and the attempts on God's life in the streets of Madrid and Barcelona are too numerous to count."[60]

The passage displays how illusory the conflict between politics and theology is. The existence and the security of the State intertwines with that of God after the main concepts of theology have been appropriated by the new secular religions of politics—and of the State. Through the words of his friend de Foxà, Malaparte pits Kafka against Carl Schmitt. Again, after the secularization of religious concepts, the State lives on as the depository of sovereign power. The State is no longer the expression of the common will of the people—if it ever was—but survives as a mere sign of its power, totally devoid of any meaning. The State lives on as a fully opaque signifier, expressing nothing but itself. Through the cynical words of the ambassadors of two Fascist states, Costantinide and de Foxà, the ideals of social and cultural reorganization that originally fostered Fascism are on the brink of collapse. The new religion of the State transforms these ideals into clericalism and blind violence. For the new totalitarian order, politics and religion are a matter of police and assassination.

Christological Figures of Sacrifice: *The Skin*

As Hannah Arendt insightfully argued, "The problem of evil will be the fundamental question of postwar intellectual life in Europe—as death became the fundamental question after the last war."[61] In Malaparte's writing, nothing redeems evil. Although the question occupies many of his pages, he never addresses the problem of evil *per se*, as an ontological category. Rather, in his books, he describes figures of victimization and sacrifice that elaborate the profound continuity of creaturely life, which Benjamin has described as pertaining not to ideology but to "natural history."[62] In *The Skin*, this "natural" continuity unreservedly questions what Malaparte calls modern "Cartesian reason," which, for him, is utterly inadequate to confront recent traumatic history and thereby understand the problem of evil as newly posed by WWII.

Against so-called Cartesian reason, Malaparte turns to Christological allegory, although in a radically immanent perspective. By projecting Christ's story of suffering and ultimate scapegoating onto the many victims of WWII, he points to creaturely life as the decisive correspondence among the many figures of sacrifice crowding his narrative. Malaparte's Christological figures are devoid of any metaphysical underpinning; the evil and suffering inflicted on their flesh are not redeemed by any superior design or ideological rationale. Their unwieldy presence and torn bodies withstand consoling interpretations—especially vulgar Marxist and liberal readings of recent history as one of emancipation and progress—and testify to the many unresolved questions haunting Europe after its downfall.

An incisive entry from Malaparte's *Secret Journal* during his stay in Finland may help illuminate this point:

The thought of death does not trouble me, even in these days so "close to death." I surprised myself, the other night, thinking that maybe I don't have a sense of death. That's the reason, maybe, for my estrangement from faith, my anarchic religiosity. De Foxà says that he has never met a man who is more religious than me. Yes, but anarchic. Who knows how all this will resolve. And who knows how it will resolve in artistic terms. Because that's where everything, in the end, is clarified and resolved. Certainly, Febo [*Malaparte's dog*] helped me a great deal to develop my religious sense. The intermediary between us and God, between man and God, is the animal.[63]

The dog Febo in *The Skin* is an explicit Christological representation, consistent with the seminal position animals hold in *Kaputt*, where the spectral dead bodies of the "Horse-Christ" appeared to the author's eyes as "our homeland."[64] Febo was Malaparte's favorite dog, which died before the war. In *The Skin*, the author invents a fictitious yet atrocious death for his dog: Febo is used as a guinea pig for a scientific experiment, his stomach surgically opened and his vocal cords cut so he can no longer make any noise.

The position of this story in the economy of the book—right after the recollection of his disturbing nightmare featuring Eastern European Jews (*Ostjuden*) crucified in Romania and before the agony of the American soldier dismembered by a land mine—points to the universality of suffering and the creaturely continuity among these heterogeneous figures, for which death is nothing but a relief. Furthermore, Febo and the American soldier are associated through the similar disquieting details of their final moments. Their atrocious deaths have the features of blasphemy. Their end also challenges natural causality and human imagination alike, as it is provoked by the peculiar "technological" cruelty of modern man and modern war. Nothing redeems the suffering of these Christological figures, connected by violent death. Through their sacrifice, Malaparte retrieved the tragic understanding of history that he would put forward once again in his movie, *The Forbidden Christ*, by placing an unredeemable conflict at the center of his modern representation.[65] His search for the tragic in modern history is in polemical dialogue with contemporary realist and Neorealist accounts, which narrate individual death in the larger scheme of a collective redemption.

In his classic study *The Death of Tragedy*, George Steiner traces the decline of the tragic genre—after the seminal works of Greco-Roman culture and its Early Modern revival—back to the aporias of the Romantics, who sought to combine the classical tragic sense of life and history with the Christian master narrative of redemption. According to Steiner, "Rousseauism close[d] the doors of hell" and laid the foundation for a positive anthropology, which relegated the responsibility for all evil to society. The result was, at best, the "sublime melodrama" of Goethe or the "apotheosis of redemption" of Wagner.[66]

After witnessing the tragedy of Europe, Malaparte interpreted Christian eschatology and technological modernity as inherently incompatible. His dismissal of the well-established tradition of the "romantic tragedy" echoes in his special treatment of Christological figurations. After the analogy of "Christ-Horse-Homeland" in *Kaputt*, in which creaturely life contrasts with the ruptures of history and ideology, this correspondence finds a new haven in *The Skin*, which Malaparte dedicates to the controversial spectacle of Italy's (and Europe's) abasement during the Allied occupation. His insistence on the spectacle of European degradation is a criticism leveled at any redemptive reading of Italy's recent past.

As I have detailed in the Introduction, every major early postwar reading of the fall of Fascism, whether Christian or secular, featured eschatological pretenses. For Croce, the "parenthesis" of Fascism stands out as a temporary break in the historical progress of the Italian nation. The "Secondo Risorgimento" rhetoric turns the moral legacy of the Risorgimento into a call for collective action and sacrifice. For Communists, the Nazi-Fascist defeat confirmed the Marxist interpretation of history, the revolutionary triumph of the Soviet "new man" and the beginning of a new era.[67] Each of these narratives distinctively projected post-Fascist Italy onto a *historical* background of national regeneration—a collective redemption from the shameful subjugation to Mussolini's regime and the suffering of the war years.

Against this ideological background, *The Skin* looked totally untimely. The novel is a visionary, baroque, self-indulgent, and highly sophisticated narrative of the new wave of moral corruption, a new plague depicted in an almost Boccaccian style, which followed the liberation of Italy. In *The Skin*, Malaparte narrates Europe's encounter with its own "other"—an *internal* other—and its many dissonant voices.[68] The author introduces this consequential encounter from the perspective of unaware outsiders—that is, of young American officials who landed in Naples, biased from their readings of Greek and Roman classics, and confident they would free European civilization from Hitler's tyranny. Malaparte portrays the dismay of the young officials when they discover instead "the other Europe," which rejects all their expectations. The Europe before their eyes is "a mysterious country, where men and the circumstances that make up their lives seemed to be governed not by reason and conscience, but by obscure subterranean forces."[69]

The contrast between the American gaze, full of expectations, and the sordid reality they discover in Naples inflates the contradiction that the author believes lies at the core of European identity. Malaparte stresses how the war violently uncovered the many aporias that ideas of progress inevitably contain. He emphasizes the numerous fallacies of "Cartesian reason" and its inadequacy to make sense of European history and its recent tragic developments. Ultimately, *The Skin* details the Enlightenment's failure to tame life and its polyphonic yet vital baroque spectacle.[70]

The overlapping of different languages and layers of reality and the juxtaposition of contrasting Europes that somehow coexisted side by side for centuries are all distinguishing features of this novel. Most commentators, however, were too concerned with the moral problems brought about by Malaparte's graphic representations to approach the novel from the position suggested by its author in the first epigraph: "If conquerors respect the temple and the gods of the conquered, they shall be saved."[71] This quotation is taken from Aeschylus's *Agamemnon*, the first tragedy of the *Oresteia* trilogy. Its solemn, religious tone is disrupted by the ironic juxtaposition of another quotation by Paul Valéry: "Ce qui m'intéresse n'est pas toujours ce qui m'importe."[72] Aeschylus's *Oresteia* cycle is a meditation on the theme of justice, from the primordial law of vengeance to the institution of civil courts able to administer justice on equal terms and, thenceforth, avoid long chains of crimes. Salvation is possible—Malaparte seems to admit—but only for the Allies, if they can overcome their differences and cease the ideological struggles that reduced Europe to rubble. Only if they can acknowledge the inherent continuity of this heterogeneous, complex, contradictory Europe, from the Champs-Elysées in Paris to the slums of Naples, from the ancient nobility of the West to the peasants of Ukraine and Russia, from Latin pastoral poetry to Hitler.

The author recognizes how national divides and ideological conflicts crushed European civilization by insisting on a total restructuring of the old society through the violent annihilation and scapegoating of its internal other—the South, the Slavs, the Jews. In the subsequent pages of *The Skin*, Malaparte addresses this fundamental issue directly. Naples is the "Levantine city" par excellence; its depiction echoes the hallucinatory portrait of Belgrade after the Nazi aerial bombings of 1941, as described in Malaparte's war reportage for the *Corriere della Sera*.[73] In his words, Naples is the mysterious—if alluring and titillating—image of this *other* Europe, its "naked ghost," alien to "Cartesian reason."[74]

Such a portrayal of Naples outraged the early postwar intelligentsia, even beyond the boundaries of Italy. For the first time, the city is represented neither as the triumph of the picturesque nor as the miserable locus of the *malavita* ("organized crime") that epitomizes the Southern question.

Malaparte does not reduce Naples to the sick limb of the nation, or of Europe, which can be cured and redeemed only through Northern paternalistic intervention. For the writer, its maladies are not dissimilar to the chronic diseases that plague Eastern European cities, as portrayed in *Kaputt*.

To fully understand *The Skin*'s novelty, one must go back to the long-standing cultural tradition of the Italian *literato*, which started with Dante but took on special relevance during and after the Risorgimento.[75] For such a tradition, which merges together classical references and Christian martyrdom, the exemplary biography of the man of letters is more significant than his own work. This obsessive rewriting of Dante's *Inferno*, with the personal trajectory from perdition to redemption, from darkness to light, finds its nemesis in the twentieth century with the works of the best Italian writers, from Pasolini to Primo Levi.

Conversely, *The Skin* questions the possibility of Christian redemption until its very last line. In the novel, Malaparte begins his voyage through a modern *Inferno* by casting his persona in the unconventional and tragic role of Virgil, the truly tragic figure of the *Divine Comedy*. Virgil is, indeed, condemned to never seeing the light of redemption, although he arguably has not sinned. At the end of *The Skin*, Malaparte accepts Virgil's destiny, which he alleges is also the destiny of European civilization. As in Aeschylus's tragedy, salvation is possible only for the winners, but only if they respect the gods of the vanquished.[76]

The true Dante of *The Skin* is instead Jack Hamilton, the American officer whom Malaparte guides during the war of liberation from Naples to Northern Italy. For the reader, the main anchor of the story is, of course, Malaparte, but *The Skin* is also the *Bildungsroman* of Jack, from his initial innocence where Europe is but "the banlieue of Paris" to the understanding of Naples as the mysterious image of "the *other* Europe." *The Skin*'s ultimate rationale is Jack's understanding—and Malaparte's contention—that "Hitler too belongs to that *other* Europe which Cartesian logic cannot penetrate."[77]

In postwar Italy, no message could be more polemical than claiming that Hitler (and Fascism) were deeply rooted in European civilization. No *Sonderweg* for the Germans and no "Hyksos invasion" in Italy, as Croce emphatically called the Fascist *ventennio*.[78] No redemption is really possible for the winners either, if only on the personal level of conscience. That strange Dante embodied by Jack, who arrived in hell without having sinned, dies on the battlefield in the final pages of the book only a few days before the war's end. Only after Jack's death is it possible to interpret the most ambiguous passage of the text, the initial dedication looming large over the entire book. In the original Italian edition, *The Skin* features the meaningful subtitle "storia e racconto" ("history and story") and is dedicated to the memory of a dead American official:

> In affectionate memory of Colonel Henry H. Cumming, of the University of Virginia, and of all the brave, good and honorable American soldiers who were my comrades-in-arms from 1943 to 1945, and who died in vain in the cause of European freedom.[79]

Here, italics are in the original. Jack Hamilton is the name Malaparte used in his novel for his friend Henry Cummings. The message is now clear, and it is not a judgment on the American military intervention in Italy and Europe. Malaparte addressed it to the vanquished: Between testimony and fiction ("history *and* story," he writes), his book argues that the winners of the war did not achieve their ultimate goal—restoring European freedom. Regardless of the liberation from Hitler and Mussolini, the author contends that Europe did not regain any substantial freedom, which would probably coincide with its lost innocence. Malaparte insists that Allied military intervention did not bring about any professed moral regeneration, as old maladies—such as factionalism, clericalism, and conservatism—still persist.[80]

Despite its huge success upon publication, *The Skin* received mixed reviews. A young Giovanni Spadolini—later Italy's Prime Minister—emphasized in *Il messaggero* that the book's focus on national defeat was truly unique in postwar Italy.[81] In *La gazzetta del popolo*, Lorenzo Gigli added: "Ultimately, *The Skin* is the thrilling account of a moral defeat [. . .]. It is not the novelized history of the defeat and degradation of a conquered people, but the story of a generation that bears all the responsibility for its past."[82] These positive appraisals were nonetheless exceptions. The general critical response can be summed up with the *stroncatura* ("slating") of the novel by the authoritative *literato* Emilio Cecchi: "[Malaparte], God forgive him, has done one of those things that really aren't done. Better silence and hypocrisy, then, than these dubious feats."[83]

While Gigli praised *The Skin* for revealing the moral disaster of the generation that wielded power, in his review he nevertheless regretted that Malaparte did not trace the responsibilities of this European abasement and its tragic consequences back to its origin—Fascism's revolt against human reason, tolerance, and freedom.[84] Malaparte always avoided taking moral responsibility for his writing, a contradiction he would never fully come to terms with. Gigli, however, stresses approvingly that *The Skin* opened a real Pandora's box in working through the war trauma in Italy. If anything, Gigli bemoans the fact that the novel did not take a more radical stand. Cecchi, instead, laments exactly the opposite. He criticizes the book by arguing for a full silencing of the past: "Unfortunately," he concludes, "we don't stand with Dalì or de Sade; we stand with Manzoni."

In opposition to *The Skin*, Cecchi advocates for the moral monumentality of the Italian literary tradition, epitomized by the rectitude of the author of *The Betrothed*. This hypocritical stance is the postwar revisitation of what Leo Bersani called "the culture of redemption": "Art redeems the catastrophe of history. To play this role, art must preserve what might be called a moral monumentality."[85] Bersani then concludes his analysis of such a strictly ideological conception of art, which is historically grounded in European modernism despite its classicist undertones, with a piercing argument: "Claims for the high morality of art may conceal a deep horror of life. And yet nothing perhaps is more frivolous than that horror, since it carries within it the conviction that, because of the achievements of culture, the disasters of history somehow do not matter."[86]

Since his 1940 article titled "Exquisite Corpses," Malaparte claimed that the moral quality of his writing lay in its "cruelty."[87] Yet his impassive depiction of the horrors of the war and their legacy betrays an uncompromising passion for life. This love for life is evident in the creaturely dimension of his recurrent Christological figures of sacrifice. Their suffering is universal, calling for compassion that is beyond any ideological or national divide. It is also beyond human boundaries, for in Malaparte animals are often depicted as—and named—the truly new Christ.

European Jews, too, figure as the new Christ, since they have been reduced by Nazi power to the creaturely residual that the new order bans. In *Kaputt*, the section "Mice" recounts the atrocities committed by the Nazis on the European Jews—the Warsaw ghetto, the Romanian pogroms, the Wehrmacht's mass executions of Ukrainian Jews, and the cattle trains en route to the concentration camps. In *The Skin*, however, a hallucinatory dream further illuminates Malaparte's understanding. Although the scene echoes the dream of the crucified horse in *Kaputt*, the crucifixion now involves Eastern European Jews ousted from the West not only through Nazi genocidal politics but also the European self-reflective gaze and politics of exclusion. Here, animals and *Ostjuden* are Christological figures, the scapegoats Europe needs to reaffirm itself while seeking to eliminate its own *other*. In prose redolent of surrealist and magical realist experiences, Malaparte represents animals and *Ostjuden* as historical victims and allegories of the surgery that Nazi-controlled Europe sought to carry out on its own body to remove the creaturely, pre-political, and pre-ideological parts of its nature.

In traditional Christian ethics, Christ is the historical *and* superhistorical, human *and* superhuman, medium between man and God. In Malaparte's approach, however, transcendence is not even considered. When he employs animals as allegories of Christ in his narrative and explicitly names them the "new Christ," their violated bodies testify to a compelling paradox, a tragic conflict that is at the heart of all his later artistic elaboration. In Malaparte's figurations, animals and WWII victims senselessly repeat the passion of Christ without any possibility of religious resurrection or ideological redemption. Stripped of superhistorical resolutions, their deaths are interpreted in a radically immanent prospective. Their individual suffering and ultimate death defy the collective or national sublimations provided by the redemptive readings of national history, from Croce to the "Secondo Risorgimento" trope.[88]

Historical contingency notwithstanding, Malaparte's "anarchic religiosity" argues for a correspondence between animals and Christ as a means to God. Consequently, he casts Christ and God in a radically secular light, where the latter is demoted to a pure sign without any attribute, not unlike Kafka's tales or the stories told by European ambassadors in *Kaputt*. In Malaparte's works, Christ is reduced to his human, if not merely animal, component. His figure resists any transcendent design, as he epitomizes not redemption but creaturely life. Christ's victimization and sacrifice are recuperated as the exemplary and universal narrative of the human condition and its frailty—primarily vis-à-vis the terroristic behavior of biopolitical power.

Still, Malaparte's Christological narrative is devoid of any aspect of faith in superhistorical justice.[89] For the author, the radical significance of Christ's sacrifice resides not in its revelation of a higher order, and even less in the metaphysical challenge that faith can constitute. Christ's sacrifice instead announces humankind's communal belonging that withstands what Arendt called "the totalitarian attempt to make man superfluous."[90] In this sense, the aforementioned analogy of "Christ-Horse-Homeland," which was pivotal in *Kaputt*, testifies against the political and technological excesses of the modern man. In the same vein, toward the end of his later novel, Malaparte concludes, "Our true country is our own skin."[91]

Malaparte's appeal to animals as Christological figures is a confirmation of his "anarchic" religious understanding of life, which requires neither institutions nor orthodoxy. Rather than subverting or emptying the original meaning associated with Christ, Malaparte carries out a deconstruction of his figure to strip it of any metaphysical—and, therefore, superhistorical—significance. The goal here is to recover the immanent religious sense of life that Malaparte thought was the basis of European civilization, as opposed to its totalitarian aberrations—a radical secularism that went hand in hand with his own attempt to highlight the tragic understanding of history. His indictment of Nazism finds evidence not only in its reckless use of violence; on a creaturely level, it signals the incompatibility of Nazi biopolitics with the ethical foundation of the state of nature, of which the animal and Malaparte's interpretation of the figure of Christ are prime examples.

Malaparte undertakes the removal of the divine by superimposing Christ and the animal. This superimposition is first a criticism of Nazi political theology. Deeply controversial, this subversive strategy was, however, rhetorically effective, though few people in Italy took it seriously when Malaparte published his works. As exemplified by Cecchi's review, the cultural establishment preferred to overlook Malaparte's radical and piercing arguments, concentrating instead on the vanity of an intellectual deeply compromised by his personal involvement in Mussolini's regime and unable to come to terms with his Fascist past. Still, Malaparte's foremost achievement lies in the double recovery of a tragic understanding of history together with the universality of the Christological message. He deploys both motifs on a secular basis as incompatible strands in conflict with one another. The conflict between the two remains unresolved, devoid as they are of any progress or any dialectically superior solution. Malaparte's rejection of the "romantic tragedy" is the primary reason he was ostracized by the postwar Italian cultural establishment.

Malaparte's Christological figures underscore the tragic fallacy behind the totalitarian secularization of religious concepts. However, *The Skin* also foregrounds how Fascism and Communism appropriated and developed the practices of the Italian Catholic Church in original ways. A passage in the novel brings to light this disturbing correspondence by focusing on the ideological struggle of the early postwar. In *The Skin*'s chapter "The Rose of Flesh," Malaparte has an animated exchange with a younger man about Marxism and Russian literature. He disparages the lack of self- and historical criticism exhibited by these young men and women born into the European middle and upper classes—a generation that, according to Malaparte, embraces Communism as if it were the latest fashion:

> One of the youths said that all Italian writers except those who were Communists were traitors and cowards. I replied that the one real merit of young Communist writers, and of young Fascist writers, was that they were children of their time, that they accepted the responsibilities of their age and environment in that they were rotten like everyone else. "That's not true!" cried the youth venomously, gazing into my face with a wrathful and menacing

expression. "Faith in Communism is a safeguard against all corruption: it is, if anything, an expiation." I replied that you might as well go to Mass. "What?" cried a young working man wearing the blue dungarees of a mechanic. "You may as well go to Mass," I repeated.[92]

Malaparte artfully disperses the responsibility of his utterances through the conflicting voices of a dialogue. In this heated exchange, he underscores the gloomy atmosphere that characterizes postwar Europe's intellectual life: If modern politics appropriated and secularized religious concepts, postwar Europe trivialized these same concepts—atonement and redemption included. The author bases the whole chapter on the idea that reality is now disguised in blasphemous ways. Transvestites and religious rituals take center stage in the unfolding of the story. According to Malaparte, the blue-collar coverall worn by his young antagonist is but a costume: His Communist faith is insincere and has no relation to his sociopolitical background. The young man will allegedly leave his new faith soon, oscillating between novel intellectual fashions as the gender roles are reversed in the carnivalesque ending of the chapter.

It is not difficult to see a reactionary defensive strategy in Malaparte's criticism. Years later, when Moravia claimed that Malaparte "was the representative of the Fascist illusion," adding that his former friend "was caught off guard by the modern world," he voiced a judgment shared by the Italian intellectual elite.[93] Moravia's conclusion is not without reason: The blatant homophobia in *The Skin*'s chapter "The Rose of Flesh" epitomizes this reactionary defensive strategy, featuring an idea of virility that the war displaced once and for all.[94] Malaparte is well aware that some of his battles, particularly on the question of masculinity, are fought at the rearguard of postwar culture. In his narrative, there is no conversation, no dialogical struggle—regardless of how passionate—in which his own character is totally involved in the struggle. The role of the witness he crafted for himself allows for this distance from his own narration, as will be fully disclosed in the subsequent chapter of *The Skin*, "The Son of Adam." Malaparte's agenda motivating this narrative and dialogic *tour de force* is not to reaffirm his own integrity but to underscore the bad faith of an entire intellectual class that eagerly collaborated with the totalitarian regime, only to profess noninvolvement and a progressive mindset once Fascism fell apart. His stress on the younger generation only adds evidence to such an indictment.

In his postwar works, Malaparte portrays Italy, Europe, and the entirety of Western civilization as a "rotten mother." *Mamma Marcia* is indeed the title of an unfinished book published posthumously (1959, but written in

1950–1952), haunted by ghosts, misunderstandings of the past, and the disavowal of the present. Incomplete and inorganically articulated, *Mamma Marcia* testifies to the anxieties of Malaparte's last season and his ambiguous engagement with the new global stage upon which Europe plays only a secondary role. This book tells of another story and another era, in which the transition in Italy is over and Malaparte, with his usual restlessness, directs his gaze outside Europe to Mao's China or the dictatorial regimes of South America, which are, in his view, the real heirs of Fascism.[95] In his final years, Malaparte shifted his focus beyond Europe, aware that the political question he raised with his WWII novels—the legacy of the political theology established by Mussolini's regime—remained unaddressed in Italian post-Fascist and post-transition culture.

Conclusion: Tearing Down the Monuments

> I would like for the Americans to be always about to arrive, and then never, ever arrive.
>
> —Mario Soldati, *Escape in Italy*

This book has sought to uncover the rich and complex intellectual networks that defined the post-Fascist transition in Italy. My inquiry encompasses a diverse range of voices and publications, which include celebrated books, neglected yet remarkable texts, and ambitious literary projects that were never completed—a sign of the uncertain circumstances intellectuals faced in those years. Among them, Alberto Savinio's *New Encyclopedia* stands out. In an entry of this odd volume, which the author claims to have written only "for personal use," Savinio provides a thought-provoking definition of history. The entry is titled "Deliberations":

> The first book of Herodotus's histories is dedicated as is proper to Clio, which in Greek is written *kleio* and means "I close." The name of the sternest of the nine muses reveals the true function of history, which is to gradually "close" our actions in the past, with the purpose of lifting their weight from our shoulders and making us rediscover every morning a new spirit, in the absence of a new world.[1]

Savinio was an enthusiastic lover of etymologies, which he regarded as evidence of the impossibility of replicating the past.[2] Profoundly influenced by another keen lover of etymologies like Nietzsche and his considerations on history, Savinio expresses here many of the concerns that characterized the heterogeneous intellectual production of Italian writers I have analyzed in my study.

Chief among them was the anxiety to discard the Fascist past to allow for moral and cultural renewal. Despite Mussolini's boasting, the regime utterly failed to achieve the promised national regeneration.³ In addition to Fascism, twentieth-century Italian history is filled with political calls for moral palingenesis: The generation of the Resistance fought for principles that went beyond mere political redemption from Mussolini's wrongdoings.⁴ For certain former believers in the Fascist palingenesis of the nation, especially the younger generation, the Resistance assigned new meaning to the revolutionary ideals that informed their failed credo. Enzo Forcella described this process as "the dialectical template of Error-Bewilderment-Redemption." This also explains the passage of many former Fascists to Communist ranks or the construction of an institutionalized memory based on the 1943–1945 war, obliterating the preceding *ventennio*.

Authors such as Carlo Levi, Alberto Moravia, Vitaliano Brancati, and Curzio Malaparte radically disagreed with this reading of recent history. For these authors, moving beyond the national past meant first disavowing European civilization as the univocal model, tradition, and *Weltanschauung*. We can also extend this conclusion to Elsa Morante's provocative claim that with *Lies and Sorcery*, she wanted to write *the last novel*. The novelistic tradition she was alluding to is indeed profoundly associated with the bourgeois Europe that perished once and for all with WWII. Far from a parenthesis of national history, Fascism, its violence, its politics of exclusion, and its false myths were integral parts of the larger development of European self-consciousness.

Recognizing this does not excuse Italy's responsibility in twentieth-century European imperialism and WWII. It is rather a full acknowledgment that the many modern claims for Italy's civilizing mission based on its past glories were rooted, as Savinio would say, in *bad readings of history*.⁵ Although the Risorgimento's moral message was not lost on the early postwar period, its tradition came to a complete close with the September 8, 1943, armistice and the ensuing disrepute of the Italian state. The *Jetztzeit*, the "Now-time" of liberated Florence, portrayed by Carlo Levi in *The Watch*, is the main counterargument to the conspicuous self-delusions that characterized the nation-state, of which Mussolini's dictatorship was the historical actualization. With his melancholic gaze, Brancati mourns the best parts of this self-delusion, aware that the other side of the coin is Fascism's vulgarity. In this regard, the naivete of Giuseppe Berto's characters evidences the intellectual courage of their author. Berto shows in his novels how Italians were tragically unprepared for the imperial "destiny" Mussolini assigned to them. Inspired by the ruins of past civilizations, such destiny was inscribed in history books but less so in the socioeconomic reality of Italy. The scene in *The Skin* in which Malaparte plays the role of a tour guide on Via Appia for the American Army entering Rome is probably the best parody of Fascism ever written.[6] It is also a bitter insight into the future of Italy—and of Europe.

Second, the critical distancing from the past advocated for by Savinio underscores a profound *intellectual weariness* for old and new historicisms, which were completely dismissed by recent events. Fascination with the myth of America, for instance, was a large part of the success of writers such as Vittorini and Pavese, both before and after the war. In many respects, America's allure affects even Carlo Levi's prose as he recounts the mixed fortunes of Southern emigrants.[7] This fascination was not simply a reaction to Fascist autarchy but the recognition that Europe—in addition to Italy—had begun to question its own mythology and was profoundly dissatisfied with its own civilization. Here again, the disillusioned Fascist Malaparte and the anti-Fascist Carlo Levi represent a fundamental polarity. From opposite sides of the political spectrum, both sought to debunk the narratives of redemption based on rhetorical concepts of life and politics, ultimately challenging the foundations of European civilization. In his tragic representations of the contrast between technological warfare and creaturely life, Malaparte introduces concerns that Fascist and anti-Fascist culture only superficially envisaged.[8] Postwar intellectual debate has thoroughly assessed the crucial role biopolitics plays in totalitarian experiments—in all modern political experiments. The representation of the biopolitical contrast between life and ideology is the main legacy of Malaparte's WWII novels.

Fascist and anti-Fascist institutional cultures were based on opposing readings of the humanistic tradition. The first blatantly distorted this tradition and advocated for the supremacy of Italian—and Western—civilization on historical grounds. This reading is nevertheless consistent with certain premises of the humanistic tradition itself, from which guiding concepts of Fascist ideology such as race, political exclusion, patriarchal power, hierarchy, and the centrality of the state were taken. Merging heterodox traditions and drawing especially from Jewish Libertarianism, Carlo Levi identified the *antibodies* of Fascism in the subaltern voices that were traditionally excluded from the polity—and not solely by totalitarian regimes. Levi's discourse is truly post-national. It criticized the assumed superiority of Western civilization and anticipated issues that would be pivotal in the postcolonial world.

Savinio's passage touches on a third and final concern: the failure of revolutionary politics. This conclusion was far from widely accepted at the end of the war. In 1945, the idea of a socialist revolution gained momentum, supported by the striking victory of the Red Army over Nazi divisions in the East and by a wave of popular consensus in Western Europe.

As Tony Judt claimed, the possibility of "a different turn had seemed very real in 1945."[9] The texts examined in this book bear relevant traces of this atmosphere. Critical editions of the manuscripts and their variants, outside the scope of my research, would probably reveal significant oscillations in the ideological positions taken by these authors in such a confusing and eventful period.

The evolution from skeptical hope to complete disavowal of revolutionary politics in Alberto Moravia's—and, to a certain extent, Guido Piovene's—output during the transition is telling in this regard. This development influences Moravia's later novels such as *The Woman of Rome* and especially *The Conformist*, in which he refined his analysis of the psychological, existential, and ultimately *private* significance of ideology and politics of exclusion, concluding with a refusal of the revolutionary myth consistent with his rejection of totalitarianism.

Savinio's remark does not address one fundamental issue: the trauma of history, which haunts the present and casts a shadow over the future of individuals and countries. Umberto Saba's experimental prose and correspondence of the period, as well as Ennio Flaiano's novel *A Time to Kill*, elucidate how the many ghosts of Fascism—such as colonial violence, the cult of the Duce, and state racism—would haunt private memory for decades, despite collective forgetting and political absolutions. In fact, this issue would continue to unfold well beyond the period scrutinized in my study, encompassing the historical transformation of the questions of guilt and responsibility addressed in these pages. In 1963, Piovene published the autobiographical novel *The Furies*, while the following year Berto published *Incubus*.[10] In these novels, the two authors painstakingly dissect the psychological strains that tormented them for decades after the war—as the explicit title of each book attests. The enormous popular success and controversial critical dispute that followed publication of Morante's *History* in 1974—a novel which emphatically embodies the viewpoint of the victims—showcases how the profound discord in the national community provoked by Fascism and the war's traumas was silenced but incredibly vivid. Like embers buried under ashes, the questions posed during the transition years were far from resolved in the subsequent decades.

Historical traumas also elicit questions regarding the formation and institutionalization of memory. As Corrado Alvaro gloomily reported in his 1945 pamphlet *Italy's Renunciation?*:

> The ground of every other nation in Europe is incomparably empty of the ruins of a great civilization; the destruction and erasures it underwent were

definitive; it had its decisive episodes that signaled a new stage in the evolution of national life [. . .]. Here, for centuries, errors have been piled on errors, ruin on ruin.[11]

Alvaro describes Italy's material *and* moral prostration after Fascism and the war. The passage also displays the author's tormented psychology and the recognition that the best years of his life were wasted under dictatorship.[12] This traumatic past required a process of critical distancing on the public and individual levels. In her 1947 novel *Artemisia*, for instance, Anna Banti not only recuperates the story of a seventeenth-century female artist that canonized history neglected; she also reflects on the epistemological break occasioned by the war, epitomized by the overwhelming presence of rubble in the Italian cityscape. In *Artemisia*, Banti integrates women's history in national history and substitutes the traditional (and then Fascist) trope of the contemplation of past ruins with an unsettling meditation on present debris.[13]

The transition from Fascism to democracy was an exceptional instance of intellectual fluidity in Italy—a time of possibilities and missed opportunities. This book has focused on writers who contested the widespread rhetoric of national redemption fostered by party politics. The analysis of reviews, private correspondence, and Liberation journals which hosted these authors' discontent, reveals how the postwar cultural establishment marginalized them despite at times spectacular public success. Nevertheless, their works did not happen in a vacuum. They were, instead, in close dialogue with Neorealism and the cultural events that typified early postwar Italy in collective and public memory.

Today, their work also sheds new light on how canonized authors experienced this eventful period, prompting contrastive interpretations. From Pavese to Calvino, most prominent Italian intellectuals felt uneasiness at the institutionalization of party politics and the new political hegemony of the Christian Democrats.[14] Even those who adhered to Communism (as Pavese and Calvino did) were dismayed by the narrowing of the intellectual debate after the 1948 general elections. Pavese's diary, *This Business of Living*, is full of sarcastic yet bitter remarks about his being a bad "compagno" ("Communist comrade"),[15] whereas Calvino's 1964 preface to his unorthodox Resistance novel, *The Path to the Spiders' Nests*, ends with a melancholic note on the intellectual challenges of the transition: "The significance of this polemic, this challenge is now rather remote from us: and even in those days, I have to admit, the book was read simply as a novel, and not as part of this debate about history's verdict on the Resistance."[16]

The intellectuals addressed in my research employed literature for its intrinsic value of expressing the "political wrong," as outlined by Rancière. Traditionally, Italian national identity coalesced around the common ground of literature. After Fascism, writers such as Saba, Morante, Moravia, and Carlo Levi wrote against self-delusional narratives of redemption with public statements and the creation of new literary languages. In their own way, they contributed to the idea of establishing, for the first time in Italy, a truly democratic space for debate. On the other hand, authors such as Brancati, Berto, Flaiano, and Malaparte, previously associated with Mussolini's regime to varying degrees, resisted the forgetting of past violence and the absolution of personal responsibility that was widespread in the early postwar period. Their works countered the distortions of a shared memory based on the political demands at the time.

Democratic ideals and contrasting memories were deeply intertwined in the early postwar attempt to use literature to resist redemptive readings of recent history. "These first works," claims Andrea Zanzotto reflecting on Berto's *The Sky Is Red*, "have the scent of truth caught in the moment, of the document that yearns to be culture and even merges with what it wants to document."[17] Political disagreement turned into literary and intellectual discontent, a lesson that would prove influential in the long postwar period. The legacy of liberal and Fascist Italy was then minimized through a selective politics of memory that often drew from the same historicist culture and monumental history that sustained the regime.[18] Still, monumental history and historicist culture, wrote Luigi Meneghello, recollecting the moral crisis that led him to join the armed Resistance against Fascism, are the "product of an education people died of."[19]

The authors I examined here reveal how this cultural heritage did not fade with the disappearance of Mussolini's portrait from the walls of the town halls, of his voice from the national radio, of his body from movie screens. Many of the protagonists of their books, from Morante's Elisa in *Lies and Sorcery* to Flaiano's lieutenant in *A Time to Kill*, eventually learn how to live with the ghosts of their past. Their long and troubled journeys do not necessarily end happily, but as flawed as these characters are, their voices elevate the need for truth over the alleged consolation of collective redemption.

Acknowledgments

This book was born and grew up as an ongoing conversation with a great deal of people in Italy and the United States, enriched by a number of other remarkable meetings I enjoyed in cafés, libraries, and archives outside my home and my elective country. I thank all the friends who cordially shared their expertise and insights in different disciplines, sparking my curiosity to know more about their work and also their lives. I hope my book's pages convey the earnest intellectual collegiality that forged it in the first place, in addition to the passionate exchange that made it possible.

My research has benefited from grants and residences awarded by institutions such as the American Academy in Rome, the National Endowment for the Humanities, the American Philosophical Society, the Andrew Mellon Foundation, the Remarque Institute at NYU, the Center for Italian Modern Art (CIMA) in New York, and the Civitella Ranieri Foundation. Research funds from New York University and Bard College were pivotal to expanding the scope of my research and then finalizing this manuscript.

I begin my long thank-you note with Stephen Twilley, who translated the Italian language passages in this book, and Jenny McPhee, who graciously allowed me to work with her translation of Elsa Morante's *Lies and Sorcery*, soon to be published by NYRB Classics. In this book I have occasionally modified published translations, especially of Italian books published in the 1940s and 1950s, as they often conspicuously changed or skipped entire paragraphs of the original Italian texts I discuss here (cases in point are Morante's *Lies and Sorcery*, so far published as *House of Liars*, and Malaparte's *Kaputt* and *The Skin*). I am also especially grateful to Chiara Sbuttoni, Iuri Moscardi, and Mildred Sanchez, who helped with the revision of the manuscript, as well as Fred Nachbaur and Günther Piehler at Fordham University Press, who believed in my book project and helped me to carry it through.

A warm thank you to the many people at NYU that were crucial for my intellectual growth, beginning with Ruth Ben-Ghiat. Ruth profoundly inspired this research of mine with her teaching and mentorship, prompting me to find my own voice through her example. I am also grateful to Tony Judt, Jane Tylus, David Forgacs, Teresa Fiore, Lidia Santarelli, Chiara Ferrari, Ara Merjian, Virginia Cox, and John Freccero for their encouragement and their advice. I was very lucky to discuss my ideas with Giuliana Bruno, Robert S. C. Gordon, and Thomas Harrison, who all provided invaluable feedback (and Giuliana, together with Andy Fierberg, also hosted lovely evenings in Rome and Wainscott). I thank all my colleagues at Bard, especially Patricia López-Gay, Oleg Minin, Wakako Suzuki, Éric Trudel, Joe Luzzi, Odile and Bruce Chilton, Elizabeth Holt, Marina Van Zuylen, Melanie Nicholson, Nicole Caso, Deirdre d'Albertis, Peter Laki, and Tom Wolf, who actively contributed with their support to the completion of this volume. And finally a long list of friends—in no particular order—whose lively conversations and personal empathy were key to the themes of my project: Raffaele Bedarida, Franca Sinopoli, Rosario Forlenza, Alberto Cellotto, Maria Anna Mariani, Nadia Grillo, Adele Carrai, Matthew Amos, Anna Baldini, Konstantina Zanou, Carmen Belmonte, Nicola Lucchi, Simona and Dan Wright, Stefano Adamo, Erica Moretti, Sara Marzioli, Giovanni Braico, Maurizio Serra, Andrea Cortellessa, Maria Pia de Paulis, Paola Italia, Fulvio Pezzarossa, Riccardo Gasperina Geroni, Martina Piperno, Luca Falciola, Massimo Rizzante, Daniele Biffanti, Valerio Angeletti, Stan Pugliese, Dan Tzahor, Riccardo Capoferro, Alessandra Crotti, Renato Camurri, Stefania Lucamante, Martino Marazzi, Raoul Bruni, Charles Leavitt, Maurizio Ciocchetti, Antonio Debenedetti, and Ruggero Savinio. I also thank many of my colleagues here for their kind invitations to publicly speak about this book when it was still a work in progress. They have been fundamental opportunities to test my ideas in front of learned and diversified audiences.

A special thanks to Dave Giovannitti and family for the "writers' retreat" in Springs, NY, in the summer of 2020, and to the following who aided my research: Laura Mattioli and the staff at CIMA; Dana Prescott, Diego Mencaroni, and Ilaria Locchi at Civitella Ranieri; Alessia Rositani Suckert and family; Matteo Noja and Carla Giacobbe at the Fondazione Biblioteca Via del Senato in Milan; Stephanie Steiker at the New York Institute for the Humanities; Nour Melehi at the Casa Museo Alberto Moravia; and the staff at the Biblioteca Cantonale di Lugano in Switzerland; the Gabinetto Vieusseux and the Biblioteca Nazionale in Florence; the Biblioteca Nazionale Centrale, the Archivio di Stato, and the Fondazione Carlo Levi in Rome.

The pages, ideas, and words in this book have traveled a lot, especially between Harlem in New York City, where I live with my family, Annandale-on-Hudson, where I teach and meet colleagues and students, and a small town called Visnadello in the province of Treviso, where I come from. I would like to acknowledge here the role of my family in Italy, especially my parents, Mariuccia and Aldo, and my siblings, Giorgio, Elisa, and Valeria Baldasso, together with my New York family, Ellin, Marc, Dan Levin, and Sam Levenstein. I purposely left Sara as the last person to thank here, for her bright smile and unconditional patience prompted me to complete this book, in the good company of Fiammetta and Davide, who recently joined us and doubled the fun of living together. To Sara, Fiammetta, and Davide, who all have American passports, this book about Italy is dedicated.

Parts of Chapter 1, "Specters of a Revolutionary Past: Curzio Malaparte," were previously published in Italian in my book *Curzio Malaparte, la letteratura crudele.* Kaputt, La pelle, *e la caduta della civiltà europea* (Rome: Carocci, 2019). A shorter version of "Autonomy and Anarchic Resistance: From *Fear of Freedom* to *Christ Stopped at Eboli*" in Chapter 4 was published in Italian as "Diventare stranieri: *Paura della libertà* di Carlo Levi tra storia, redenzione e identità ebraica." *Allegoria* 81, no. 1 (2020): 165–79. Finally, a much shorter version of Chapter 5 was published as "Curzio Malaparte and the Tragic Understanding of Modern History," *Annali d'Italianistica* 35 (2017): 279–303. I am grateful to Carocci Editore and the editorial boards of the journals *Allegoria* and *Annali d'Italianistica* for their collaboration.

Notes

Introduction: Ruins and Debris of a Contested History

1. Elsa Morante, "Pagine autobiografiche postume," in *Opere, Vol. 1*, ed. Carlo Cecchi and Cesare Garboli (Milan: Mondadori, 1988), l–li. Italics are in the original text.

2. Benedetto Croce, *Scritti e discorsi politici (1943–1947), Vol. 1*, ed. Angela Carella (Naples: Bibliopolis, 1993), 61.

3. Among the many possible examples of this trend, see Roberto Rossellini's films *Rome Open City* (1945) and *Paisan* (1946); novels such as Vasco Pratolini's *A Tale of Poor Lovers* (*Cronache di poveri amanti*, 1947) and Renata Viganò's *L'Agnese va a morire* (1949); and, finally, influential memoirs such as Paolo Monelli's *Roma 1943* (1945).

4. For a historical account of the representations of the "Italian character" in modern Italy, see Silvana Patriarca, *Italian Vices: Nation and Character from the Risorgimento to the Republic* (New York: Cambridge University Press, 2010). See also Giulio Bollati, *L'italiano. Il carattere nazionale come storia e come invenzione* (Turin: Einaudi, 1983).

5. Curzio Malaparte, "Letter to Prezzolini, September 15, 1946," in Curzio Malaparte, *Malaparte, Vol. 7: 1946–1947*, ed. Edda Ronchi Suckert (Florence: Ponte alle Grazie, 1993), 148.

6. Malaparte, "Letter to Prezzolini," 148.

7. On the subject, see Filippo Focardi, *La guerra della memoria. La Resistenza nel dibattito politico italiano dal 1945 ad oggi* (Bari-Rome: Laterza, 2005); Philip Cooke, *The Legacy of the Italian Resistance* (New York: Palgrave Macmillian, 2011); and James Foot, *Italy's Divided Memory* (New York: Palgrave Macmillian, 2003).

8. Giovanni Falaschi claimed that "debating Neorealism meant discussing the pivotal historical question of contemporary Italy, the transition from Fascism to today's democratic-bourgeois state." Giovanni Falaschi, *Realtà e retorica. La letteratura del neorealismo italiano* (Messina: Casa Editrice D'Anna, 1977), 7. On the cinematic level, however, important reflections on the difficulty of determining Neorealism's unifying paradigm over its composite nature are explored in Alessia Ricciardi, "The Italian Redemption of Cinema: Neorealism from Bazin to Godard," *Romanic Review* 97, nos. 3–4 (2006): 483–500.

9. As Ruth Ben-Ghiat explains, the dramatic power of Neorealism lies in capturing "the abyss between aspirations for normalcy and the psychic and material devastation wrought by the war." Ruth Ben-Ghiat, "Italian Cinema and the Transition from Dictatorship to Democracy," in *Histories of the Aftermath: The Legacy of the Second World War in Europe*, ed. Frank Biess and Robert G. Moeller (New York: Berghahn, 2010), 160. Among the vast body of scholarship on the two filmmakers, for the themes studied here, see David Forgacs et al., eds., *Rossellini: Magician of the Real* (London: British Film Institute, 2001); P. Adams Sitney, *Vital Crises in Italian Cinema: Iconography, Stylistics, Politics* (New York: Oxford University Press, 2013); and Noa Steimatsky, *Italian Locations: Reinhabiting the Past in Postwar Cinema* (Minneapolis: University of Minnesota Press, 2008).

10. Charles L. Leavitt IV, *Italian Neorealism: A Cultural History* (Toronto: University of Toronto Press, 2020), 169.

11. See Gian Piero Brunetta, *L'Italia sullo schermo. Come il cinema ha raccontato l'identità nazionale* (Rome: Carocci 2020). For an interpretation of the display of violence in Neorealist cinema, see Karl Schoonover, *Brutal Vision: The Neorealist Body in Postwar Italian Cinema* (Minneapolis: University of Minnesota Press, 2012).

12. "For at least ten years from the end of the conflict, Italian literature strove to discredit the myths of Fascism, to underline its moral poverty, to speak of its military unpreparedness in the African deserts and on the steppes of Russia, to exalt an Italian heroism—that of the poor, of the defeated, and finally of the resistants—against the tin gods of the Fascist pantheon. In the Italy emerging from war and civil war, for maybe the first time in its history, literary invention and autobiographical and documentary writing meet on the terrain of the epic." Walter Barberis, "Primo Levi e un libro 'fatale,'" in *Atlante della letteratura italiana, Vol. 3: Dal Romanticismo a oggi*, ed. Sergio Luzzatto, Gabriele Pedullà, Domenico Scarpa (Turin: Einaudi, 2012), 756.

13. Elio Vittorini, "Una nuova cultura," *Il Politecnico* 1, no. 1 (1945), now in Elio Vittorini, *Letteratura arte società, Vol. 2: Articoli e interventi 1938–1965*, ed. Raffaella Rodondi (Turin: Einaudi, 2008), 235. For a reappraisal of Neorealism and its hermeneutic categories on the score of Pierre Bourdieu's sociology, see Anna Baldini, *Il Comunista. Una storia letteraria dalla Resistenza agli anni Settanta* (Turin: UTET, 2008), 3–40.

14. Romano Luperini, *Gli intellettuali di sinistra e l'ideologia della ricostruzione nel dopoguerra* (Rome: Edizioni di ideologie, 1971).

15. Enzo Forcella, *La Resistenza in convento* (Turin: Einaudi, 1999), 231.

16. Neorealist filmmakers themselves did not all abide by this redemptive reading of the recent past. A film like Vittorio De Sica's *Bicycle Thieves* (1948) sensibly takes a different direction. Its tragic understanding of postwar everyday man's vicissitudes is far from Rossellini's spiritual *quête* or Visconti's cinematic epic. It is worth mentioning how an eccentric figure like Malaparte, whose work is in constant polemical dialogue with Neorealism, called *Bicycle Thieves* an

"Aeschylean tragedy." Cited in Luigi Martellini, "Introduzione. La croce, alcuni segni, un eroe," in Curzio Malaparte, *Il Cristo proibito*, ed. Luigi Martellini (Naples: ESI, 1992), 58. For the idea of "chorality" in Neorealist cinema, see Joseph Luzzi, *A Cinema of Poetry: Aesthetics of the Italian Art Film* (Baltimore, MD: Johns Hopkins University Press, 2014), 19–35; and Charles L. Leavitt IV, *Italian Neorealism*, 128–70.

17. For an accurate account of this process and its historiography, see Silvio Lanaro, *Storia dell'Italia repubblicana* (Venice: Marsilio, 1992), especially the first chapter, "Il lungo dopoguerra," 9–236; Claudio Pavone, *Alle origini della Repubblica. Scritti su fascismo, antifascismo e continuità dello stato* (Turin: Bollati Boringhieri, 1995); Christopher Duggan, "Italy in the Cold War Years and the Legacy of Fascism," in *Italy in the Cold War: Politics, Culture and Society 1948–58*, ed. Christopher Duggan and Christopher Wagstaff (Oxford: Berg, 1995), 1–24. For the juridical aspects of the continuity of the state, see Michele Battini, *The Missing Italian Nuremberg: Cultural Amnesia and Postwar Politics* (New York: Palgrave Macmillan, 2007).

18. For a detailed overview of the period, see Pier Giorgio Zunino, *La Repubblica e il suo passato* (Bologna: il Mulino, 2003); for the war's traumatic effects on Italian literature and film, see Anna Maria Torriglia, *Broken Time, Fragmented Space: A Cultural Map for Postwar Italy* (Toronto: University of Toronto Press, 2002); and Giancarlo Alfano, *Ciò che ritorna. Gli effetti della guerra nella letteratura italiana del Novecento* (Florence: Cesati, 2014).

19. Rosario Forlenza, *On the Edge of Democracy: Italy, 1943–1948* (Oxford: Oxford University Press, 2019), 153.

20. Though neither Gentile nor Volpe were hegemonic during the *ventennio*, their original development of Croce's historicism evidenced a profound continuity with the culture of the liberal regime. See Claudio Fogu, *The Historic Imaginary: Politics of History in Fascist Italy* (Toronto: University of Toronto Press, 2003). This continuity will be singled out and harshly criticized by the intellectuals I examine here (see Chapter 3).

21. Regarding the concept of "creaturely life," see Eric Santner, *On Creaturely Life: Rilke, Benjamin, Sebald* (Chicago: University of Chicago Press, 2006).

22. Daniela La Penna, "The Rise and Fall of Benedetto Croce: Intellectual Positioning in the Italian Cultural Field, 1944–1947," *Modern Italy* 21, no. 2 (2016): 141.

23. Harald Wydra's considerations on the tight bonds between politics and the sacred are especially pertinent here: "Quests for salvation and redemption are strongly felt but hazy aspirations, whose final purpose eludes human beings. Such meanings can only be valid if they are practised, performed, and believed. Such markers of certainty are not gained by deliberation, scrutiny, or critique. The key to collective identity is therefore often in vanishing points or ultimate ends, which transcend the profane reality of measurement and rationality." Harald Wydra, *Politics and the Sacred* (Cambridge: Cambridge University Press, 2015), 6.

24. For the construction of Catholic and Communist national ideologies in Italy, see Rosario Forlenza and Bjørn Thomassen, *Italian Modernities: Competing Narratives of Nationhood* (New York: Palgrave Macmillan, 2016).

25. Corrado Alvaro, *Il nostro tempo e la speranza. Saggi di vita contemporanea* (Milan: Bompiani, 1952), 56.

26. "Fascism didn't deserve to have against it the stupid, the frightened, and the sycophantic, not even after death! Who was so foolish as to gift it such enemies? Probably Pure Anti-Fascism: official, codified, and vindictive." Vitaliano Brancati, "La lettera anonima," in *I fascisti invecchiano* (1946), now in *Opere 1932–1946*, ed. Leonardo Sciascia (Milan: Bompiani, 1987), 1134.

27. Fogu, *Historic Imaginary*.

28. On this subject, see Richard J. B. Bosworth, *Whispering City: Modern Rome and Its Histories* (New Haven, CT: Yale University Press, 2011). For the concept of "Romanità" in Fascist Italy, see Joshua Arthurs, *Excavating Modernity: The Roman Past in Fascist Italy* (Ithaca, NY: Cornell University Press, 2012).

29. On the rhetorical myth of the Italian nation, see Emilio Gentile, *La Grande Italia: The Myth of the Nation in the Twentieth Century* (Madison: University of Wisconsin Press, 2009).

30. On the organization of mass parties in Italy in the postwar period, Giovanni De Luna interestingly comments: "The mistrust of anything that was spontaneous, unorganized, or not centralized inspired the trade unionism of Catholics and Communists alike; both adapted themselves in an almost natural, physiological way to continuity with the Fascist unions, inheriting from them their centralizing structure and their preoccupation with collective bargaining from the top." De Luna, *La Repubblica inquieta. L'Italia della Costituzione, 1946–1948* (Milan: Feltrinelli, 2017), 237.

31. The mutual influence of rhetoric and politics on the foundation of the new post-Fascist state in Italy has been expressed in Silvio Lanaro, *Retorica e politica. Alle origini dell'Italia contemporanea* (Rome: Donzelli, 2011).

32. Despite its prominence during the civil war and in the years immediately following national Liberation, the "Secondo Risorgimento" narrative has a multilayered history which predates WWII and will continue in the ensuing decades of the Republican state, through the processes of memorialization of the Resistance. On this topic, see Michela Ponzani, "Il mito del Secondo Risorgimento nazionale. Retorica e legittimità della Resistenza nel linguaggio politico istituzionale," *Annali della Fondazione Luigi Einaudi* 37 (2003): 199–258; Philip Cooke, "La Resistenza come 'Secondo Risorgimento.' Un *topos* retorico senza fine?," in *Resistenza e autobiografia della nazione. Uso politico, rappresentazione, memoria*, ed. Aldo Agosti and Chiara Colombani (Turin: SEB, 2012), 61–79. Forlenza (*On the Edge of Democracy*, 157) traces the trope back to Carlo Rosselli, "Primo Programma di Giustizia e Libertà," *Giustizia e Libertà* 1 (1929), cited in Carlo Rosselli, *Socialismo Liberale* (Rome: Edizioni U, 1944–1945 [1930]), 15.

33. Leone Ginzburg, "La tradizione del Risorgimento," *Aretusa* 2, no. 8 (1945): 1–16. Now in Leone Ginzburg, *Scritti* (Turin: Einaudi, 1964), 114.

34. Remarkably, the Risorgimento was a rhetorical reference also for the Fascist, as in Giovanni Gentile, *I profeti del Risorgimento italiano* (Florence: Vallecchi, 1923).

35. Giaime Pintor, "L'ora del riscatto" (1943), in *Il sangue d'Europa (1939–43)*, ed. Valentino Gerratana (Turin: Einaudi, 1950), 241.

36. For an account of Communist Resistance narratives in Italy, see Donald Sassoon, "Italy after Fascism: The Predicament of Dominant Narratives," in *Life after Death: Approaches to a Cultural and Social History of Europe during the 1940s and 1950s*, ed. Richard Bessel and Dirk Schumann (Cambridge: Cambridge University Press, 2003), 259–90; for its legacy and aftermath, see Stephen Gundle, "The 'Civic Religion' of the Resistance in Post-War Italy," *Modern Italy* 5, no. 2 (2000): 112–32. For a more nuanced assessment of the Italian case in the broader context of the emerging Cold War, see Tony Judt, *Postwar: A History of Europe since 1945* (New York: Penguin, 2005), especially "Part one: Post-War: 1945–1953," 13–237.

37. David Ward, *Antifascisms: Cultural Politics in Italy, 1943–46* (Madison, NJ: Fairleigh Dickinson University Press, 1996).

38. Luca La Rovere, *L'eredità del fascismo. Gli intellettuali, i giovani e la transizione al postfascismo* (Turin: Bollati Boringhieri, 2008).

39. Recent intellectual histories of the transition, such as Mirella Serri's *I redenti. Gli intellettuali che vissero due volte. 1938–1948* (Milan: Corbaccio, 2006) and, with a focus on the art world, Alessandro Masi, *Idealismo e opportunismo nella cultura italiana 1943–1948* (Milan: Mursia, 2018), attempt to problematize the period by following the careers of prominent artists and intellectuals, such as Carlo Muscetta, Mario Alicata, Elio Vittorini, and Renato Guttuso. Serri's and Masi's studies retrace the trajectories of these intellectuals from the journal *Primato*—launched and directed by Fascist Minister of National Education Giuseppe Bottai in 1940 to "spiritually" support the war struggle—to Communist outlets such as *Rinascita, Società*, and *Il Politecnico*, and to the alignment with the PCI. Though necessary to complete the context of my discourse here, this approach falters by restricting the terms of the overall inquiry to a broader collective repression of the Fascist past (and the related racial laws). It also reiterates the postwar teleological reading ("Error-Bewilderment-Redemption") that it seeks to criticize but avoids widening the investigation to include voices that contested this redemptive narrative.

40. Forcella, *Resistenza in convento*, 231.

41. Italo Calvino, "Preface," in *The Path to the Spiders' Nests*, trans. Archibald Colquhoun (New York: Ecco Press, 2000 [*Il sentiero dei nidi di ragno*, 1947]), 8. Primo Levi also vividly recalls this obsessive urge, though motivated by the radically different experience of the Nazi camps: "The need to tell our story to

'others,' to make 'others' share it, took on for us, before our liberation and after, the character of an immediate and violent impulse." Primo Levi, *If This Is a Man*, in *The Complete Works of Primo Levi, Vol. 1*, ed. Ann Goldstein, trans. Stuart Woolf (New York: Liveright, 2015 [*Se questo è un uomo*, 1947]), 6. On Calvino's 1964 "Preface," see Anna Baldini, "Il Neorealismo. Nascita e usi di una categoria letteraria," in *Letteratura italiana e tedesca 1945–1970. Campi, polisistemi, transfer*, ed. Michele Sisto and Irene Fantappiè (Rome: Istituto italiano di studi germanici, 2013).

42. Natalia Ginzburg, *Family Lexicon*, trans. Jenny McPhee (New York: NYRB Classics, 2017), 152. The translation here has been modified by the author.

43. De Luna, *Repubblica inquieta*, 184.

44. Mercurio [Alba de Céspedes], "Caro lettore," *Mercurio* 4, 34 (1948): 5.

45. Lanaro, *Storia*, 66.

46. On this specific subject, see note 7.

47. See "On Living among Ghosts: Elsa Morante" in Chapter 3, and Chapter 4.

48. On the issue of modernity's periodization, I refer here to Remo Ceserani to clarify my way of proceeding in the study of specific years. To understand a year's significance, Ceserani argues for the necessity "to look not only at the year in question but also at the preceding and the following ones." In support of his point, Ceserani mentions Giacomo Debenedetti, who explained his critical methodology with a memorable image "to act in the same way as when one cuts the trunk of a tree and looks at the rings in it, at the sap that mounts from the bottom, coming from what was before, and rising toward what will come after." Quoted in Remo Ceserani, "Italy and Modernity: Peculiarities and Contradictions," in *Italian Modernism: Italian Culture between Decadentism and Avant-Garde*, ed. Luca Somigli and Mario Moroni (Toronto: University of Toronto Press, 2004), 52. From a historiographical perspective, La Rovere recently criticized the cliché of the lack of a discussion on Italy's responsibility in WWII and of an overall repression of the Fascist past, especially in the early postwar debate. In particular, he suggested that the repression paradigm was successful also because the voices in this debate were not easily recognizable in a univocal discourse and resisted comprehensive labels (*Eredità del fascismo*, 51). On this issue, see also the compelling reflections in Mariuccia Salvati, *Passaggi. Italiani dal fascismo alla Repubblica* (Rome: Carocci, 2016), 95–120.

49. Jacques Rancière, *The Names of History: On the Poetics of Knowledge* (Minneapolis: University of Minnesota Press, 1994), 30.

50. Jacques Rancière, *Disagreement: Politics and Philosophy* (Minneapolis: University of Minnesota Press, 1999).

51. On the subject, Luisa Mangoni cites an interesting letter by Giulio Einaudi to Vittorio De Sica, dated February 3, 1955: "I remember a walk one night through the streets of Milan, chatting about everything and anything. It was the time of *Miracle in Milan* and of Carlo Levi's *The Watch*. Two events for Italy." Luisa Mangoni, "Da *Cristo si è fermato a Eboli* a *L'Orologio*: note su Carlo Levi e la casa

editrice Einaudi," in *Carlo Levi. Gli anni fiorentini 1941–1945*, ed. Piero Brunello and Pia Vivarelli (Rome: Donzelli, 2003), 207. Important exceptions are the special issue dedicated to the novel of *Poetiche* 17, no. 42 (1 2015), ed. Fabio Camilletti and Filippo Trentin; and Riccardo Gasperina Geroni, *Il custode della soglia. Il sacro e le forme nell'opera di Carlo Levi* (Milan: Mimesis, 2018).

52. This does not imply that Carlo Levi had no faith in the possible representation of traumatic experience—quite the contrary, as I will detail in Chapter 4.

53. In her recent monograph on *Mercurio*, Laura Di Nicola argues that the journal directed by de Céspedes anticipates many of the themes of Vittorini's *Il Politecnico*. Thanks to the authority of its director and collaborators, and the much-quoted polemics between him and Togliatti, *Il Politecnico* took center stage in all discussions regarding Italian intellectuals during the transition. Laura Di Nicola, *"Mercurio." Storia di una rivista 1944–1948* (Milan: il Saggiatore/Fondazione Mondadori, 2012), 12. More recently, Salvati convincingly insisted on the national relevance of Rome's intellectual exchange after the Liberation in her *Passaggi*, esp. 59–79.

54. Umberto Saba, *Scorciatoie e raccontini*, in *Tutte le prose*, ed. Arrigo Stara (Milan: Mondadori, 2001 [1946]). A vast selection, translated as *From Shortcuts and Very Short Stories*, can be read in *The Stories and Recollections of Umberto Saba*, trans. Estelle Gibson (Riverdale-on-Hudson: The Sheep Meadow Press, 1993), 163–92.

55. Denis Hollier, *The College of Sociology* (Minneapolis: University of Minnesota Press, 1988).

56. During the transition, many of the authors I examine here, such as Carlo Levi, Moravia, and Saba, were indeed close to the Action Party—at least until its early demise in 1947. See Giovanni De Luna, *Storia del Partito d'Azione, 1942–1947* (Turin: UTET, 2006).

57. Vitaliano Brancati, *Diario romano*, in *Opere 1947–1954*, ed. Leonardo Sciascia (Milan: Bompiani, 1992), 424.

58. Already in 1963, Eugenio Garin characterized the period as "Crocean diaspora." Eugenio Garin, *La cultura italiana tra '800 e '900* (Bari-Rome: Laterza, 1963), 205.

59. Giacomo Debenedetti, "Probabile autobiografia di una generazione" (1949), in *Saggi* (Milan: Mondadori, 1999), 109.

60. Sapegno's assessment would not go uncontested. For the heated debate about his position—especially after Luigi Russo's critical reply—see La Penna, "Rise and Fall of Benedetto Croce," and Charles L. Leavitt IV, "Probing the Limits of Creocean Historicism," *The Italianist* 37, no. 3 (2017): 387–406.

61. On Croce's influence on Marxist critics, see Leavitt, *Italian Neorealism*, 106–22.

62. "For promoters of the Risorgimento movement (from Cuoco to Foscolo, from Manzoni to Mazzini, etc.) it is the Italian language and Italian literature that testify to the existence of the Italian nation, and that provide the basis for

ambitions of political redemption." Alberto Mario Banti, *Sublime madre nostra. La nazione italiana dal Risorgimento al fascismo* (Bari-Rome: Laterza, 2011), 7. On the topic, see also Francesco De Sanctis, *History of Italian Literature* (New York: Harcourt, 1931 [*Storia della letteratura italiana*, 1870]); Ezio Raimondi, *Letteratura e identità nazionale* (Milan: Bruno Mondadori, 1998); Romano Luperini, "Letteratura ed identità nazionale: la parabola novecentesca," in *Letteratura ed identità nazionale nel Novecento*, ed. Romano Luperini and Daniela Brogi (San Cesario di Lecce: Manni, 2004), 7–33.

63. Stefano Jossa, *L'Italia letteraria* (Bologna: il Mulino, 2006), 84.

64. On Gramsci's notion of "national-popular literature" and its lack in Italy, see his *Prison Notebooks, Vols. 1–3*, trans. Joseph Buttigieg (New York: Columbia University Press, 2011 [*Quaderni dal carcere*, 1948–1951]); and more specifically, Antonio Gramsci, *Letteratura e vita nazionale*, ed. Felice Platone (Rome: Editori Riuniti, 1996 [1950]).

65. Luperini, *Intellettuali di sinistra*, 19. On the publication of Gramsci's works in the late 1940s, La Penna adds: "The timely republication of some of his works starting in 1947 with Einaudi, constituted the single most important cultural event of the period. This cultural operation quickly galvanized the intellectuals close to the Communist Party and persuaded others to join its ranks. The release of these texts contributed significantly to the erosion of Benedetto Croce's influence over the intellectual field." La Penna, "Rise and Fall of Benedetto Croce," 140. See also Andrea Scapolo, "Scattered Ashes: The Reception of the Gramscian Legacy in Postwar Italy," in *Gramsci in the World*, ed. Roberto Dainotto and Fredric Jameson (Durham, NC: Duke University Press, 2020), 93–112. Roberto Battaglia, *Un uomo un partigiano* (Rome: Edizioni U, 1946).

66. Given their difference in aesthetic choices and contrastive political ideas, their writings do not preclude possible self-indulgent populist tones of a different nature and political agenda than Neorealist populism. Such is the case of Malaparte, especially in his journalistic works in the late 1940s–1950s. The conundrum of revolutionary politics, populism, and narcissism, however, would become a thought-provoking plotline of Elsa Morante's *Lies and Sorcery*, trans. Jenny McPhee (New York: NYRB Classics, forthcoming [*Menzogna e sortilegio*, 1948]), embodied in particular in the character of Francesco De Salvi.

67. In this study, I follow Rancière's definition of literature as "a new system of identification in the art of writing. A system of identification of an art is a system of relationships between practices, the forms of visibility of such practices, and modes of intelligibility." Jacques Rancière, *The Politics of Literature* (Cambridge: Polity Press, 2011), 7.

68. This explains, among other things, the moral suasion that quotations from Dante and other classics of Italian literature have in works such as Primo Levi's *If This Is a Man* or Carlo Levi's *Christ Stopped at Eboli*.

69. For the notion of "transitional objects," see Fredric Jameson, "The Vanishing Mediator; or, Max Weber as Storyteller," in *The Ideologies of Theory, Vol. 2* (Minneapolis: University of Minnesota Press, 1988), 3–34.

70. Frank Biess, introduction, *Histories of the Aftermath: The Legacy of the Second World War in Europe*, ed. Frank Biess and Robert G. Moeller (New York: Berghahn, 2010), 3.

71. Judt, *Postwar*, 6.

72. Curzio Malaparte, *Kaputt* (1944), trans. Cesare Foligno (New York: NYRB Classics, 2005), 390.

73. Recent assessments of the early responses to the fall of Mussolini can be found in Giuseppe Tosi, "*Morte della patria* and Mourning Elaboration: Memoirs and State of Consciousness after 8 Settembre's Italy," in *Italy and the Bourgeoisie: The Re-Thinking of a Class*, ed. Stefania Lucamante (Madison, NJ: Fairleigh Dickinson University Press, 2009), 63–75; and Joshua Arthurs, "Settling Accounts: Retribution, Emotion, and Memory during the Fall of Mussolini," *Journal of Modern Italian Studies* 20, no. 5 (2015): 617–39.

74. In a recent study, Simon Levis Sullam points out that "the phenomenon of the Resistance as a foundational myth, substituting for individual responsibilities and thus serving to exculpate, was not only an Italian or French phenomenon, but a European one." Simon Levis Sullam, *I fantasmi del fascismo. Le metamorfosi degli intellettuali italiani nel dopoguerra* (Milan: Feltrinelli 2021), 136.

75. The troublesome story of the publication of Primo Levi's *If This Is a Man* (first Italian edition: 1947) can be an insightful instance of the difficulties writers and intellectuals found at the time, if they attempted to raise such issues in the public sphere. For a detailed account of Levi's first publication, see Ian Thomson, *Primo Levi: A Life* (London: Hutchinson, 2002).

76. A more nuanced discourse has to be made regarding Malaparte and his writing. While gesturing against this kind of melancholic gaze in *Kaputt*, Malaparte will employ this tone in a specifically literary fashion in his unfinished *Diary of a Foreigner in Paris*, trans. Stephen Twilley (New York: NYRB Classics, 2020 [*Diario di uno straniero a Parigi*, 1966]). On this topic, see Chapter 5.

77. See Zunino, *Repubblica*, 557–77.

78. Guido Piovene, *I falsi redentori*, in *Opere narrative*, vol. 2, ed. Clelia Martignoni (Milan: Mondadori, 1976), 17.

79. Salvatore Satta, *De Profundis* (Milan: Adelphi, 1980 [1948]).

80. The most thought-provoking meditation on past ruins—itself a traditional topic in European literature—to appear in early postwar Italy is Anna Banti's *Artemisia*, trans. Shirley D'Ardia Caracciola (London: Serpent's Tail, 2003 [*Artemisia*, 1947]).

81. Giuseppe Berto, *The Sky Is Red*, trans. Angus Davidson (New York: New Directions, 1947); Vitaliano Brancati, *Beautiful Antonio*, trans. Stanley Hochman (New York: F. Ungar, 1978).

82. Bruno Romani, "A Parigi si leggono opere di scrittori italiani," *Il Tempo* (April 1948). Now in Malaparte, *Malaparte, Vol. 8: 1948–1949*, 104–6.

83. Romani, "Parigi," 105. On the centrality of Paris for the affirmation and international success of modern literature, see Pascal Casanova, *The World Republic of Letters* (Cambridge, MA: Harvard University Press, 2007).

84. Dario Biagi, *Vita scandalosa di Giuseppe Berto* (Turin: Bollati Boringhieri, 1999), 110. Giuseppe Berto, *The Brigand*, trans. Angus Davidson (New York: New American Library, 1953 [*Il brigante*, 1951]).

85. In one of the early reviews of postwar fiction in Italy, published in the influential Marxist journal *Società*, Malaparte is not even named and Berto is barely mentioned, setting the standard for a long critical tradition. Niccolò Gallo, "La narrativa italiana del dopoguerra," *Società* 6, no. 2 (1951): 324–41.

86. Michel-Rolph Trouillot, *Silencing the Past: Power and the Production of History* (Boston: Beacon Press, 1995), 49.

87. Among this vast bibliography on the military defeat, recent important contributions focused on the memory of the defeated soldiers returning from the many fronts, such as Agostino Bistarelli, *La storia del ritorno. I reduci italiani del secondo dopoguerra* (Turin: Bollati Boringhieri, 2007); and Gabriella Gribaudi, *Combattenti, sbandati, prigionieri. Esperienze e memorie dei reduci della seconda guerra mondiale* (Rome: Donzelli, 2016).

88. Indro Montanelli, *Qui non riposano* (Venice: Marsilio, 1982 [1945]); and Ruggero Zangrandi, *Il lungo viaggio. Contributo alla storia di una generazione* (Turin: Einaudi, 1948); then, with substantial changes, *Il lungo viaggio attraverso il fascismo. Contributo alla storia di una generazione* (Milan: Feltrinelli, 1962).

89. La Rovere, *Eredità del fascismo*, 29.

90. Giovanni Spadolini, review of *La pelle*, by Curzio Malaparte, *Il Messaggero*, February 9, 1950.

91. On the journal *Società* and the poetics of the chronicle, see Lucia Re, *Calvino and the Age of Neorealism: Fables of Estrangement* (Stanford, CA: Stanford University Press, 1990), and Leavitt, *Italian Neorealism*. In particular, Robert Gordon stresses the relevance of Giacomo Debenedetti's "16 Ottobre 1943," "as a model for the early postwar decades." Robert S. C. Gordon, *The Holocaust in Italian Culture, 1944–2010* (Stanford, CA: Stanford University Press, 2012), 47.

92. Cooke, *Legacy*, 33.

93. Italo Calvino, "La letteratura italiana sulla Resistenza," *Movimento di liberazione in Italia* 1 (1949): 40–46, cited in Cooke, *Legacy*, 32.

94. Cooke, *Legacy*, 29.

95. Claudio Fogu, "*Italiani brava gente*: The Legacy of Fascist Historical Culture on Italian Politics of Memory," in *The Politics of Memory in Postwar Europe*, ed. Richard Ned Lebow, Wulf Kasteiner, and Claudio Fogu (Durham, NC: Duke University Press, 2006), 147–76.

96. Guri Schwarz, *Tu mi devi seppellir. Riti funebri e culto nazionale alle origini della Repubblica* (Turin: UTET, 2010), 280.

97. Léon Blum's speech is cited in John C. Cairns, "Along the Road Back to France 1940," *American Historical Review* 64, no. 3 (April 1959): 590.

98. See Banti, *Sublime madre nostra*; and Gentile, *Grande Italia*.

99. On the rhetoric of national redemption arguing for Italy's intervention in WWI, see Patriarca, *Italian Vices*, 117.

100. Adriana M. Baranello, "Giovanni Pascoli's *La grande proletaria si è mossa*: A Translation and Critical Introduction," *California Italian Studies* 2, no. 1 (2011). Accessed January 25, 2022, https://escholarship.org/uc/item/6jho7474. On the invasion of Ethiopia as a "redemptive" war, see Maurizio Serra, *Malaparte. Vite e leggende* (Venice: Marsilio, 2012), 259.

101. La Rovere, *Eredità del fascismo*. Gian Enrico Rusconi aptly described the popular participation to the life of the nation during the transition, with the term "expiatory patriotism": "It's a way of participating in the sorrows of the nation characterized by a vague sense of guilt that is not personal (individually, in fact, one feels like an innocent victim), but collective. It's as if the traditional sense of national victimhood now found good reasons to justify itself. The adversities of a political-military nature that strike the country [...] appear to be the price that the community must pay for its own redemption from the consent given to the Fascist regime that led to the catastrophe." Gian Enrico Rusconi, *Possiamo fare a meno di una religione civile?* (Bari-Rome: Laterza: 1999), 51.

102. Cited in Forlenza, *On the Edge of Democracy*, 117.

103. Regarding a national Catholic ideology and how deeply rooted Catholic values and mindset were even in Communist Italy, see De Luna, *Repubblica inquieta*, 242, 251.

104. A few days after the end of the war, the liberal philosopher Guido De Ruggiero writes, "We need to begin with erasing from the veterans' spirit the upsetting and unjust impression that their sacrifice was in vain and that the country is released from any obligation of gratitude for what they did and suffered [...]. The opposition between Fascism and anti-Fascism must not apply in their regard." This excerpt is from one of the few articles of the time addressing the political and social problem of the Italians coming home from internment. See Guido De Ruggiero, "I reduci," *La Nuova Europa* 2, no. 21 (May 27, 1945): 1–2.

105. Claudio Pavone, *A Civil War: A History of the Italian Resistance* (London: Verso, 2014).

106. Robert S. C. Gordon, "The Italian War," in *The Cambridge Companion to the Literature of World War II*, ed. Marina Mackay (Cambridge: Cambridge University Press, 2011), 130. Starting from the brief and obscure experience of Primo Levi as a partisan, Sergio Luzzato poses the question of anti-Fascist violence's morality in compelling terms, in particular exploring its local and national memory, in his *Primo Levi's Resistance: Rebels and Collaborators in Occupied Italy* (New York: Metropolitan Books, 2016).

107. Celebrated novels such as Cesare Pavese's *The House on the Hill* (*La casa in collina*, 1948) and Italo Calvino's *The Path to the Spiders' Nests* (*Il sentiero dei nidi di ragno*, 1947) are fitting examples. Though part of the anti-Fascist canon, they display an uneasiness in aligning with the political dicta of the period. See also Daniela Brogi, *Giovani. Vita e scrittura tra fascismo e dopoguerra* (Palermo: Duepunti, 2012).

108. Leonardo Paggi, *Il "popolo dei morti." La repubblica italiana nata dalla guerra (1940–1946)* (Bologna: il Mulino, 2009), 30.

109. Wolfgang Schivelbusch, *The Culture of Defeat: On National Trauma, Mourning, and Recovery* (New York: Metropolitan, 2001), 10–11.

110. See Paolo Macry, *Gli ultimi giorni. Stati che crollano nell'Europa del Novecento* (Bologna: il Mulino, 2009).

111. Eric Santner, *Stranded Objects: Mourning, Memory, and Film in Postwar Germany* (Ithaca, NY: Cornell University Press, 1993), 6.

112. See Gentile, *Grande Italia*.

113. See Lanaro, *Storia*, 11–43.

114. Carlo Emilio Gadda, *Eros e Priapo. Versione integrale*, ed. Paola Itala and Giorgio Pinotti (Milan: Adelphi, 2016), 164.

115. Gadda, *Eros e Priapo*, 13.

116. Gadda, *Eros e Priapo*, 24.

117. Andrea Zanzotto, "Giuseppe Berto tra 'Il cielo è rosso' e 'Il brigante,'" *La provincia di Treviso* 5, no. 2 (1962): 30.

118. Alberto Asor Rosa, "Lo stato democratico ed i partiti politici," in *Letteratura Italiana, Vol. 1: Il letterato e le istituzioni*, ed. Alberto Asor Rosa (Turin: Einaudi, 1982), 580.

119. Yet "totalitarianism" was well present as a political term in the debate of the period. Giovanni De Luna exposes how before the 1948 elections, the Communist journal *Rinascita* was accusing the Christian Democrats of "totalitarianism": "In Italian political history there has never been a party or grouping (except maybe Fascism) that demonstrated [. . .] such a strong propensity for totalitarianism." De Luna, *Repubblica inquieta*, 193.

120. Vittorio Zincone, *Lo stato totalitario* (Rome: Ideazione, 1999 [1947]); Curzio Malaparte, *Il Volga nasce in Europa* (Milan: Bompiani, 1943), and *Das Kapital*, trans. and ed. Mario Maranzana (Milan: Mondadori, 1980 [1949]). However, Malaparte's relationship with Communism and the PCI establishment was complex and changed over time. His collaboration with the Communist daily *l'Unità* in 1944 and his friendship with Togliatti rapidly turned to sharp criticism in the aforementioned books and the disparaging political fiction of a Communist takeover in Italy in *Storia di domani* (Rome: Aria d'Italia, 1949).

121. Alberto Moravia, *Man as an End: A Defense of Humanism. Literary, Social, Political Essays*, trans. Bernard Wall (New York: Farrar, Straus and Giroux, 1966 [*L'uomo come fine*, 1953]); and "La speranza ossia cristianesimo e comunismo," in *Impegno controvoglia. Saggi, articoli, interviste: Trentacinque anni di scritti politici* (Milan: Bompiani, 2008 [1980]), 11–29.

122. Carlo Levi, *Christ Stopped at Eboli*, trans. Frances Frenaye (New York: Farrar, Straus and Giroux, 1998 [*Cristo si è fermato a Eboli*, 1945]).

123. Carlo Levi, *Fear of Freedom*, trans. Adolphe Gourevitch (New York: Columbia University Press, 2008 [*Paura della Libertà*, 1946]); and *The Watch*, trans. John Farrar and Marianna Gifford (New York: Farrar, Straus and Young, 1951 [*L'orologio*, 1950]).

124. Milan Kundera, "The Skin: Malaparte's Arch-Novel," in *Encounter* (New York: HarperCollins, 2010), 160.

1. After Italian Totalitarianism

1. Alberto Asor Rosa, "Lo Stato democratico e i partiti politici," in *Letteratura Italiana, Vol. 1: Il letterato e le istituzioni*, ed. Alberto Asor Rosa, (Turin: Einaudi, 1982), 580.

2. Enzo Traverso, *Il totalitarismo. Storia di un dibattito* (Milan: Bruno Mondadori, 2002), 19; see also Bruno Bongiovanni, "Totalitarianism: The Word and the Thing," *Journal of Modern European History* 3, no. 1 (2005): 5–17.

3. See Benito Mussolini, *Opera Omnia, Vol. 21*, ed. Edoardo Susmel and Duilio Susmel (Florence: La Fenice, 1967), 425.

4. For a general assessment, see Sigrid Meuschel, "The Institutional Frame: Totalitarianism, Extermination, and the State," in *The Lesser Evil: Moral Approaches to Genocide Practices*, ed. Helmut Dubiel and Gabriel Motzkin (London: Routledge, 2004), 109–24. For a comprehensive interpretation of Italian Totalitarianism, see Emilio Gentile, *La via italiana al totalitarismo. Il partito e lo Stato nel regime fascista* (Rome: Carocci, 2008).

5. See Stefano Cavazza, "La transizione difficile: l'immagine della guerra e della resistenza nell'opinione pubblica dell'immediato dopoguerra," in *La grande cesura. La memoria della guerra e della resistenza nella vita europea del dopoguerra*, ed. Giovanni Miccoli, Guido Neppi Modona, and Paolo Pombeni (Bologna: il Mulino, 2001), 427–64; Filippo Focardi, *La guerra della memoria. La Resistenza nel dibattito politico italiano dal 1945 ad oggi* (Bari-Rome: Laterza, 2005); John Foot, *Italy's Divided Memory* (New York: Palgrave Macmillian, 2003).

6. Paolo Alatri, "Morte apparente del fascismo," *La Nuova Europa* 2, no. 24 (1945): 10.

7. Filippo Focardi, "'Bravo italiano' e 'cattivo tedesco': riflessione sulla genesi di due immagini incrociate," *Storia e memoria* 1 (1996): 55–83; Ruth Ben-Ghiat, "A Lesser Evil? Italian Fascism in/and the Totalitarian Equation," in *The Lesser Evil: Moral Approaches to Genocide Practices*, ed. Helmut Dubiel and Gabriel Motzkin (London: Routledge, 2004), 137–53.

8. See Silvana Patriarca, *Italian Vices: Nation and Character from the Risorgimento to the Republic* (Cambridge: Cambridge University Press, 2010). This question does not pertain solely to Italian historiography. Foreign press and scholarly work substantially contributed to the building and the perpetuation of these stereotypes until today. Without delving into this long tradition here, it is worth mentioning one recent publication, Ian Buruma, *Year Zero: A History of 1945* (New York: Penguin, 2013). In Buruma's volume, Italy and its history are so ill-documented that Italian Fascism does not even figure among the regimes that unleashed World War II. Moreover, the momentous events of Italy's eastern border—Fascist massacres of civilians of Slavic origins; the Nazi, Titoist, and

then Allied occupation of Trieste; the attempted ethnic cleansing of Italian inhabitants of the Istrian peninsula perpetrated by Tito's army, followed by the so-called Foibe ("sinkholes") and the forced mass migration of about 300,000 Italians—are not even mentioned. On these issues, see Marina Cattaruzza, *L'Italia e il confine orientale. 1866–2006* (Bologna: il Mulino, 2007); and Guido Crainz, *Il dolore e l'esilio. L'Istria e le memorie divise d'Europa* (Rome: Donzelli, 2007). For a well-documented approach to the "Year Zero" in Italy, see Guido Crainz, *L'ombra della guerra. Il 1945, l'Italia* (Rome: Donzelli, 2007).

9. See Claudio Fogu, "*Italiani brava gente*: The Legacy of Fascist Historical Culture on Italian Politics of Memory," in *The Politics of Memory in Postwar Europe*, ed. Richard Ned Lebow, Wulf Kasteiner, and Claudio Fogu (Durham, NC: Duke University Press, 2006); Thomas Schlemmer, *Invasori, non vittime. La campagna italiana in Russia 1941–1943* (Bari-Rome: Laterza, 2009).

10. See Davide Rodogno, *Fascism's European Empire: Italian Occupation during the Second World War* (Cambridge: Cambridge University Press, 2006); Davide Conti, *L'occupazione italiana dei Balcani. Crimini di guerra e mito della "brava gente" (1940–1943)* (Rome: Odradek, 2008); Bastian Matteo Scianna, *The Italian War on the Eastern Front, 1941–1943: Operations, Myths, and Memories* (New York: Palgrave Macmillan, 2019).

11. See Michele Sarfatti, *The Jews in Mussolini's Italy: From Equality to Persecution* (Madison: University of Wisconsin Press, 2006).

12. Among the many recent academic contributions to these subjects, see Pamela Ballinger, *The World Refugees Made: Decolonization and the Foundation of Postwar Italy* (Ithaca, NY: Cornell University Press, 2021); Stephanie Malia Hom, *Empire's Mobius Strip: Historical Echoes in Italy's Crisis of Migration and Detention* (Ithaca, NY: Cornell University Press, 2019); and Ruth Ben-Ghiat, Stephanie Malia Hom, eds., *Italian Mobilities* (London: Routledge, 2016).

13. See also Paolo Monelli, *Roma 1943* (Turin: Einaudi, 2012 [1948]). For Croce during the postwar transition, see Fabio Fernando Rizi, *Benedetto Croce and the Birth of the Italian Republic, 1943–1952* (Toronto: University of Toronto Press, 2019).

14. Benedetto Croce, "The Fascist Germ Still Lives," *New York Times*, November 28, 1943.

15. Carlo Sforza, *The Real Italians: A Study in European Psychology* (New York: Columbia University Press, 1942), 138.

16. On the Italian spiritual brand of racism, see Aaron Gillette, *Racial Theories in Fascist Italy* (London: Routledge, 2002). On *Strapaese*, see Andrea Righi, *Italian Reactionary Thought and Critical Theory: An Inquiry into Savage Modernities* (New York: Palgrave Macmillan, 2015), esp. 79–153.

17. "An element of farce had never been lacking even in Italy's most serious efforts to adjust to its powerful friend and ally." Hannah Arendt, *Eichmann in Jerusalem: A Report on the Banality of Evil* (New York: Penguin, 1963), 178.

18. For the popular myth of the USSR and Stalin in Italy during the transition, see Rosario Forlenza, "The Soviet Myth and the Making of Communist Lives in Italy, 1943–56," *Journal of Contemporary History* 57, no. 3 (2022): 645–68.

19. Traverso, *Totalitarismo*, 77–86.

20. Alberto Moravia, "Man as an End," in *Man as an End: A Defense of Humanism. Literary, Social, Political Essays*, trans. Bernard Wall (New York: Farrar, Straus and Giroux, 1966 [*L'uomo come fine*, 1953]), 13–63.

21. Among the many contributions regarding the postwar return to humanism, the most influential were Jean-Paul Sartre, *Existentialism and Humanism* (1946); and Martin Heidegger, *Letter on "Humanism"* (1949). In Italy, two pivotal contributions were Cesare Pavese, "Ritorno all'uomo," *l'Unità* (May 20, 1945), now in *La letteratura americana e altri saggi* (Turin: Einaudi, 1991), 197–99; and Elio Vittorini, *Men and Not Men*, trans. Sarah Henry (Marlboro, VT: Marlboro Press, 1985 [*Uomini e no*, 1945]). The "return to humanism" was also a major theme in Neorealist film production—certainly more artistically successful and culturally influential than its literary counterpart. See Luchino Visconti, "Cinema antropomorfico," *Cinema* 8 (1943): 108–9; and Umberto Barbaro, *Il cinema e l'uomo moderno* (Milan: Edizioni Sociali, 1950).

22. Moravia was so prolific at the time—writing was his only source of income—that in the first issue of *Società*, an anonymous reviewer comments about the "usual Moravia, who is by now impossible not to find in any magazine of any party, or even of the independents." "Recensioni," *Società* 1–2 (1945): 349.

23. Maurizio Serra, *Malaparte. Vite e leggende* (Venice: Marsilio, 2012), 116.

24. "I was Fascist with a 'Protestant mentality,'" claimed Malaparte after the war, cited in Luigi Martellini, introduzione, in Curzio Malaparte, *Opere scelte*, ed. Luigi Martellini (Milan: Mondadori, 1997), lvii. The writer was also under special surveillance by Fascist secret police, particularly during the war and after his unorthodox reports from the Eastern Front. On this question, see Fabio Fattore, "Malaparte, corrispondente di guerra," *Nuova storia contemporanea* 14 (2010): 93–108.

25. Pier Giorgio Zunino, *Repubblica* (Bologna: il Mulino, 2003), 579.

26. Giorgio Napolitano, "Era quasi una replica di Kaputt che si svolgeva sotto i miei occhi . . . ," in Serra, *Malaparte*, 547–50.

27. See Emilio Gentile, *The Sacralization of Politics in Fascist Italy* (Cambridge, MA: Harvard University Press, 1996); and, by the same author, "The Sacralisation of Politics: Definitions, Interpretations, and Reflections on the Question of Secular Religion and Totalitarianism," *Totalitarian Movements and Political Religions* 1, no. 1 (2000): 18–55.

28. See Meuschel, "Institutional Frame;" and Enzo Traverso, *Il secolo armato. Interpretare le violenze del Novecento* (Milan: Feltrinelli, 2012), esp. 65–86.

29. See Roger Griffin, *Modernism and Fascism: The Sense of a Beginning under Mussolini and Hitler* (New York: Palgrave Macmillan, 2007).

30. Serra, *Malaparte*, 194–204.

31. Curzio Malaparte, *Mamma Marcia* (Florence: Vallecchi, 1959), 293.

32. According to Lorenzo Greco, in the early 1930s Vittorini worked as a ghost writer for some of Malaparte's Fascist pamphlets. See Lorenzo Greco, *Censura e scrittura. Vittorini, lo pseudo-Malaparte, Gadda* (Milan: il Saggiatore, 1983). On many occasions, Carlo Emilio Gadda claimed that his distance from the regime grew after the Italo-Ethiopian War. In a study of Gadda's journalistic work in the 1930s and 1940s, Robert Dombroski demonstrated instead how, as far as 1943, the writer was still in full support of the regime with fervid propaganda press. Robert S. Dombroski, *Creative Entaglements: Gadda and the Baroque* (Toronto: University of Toronto Press, 1999), 117–34. Notoriously, both Ungaretti and Pirandello were acclaimed as "Accademici d'Italia" under the regime.

33. Malaparte, "Nostro peccato," *Prospettive* 4, no. 4 (1940): 3.

34. "Literature is, in a certain sense, outside history; it develops, that is, independently of everything that is extraneous to it. And precisely to the extent that it denies everything that is extraneous to it, precisely to the extent that it refuses history, it reveals its particular morality, its intrinsic nature, the intimate reasons behind its demands and behaviors [. . .] an autonomy finally rediscovered and conquered in itself." Malaparte, "Cadaveri squisiti," *Prospettive* 4, no. 6–7 (1942): 4. For a detailed overview of the journal, see Luigi Martellini, *Le "Prospettive" di Malaparte. Una rivista tra cultura fascista, europeismo e letteratura* (Naples: ESI, 2014).

35. Curzio Malaparte, *The Skin*, trans. David Moore (New York: NYRB Classics, 2013 [*La pelle*, 1949]), 283.

36. See Giordano Bruno Guerri, *L'arcitaliano. Vita di Curzio Malaparte* (Milan: Mondadori, 2000), 206; Giuseppe Pardini, *Curzio Malaparte. Biografia politica* (Milan: Luni, 1998), 297–300; and Serra, *Malaparte*, 312–17.

37. Curzio Malaparte, Letter to Valentino Bompiani, Capri, March 12, 1943 XXI, reprinted in Enzo Laforgia, *Malaparte scrittore di guerra* (Florence: Vallecchi, 2011), 236.

38. Curzio Malaparte, Letter to Valentino Bompiani, Capri, August 21, 1943, reprinted in Laforgia, *Malaparte scrittore di guerra*, 238.

39. Curzio Malaparte, *The Volga Rises in Europe*, trans. David Moore (London: Redman, 1957) follows the 1951 Italian edition. Here I will quote from the original 1943 edition, Curzio Malaparte, *Il Volga nasce in Europa* (Milan: Bompiani, 1943). Translation is mine.

40. Malaparte, *Volga*, 11.

41. In these correspondences, Malaparte blends orientalist clichés with stereotypes about the "savage nature" of Balkan countries, conceived as a "bridge" between Western Europe and "the Orient." On Malaparte's war correspondence from the Balkans, see Franco Baldasso, "Curzio Malaparte e la guerra nei Balcani. Letteratura, propaganda, censura," in *Curzio Malaparte e la ricerca dell'identità*

europea (1920–1950), ed. Beatrice Baglivo et al. (Chambéry: Presses de l'Université Savoie Mont Blanc, 2020), 191–222.

42. "Among bourgeois prejudices about Soviet Russia, the most stubborn is the one that considers Bolshevism a typically Asiatic phenomenon," Malaparte states in the preface to his book. "The title of this book, *The Volga Rises in Europe*, is meant precisely as a rebuke of that petty prejudice." Malaparte, *Volga*, 10–11.

43. See Malaparte, *Volga*, 10–12.

44. See Baldasso, "Curzio Malaparte e la guerra nei Balcani," especially 201–8.

45. Malaparte, *Volga*, 67–69. This passage was originally in "Battaglia nei campi ucraini," *Corriere della Sera*, July 11, 1941.

46. Curzio Malaparte, "Cadaveri squisiti," *Prospettive* 4, no. 6–7 (1940): 5.

47. Indro Montanelli, *Qui non riposano* (Venice: Marsilio, 1982 [1945]); Leo Longanesi, *Parliamo dell'elefante. Frammenti di un diario* (Milan: Longanesi, 1947).

48. Malaparte, "Cadaveri squisiti," 4; 6. For Malaparte's war reportages, see Fattore, "Curzio Malaparte"; and Laforgia, *Malaparte scrittore di guerra*.

49. Malaparte explicitly calls *Kaputt*, "un libro crudele," now in Curzio Malaparte, *Opere scelte*, ed. Luigi Martellini (Milan: Mondadori, 1997), 430. The available translation in English reads: "*Kaputt* is a horribly gay and gruesome book." Curzio Malaparte, *Kaputt*, trans. Cesare Foligno (New York: NYRB Classics, 2005), 3.

50. On Malaparte's articles from Greece, see Mario Isnenghi, "I due occhi di Malaparte giornalista e fotografo," in *Da Malaparte a Malaparte. Malaparte fotografo*, ed. Sauro Lusini (Prato: Comune di Prato, 1987). On his relations with French culture, see Maria Pia de Paulis, ed., *Cahier Malaparte* (Paris: Éditions de l'Herne, 2018); and Martina Grassi, ed., *"La Bourse des idées du monde." Malaparte e la Francia* (Florence: Olschki, 2008).

51. See Giuseppe Pardini, "Malaparte, Moravia e 'Prospettive,'" *Nuova storia contemporanea* 3 (1999): n108. Moravia was not the only writer of Jewish origin who published in *Prospettive* after the promulgation of the racial laws. Elsa Morante, Alberto Vigevani, and Guido Seborga also wrote for the journal. This, however, did not prevent Malaparte from using anti-Semitic tones in his *Corriere della Sera* articles of the same time. See Annalisa Capristo, "'Spettacolo più tetro non vidi mai.' La persecuzione antiebraica nell'Est europeo nei giornali italiani: il 1941," *Rassegna mensile di Israel* 84, nos. 1–2 (2018): 179–218.

52. Curzio Malaparte, "Lana Caprina," *Prospettive* 4, 5 (1940): 4.

53. Pardini, "Malaparte, Moravia," 109.

54. Czesław Miłosz, *The Captive Mind* (New York: Vintage, 1990 [1951]); Danilo Kiš, "Censorship/Self-Censorship," in *Homo Poeticus: Essays and Interviews* (New York: Farrar, Strauss and Giroux, 2003 [1985]), 91–92.

55. Guido Piovene, "Gli intellettuali sono proletari," cited in Sandro Gerbi, *Tempi di Malafede. Guido Piovene ed Eugenio Colorni. Una storia italiana tra fascismo e dopoguerra* (Milan: Hoepli, 2012), 167; Moravia, "Speranza," 11–29;

and Alberto Savinio, "Sorte dell'Europa," in *Sorte dell'Europa* (Milan: Adelphi, 2005 [1945]), 89–90. For the "metamorphosis" of Italian intellectuals after Fascism, see Simon Levis Sullam, *I fantasmi del fascismo. Le metamorfosi degli intellettuali italiani nel dopoguerra* (Milan: Feltrinelli, 2021), especially 106–31 on Moravia.

56. Curzio Malaparte "La lezione di Firenze. I fiorentini delle 'cronache,'" *l'Unità*, August 23, 1944. Now in *Malaparte, Vol. 6: 1942–1945*, ed. Edda Ronchi Suckert (Florence: Ponte alle Grazie, 1991–1996), 513.

57. After its first publication in 1921, Malaparte revised *Viva Caporetto!* and changed its title to *La rivolta dei santi maledetti* (1923) because of censorship problems. That revision can be found in Malaparte, *Opere scelte*.

58. John Gatt-Rutter, "Liberation and Literature: Naples 1944," *Journal of Modern Italian Studies* 1 (1996): 249.

59. For his critique of Stalinism, see also Curzio Malaparte, *The Kremlin Ball*, trans. Jenny McPhee (New York: NYRB Classics, 2018 [1971]).

60. Curzio Malaparte, *Das Kapital, pièce en trois actes; précédée de Du côté de chez Proust, impromptu en un acte* (Paris: Denoël, 1951). Information on the scandal *Das Kapital* caused in Paris, including the mentioned remark, are in Serra, *Malaparte*, for whom *Das Kapital* is the "most modern [work] that Malaparte ever wrote" (431).

61. The article was published as C. E. Suckert, "Gli eroi capovolti," *La Rivoluzione liberale* 1, no. 23 (1922): 85–86.

62. In his biography, Guerri documents Malaparte's deep knowledge and appreciation of classic Greek tragedy. See Guerri, *Arcitaliano*, 237–38.

63. Walter Benjamin, *On the Concept of History*, in *Selected Writings, Vol. 4, 1938–1940* (Cambridge, MA: The Belknap Press of Harvard University Press, 2004 [1940]), 115.

64. On the philosophical inquiry regarding the ontological possibility of a "new origin," see Roberto Esposito, *Living Thought: The Origins and Actuality of Italian Philosophy* (Stanford, CA: Stanford University Press, 2012).

65. Silvio D'Amico, "Vanno in scena a Parigi due commedie di Malaparte," *Il Tempo*, October 25, 1948. Now in Malaparte, *Malaparte, Vol. 8: 1948–1949*, 229.

66. Malaparte, *Das Kapital*, 87; 140.

67. "Jesus Christ is Marx's antagonist, the interlocutor of his conscience, and is represented by a strange character with the duties of a secretary, dressed all in black, mysterious and surprising. He tells Marx that justice is not the work of men, but of God . . . " Gianni Granzotto, "La politica a teatro. Parigi decreta il successo a 'Das Kapital' di Curzio Malaparte," *Il Tempo*, January 30, 1948. Now in Malaparte, *Malaparte, Vol. 8: 1948–1949*, 338.

68. See "Christological Figures of Sacrifice: *The Skin*" in Chapter 5.

69. Malaparte, *Das Kapital*, 87.

70. See Michael Löwy, *Redemption and Utopia: Jewish Libertarian Thought in Central Europe* (Stanford, CA: Stanford University Press, 1992).

71. The opposition between "justice" and "charity" at the center of *Das Kapital* is also key to interpreting the novel *The Kremlin Ball*, which Malaparte was writing in those very years. Unfinished and published only posthumously, the novel portrays how terror and political violence ruled society in Soviet Russia. Malaparte, *Kremlin Ball*.

72. Salvatore Quasimodo, "Carlo Marx resuscitato da Malaparte," *Tempo*, February 5–12, 1949. Now in Malaparte, *Malaparte, Vol. 8: 1948–1949*, 375.

73. Silvio D'Amico, "Vanno in scena a Parigi due commedie di Malaparte," *Il Tempo*, October 25, 1948, now in Malaparte, *Malaparte, Vol. 8: 1948–1949*, 227–29.

74. Milan Kundera, "The Skin: Malaparte's Arch-Novel," in *Encounter* (New York: Harper Collins, 2010), 176.

75. For a general assessment of the Action Party politics and the debate on the issue of the "purge" of Fascist representatives—not only in politics but also in Italian civil society—see Giovanni De Luna, *Storia del Partito d'Azione, 1942–1947* (Turin: UTET, 2006).

76. Elio Vittorini, "Fascisti i giovani?," *Il Politecnico* 15 (1946), 69–73. For an analysis of Vittorini's populism and redemptive narratives, see Chiara Ferrari, *The Rhetorics of Violence and Sacrifice in Fascist Italy: Mussolini, Gadda, Vittorini* (Toronto: University of Toronto Press, 2013).

77. Ruggero Zangrandi, *Il lungo viaggio. Contributo alla storia di una generazione* (Turin: Einaudi, 1948). Relevant reflections on the concept of "generation" for historiography can be found in Mariuccia Salvati, *Passaggi. Italiani dal fascismo alla Repubblica* (Rome: Carocci, 2016), 121–42.

78. Luca La Rovere, *L'eredità del fascismo. Gli intellettuali, i giovani e la transizione al postfascismo* (Turin: Bollati Boringhieri, 2008), especially 134–257.

79. Vittorio Zincone, *Lo stato totalitario* (Rome: Ideazione, 1999 [1947]), 187.

80. Zincone, *Stato totalitario*, 92.

81. Zincone, *Stato totalitario*, 123–24.

82. Zincone, *Stato totalitario*, 204.

83. See Enzo Traverso, *Il secolo armato. Interpretare le violenze del Novecento* (Milan: Feltrinelli, 2012).

84. La Rovere, *Eredità del Fascismo*, 286.

85. See La Rovere, *Eredità del Fascismo*; and Mirella Serri, *I redenti. Gli intellettuali che vissero due volte. 1938–1948* (Milan: Corbaccio, 2006).

86. Vittorio Zincone "Quello che manca alla Costituzione," *Mercurio* 3, nos. 25–26 (1946): 14–18.

87. Zincone "Quello che manca," 16.

88. See Piero Calamandrei, *Uomini e città della Resistenza. Discorsi, scritti ed epigrafi* (Bari-Rome: Laterza, 1955).

89. Piero Calamandrei, *Il fascismo come regime della menzogna* (Bari-Rome: Laterza, 2014), 18–19.

90. Calamandrei, *Fascismo come regime*, 17.

91. For an analysis of Calamandrei's work during the dictatorship through postwar Italy, see Levis Sullam, *Fantasmi*, especially 52–79.

92. Gabriele Pedullà, "Piero Calamandrei e la Resistenza come narrazione civile," *Contemporanea*, 14, no. 2 (2011): 272.

93. Alberto Moravia and Alain Elkann, *Life of Moravia*, trans. William Weaver (South Royalton, VT: Steerforth Italia, 2000), 132. Translation here is mine.

94. Simone Casini, "Moravia e il fascismo. A proposito di alcune lettere a Mussolini e a Ciano," *Studi italiani* 38, no. 2 (2007): 214. See also Simon Levis Sullam, "Gli indifferenti 'ebraizzati,'" in *Atlante della letteratura italiana, Vol. 3: Dal Romanticismo a oggi*, ed. Sergio Luzzato, Gabriele Pedullà, and Domenico Scarpa (Turin: Einaudi, 2021), 551–58.

95. "This illness was the most important fact of my life. The second fact was Fascism. I attribute a great deal of importance to the illness and to Fascism because due to the illness and to Fascism I had to undergo and do things that otherwise I would not have done. What shapes our character are the things we are forced to do, not those that we do of our own free will." Alberto Moravia, "Autobiografia in breve di Alberto Moravia," quoted in Casini, "Moravia e il fascismo," 192.

96. In the article "Recalling *Time of Indifference*," first published in 1945 in *La Nuova Europa* Moravia claims: "At this point someone will want to know why I don't talk about the social or furtively political aims of anti-bourgeois critique that many attribute to the novel. I reply that I don't talk about them because they weren't there." Alberto Moravia, "Recalling *Time of Indifference*," in *Man as an End: A Defense of Humanism. Literary, Social, and Political Essays*, trans. Bernard Wall (New York: Farrar, Straus and Giroux, 1966 [1953]), 80. Translation here is mine.

97. According to the official biographer Yvon de Begnac, Mussolini commented on Moravia's *The Time of Indifference*: "That book, the debut work of a very young man, written in a mediocre Italian but powerful in its account of a Roman environment whose survival I never would have suspected, had revealed to me the presence of the real world of anti-Fascism, of the anti-Fascism that does not speak, that does not reveal its own presence. Its shadow slips beside you, you notice its terrifying tremor." Yvon De Begnac, *Taccuini Mussoliniani* (Bologna: il Mulino, 1990), 483–84.

98. See Guido Bonsaver, *Censorship and Literature in Fascist Italy* (Toronto: University of Toronto Press, 2007).

99. Moravia, "Man as an End," 49.

100. See Ruth Leys, *From Guilt to Shame: Auschwitz and After* (Princeton, NJ: Princeton University Press, 2007).

101. Moravia, "Man as an End," 57–58.

102. See Zygmunt Bauman, *Modernity and the Holocaust* (Ithaca, NY: Cornell University Press, 2006); and Giorgio Agamben, *Homo Sacer: Sovereign Power and Bare Life* (Stanford, CA: Stanford University Press, 1998).

103. Moravia, "Man as an End," 54.

104. See Simone Casini, Introduction, in Alberto Moravia, *I due amici. Frammenti di una storia fra guerra e dopoguerra*, ed. Simone Casini (Milan: Bompiani, 2007), xxvii.

105. Maurizio Ciocchetti, *Percorsi paralleli. Moravia e Piovene tra giornali e riviste del dopoguerra* (Pesaro: Metauro, 2010).

106. In his biography of Moravia, René De Ceccatty mentions "Diario politico" only briefly. In the months following the liberation of Rome in June 1944, Moravia published his political pamphlet *La speranza* and a collection of short stories entitled *L'epidemia* for the small but dynamic "Edizioni Documento." For the same publication, Moravia planned and announced a forthcoming *Diario politico* in 1944 that was never released. See René De Ceccatty, *Alberto Moravia* (Paris: Flammarion, 2010); and Gioia Sebastiani, "Editori a Roma dopo la Liberazione: *Le Edizioni Documento*," in *Gli archivi degli editori, studi e prospettive di ricerca*, ed. Gianfranco Tortorelli (Bologna: Patron, 1998), 170.

107. Alberto Moravia, "Folla e demagoghi," *Il Popolo di Roma*, August 25, 1943, now in *Impegno controvoglia. Saggi, articoli, interviste: Trentacinque anni di scritti politici* (Milan: Bompiani, 2008 [1980]), 6.

108. On the journal, see Daniela La Penna, "*Aretusa*: Continuity, Rupture, and Space for Intervention (1944–1946)," *Journal of Modern Italian Studies* 21, no. 1 (2016): 19–34.

109. Alberto Moravia, "Diario politico," *Aretusa* 1, no. 2 (1944): 42.

110. Alberto Moravia, "La speranza, ossia cristianesimo e comunismo" (1944), in *Impegno controvoglia*, 11–29.

111. Beginning with Max Weber's notion of "disenchantment of the world," social theorists have described this larger process, which was also driven by capitalism and rationalization, as "secularization." For a broader interpretation of secularization, see Charles Taylor, *A Secular Age* (Cambridge, MA: The Belknap Press of Harvard University Press, 2007).

112. Moravia, "Speranza," 11.

113. Simone Casini "Lo scrittore e l'intellettuale," introduzione to Moravia, *Impegno controvoglia*, xix.

114. Alain Badiou, *Ethics: An Essay on the Understanding of Evil* (New York: Verso, 2002).

115. Moravia, "Speranza," 29.

116. Vittore Branca, review of *La Speranza*, by Alberto Moravia, *Il Ponte* 1, no. 2, (1945): 158.

117. Il pigro, [Alberto Moravia], "Rivoluzione e pessimismo," *Città*, November 23, 1944, 14.

118. Il pigro [Moravia], "Rivoluzione e pessimismo," 14.

119. While Gramsci's ideas circulated widely in postwar Italy—first in the Communist journal *Rinascita*, then in *Letters from Prison* (1947), and finally in volumes such as *Note sul Machiavelli, sulla politica e sullo Stato moderno* (1949)—

there is no evidence that they circulated in Rome in the months following the June 1944 Liberation, when Moravia's "Rivoluzione e pessimismo" was published.

120. Alberto Moravia, "Diario politico," *La Nuova Europa* 2, no. 2 (1945): 6. Moving from *Aretusa*—a journal under the influence of Croce and his intellectual circle—to the more progressive *La Nuova Europa*, Moravia's "Political Diary" becomes increasingly experimental both in content and in form.

121. Alberto Moravia, "Diario politico," *La Nuova Europa* 2, no. 6 (1945): 7.

122. Alberto Moravia, "Diario politico," *La Nuova Europa* 2, no. 20 (1945): 9.

123. Alberto Moravia, "Nazismo e nazione," *Libera Stampa*, April 11, 1945, 1.

124. Alberto Moravia, "Questo dopoguerra," *Libera Stampa*, June 5, 1945, 1.

125. Alberto Moravia, "Sull'Europa," *La città libera*, June 14, 1945, 8; and "Sulle masse," *La città libera*, July 19, 1945, 3.

126. See Guri Schwarz, *Tu mi devi seppellir. Riti funebri e culto nazionale alle origini della Repubblica* (Milan: UTET, 2010), 93–98.

127. Gaetano Salvemini, "Salvemini a Rossi e a Valiani, 10 agosto 1946," *Lettere dall'America, Vol. 1, 1944–1946*, ed. Alberto Merola (Bari-Rome: Laterza, 1967), 356–57. Quoted in Zunino, *Repubblica*, 502.

128. Alberto Moravia, "Quaderno politico" *La città libera*, September 13, 1945, 4.

129. Moravia, "Quaderno politico," 4.

2. The Language of Responsibility

1. Dario Biagi, *Vita scandalosa di Giuseppe Berto* (Turin: Bollati Boringhieri, 1999), 127.

2. Biagi, *Vita scandalosa*, 78; see also Evaldo Violo, "La fortuna editoriale e il pubblico di Berto," in *Giuseppe Berto. La sua cultura, il suo tempo*, ed. Everardo Artico and Laura Lepri (Venice: Marsilio; Olschki, 1989), 285–96.

3. Giancarlo Vigorelli, "Review of *Il cielo è rosso* by Giuseppe Berto," *Oggi*, February 11, 1947; cited in Biagi, *Vita scandalosa*, n245. Publisher Leo Longanesi took interest in the novel after a letter from famed author Giovanni Comisso, who wrote, "I assure you it represents a turning point in Italian literature," and strongly recommended publication. Cited in Domenico Scarpa, "Prefazione. Un volontario sincero," in Giuseppe Berto, *Il cielo è rosso* (Turin: UTET, 2007), xviii.

4. Sereni also reflects on his war experience in some of his early proses. See Vittorio Sereni, *La tentazione della prosa*, ed. Giulia Raboni (Milan: Mondadori, 1998).

5. Ernesto Galli della Loggia, *La morte della patria. La crisi dell'idea di nazione tra Resistenza, antifascismo e Repubblica* (Bari-Rome: Laterza, 1996), 93.

6. For a reconstruction of the debate ensuing the publication of Galli della Loggia's essay, see Filippo Focardi, *La guerra della memoria. La Resistenza nel dibattito politico italiano dal 1945 ad oggi* (Bari-Rome: Laterza, 2005), 65. See also Leonardo Paggi's reflections on the devastating consequences of Allied bombings

for the consensus of Italian people with Mussolini's regime, in his *Il "popolo dei morti." La repubblica italiana nata dalla guerra (1940–1946)* (Bologna: il Mulino, 2009), 11. For a military assessment of Italy in WWII up to the fall of Mussolini, see John Gooch, *Mussolini's War: Fascist Italy from Triumph to Collapse: 1935–1943* (New York: Pegasus, 2020).

7. See Davide Rodogno, *Fascism's European Empire: Italian Occupation during the Second World War* (Cambridge: Cambridge University Press, 2006).

8. See Victoria de Grazia, *The Culture of Consent: Mass Organization of Leisure in Fascist Italy* (Cambridge: Cambridge University Press, 2002).

9. Alberto Moravia, "La borghesia," in *Dopo il diluvio. Sommario dell'Italia contemporanea*, ed. Delio Terra (Garzanti: Milano, 1947), 214.

10. Mario Soldati, "La capitolazione," in *Corrispondenti di guerra*, ed. Emiliano Morreale (Palermo: Sellerio, 2009 [1943]), 72.

11. Bonaventura Tecchi, "I vantaggi della sconfitta," *La Nuova Europa* 2, no. 41 (1945): 5.

12. See Mirella Serri, *I redenti. Gli intellettuali che vissero due volte. 1938–1948* (Milan: Corbaccio, 2006); and Luisa Mangoni, ed., *Primato, 1940–1943: Antologia* (Bari: De Donato, 1977).

13. Stephen Gundle, "The Legacy of the Prison Notebooks: Gramsci, the PCI, and Italian Culture in the Cold War Period," in *Italy in the Cold War: Politics, Culture, and Society 1948–58*, ed. Christopher Duggan and Christopher Wagstaff (Oxford: Berg, 1995), 131–47; and Roberto Dainotto and Fredric Jameson, eds., *Gramsci in the World* (Durham, NC: Duke University Press, 2020).

14. Robert Ventresca, *From Fascism to Democracy: Culture and Politics in the Italian Election of 1948* (Toronto: University of Toronto Press, 2004).

15. Sandro Gerbi, *Tempi di Malafede. Guido Piovene ed Eugenio Colorni. Una storia italiana tra fascismo e dopoguerra* (Milan: Hoepli, 2012); Serri, *Redenti*.

16. Vitaliano Brancati, "Istinto e intuizione," in *I fascisti invecchiano*, in *Opere 1932–1946*, ed. Leonardo Sciascia (Milan: Bompiani, 1987), 1135.

17. Vittorio Sereni, "Appunti da un sogno," in *Diario d'Algeria* (Milan: Mondadori, 1965 [1947]), 70.

18. Giuseppe Berto, *The Sky Is Red*, trans. Angus Davidson (New York: New Directions, 1948 [*Il cielo è rosso*, 1947]); and *The Works of God and Other Stories*, trans. Angus Davidson (New York: New Directions, 1950 [*Le opere di Dio*, 1948]).

19. Biagi, *Vita scandalosa*, 126.

20. Biagi, *Vita scandalosa*, 66.

21. Berto is not referring here to the combatants of the "Repubblica di Salò," of which he probably had a proper knowledge only after his return from his imprisonment in Texas, but more broadly to Italian Army's soldiers and volunteers involved in the war. Giuseppe Berto, *Guerra in camicia nera* (Venice: Marsilio, 1985 [1955]), 10.

22. Giuseppe Berto, "L'inconsapevole approccio" (1965), in *Le opere di Dio* (Milan: Mondadori, 1980), 67–68.

23. Berto, "Inconsapevole approccio," 73.

24. Andrea Zanzotto, "Giuseppe Berto tra 'Il cielo è rosso' e 'Il brigante.'" *La provincia di Treviso* 5, no. 2 (1962): 30.

25. In the novel Berto describes the bombings from American pilots' point of view as well: "And the stars fly too; they fly at a fantastic speed towards the places to which those men belong, in another part of the earth. In a matter of a few hours, the stars which are now above their heads will be above Kentucky, Missouri, California. And each of those men who have destroyed houses and living creatures can still think lovingly of other houses and other living creatures." Berto, *Sky Is Red*, 62–63. See also Paola Culicelli, *La coscienza di Berto* (Florence: Le Lettere, 2012), 61.

26. Giancarlo Alfano hinted at this direction in his book *Ciò che ritorna: Gli effetti della guerra nella narrativa italiana del Novecento* (Florence: Cesati, 2014).

27. Giorgio Barberi Squarotti, "Quale rosso del cielo," in *Giuseppe Berto vent'anni dopo. Atti del convegno. Padova—Mogliano Veneto 23–24 ottobre 1998*, ed. Beatrice Bartolomeo and Saveria Chemotti (Pisa-Rome: Istituti Editoriali e Poligrafici Internazionali, 2000), 32.

28. Berto, "Inconsapevole approccio," 62.

29. Donald Heiney, *America in Modern Italian Literature* (New Brunswick, NJ: Rutgers University Press, 1964), 161.

30. Translation here is by the author. In fact, the 1948 English translation omits the reference to Jesus altogether, thus distorting the meaning of the entire novel. Censorship and conspicuous omissions were the norm in early postwar American translations of Italian books. It is no coincidence that other novels that are key for this study—such as Morante's *Lies and Sorcery* (translated in 1951 as *House of Liars*) and Malaparte's *The Skin*—were heavily cut, presumably on moral grounds (see, respectively, "On Living among Ghosts: Elsa Morante" in Chapter 3 and "Christological Figures of Sacrifice: *The Skin*" in Chapter 5). Berto, *Sky Is Red*, 395.

31. "Daniele wants to die in the manner of Christ, and therefore basically *mimics* Christ's sacrifice, even if he mimics it in its external features, more than in its substance. [His] gesture is a desperate one, and thus only formally Christian." Giorgio Pullini, "Dialettica di due forme terapeutiche: l'afflato cristiano e l'autonomia," in *Giuseppe Berto. La sua opera, il suo tempo*, ed. Everardo Artico and Laura Lepri (Venice: Marsilio; Olschki, 1989), 60–61.

For a general overview of these themes in Berto's production, see Giorgio Pullini, *Giuseppe Berto: da "Il cielo è rosso" a "Il male oscuro"* (Modena: Mucchi, 1991).

32. Biagi, *Vita scandalosa*, 54–55.

33. See Ruth Ben-Ghiat, *Fascist Modernities: Italy 1922–1945* (Berkeley: University of California Press, 2001), 195–96; and Noa Steimatsky, *Italian Locations: Reinhabiting the Past in Postwar Cinema* (Minneapolis: University of Minnesota Press, 2005), 79–116.

34. Berto, "Inconsapevole approccio," 64.
35. Italics added.
36. Traverso, *Il secolo armato. Interpretare le violenze del Novecento* (Milan: Feltrinelli, 2012), 154. On the significance of melancholic gaze for historical interpretation, see Michael Löwy, *Fire Alarm: Reading Walter Benjamin's 'On the Concept of History'* (New York: Verso, 2005); and, again: Traverso, *Secolo armato*, 189–195.
37. Giuseppe Berto, "Economia di candele," "Il seme tra le spine," "Gli eucaliptus cresceranno," in *Tutti i racconti* (Milan: Rizzoli, 2012).
38. Berto, *Sky Is Red*, 370–71.
39. Berto, *Sky Is Red*, 371.
40. Berto, *Sky Is Red*, 396.
41. Fortini's *Agonia di Natale* was republished with a new title in 1972: Franco Fortini, *Giovanni e le mani* (Turin: Einaudi, 1972 [1948]).
42. Fortini, *Giovanni e le mani*, 85.
43. Walter Benjamin, "The Storyteller: Reflections on the Works of Nikolai Leskov," in *Illuminations: Essays and Reflections* (New York: Schocken, 2007), 86.
44. Eduardo De Filippo, *Naples Get Rich (Napoli milionaria!)*, in *Four Plays*, trans. Maria Tucci (Hanover, NH: Smith and Kraus, 2002 [1945]). For an analysis of De Filippo's play in revealing contrast to Malaparte's novel *The Skin* (1949), see Ruth Glynn, "Naples and the Nation in Cultural Representations of the Allied Occupation," *California Italian Studies* 7, no. 2 (2017), accessed June 5, 2021, https://escholarship.org/uc/item/1vp8t8dz.
45. James J. Sheehan, *Where Have All the Soldiers Gone? The Transformation of Modern Europe* (Boston: Mariner, 2009).
46. Carlo Mazzantini's harrowing WWII memoir *In Search of a Glorious Death* (Manchester: Carcanet, 1992 [*A cercar la bella morte*, 1986]) hints precisely in this direction.
47. Berto, "Gli eucaliptus cresceranno," in *Tutti i racconti*, 116.
48. For this specific topic in Benjamin, see Martin Jay, "Walter Benjamin, Remembrance, and the First World War," *Review of Japanese Culture and Society* 11–12 (1999–2000): 18–31.
49. Hannah Arendt, *The Origins of Totalitarianism* (New York: Harvest, 1976 [1951]), 458.
50. David Michel, "La psicologia nell'opera narrativa di Berto," in *Giuseppe Berto. La sua cultura, il suo tempo*, ed. Everardo Artico and Laura Lepri (Venice: Marsilio; Olschki, 1989), 126.
51. Mangano's babbling in *The Works of God* confirms the centrality of this motif in Berto's reflections on the consequences of the war.
52. Gerbi, *Tempi di malafede*, 71–108.
53. Pierre Loewel, "Romanciers Italiens," *L'Aurore*, October 28, 1948.
54. Gerbi, *Tempi di malafede*, 167.
55. Guido Piovene, "Non furono tetri," *Mercurio* 1, no. 4 (1944): 287.

56. Franco Cordelli, *L'ombra di Piovene* (Florence: Le Lettere, 2011), 49–50.

57. Piovene's early postwar novels, indeed, received mixed reviews once published. See Gianfranco Piazzesi, "Review of *Pietà contro pietà* by Guido Piovene," *Il Ponte* 2, nos. 7–8 (1946): 873.

58. Gerbi, *Tempi di malafede*, 135.

59. Guido Piovene, "Gli amanti della malafede," *Città* 1, no. 1 (November 11, 1944): 12.

60. Guido Piovene, "Gli interprovinciali," *Città*, 1, no. 2 (November 23, 1944): 10.

61. Guido Piovene, "Est, est: non, non," *La città libera* 1, no. 16 (May 31, 1945): 8–9.

62. Guido Piovene, "Sinistra e destra nell'arte," *Il Tempo*, July 11, 1944, 2.

63. Guido Piovene, *Pietà contro pietà*, in *Opere narrative*, Vol. 1, ed. Clelia Martignoni (Milan: Mondadori, 1976), 841.

64. Vittorio Alfieri, *The Life of Vittorio Alfieri Written by Himself*, trans. Sir Henry McAnally (Lawrence: University of Kansas Press, 1953 [*Vita scritta da esso*, 1804]); Italo Svevo, *Zeno's Conscience*, trans. William Weaver (London: Penguin, 2019 [1923]).

65. Piovene, *Pietà contro pietà*, 945.

66. Piovene, *Pietà contro pietà*, 889.

67. Leo Bersani, *The Culture of Redemption* (Cambridge, MA: Harvard University Press, 1990), 2.

68. Marcello Ciocchetti, *Percorsi paralleli. Moravia e Piovene tra giornali e riviste del dopoguerra* (Pesaro: Metauro, 2010), 66.

69. Guido Piovene, "La chiesa," in *Dopo il diluvio. Sommario dell'Italia contemporanea*, ed. Delio Terra (Milan: Garzanti, 1947), 37.

70. See Nino Borsellino, "Metamorfosi del comico," in *Vitaliano Brancati. Da Via Etnea a Via Veneto*, ed. Daniela Battiati and Immacolata Magnano (Rome: Fahrenheit 451, 2001), 27–32.

71. For Brancati's relations with Italian cinema, see Orio Caldiron, "La lente smisurata di Vitaliano Brancati," in *Dalla Sicilia all'Europa. L'Italia di Vitaliano Brancati*, ed. Marco Dondero (Rome: De Luca, 2005).

72. It is no chance that a highly politicized film critic such as Goffredo Fofi, in more recent years admitted that he found the novel "frivolous" when he first read it. See Goffredo Fofi, "Vitaliano Brancati," in *Vitaliano Brancati. Da Via Etnea a Via Veneto*, ed. Daniela Battiati and Immacolata Magnano (Rome: Fahrenheit 451, 2001), 107–18.

73. Brancati, "Istinto e intuizione," in *I fascisti invecchiano*, 1135.

74. Brancati, "Istinto e intuizione," in *I fascisti invecchiano*, 1136–37.

75. Leonardo Sciascia, "Del dormire con un occhio solo," in Vitaliano Brancati, *Opere 1932–1946*, ed. Leonardo Sciascia (Milan: Bompiani, 1987), xiii.

76. Vitaliano Brancati, "La lettera anonima," in *I fascisti invecchiano*, in *Opere 1932–1946*, ed. Leonardo Sciascia (Milan: Bompiani, 1987), 1134.

77. Brancati, *Diario romano*, in *Opere 1947–1954*, ed. Leonardo Sciascia (Milan: Bompiani, 1992), 415.
78. Sciascia, "Del dormire," xiii.
79. Brancati, *Diario romano*, 431.
80. Vitaliano Brancati, "La capitale," in *Il borghese e l'immensità. Scritti 1930/1954*, ed. Sandro De Feo and G. A. Cibotto (Milan: Bompiani, 1973), 185.
81. Brancati, *Diario romano*, 424.
82. Brancati, "I piaceri del conformismo," in *Borghese e l'immensità*, 153.
83. Brancati, "Non amo la mia epoca," in *Borghese e l'immensità*, 164; 163.
84. Brancati, "Riperderemo il tempo perduto?," in *Borghese e l'immensità*, 157.
85. Brancati, *Beautiful Antonio*, trans. Stanley Hochman (New York: F. Ungar, 1978 [*Il bell'Antonio*, 1949]), 224.
86. Fabio Cusin, *Antistoria d'Italia* (Milan: Mondadori, 1972 [1948]).
87. Leo Longanesi, *Parliamo dell'elefante. Frammenti di un diario* (Milan: Longanesi, 1947), 254–56.
88. Brancati, *Diario romano*, 409.
89. Brancati, *Diario romano*, 425.
90. Brancati, *Diario romano*, 543.
91. Vitaliano Brancati, "I nomignoli," in *I fascisti invecchiano*, in *Opere 1932–1946*, 1157.
92. Vitaliano Brancati, "Filadelfo Rapisardi," in *I fascisti invecchiano*, in *Opere 1932–1946*, 1145.
93. For a genealogy of Brancati's intellectual position *vis-à-vis* twentieth-century European bourgeois culture, see Sonia Gentili, "Personaggio letterario e carattere 'sopraindividuale.' T. Mann, G. A. Borgese, V. Brancati," in *Cultura della razza e cultura letteraria nell'Italia del Novecento*, ed. Sonia Gentili and Simona Foà (Rome: Carocci, 2010), 247–70.
94. Brancati, "Riperderemo il tempo perduto?," in *Borghese e l'immensità*, 158.
95. Brancati, *Beautiful Antonio*, 195.
96. Brancati, *Beautiful Antonio*, 226.
97. Brancati, "Istinto e intuizione," in *I fascisti invecchiano*, 1140.

3. Ghosts from a Recent Past

1 Stefano Dal Bianco, "Rigurgiti di Arcadia," in *Atlante della letteratura italiana, Vol. 3: Dal Romanticismo a oggi*, ed. Sergio Luzzatto, Gabriele Pedullà, and Domenico Scarpa (Turin: Einaudi, 2012), 724.
2. For the historical and intellectual trajectory of the Action Party, see Giovanni De Luna, *Storia del Partito d'Azione, 1942–1947* (Turin: UTET, 2006); for the anti-Fascist experience of the Actionists in the Giustizia and Libertà group, see Marco Bresciani, *Quale antifascismo? Storia di Giustizia e Libertà* (Rome: Carocci, 2017).
3. Croce employed the parenthesis trope for the first time in a speech titled "La libertà italiana nella libertà del mondo," delivered in Bari, on January 28,

1944. On the occasion, the philosopher emphatically asked his audience: "In our history, what is a parenthesis of twenty years? And is this parenthesis entirely Italian history, or European and world history as well?" The text can be found in Benedetto Croce, *Scritti e discorsi politici, Vol. 1*, ed. Angela Carella (Naples: Bibliopolis, 1993), 61. However, as outlined by Pier Giorgio Zunino, Croce employed the parenthesis trope as an instrument to argue for the country's inclusion among the victors at the end of the war. Pier Giorgio Zunino, *La Repubblica e il suo passato* (Bologna: il Mulino, 2003), 284–86. For the early postwar response to Croce's trope, see also Charles L. Leavitt IV, "'An Entire New Land'? Italy's Post-War Culture and Its Fascist Past," *Journal of Modern Italian Studies* 21, no. 1 (2016): 4–18.

4. On this trajectory, see Daniela La Penna, "*Aretusa*: Continuity, Rupture, and Space for Intervention (1944–1946)," *Journal of Modern Italian Studies* 21, no. 1 (2016): 19–34; and Mirella Serri, *I Redenti. Gli intellettuali che vissero due volte, 1938–1948* (Milan: Corbaccio, 2005), esp. 187–204. On Rome after the Liberation, see Mariuccia Salvati, *Passaggi. Italiani dal fascismo alla Repubblica* (Rome: Carocci, 2016), esp. 59–79.

5. The founders of *Città* were Paola Masino, Massimo Bontempelli, Goffredo Bellonci, Ercole Maselli, Guido Piovene, Alberto Savinio, and Alberto Moravia. On Masino and *Città*, see Laura Di Nicola, "L'attività giornalistica di Paola Masino negli anni del secondo dopoguerra. L'esperienza di 'Città,'" *Atti della Accademia roveretana degli Agiati* 8, no. 2 (2008): 73–90. On De Céspedes and *Mercurio*, see Laura Di Nicola, *"Mercurio." Storia di una rivista 1944–1948* (Milan: il Saggiatore/ Fondazione Mondadori, 2012).

6. See, for instance: Giansiro Ferrata, "Le scorciatoie di un poeta saggio," *Il Politecnico*, March 30, 1946; and Guido Piovene, "Scorciatoie di Saba," *Corriere della Sera*, November 3 1946.

7. In his informed study on Flaiano, Gino Ruozzi points out that 1947 was a watershed year for Italian literature in terms of the great number of groundbreaking texts published. Gino Ruozzi, *Ennio Flaiano, una verità personale* (Rome: Carocci, 2016), 61.

8. Umberto Saba, "From *Shortcuts and Very Short Stories*," in *The Stories and Recollections of Umberto Saba*, trans. by Estelle Gibson (Riverdale-on-Hudson, NY: Sheep Meadow Press, 1993), 165. All changes from Gilson's translation are mine.

9. Guido De Ruggiero, "Al di là dello storicismo," *La Nuova Europa* 2, no. 4 (January 28, 1945): 9.

10. Guido De Ruggiero, "La fase crociana," *La Nuova Europa* 2, no. 3 (January 21, 1945): 9.

11. Guido De Ruggiero, "Come scrivere la storia per le scuole," *La Nuova Europa* 2, no. 16 (April 22, 1945): 9.

12. As Daniela La Penna argued: "Appropriation of Crocean tropes, the polemical dismantlement of Croce's role during Fascism, and the absorption of Crocean intellectuals had been the main strategies carried out by the PCI to

infiltrate and then dominate the post-war intellectual field." La Penna, "The Rise and Fall of Benedetto Croce: Intellectual Positioning in the Italian Cultural Field, 1944–1947," *Modern Italy* 21, no. 2 (2016): 152.

13. "The dissolution of Hegelianism, in the second half of the nineteenth century, did not signal a break in this tendency; on the contrary [. . .] the very overturning of idealism in the materialism of Marx preserved the historicist and dialectical character of the original doctrine." Guido De Ruggiero, "Lo storicismo. I precedenti," *La Nuova Europa* 2, no. 2 (January 14, 1945): 10.

14. Fabio Cusin, *Antistoria d'Italia* (Milan: Mondadori, 1972 [1948]). On Cusin's idea of history, see Giuseppe Trebbi, "Italia ed Europa nel pensiero di Fabio Cusin," in *Attilio Tamaro e Fabio Cusin nella storiografia triestina. Atti del Convegno in ricordo di Arduino Agnelli, Trieste 15–16 ottobre 2005*, ed. Silvano Cavazza and Giuseppe Trebbi (Trieste: Deputazione di Storia Patria per la Venezia Giulia, 2007), 213–47; and Sante Marelli, *Scrittori dell'antistoria* (Rimini: Panozzo Editore, 1984).

15. Charles L. Leavitt IV argued that in the contested field of how to navigate the transition to post-Fascism "the break with Croce thus became a kind of foundation, an inauguration for the intellectual and political work of the post-war period." Leavitt, "Probing the Limits of Crocean Historicism," *The Italianist* 37, no. 3 (2017): 393.

16. Cusin, *Antistoria d'Italia*, xiii.

17. Cusin, *Antistoria d'Italia*, xvii.

18. On the "Italiani brava gente" trope, see Angelo Del Boca, *Italiani brava gente?* (Vicenza: Neri Pozza, 2005); and Filippo Focardi, "'Bravo italiano' e 'cattivo tedesco': riflessioni sulla genesi di due immagini incrociate,'" *Storia e memoria* 5, no. 1 (1996): 55–83.

19. Cusin, *Antistoria d'Italia*, xiv.

20. La Penna, "Rise and Fall," 140.

21. Umberto Saba, *Scorciatoie e raccontini* (1946), in *Tutte le prose*, ed. Arrigo Stara (Milan: Mondadori, 2001), 79.

22. For Savinio's relations with Fascism, see Paola Italia, *Il pellegrino appassionato. Savinio scrittore (1915–1925)* (Palermo: Sellerio 2004); and Lucilla Lijoi, *Il sognatore sveglio. Alberto Savinio 1933–1943* (Milan: Mimesis 2021).

23. Alberto Savinio, "Inquieti adolescenti," in *Scritti dispersi (1943–1952)*, ed. Paola Italia (Milan: Adelphi 2004), 170.

24. Copernicus and Ptolemy return in critical terms even in Gadda's *Eros and Priapus*, written in those very years: "We can read Copernicus and Ptolemy, but we cannot be Copernican and Ptolemaic at the same time. The ethical act or even simple mental resolve, assent or dissent, involves at certain moments a choice: that is, an acquisition or a relinquishment." Gadda, *Eros e Priapo. Versione integrale*, ed. Paola Italia and Giorgio Pinotti (Milan: Adelphi, 2016 [1967]), 167.

25. Alberto Savinio, "Illusione del definitivo," in *Scritti dispersi 1943–1952*, ed. Paola Italia (Milan: Adelphi, 2004), 159. On Copernicus and Ptolemy in Savinio,

see Martin Weidlich, *Tramonti e aurore di Alberto Savinio. Percorso meandrico di un intellettuale europeo del '900* (Milan: Scalpendi, 2017), 35; and Lijoi, *Sognatore sveglio*, 263.

26. Alberto Savinio, *Sorte dell'Europa* (Milan: Adelphi, 2005 [1945]), 34–35.

27. Savinio, *Sorte dell'Europa*, 90.

28. Alberto Savinio, "Conclusione." Archivio contemporaneo Gabinetto G. P. Vieusseux, Carte A. Savinio, AS II. 20.49.

29. Alberto Savinio, "Tommaso Moro e l'utopia," in *Scritti dispersi 1943–1952*, ed. Paola Italia (Milan: Adelphi, 2004), 102.

30. On Nietzsche's profound impact on Savinio's intellectual agenda and method of inquiry, see Franco Baldasso, "Alberto Savinio and the Myth of Babel: Homecoming, Genealogies, and Translation in *Hermaphrodito*," *The Italianist* 40, no. 1 (2020): 44–65.

31. Savinio, "Inquieti adolescenti," 170.

32. Here are some meaningful passages from reviews of Savinio's *Sorte dell'Europa*. Su *Mondo Europeo* (Rome: December 1945), A.A. comments: "Only in the conclusion does Savinio write that the idea that will unify Europe will be that of the 'social community'; but the idea is vague and hardly in line with the author's liberalism." On *La città libera* (Rome: September 20, 1945), Enzo Forcella writes: "For Savinio too, in fact, as for all the sharpest minds capable of reading into the events of recent years, the war the world fought is consigned to history with just this precise and distinctive character: of a war fought for the *idea* of the social community, our century's only fruitful and practical idea, just as the *practical* idea of the previous century was the *liberal* idea." From a different standpoint, Giulio Parigi on *L'Universo* (Florence: Mar–Apr 1948): "An intellectual, S. turns to thought for a reform of the educational system, urging liberation from the narrow, dogmatic partisan mindset, freeing man from the grips of 'centripetal motion' to freely launch him into the expansive 'centrifugal motion.'" On *Studium* (Rome: June 1945), a.m. concludes, "The final appeal to the partisans of united Europe sounds, after the latest events on our eastern and western frontiers, particularly tone-deaf."

33. De Ruggiero, "Lo storicismo. I precedenti."

34. Umberto Saba, "Poesia, filosofia, psicanalisi," in *Tutte le prose*, ed. Arrigo Stara (Milan: Mondadori, 2001), 965.

35. Saba, "Poesia, filosofia, psicanalisi," in *Tutte le prose*, 973.

36. On the trope of the early postwar return to the "human," see fundamental texts by Croce, *Scritti e discorsi politici*; for the debate in France and the role of Sartre, see Edward Baring, "Humanist Pretensions: Catholics, Communists, and Sartre's Struggle for Existentialism in Postwar France," *Modern Intellectual History* 7, no. 3 (2010): 581–609.

37. Saba, "Poesia, filosofia, psicanalisi," in *Tutte le prose*, 973.

38. Walter Pedullà, *Alberto Savinio. Scrittore ipocrita e privo di scopo* (Treviso: Anordest 2011), 117.

39. Alberto Savinio, "Voltaire e Federico II," in *Scritti dispersi 1943–1952*, ed. Paola Italia (Milan: Adelphi, 2004), 188–212.

40. On Savinio's concept of "hermaphroditism," see Paolo Baldacci, *De Chirico: The Metaphysical Period 1888–1919* (Boston: Bulfinch Press, 1997), 18.

41. To be fair, Savinio's discourse on homosexuality can also be seen as an essentialism. However, it is important to highlight how a heterosexual intellectual published an article openly supporting homosexuality in the very years when Christian Democrats in Italy were rebuilding the shattered Italian community on "eternal" values such as the traditional family—a value that was at the center of Fascist propaganda as well. Savinio's novelty is not in his opposition to the traditional family—he himself had a fairly traditional one—but in his assertion that it can coexist with other kinds of families.

42. Alberto Savinio, *Maupassant e l'"Altro'* (Milan: Adelphi 1975), 22.

43. Savinio, "Voltaire e Federico II." In the short story "Zinc," Levi claims: "For the wheel to turn, for life to live, impurities are needed, and the impurities of impurities: in the earth, too, as we all know, if it is to be fertile. We need dissent, difference, the grain of salt, the mustard seed. Fascism doesn't want them, forbids them, and so you're not a Fascist; it wants everyone to be the same, and you are not the same." Primo Levi, *The Periodic Table*, trans. Ann Goldstein, in *The Complete Works of Primo Levi, Vol. 2* (New York: Liveright, 2015), 780.

44. One of Savinio's comments on *writing history* in his unpublished papers is especially significant here: "Among other maxims and reflections by Wolfgang Goethe, some days ago I happened to read the following maxim on history: 'Writing history is a way to get the past off your shoulders,'" The author then concludes that reading Goethe's remark, "It was of great comfort, because I don't seek originality in thoughts, but truth." Archivio contemporaneo Gabinetto G. P. Vieusseux, Carte A. Savinio, Ad. II. 52. 61.

45. It is no coincidence that one of the greatest admirers of Savinio was Leonardo Sciascia. Though distant from neo-avant-garde movements, he was—like Savinio—an avid reader of Voltaire and French Enlightenment. In fact, Sciascia edited the first comprehensive reprint of Savinio's uncollected articles, paving the way for his critical rediscovery. See Alberto Savinio, *Opere: Scritti dispersi tra guerra e dopoguerra (1943–1952)*, ed. Leonardo Sciascia and Franco De Maria (Milan: Bompiani, 1989).

46. Umberto Saba, "Gratitudine," in *Il Canzoniere* (Turin: Einaudi 2014 [1961]), 523.

47. Umberto Saba, "A Linuccia, 31 dicembre 1944," in *La spada d'amore. Lettere scelte 1902–1957*, ed. Aldo Marcovecchio (Milan: Mondadori 1983), 120.

48. Elsa Morante, "Il poeta di tutta la vita," in *Pro o contro la bomba atomica* (Milan: Adelphi 1987), 39.

49. Natalino Sapegno articulated his ideas on Croce in the 1945 article "Marxismo, cultura, poesia." *Rinascita* 2, nos. 7–8 (1945): 182–84. Regarding this article, La Penna comments that "by condemning Croce's approach to history as

ahistorical, and by declaring Marxism to be 'integral historicism,' Sapegno outlined the agenda of the Marxist literary historian who, advancing in the opposite direction from the one indicated by Crocean aesthetics, should link works of art to their historical context and to the agents that contributed to artistic production" (La Penna, "Rise and Fall," 147). The debate in Marxist circles on how to overcome Croce—and implicitly convert his acolytes to Communism—is of course much more complex and nuanced than what can be examined here.

50. Umberto Saba, "Umberto Saba a Primo Levi. Trieste, 3 Novembre 1948," in Massimo Bucciantini, *Esperimento Auschwitz—Auschwitz Experiment* (Turin: Einaudi, 2011), 159.

51. On this aspect, see Walter Barberis, "Primo Levi e un libro 'fatale,'" in *Atlante della letteratura italiana, Vol. 3: Dal Romanticismo a oggi*, ed. Sergio Luzzatto, Gabriele Pedullà, and Domenico Scarpa (Turin: Einaudi, 2012), 756.

52. Elena Loewenthal, *Scrivere di sé. Identità ebraiche allo specchio* (Turin: Einaudi, 2007), 80, 95.

53. See Gordon, *Holocaust in Italian Culture*, but for a larger assessment of how Holocaust testimony became part of public discourse in Europe and the US, see Annette Wieviorka, *The Era of the Witness* (Ithaca, NY: Cornell University Press, 2006); and how it impacted on postcolonial narratives, see Michael Rothberg, *Multidirectional Memory: Remembering the Holocaust in the Age of Decolonization* (Stanford, CA: Stanford University Press, 2009).

54. On this, see also Levi's response to Saba: Primo Levi, "Primo Levi a Umberto Saba. Torino, 10 gennaio 1949," in Bucciantini, *Esperimento Auschwitz*, 161.

55. Saba, "From *Shortcuts and Very Short Stories*," 176.

56. For Levi's biography, see Ian Thomson, *Primo Levi: A Life* (London: Hutchinson, 2002); and Berel Lang, *Primo Levi: The Matter of a Life* (New Haven, CT: Yale University Press, 2013).

57. A first approach on the question of the Holocaust in Saba can be found in Ettore Janulardo, "Saba: Scorciatoie dopo Majdanek," *Studi e ricerche di storia contemporanea* 64 (2005): 63–67; while the correspondence Saba–Levi is commented in Alberto Cavaglion, *Notizie su Argon. Gli antenati di Primo Levi da Francesco Petrarca a Cesare Lombroso* (Turin: Instar 2006), 104; and Andrea Rondini, "Da Umberto Saba a Primo Levi," *Rivista di letteratura italiana* 26, nos. 2–3 (2008): 45–53.

58. Saba, "From *Shortcuts and Very Short Stories*," 186.

59. Georges Bataille, *Sartre*, in *Oeuvres complètes* (Paris: Gallimard 1988), t. XI, 226, cited in Enzo Traverso, *Auschwitz e gli intellettuali* (Bologna: il Mulino, 2004).

60. On the specific impact of the news of Majdanek in Italy, see Antonella Filippi and Lino Ferracin, *Deportati italiani nel campo di Majdanek* (Turin: Zamorani, 2013). For the early press coverage of the Holocaust in Italy, see Sara Fantini, *Notizie dalla Shoah. La stampa italiana nel 1945* (Bologna: Pendragon 2005).

61. Dan Diner, *Beyond the Conceivable. Studies on Germany, Nazism, and the Holocaust* (Berkeley: University of California Press, 2000), 2–4.

62. David Rousset, *L'Univers concentrationnaire* (Paris: Editions du Pavois 1946); partially translated into English as *The Other Kingdom* (New York: Reynal and Hitchcock, 1947).

63. A more comprehensive approach to this crisis of representation will be offered through Günther Anders's critical assessment in the section "Creaturely Life and Technological Warfare: *Kaputt*," in Chapter 5.

64. On the terminology employed to name Nazis' destruction of European Jewry, see Anna-Vera Sullam Calimani, *I nomi dello sterminio. Definizioni di una tragedia* (Bologna: Marietti, 2019).

65. Saba's remarks on his Jewishness are always personal and often provocative, especially in his letters. See Stefano Carrai, *Saba* (Naples: Salerno, 2017), 214.

66. Umberto Saba, "Lettera a Flescher. 5 Ottobre, 1946," in *Lettere sulla psicanalisi. Carteggio con Joachim Flescher 1946–1949* (Milan: SE 2007), 12.

67. On Saba's Jewish humor, see Paola Frandini, *Il poeta, il cane e la gallina. Scorciatoie e raccontini di Umberto Saba tra umorismo ebraico e Shoah* (Florence: Le Lettere, 2011); on the concept of *Witz*, see Barbara Cassin et al., eds., *Dictionary of Untranslatables: A Philosophical Lexicon* (Princeton, NJ: Princeton University Press, 2014), 489.

68. Walter Barberis corroborates this interpretation affirming that in his letter to the young writer, Saba "was emphasizing his opinion that Levi had carried the theme of the extermination of the Jewish people outside the contingencies of a war, albeit a world war marked by a loss of moral reference points like never before." Barberis, "Primo Levi e un libro 'fatale,'" 754.

69. Saba, "From *Shortcuts and Very Short Stories*," 165. Changes are mine.

70. Saba, "From *Shortcuts and Very Short Stories*," 166.

71. Saba, "From *Shortcuts and Very Short Stories*," 176.

72. Saba, "A Linuccia, 30 novembre 1945," in *Spada d'amore*, 137.

73. For the intellectual debate on the aftermath of the Holocaust, see Traverso, *Auschwitz e gli intellettuali*.

74. Saba, "A Giuseppe De Robertis, 22 settembre 1946," in *Spada d'amore.*, 176–77.

75. Saba, *Scorciatoie*, in *Tutte le prose*, 43.

76. Robert Antelme, *The Human Race* (Evanstone, IL: Marlboro Press, 1998 [*L'éspèce humaine*, 1947]).

77. Saba, "From *Shortcuts and Very Short Stories*," 175.

78. Saba, "A Linuccia, 7 giugno 1946," in *Spada d'amore*, 160.

79. Saba, "A Vittorio Sereni, 1 marzo 1948," in *Spada d'amore*, 190.

80. Saba, "A Linuccia, 30 novembre 1945," in *Spada d'amore*, 138.

81. One exception is Martino Marazzi, "Il Saba di 'Scorciatoie e raccontini' tra Nietzsche e Freud," *Autografo* 7, no. 20 (1990): 43.

82. Saba, "From *Shortcuts and Very Short Stories*," 186. Changes are mine.

83. Robert S. C. Gordon, *Holocaust in Italian Culture 1944-2010* (Stanford, CA: Stanford University Press, 2012), 47.

84. "Saba's poetry is helpful, in the highest meaning of the term: a poetry that helps and illuminates men [*in the*] job of living. To achieve such a result, it took a man capable of performing, with an almost paradoxical specialization, that job of living. Saba took upon himself, or rather underwent, by temperament and by desire, this task." Giacomo Debenedetti, "Il grembo della poesia," in *Intermezzo* (Milan: il Saggiatore, 1972), 47.

85. Saba, "A Giuseppe De Robertis, 22 settembre 1946," in *Spada d'amore*, 176–77.

86. Umberto Saba, *Songbook. The Selected Poems of Umberto Saba*, trans. George Hochfield and Leonard Nathan (New Haven, CT: Yale University Press, 2008 [*Il Canzoniere*, 1961]): 472–73.

87. Alberto Cavaglion, "Il grembo della Shoah. Il 16 ottobre 1943 di Umberto Saba, Giacomo Debenedetti, Elsa Morante," in *Dopo i testimoni. Memorie, storiografie e narrazioni della deportazione razziale*, ed. Marta Baiardi and Alberto Cavaglion (Rome: Viella, 2014), 191.

88. On Saba's influence on Pasolini and Morante, see Francesca Cadel, "Umberto Saba, Pierpaolo Pasolini ed Elsa Morante. Scorciatoie anticanoniche nell'Italia del dopoguerra," *Italica* 89, no. 2 (2012): 253–69.

89. Umberto Saba, "A Weiss, 19 marzo 1949," in *Lettere sulla psicanalisi*, 78.

90. Ennio Flaiano, *A Time to Kill*, trans. Stuart Hood (London: Quartet, 1992 [*Tempo di uccidere*, 1947]). Translation here is mine.

91. Ruozzi, *Ennio Flaiano*, 43. Interestingly, *The Short Cut* was the title used for the first American edition of Flaiano's novel, translated by Stuart Hood (New York: Pellegrini and Cudahi, 1950).

92. Flaiano, *A Time to Kill*, 54.

93. For the history of Italian colonialism in Eastern Africa, see Angelo Del Boca, *Gli Italiani in Africa Orientale, Vol. 1–4* (Bari-Rome: Laterza, 1976–1984); Ruth Ben-Ghiat and Mia Fuller, eds., *Italian Colonialism* (New York: Palgrave, 2005); and Nicola Labanca, *Oltremare. Storia dell'espansione coloniale italiana* (Bologna: il Mulino, 2007). Remarkable comments on how critics have—even recently—failed to recognize the sexual violence at the center of *A Time to Kill* are in Lucia Re, "Italy's First Postcolonial Novel and the End of (Neo)realism," *The Italianist* 37, no. 3 (2017): 416–35. Significant notes on the legacy of Italian imperialism in Africa and its representations are in Charles Burdett, "Addressing the Representation of the Italian Empire and Its Afterlife," in *Transnational Italian Studies*, ed. Charles Burdett and Loredana Polezzi (Liverpool: Liverpool University Press, 2020), 249–65.

94. Flaiano, *A Time to Kill*, 259.

95. Flaiano, *A Time to Kill*, 77, 110.

96. Relevant critical contributions on the author's multidisciplinary production can be found in Ruozzi, *Ennio Flaiano*; and Marisa Trubiano, *Ennio Flaiano and his Italy* (Madison, NJ: Fairleigh Dickinson University Press, 2010).

97. As an instance, "Aucor," pseudonym reviewer of Flaiano's novel in *La Sicilia* (July 29, 1947) states: "It is, let's be clear, the repudiation of Africa and maybe of any land of conquest."

98. In fact, *Tempo di uccidere* was published when Italy's diplomacy, despite military defeat, was still claiming these territories on an international level: all the parties of the constitutional arc supported this policy. On this question, see Labanca, *Oltremare*, 430–40.

99. Stefani Frati (Giovanni Ansaldo), review of *Tempo di Uccidere*, by Ennio Flaiano, *Il libraio*, June 15, 1947, 12.

100. "Flaiano, after hundreds of 'colonial novels,' all failures, gives us the first true and powerful and beautiful Italian colonial novel; and it's a novel of clear and deep rejection of Africa." Stefano Frati (Giovanni Ansaldo), review of *Tempo di Uccidere*, by Ennio Flaiano, *Il libraio*, June 15, 1947, 3.

101. Gino Nogara, "Galleria delle riedizioni. *Tempo di uccidere*," *La fiera letteraria*, November 28, 1954.

102. Derek Duncan put the question of the representation of Mariam through the lieutenant's gaze in a crystal clear way: "The narrator's chance sighting of the naked woman bathing is a classic instance of imperialist scopophilia (...). Innocent even of her own beauty, the woman exists only and through the soldier's gaze. Flaiano, however, ensures that the reader understands that the encounter is fully embedded in the erotics and economics of colonialism." Derek Duncan, "Italian Identity and the Risks of Contamination: The Legacies of Mussolini's Demographic Impulse in the Works of Comisso, Flaiano, and Dell'Oro," in *Italian Colonialism: Legacy and Memory*, ed. Jaqueline Andall and Derek Duncan (Oxford: Peter Lang, 2005), 110. In the same volume, see the discussion of images of black femininity from the nineteenth century to today's advertising practices in Sandra Ponzanesi, "Beyond the Black Venus: Colonial Sexual Politics and Contemporary Visual Practices," in *Italian Colonialism*, 165–89.

103. Roberta Orlandini, "(Anti)colonialismo in *Tempo di uccidere* di Ennio Flaiano," *Italica* 69, no. 4 (1992): 478–88.

104. Umberto de Federicis, review of *Tempo di Uccidere*, *l'Avanti!* (Milan edition), July 27, 1947.

105. On this specific aspect, see Giovanna Tomasello, "Flaiano e gli incubi della coscienza," in *L'Africa tra mito e realtà. Storia della letteratura coloniale italiana* (Palermo: Sellerio, 2004), 208–15.

106. Duncan, "Italian Identity," 102.

107. Flaiano, *A Time to Kill*, 26. Changes from Hood's translation are mine.

108. On the topic, see Angelo Del Boca, *Gli italiani in Africa Orientale, Vol. 4: Nostalgia delle colonie* (Bari-Rome: Laterza, 1984); and Nicola Labanca, *La guerra d'Etiopia 1935–1941* (Bologna: il Mulino, 2015), esp. 101–22.

109. As Tomasello reports, the diary was written between Fall 1935 and May 1936 and published only in 1973 on *Il Mondo* (Tomasello, *Africa tra mito e realtà*, 209). Regarding the crimes committed by the occupying army, Ruozzi has correctly argued that the harrowing passage in "Aethiopia. Appunti per una canzonetta" (now in Ennio Flaiano, *Tempo di uccidere* [Milan: Rizzoli, 2014], 299) in which Flaiano describes mass killing and rape of civilians is the basis for a page of his *Nocturnal Diary* (*Diario Natturno*, 1956). In the later book Flaiano elides the graphic details of the first description for a broader reflection on war and its ills (Ruozzi, *Ennio Flaiano*, 60). I would add, however, that Flaiano's compassion for the victims in this second version has also the effect of glossing over Italian responsibility in war crimes in Africa. Ennio Flaiano, *Diario Notturno* (Milan: Adelphi, 1994), 119–20.

110. Flaiano, "Aethiopia," 289–90.

111. Ennio Flaiano, "Flaiano a Tamburi 16. Axum, 11 aprile 1936," Fondo Orfeo Tamburi, Faldone Ennio Flaiano, Archivio Prezzolini, Biblioteca Cantonale di Lugano (Switzerland).

112. On this topic, see Ruth Ben-Ghiat. *Italian Fascism's Empire Cinema* (Bloomington: Indiana University Press, 2014).

113. Ennio Flaiano, "I grandi precursori," *Il Secolo XX* (October 16, 1945), now in *L'Occhiale indiscreto*, ed. Anna Longoni (Milan: Adelphi, 2019), 140–41.

114. Flaiano, *A Time to Kill*, 233.

115. Angelo Del Boca, *Gli italiani in Africa orientale, Vol. 3: la caduta dell'impero*, 239; see also Barbara Sòrgoni, *Parole e corpi: antropologia, discorso giuridico e politiche sessuali interrazziali nella colonia Eritrea (1890–1941)* (Naples: Liguori Editori, 1998), 214.

116. Flaiano himself hints at this identification as he participated in the Ethiopian campaign in the rank of sublieutenant.

117. Flaiano, *A Time to Kill*, 120.

118. Flaiano, *A Time to Kill*, 264. During this conversation, the protagonist understands his killing of Mariam in a completely different light: "The killing of Mariam now seemed to me an inevitable crime [. . .]. More than a crime, in fact, it appeared to me like a crisis, an illness, which would protect me forever by revealing me to myself." This last exchange confirms the character's difficulty in conceiving Mariam as a fully autonomous person—even beyond their encounter. Such a circumstance is anticipated by the sublieutenant a few lines earlier, in which he ironically comments: "Like every story in this world yours, too, defies analysis. Unless one wishes to admit that the 'unfortunate circumstances' followed you because they were part of your person." (Flaiano, *A Time to Kill*, 262).

119. Flaiano, *A Time to Kill*, 264.

120. For the complex relationship between the two authors, see Anna Folli, *MoranteMoravia. Storia di un amore* (Vicenza: Neri Pozza, 2018).

121. Moravia's novel *Two Women* (*La Ciociara*, 1957), later a celebrated film with Sophia Loren, revolves around occupiers' violence perpetrated against local

women. For a detailed assessment of the violence against civilians during Nazi and Allied occupation of the South, see Gabriella Gribaudi, *Guerra totale: Tra bombe alleate e violenze naziste. Napoli e il fronte meridionale 1940–1944* (Turin: Bollati Boringhieri, 2005).

122. For information regarding the manuscript and the publication of the novel, see Carlo Cecchi and Cesare Garboli, "Cronologia," in Elsa Morante, *Opere, Vol. 1*, ed. Carlo Cecchi and Cesare Garboli (Milan: Mondadori, 1988), esp. xliv–lvii. Elsa Morante's *Menzogna e Sortilegio* first appeared in English as *House of Liars*, trans. Adrienne Foulke (New York: Harcourt Brace, 1951). Here I quote from the new translation by Jenny McPhee, soon to be published as *Lies and Sorcery* (New York: NYRB Classics, forthcoming).

123. According to Cesare Garboli, "One didn't easily forgive a 1948 novel of being at the same time fable-like and realistic, indebted to reality and to its opposite." Cesare Garboli, *Il gioco segreto. Nove immagini di Elsa Morante* (Milan: Adelphi, 1995), 38.

124. Andrea Barbato, "Una finestra sul Danubio," *l'Espresso*, May 20, 1962, 13.

125. Cited in Marco Bardini, *Morante Elsa: italiana: di professione, poeta* (Pisa: Nistri-lischi, 1999), 147–48. For Lukàcs's comments on Morante, see Leonardo Lattarulo, "Il giudizio di Lukàcs su Elsa Morante," in *Le stanza di Elsa. Dentro la scrittura di Elsa Morante*, ed. Giuliana Zagra and Simonetta Buttò (Rome: Colombo, 2006), 67–72.

126. Natalia Ginzburg, "Menzogna e sortilegio," in *Festa per Elsa*, ed. Goffredo Fofi and Adriano Sofri (Palermo: Sellerio, 2011), 27.

127. Years later, Morante thus remembered that period: "Some of her beloved war stories (which then, in the disorder of those years, ended up being lost) were turned down—as not conforming to the obligatory aesthetic modes of the time—by the first magazine of the new political-literary avant-garde of the time, to which the young author, in her fresh enthusiasm for social and human recovery, aspired in those days as an honor and a prize. Set aside in this way [. . .] she thus withdrew to write her first novel, *Lies and Sorcery*." Morante, *Opere, Vol. 1*, xlix.

128. Morante, *Opere, Vol. 1*, xliv. Among these critics, Giansiro Ferrata heavily dismissed *Lies and Sorcery*, detailing all his frustration while reading it, claiming that he was "very much unsure" whether the novel would ever really begin. Giansiro Ferrata, "Menzogne di Elsa e canti di Sibilla," *l'Unità*, Milan Edition, August 24, 1948.

129. On fiction and made-up reality in the novel, see Emanuella Scarano, "La 'fatua veste' del vero," in *Per Elisa. Studi su "Menzogna e sortilegio,"* ed. Lucio Lugnani et al. (Pisa: Nistri Lischi, 1990), 95–171; Morante's acquaintance with Freud is discussed in Marco Bardini, "Dei 'fantastici doppi' ovvero la mimesi narrativa dello spostamento psichico," in *Per Elisa*, ed. Lugnani et al., 173–299.

130. Morante, *Lies and Sorcery* (forthcoming).

131. Remarkable insights into the sense of tragedy in Morante—and of her unique way of moving beyond the tragic register of her fiction—can be found in

Giorgio Agamben, "Il congedo della tragedia," in *Festa per Elsa*, ed. Goffredo Fofi and Adriano Sofri (Palermo: Sellerio, 2011), 56–59.

132. Morante, *Lies and Sorcery* (forthcoming)

133. Sigmund Freud, "Family Romances," in *The Standard Edition of the Complete Psychological Works of Sigmund Freud, Volume 9 (1906–1908): Jensen's 'Gradiva' and Other Works* (London: Hogarth Press 1959), 239.

134. Morante, *Opere, Vol. 1*, li.

135. An example of critical misunderstanding of the novel is in the response of Emilio Cecchi, who condescendingly described it as "imaginative exercise and amusement" and "picturesque pile of adventures." Cited in Carlo Cecchi and Cesare Garboli, "Fortuna critica," in Morante, *Opere, Vol. 2*, (Milan: Mondadori, 1988), 1662. For Morante's relationship with Proust, see Stefania Lucamante. *Elsa Morante e l'eredità proustiana* (Fiesole, FI: Cadmo, 1998). See also Raffaele Donnarumma, "*Menzogna e sortilegio*. Oltre il bovarismo," *Allegoria* 9, no. 31 (1999): 121–35.

136. Morante, *Lies and Sorcery* (forthcoming).

137. Garboli, *Gioco segreto*, 38.

138. Sharon Wood, "Models of Narrative in *Menzogna e sortilegio*," in *Under Arturo's Star. The Cultural Legacies of Elsa Morante*, ed. Stefania Lucamante and Sharon Wood (West Lafayette, IN: Purdue University Press, 2006), 94–111.

139. This nexus is explored as hermeneutic category in Marianne Hirsch, *The Mother/Daughter Plot: Narrative, Psychoanalysis, Femminism* (Bloomington: Indiana University Press, 1989). Among the many critical contributions examining such nexus as a key aspect of Morante's first novel, see Tiziana De Rogatis, "Realismo stregato e genealogia femminile in *Menzogna e sortilegio*," *Allegoria* 31, no. 80 (2019): 97–124; and, more generally, Graziella Barnabò, *La fiaba estrema. Elsa Morante tra vita e scrittura* (Rome: Carocci, 2016). On this topic, see also Luisa Muraro, *The Symbolic Order of the Mother* (Albany; NY: State University of New York Press, 2018).

140. Morante, *Lies and Sorcery* (forthcoming).

141. Morante, *Lies and Sorcery* (forthcoming).

142. Morante, *Lies and Sorcery* (forthcoming).

143. Morante, *Lies and Sorcery* (forthcoming).

144. Morante, *Lies and Sorcery* (forthcoming).

145. Morante, *Lies and Sorcery* (forthcoming).

146. Morante, *Lies and Sorcery* (forthcoming).

147. Unfortunately, an in-depth analysis of this fascinating scene is not possible here. Feminist criticism beginning with Judith Butler, Jacques Lacan's psychoanalysis, and René Girard's theory of mimetic desire, as well as his ensuing discourse on the sacred, would help unravel the intricated tangle of status, desire, narcissism, hetero- and homoeroticism of this passage. After Edoardo envisions the possibility that their play might unsettle not just gender but also status difference and ultimately erode his privilege, he comments that the state of

exception the two created by crossing gender boundaries belongs to a special norm inscribed in the almost sovereign status he assigns to his persona. Aware of how destabilizing their game could be, he hurries to describe their exception as inscribed in the "sacred" sovereign law that he embodies, as reported in his mentioned remark, ultimately to keep control of Anna's subjugation. Morante, *Lies and Sorcery* (forthcoming).

148. Wood, "Models of Narrative," 97.

149. Received images of women and motherhood are also critically addressed by Elena Ferrante in her essay "Frantumaglia," in which she places *Lies and Sorcery* as a model for her own narrative. Elena Ferrante, *Frantumaglia* (New York: Europa Editions, 2016).

150. Morante, *Lies and Sorcery* (forthcoming).

151. In the same year of the publication of *Lies and Sorcery* the journal *Mercurio* hosted a remarkable exchange between Natalia Ginzburg and Alba de Cèspedes concerning women's bereaved condition. Natalia Ginzburg, "Discorso sulle donne," *Mercurio* 5, nos. 36–39 (1948): 105–10; and Alba de Céspedes, "Lettera a Natalia Ginburg," *Mercurio* 5, nos. 36–39 (1948): 110.

152. Morante's critique of traditional social structures shaping heterosexual male desire is exceptional even if confronted with remarkable works published during the transition by female authors, such as Paola Masino's *Birth and Death of the Housewife* (*Vita e morte della massaia*, first edition published as a volume 1945); Anna Banti's *Artemisia* (1947); Natalia Ginzburg's *The Dry Heart* (*È stato così*, 1947); and Alba de Céspedes's *The Best of Husbands* (*Dalla parte di lei*, 1949). Morante's novel purposely transcended the more conventionally bourgeoise and modernist perspective of the aforementioned women writers—*Lies and Sorcery*'s female characters encompass the entire social hierarchy. I will analyze the political consequences of Morante's radical approach in the next paragraphs.

153. Morante, *Lies and Sorcery* (forthcoming).

154. Morante, *Lies and Sorcery* (forthcoming).

155. Morante, *Lies and Sorcery* (forthcoming).

156. For Kafka's influence on Morante, see Saskia Ziolkowski, *Kafka's Italian Progeny* (Toronto: University of Toronto Press, 2020).

157. I think, in particular, of György Lukàcs, "L'ottobre e la letteratura," *Rinascita* 42 (October 27, 1967): 23–27; Cesare Cases, "*La Storia*. Un confronto con *Menzogna e sortilegio*," (1974), now in *Patrie lettere* (Turin: Einaudi, 1987), 104–25; and Garboli, *Gioco segreto*.

158. Italo Calvino, "Un romanzo sul serio," *L'Unità*. Turin Edition, August 17, 1948.

159. Goffredo Bellonci, "Elsa e i suoi critici," *Giornale d'Italia*, March 24, 1949, 3.

160. Edda and Carlo Sgorlon, "Profilo di Elsa Morante," in *Cahiers Elsa Morante*, ed. Jean-Noel Schifano and Tjuna Notarbartolo (Naples: ESI 1993), 19–20.

161. Morante, *Lies and Sorcery* (forthcoming).

162. I consciously wrote Anna instead of Edoardo as exponent of the language of privilege connected with frustrated social and personal desire. In the novel, Edoardo *is* the embodiment of privilege, living only in an eternal present of bliss and self-adoration (until the moment the despised prostitute Rosaria shamelessly tells him how he looks sick). For this reason, Edoardo's language cannot be fully considered the antecedent of Fascist rhetoric. In fact, he believes his superiority is part of the natural order of things; there is no vengeance or retribution in his words. In this sense, he is much more a first—though ostensibly less likable—embodiment of other male young characters of Morante's fiction, such as Arturo (from *Arturo's Island* [*L'isola di Arturo*, 1957]) and Nino (*History: A Novel* [*La Storia*, 1974]).

163. Remarkable comments in this direction are in Cases, "*La Storia*. Un confronto con *Menzogna e sortilegio*."

164. On this point, see the engrossing epistolary exchange between Calvino and Morante, now in Daniele Morante, ed., *L'amata. Lettere di e a Elsa Morante* (Turin: Einaudi, 2012), esp. 277–83.

165. Morante, *Lies and Sorcery* (forthcoming).
166. Morante, *Lies and Sorcery* (forthcoming).
167. Morante, *Lies and Sorcery* (forthcoming).

4. Carlo Levi on the Religion of the State

1 The two main references for Levi's intellectual trajectory are Nicola Carducci, *Storia intellettuale di Carlo Levi* (Lecce: Pensa MultiMedia, 1999); and Riccardo Gasperina Geroni, *Il custode della soglia. Il sacro e le forme nell'opera di Carlo Levi* (Milan: Mimesis, 2018).

2. The most influential reviews—as I will examine in detail later—were Carlo Muscetta, "Leggenda e verità di Carlo Levi," now in *Realismo neorealismo controrealismo* (Milan: Garzanti, 1976 [1946]), 52–67; and Mario Alicata, "Il meridionalismo non si può fermare a Eboli," now in *Antropologia culturale e questione meridionale. Ernesto De Martino e il dibattito sul mondo popolare subalterno negli anni 1948–1955*, ed. Carla Pasquinelli (Florence: La Nuova Italia, 1977 [1954]), 175–99.

3. For comprehensive overviews of the "Southern question" in Italy, see Guido Pescosolido, "Italy Southern Question: Long-Standing Thorny Issues and Current Problems," *Journal of Modern Italian Studies* 23, no. 3 (2019): 441–55; and Jane Schneider, ed., *Italy's "Southern Question": Orientalism in One Country* (London: Routledge, 1998).

4. David Ward, *Antifascisms: Cultural Politics in Italy, 1943–46* (Madison, NJ: Fairleigh Dickinson University Press, 1996), 158.

5. "Thus it was for Carlo Levi, who will remain the author of *Christ Stopped at Eboli*." Giancarlo Vigorelli, "Diario di un romantico," *Oggi*, February 18, 1947.

6. Giovanni De Luna, "'L'Orologio' di Carlo Levi e l'Italia del Dopoguerra," in *"L'Orologio" di Carlo Levi e la crisi della Repubblica*, ed. Gigliola De Donato (Manduria, BA: Piero Lacaita, 1996), 42.

7. Cesare Pavese, *This Business of Living. Diaries 1935–1950*, trans. A. E. Murch (Abingdon, UK: Routledge, 2009 [*Il mestiere di vivere*, 1952]), 288–89.

8. Luisa Mangoni, "Da *Cristo si è fermato a Eboli* a *L'Orologio*: note su Carlo Levi e la casa editrice Einaudi," in *Carlo Levi. Gli anni fiorentini 1941–1945*, ed. Piero Brunello and Pia Vivarelli (Rome: Donzelli, 2003), 205.

9. Muscetta, "Leggenda e verità," 52.

10. Gianfranco Piazzesi, review of *Cristo si è fermato a Eboli*, by Carlo Levi, *Società* 5 (1946): 260.

11. Ranuccio Bianchi Bandinelli, review of *L'Orologio*, by Carlo Levi, *Società* 3 (1950), 554. As I discuss in my "Diventare stranieri: *Paura della libertà* di Carlo Levi tra storia, redenzione e identità ebraica," *Allegoria* 81, no. 1 (2020): 165–79, Bianchi Bandinelli's review also features anti-Semitic undertones.

12. For reference, see Giovanni De Luna, *Storia del Partito d'Azione, 1942–1947* (Rome: Editori Riuniti, 1997).

13. Mangoni, "Da *Cristo*," 195–209; Leonardo Sacco, *L'Orologio della Repubblica. Carlo Levi e il caso Italia* (Lecce: Argo, 1996), esp. 7–30.

14. Raffaele Liucci, for instance, described Levi's postwar reflections on politics as an isolated "flash in the pan" in his production, ignoring his articles in the 1930s published on *Giustizia e Libertà*. Raffaele Liucci, *Spettatori di un naufragio. Gli intellettuali Italiani nella Seconda Guerra Mondiale* (Turin: Einaudi, 2011), 15.

15. Mangoni, "Da *Cristo*," 196.

16. "The political implications, certainly present in the book, were either immoderately swelled into operational suggestions, in order to more easily dismiss them, or just as excessively impoverished, in order to neutralize its recognized literary values." Carducci, *Storia intellettuale*, 144.

17. Gigliola De Donato, Sergio D'Amaro, *Un torinese del Sud: Carlo Levi. Una biografia* (Milan: Baldini and Castoldi, 2001), 160–74.

18. Carlo Levi, *The Watch*, trans. John Farrar and Marianna Gifford (New York: Farrar, Straus and Young, 1951 [*L'orologio*, 1950]), 31.

19. Carlo Levi, *Christ Stopped at Eboli*, trans. Frances Frenaye (New York: Farrar, Straus and Giroux, 1998 [*Cristo si è fermato a Eboli*, 1945]), 4.

20. According to Carlo Muscetta, Levi's books depicted "the legend of the Resistance as it dies in political apathy," while in his figure "the latest type of the modern superman [was] reproposed in a 'popular' (that is, traditional) language"; Muscetta, "Leggenda e verità," 67, 66.

21. Corrado Tumiati, review of *Cristo si è fermato a Eboli*, by Carlo Levi, *Il Ponte*, 2 (1946): 182–83.

22. Tommaso Fiore, "La piccolo borghesia. Voilà l'ennemi," review of *Cristo si è fermato a Eboli*, by Carlo Levi, *La gazzetta del mezzogiorno*, February 14, 1946.

23. Vittore Branca, "Lucania magica e desolata," review of *Cristo si è fermato a Eboli*, by Carlo Levi, *La Nazione del popolo*, March 21, 1946.

24. Levi, *Christ Stopped at Eboli*, 250, 253–54.

25. In a letter to Natalino Sapegno, dated February 27, 1926, Levi recalls Gobetti: "He was the one, really, to open the doors of youth for me: it's to him, really, that I owe all of what little I am." Cited in Piero Brunello, "Autonomia e autogoverno negli scritti di Carlo Levi: dalla Torino di 'Rivoluzione liberale' alla Firenze de 'La Nazione del Popolo,'" in *Carlo Levi. Gli anni fiorentini 1941–1945*, ed. Piero Brunello and Pia Vivarelli (Rome: Donzelli, 2003), 176.

26. For Levi's political thought, see David Ward, *Carlo Levi. Gli italiani e la paura della libertà* (Florence: La Nuova Italia, 2002); Brunello, "Autonomia e autogoverno"; and Brian Moloney, "*Cristo si è fermato a Eboli*, and the problem of the North," in *The Voices of Carlo Levi*, ed. Joseph Farrell (Oxford: Peter Lang, 2007), 99–118. On Carlo Rosselli, his life and political ideas, see Stanislao Pugliese, *Carlo Rosselli: Social Heretic and Antifascist Exile* (Cambridge, MA: Harvard University Press, 1999).

27. Filippo Benfante "'Risiede sempre a Firenze.' Quattro anni nella vita di Carlo Levi (1941–1945)," in *Carlo Levi. Gli anni fiorentini 1941–1945*, ed. Piero Brunello and Pia Vivarelli (Rome: Donzelli, 2003), 21.

28. Carlo Levi, Leone Ginzburg, "Il concetto di autonomia nel programma di G.L." (1932), in Carlo Levi, *Scritti politici* (Turin: Einaudi, 2001), 72–80.

29. David Ward, *Antifascisms: Cultural Politics in Italy, 1943–46* (Madison, NJ: Fairleigh Dickinson University Press, 1996), 158.

30. Carlo Levi, "La città," in *Dopo il diluvio. Sommario dell'Italia contemporanea*, ed. Dino Terra (Garzanti: Milano, 1947), 21.

31. Eugenio Montale, "Un pittore in esilio" (1946), in *Auto da fè. Cronache in due tempi* (Milan: il Saggiatore, 1966), 38.

32. Michael Löwy, *Redemption and Utopia: Jewish Libertarian Thought in Central Europe* (Stanford, CA: Stanford University Press, 1992), 3.

33. Carlo Levi, *Fear of Freedom*, trans. Adolphe Gourevitch (New York: Columbia University Press, 2008 [*Paura della Libertà*, 1946]).

34. Levi, *Fear of Freedom*, 1.

35. See, at least, Giorgio Agamben, *Homo Sacer: Sovereign Power and Bare Life* (Stanford, CA: Stanford University Press, 2020); René Girard, *Violence and the Sacred* (Baltimore, MD: Johns Hopkins University Press, 1977).

36. On Levi's sources, see Carducci, *Storia intellettuale*, and Gasperina Geroni, *Custode della soglia*.

37. Levi, *Fear of Freedom*, 34–35.

38. Levi, Ginzburg, "Concetto di autonomia," 73–74. See also David Bidussa, "Prima di Eboli. La riflessione civile e politica di Carlo Levi negli anni del fascismo e dei totalitarismi," in Levi, *Scritti politici*, v–xxxiii.

39. It is noteworthy how, a few paragraphs later, Levi and Ginzburg criticize Italians' "old anarchic tendency" as one of the sources of the Fascist dictatorship.

However, they conclude that, against Fascism, "we must create a State using anarchy's means." Levi, Ginzburg, "Concetto di autonomia," 77.

40. Levi, *Fear of Freedom*, 86.

41. Levi, *Christ Stopped at Eboli*, 250; 253–54.

42. Italo Calvino, "Carlo Levi, *Paura della libertà*," *l'Unità*, December 15, 1946, now in *Saggi: 1945–1985, Vol. 1*, ed. Mario Barenghi (Milan: Mondadori, 1995), 1115. Calvino will completely reverse his judgment in a 1967 article, "La compresenza dei tempi," *Galleria* 17, nos. 3–6 (1967): 237–40 (now in *Saggi: 1945–1985, Vol. 1*, 1122–25). On the reception of Levi's book, see Giorgio Agamben, "Attualità di Carlo Levi," in Levi, *Paura della libertà* (Vicenza: Neri Pozza, 2018), 7–25; and Filippo La Porta, "Carlo Levi. Liberarsi dalla politica attraverso la politica," in *Oltre la paura. Percorsi nella scrittura di Carlo Levi*, ed. Gigliola De Donato (Rome: Donzelli, 2008), 113–19.

43. As Aldo Bizzarri typically concluded in *La Fiera letteraria*: "Carlo Levi's gaze does not linger on the aspect of the material conditions of life, on what is usually called 'economic' fact." Aldo Bizzarri, "Un saggio di Carlo Levi," review of *Paura della libertà*, by Carlo Levi, *La Fiera letteraria*, February 13, 1947. The only positive review that I could find on the essay recognized Levi's attempt to work out a theory of totalitarianism. In *Il Ponte*, Leone Bortone wrote that in *Paura della libertà*, Levi "sketches out a sort of theory of totalitarianism, penetrating into that 'ambiguous inferno' in which the man of today wanders." Leone Bortone, review of *Paura della Libertà*, by Carlo Levi, *Il Ponte* 6 (1947): 592–93.

44. Giancarlo Vigorelli, review of *Paura della libertà*, by Carlo Levi, *Oggi*, February 2, 1947. Interestingly, a similar reading can be found in contemporary commentators such as Pier Giorgio Zunino, when in his work on post-Fascist Italy he writes about Levi: "Other passages consist of thought doodles frequently resolved in sophistries of a Judaicizing ('ebraicizzante') psychoanalytical rhetoric based on the 'fear of freedom' considered intrinsic to human being," in which the adjective "ebraicizzante" has a clear pejorative tone. Pier Giorgio Zunino, *La Repubblica e il suo passato* (Bologna: il Mulino, 2003), 486.

45. To my knowledge, no research has been conducted on the anti-Semitism of books such as Salvatore Satta's *De Profundis*, cited in all cultural-historical accounts of the transition in Italy, especially for its landmark concept of "death of the fatherland." Salvatore Satta, *De Profundis* (Milan: Adelphi, 1980 [1948]).

46. Quoted in Carducci, *Storia intellettuale*, 62. "Many Levi interpreters," writes Conni-Kay Jørgensen, "take it for granted that the writer composed his text 'with the sole escort,' as he would say, of the Bible and [Vico's] *New Science*. We were not able to ascertain the origin of this information, which circulated in various forms." Conni-Kay Jørgensen, *L'eredità vichiana nel Novecento letterario. Pavese, Savinio, Levi, Gadda* (Naples: Guida, 2008), 131.

47. Carducci noted an affinity between Levi and Ernst Bloch in their "visionary and biblic hermetism," without however expanding this insight beyond a footnote. Carducci, *Storia intellettuale*, n81. References to the Bible are

instead key in an article on Levi's reflections on painting: Guido Sacerdoti, "I transeunti Dei del nostro tempo," in *Oltre la paura. Percorsi nella scrittura di Carlo Levi*, ed. Gigliola De Donato (Rome: Donzelli, 2008), 41–58. See also Riccardo Gasperina Geroni, "La Sacra Bibbia di Diodati nell'autografo di *Paura della libertà* di Carlo Levi," in *Esperienze letterarie* 40, no. 3 (2015): 103–22.

48. Levi, *Fear of Freedom*, 43–44.

49. In her study on Levi, Giovanna Faleschini Lerner asserts that "in his theoretical writings, he privileges inclusion rather than systematization and exclusion, seeking to establish forms of coexistence—rather than coherence—among contradictory elements." Giovanna Faleschini Lerner, *Carlo Levi's Visual Poetics: The Painter as Writer* (New York: Palgrave Macmillan, 2012), 1. See also Giovanni Tesio, "*L'Orologio* di Carlo Levi tra Giona e Narciso," in *The Voices of Carlo Levi*, ed. Joseph Farrell (Oxford: Peter Lang, 2007), 55–66.

50. Carlo Levi, "Appunti sul 'Dittatore,'" now in *La strana idea di battersi per la libertà. Dai giornali della Liberazione (1944–1946)*, ed. Filippo Benfante (Santa Maria Capua Vetere, CE: Spartaco, 2007), 71.

51. Levi, "Appunti sul 'Dittatore,'" 74.

52. Levi, "Appunti sul 'Dittatore,'" 75.

53. Vittorio Giacopini, *Scrittori contro la politica* (Turin: Bollati Boringhieri, 1999), 103.

54. Levi, *Fear of Freedom*, 13–14.

55. Levi's intuitions anticipate later and more comprehensive studies like the aforementioned Girard, *Violence and the Sacred*, but also the philosophical analysis of Roberto Esposito, *Immunitas: The Protection and Negation of Life* (Cambridge: Polity Press, 2011).

56. Exceptions are Bidussa, "Dopo Eboli," and Gasperina Geroni, *Custode*. For the impact of Spengler's and particularly Ortega y Gasset's ideas on Levi, see Carducci, *Storia intellettuale*. For the decisive influence of eminent "meridionalisti," such as Gaetano Salvemini and Guido Dorso on Levi, see Brian Moloney, "*Cristo si è fermato a Eboli* and the Problem of the North," in *The Voices of Carlo Levi*, ed. Joseph Farrell (Oxford: Peter Lang, 2007), 112.

57. Agamben, *Homo Sacer*, 83.

58. Roger Caillois, *Man and the Sacred* (Glencoe, IL: Free Press of Glencoe, 1960), 30.

59. Levi, *Fear of Freedom*, 14.

60. On the elaboration of Arendt's ideas on totalitarianism in the 1940s, see Elizabeth Young-Bruehl, *Hannah Arendt: For the Love of the World* (New Haven, CT: Yale University Press, 1982), esp. 199–200.

61. Levi, *Fear of Freedom*, 32.

62. Carlo Levi, "Razzismo e idolatria statale," in *Il dovere dei tempi. Prose politiche e civili*, ed. Luisa Montevecchi (Rome: Donzelli, 2004), 63–64.

63. See Benfante, "'Risiede sempre a Firenze,'" 11–103.

64. On Gobetti's influence on Levi, see Ward, *Carlo Levi*. For an analysis of Buber's "theo-political approach," as opposed to Carl Schmitt's "political-theological"

concepts, see Samuel H. Brody, *Martin Buber's Theopolitics* (Bloomington: Indiana University Press, 2018).

65. Martin Buber, *Pfade in Utopia* (1950); all of Buber's citations are taken from Löwy, *Redemption and Utopia*, 56.

66. Löwy, *Redemption and Utopia*.

67. Gershom Scholem is cited in Löwy, *Redemption and Utopia*, 64.

68. Ernst Bloch, *The Spirit of Utopia* (1918), cited in Löwy, *Redemption and Utopia*, 102.

69. "*Fear of Freedom* represents a paradoxical anarchical critique of social spontaneity; that is, a strange anarchy without anarchism." Giacopini, *Scrittori*, 103. Calvino, too, spoke of Levi as "anarchist" in his 1946 review: "He is an anarchist [...] in the tumultuous and aestheticizing Nietzschean sense." Calvino, "Carlo Levi, *Paura della libertà*," 1115.

70. For Vico's influence on Levi, see Andrea Battistini, "La presenza di Vico in *Paura della libertà* di Carlo Levi," in *Encyclopedia Mundi. Studi di letteratura italiana in onore di Giuseppe Mazzotta*, ed. Ugo Baldassarri e Alessandro Polcri (Florence: Le Lettere, 2013), 3–20; and Martina Piperno, "Con Vico ne *L'Orologio*," in *Poetiche* 17, no. 42 (1 2015): 53–74.

71. "Jewish messianism is in its origins and by its nature (...) a theory of catastrophe." Gershom Scholem, "Toward an Understanding of the Messianic Idea in Judaism," cited in Löwy, *Redemption and Utopia*, 18.

72. See, at least, Levi, "Città."

73. Ward, *Antifascisms*, 173.

74. Levi, *Christ Stopped at Eboli*, 116. In his polemical reading of Levi's books, Muscetta completely misinterpreted this passage, which is a veiled reference to the state of prostration Jewish citizens suffered during Fascism: "He is convinced that he has inside himself a double nature, 'half baron and half lion' like his dog. Also, this strange being (which he depicts fantastically), with its mysterious nature, with the evocative, magical power it exerts on the Gaglianesi, will allow him to establish a supernatural communion with the peasant world immersed in its 'animal enchantment.'" Muscetta, "Leggenda e verità," 55–56.

75. Levi, *Christ Stopped at Eboli*, 4.

76. Levi, *Christ Stopped at Eboli*, 112.

77. Peregrine Horden and Nicholas Purcell, *The Corrupting Sea: A Study of Mediterranean History* (Oxford: Blackwell, 2000), 469. In his landmark study on the Mediterranean world, Braudel recalled Levi's Lucania as "this isolated archaic little universe." Fernand Braudel, *The Mediterranean and the Mediterranean World in the Age of Philip II* (Berkeley: University of California Press, 1995), 1240.

78. Carlo Levi, "Don Luigino guadagnato alla democrazia," in *Il dovere dei tempi. Prose politiche e civili*, ed. Luisa Montevecchi (Rome: Donzelli, 2004), 119.

79. Mario Alicata, "Meridionalismo," 190. In many passages, Alicata looks to the canon of social realism to find evidence for his arguments: "Should this not suffice to warn us, and to warn Levi and other friends and comrades of his and

ours, of the danger of never abandoning, both in poetic representations of the south and in judgments about these representations, the yardstick of realism?" Alicata, "Meridionalismo," 189.

80. Jacques Rancière, *The Politics of Literature* (Cambridge: Polity, 2011), 7.

81. Walter Benjamin, *Paralipomena to "On the Concept of History,"* in *Selected Writings, Vol. 4, 1938–1940*, ed. Howard Eiland and Michael W. Jennings (Cambridge, MA: The Belknap Press of Harvard University Press, 1996–2003), 402.

82. Giorgio Agamben, *Infancy and History: On the Destruction of Experience*, trans. Liz Heron (London: Verso, 2007), 91.

83. Löwy, *Redemption and Utopia*, 102, 96.

84. Levi, *The Watch*, 19.

85. See Erich Auerbach, "The Knight Sets Forth," in *Mimesis: The Representation of Reality in Western Literature* (Princeton, NJ: Princeton University Press, 2013), 123–42.

86. "Don Quixote, eternal and immortal hero of these peasant lands, tragically certain of his own truth and justice, even when time and events cause him to hide under the long black coat of an opportunist landowner." Levi, *The Watch*, 48.

87. Levi, *The Watch*, 34.

88. Ernst Bloch, "Nonsynchronism and the Obligation to Its Dialectics," *New German Critique* 11 (1977): 22.

89. Levi, *The Watch*, 82.

90. Levi, "Città," 20.

91. Alberto Savinio, "Difesa dell'intelligenza," in *Sorte dell'Europa* (Milan: Adelphi, 2005 [1945]), 26–27.

92. Levi, *The Watch*, 186–87.

93. See Silvana Patriarca, *Italian Vices: Nation and Character from the Risorgimento to the Republic* (Cambridge: Cambridge University Press, 2010); Walter L. Adamson, *Avant-Garde Florence: From Modernism to Fascism* (Cambridge, MA: Harvard University Press, 1993). For Mussolini and his concept of Rome, see Emilio Gentile, *La Grande Italia: The Myth of the Nation in the Twentieth Century* (Madison: University of Wisconsin Press, 2009), esp. 123–92.

94. See Simon Levi Sullam, *Giuseppe Mazzini and the Origins of Fascism* (New York: Palgrave Macmillan, 2015).

95. "The truly modern men and peoples," wrote the nationalist Enrico Corradini in 1904, "inspire a sense of *Romanità*," cited in Giovanni Belardelli, *Il Ventennio degli intellettuali. Cultura, politica, ideologia nell'Italia fascista* (Bari-Rome: Laterza, 2005), 219.

96. Giovanni Papini, "Contro Roma," in *La cultura italiana del '900 attraverso le riviste, Vol. 4: "Lacerba" "La Voce" (1914–1916)*, ed. Gianni Scalia (Turin: Einaudi, 1961); Bottai is cited in Joshua Arthurs, "The Eternal Parasite: Anti-Romanism in Italian Politics and Culture since 1860," *Annali d'Italianistica* 28 (2010): 127.

97. Gentile, *Grande Italia*, 47; 163. On the literary aspects of the Fascist myth of *Romanità*, Belardelli interestingly commented: "In carrying out these Mussolinian intentions, furthermore, the regime ultimately delineated a false image of ancient Rome destined to last well beyond Fascism. It is possible to establish a relationship between the will to isolate Roman monuments and the construction on the Fascists' part of genealogies of precursors, from Dante to Machiavelli, from Vico to Mazzini, from Carducci to Crispi." Belardelli, *Ventennio degli Intellettuali*, 214.

98. *Romanità*'s legacy in postwar Italy has been variously debated. Joshua Arthurs argues that after the demise of Fascism, "in Italy, the discrediting of *Romanità* prompted deeper introspection and a return to the anti-Roman rhetoric of the pre–Fascist period." Arthurs, *Excavating Modernity*, 156. Richard J. B. Bosworth highlighted, instead, the hegemonic role the Catholic Church had in shaping Rome's culture and identity not only after the fall of Fascism but also during Mussolini's rule. Bosworth, *Whispering City: Modern Rome and Its Histories* (New Haven, CT: Yale University Press, 2011). Finally, Emilio Gentile underscores how, in the early postwar period, the two main Italian parties, the DC and the PCI, rooted their respective international ideologies, founding myths, and civilizing missions in national narratives. These narratives were based on a new formulation of the idea of the nation, putting forth, at the same time, a novel concept of *Romanità*. Gentile, *Grande Italia*, esp. 347–75.

99. Levi, *Christ Stopped at Eboli*, 76.

100. Levi, *The Watch*, 261–62.

101. Bosworth, *Whispering City*, 211.

102. Levi, *The Watch*, 267.

103. Altiero Spinelli, *Il Manifesto di Ventotene* (Bologna: il Mulino, 1991 [1943]).

104. Muscetta, "Leggenda e verità," 66.

105. On this passage, see Giovanni De Luna and Marco Revelli, *Fascismo/Antifascismo. Le idee, le identità* (Florence: La Nuova Italia, 1995); Leonardo Sacco, "Contadini e luigini," in *"L'Orologio" di Carlo Levi e la crisi della Repubblica*, ed. Gigliola De Donato (Manduria, BA: Piero Lacaita, 1996), 97–106; Ward, *Carlo Levi*, esp. 92–122.

106. Levi, *The Watch*, 228–29.

107. Levi, *The Watch*, 229–30.

108. In the novel, Levi depicts Antonio Gramsci explicitly as a "Contadino," implicitly suggesting that Communist politicians betrayed Gramsci's true spirit by turning his party, originally a "Contadino" party, in a truly "luiginal" organization. Levi, *The Watch*, 232.

109. Levi, *The Watch*, 70.

110. See Michael Rothberg, *Traumatic Realism: The Demands of Holocaust Representation* (Minneapolis: University of Minnesota Press, 2000).

111. On the references to the Holocaust in Levi's works, see Nancy Harrowitz, "Carlo Levi: Watching the Future of Holocaust Representation," in *The Voices of Carlo Levi*, ed. Joseph Farrell (Oxford: Peter Lang, 2007), 147–58.

112. Levi, *The Watch*, 59.

113. The article is titled "Malaparte e Bonaparte, ossia l'Italia letteraria," and was published in *Giustizia e Libertà*. It polemically reviews Malaparte's *Technique du coup d'état* (see "Specters of a Revolutionary Past: Curzio Malaparte" in Chapter 1). Now in Carlo Levi, *Prima e dopo le parole: scritti e discorsi sulla letteratura*, ed. Gigliola De Donato and Rosalba Galvagno (Rome: Donzelli, 2001), 115–22.

114. Giulio Einaudi to Carlo Levi, March 9, 1950, folder 253, Carlo Levi Papers, Archivio Einaudi, Turin, Archivio di Stato.

115. On Malaparte's *Forbidden Christ*, see Franco Baldasso, *Curzio Malaparte, la letteratura crudele. Kaputt, La pelle, e la caduta della civiltà europea* (Rome: Carocci, 2019), 77–97. On Coletti's *The Earth Cries Out*, see Millicent Marcus, *Italian Film in the Shadow of Auschwitz* (Toronto: University of Toronto Press, 2007), 32–33.

116. Manlio Rossi-Doria, "La crisi del governo Parri nel racconto di Carlo Levi," in *"L'Orologio" di Carlo Levi e la crisi della Repubblica*, ed. Gigliola De Donato (Manduria, BA: Piero Lacaita, 1996), 191.

5. Curzio Malaparte, a Tragic Modernity

1 Milan Kundera, "The Skin: Malaparte's Arch-Novel," in *Encounter* (New York: Harper Collins, 2010), 173–74.

2. See "The Italian Experience within the Totalitarian Paradigm" in Chapter 1.

3. On the transnational legacy of Malaparte, see Martina Grassi, ed.,*"La bourse des idées du monde." Malaparte e la Francia* (Florence: Olschki, 2008); Michèle Coury and Emmanuel Mattiato, eds., *Curzio Malaparte, témoin et visionnaire*, special issue of *Cahiers d'études italiennes* 24 (2017); Maria Pia De Paulis-Dalembert, ed., *Curzio Malaparte. Esperienza e scrittura*, special issue of *Chronique italiennes* 35, no. 1 (2018); and Beatrice Baglivo, et al., eds., *Curzio Malaparte e la ricerca dell'identità europea (1920–1950)* (Chambéry: Presses de l'Université Savoie Mont Blanc, 2020).

4. In a 1982 interview, Alberto Moravia claimed: "Malaparte belongs to a very particular tradition, typical of Italy: namely, that of men who did not serve Literature, but made use of it as a pedestal to raise up the statue of their own 'I,' to create a cult of their own personality." Michele Buonuomo, "Un colloquio con Alberto Moravia," in *Malaparte. Una proposta*, ed. Michele Buonuomo (Rome: De Luca, 1982), 11. Relevant avenues of research about Malaparte's intellectual figure were indicated by Nicola Merola in a 1998 review: "Who knows if Malaparte won't end up being useful for a better understanding of Gadda and Pasolini." Nicola Merola, "Al banchetto dei potenti," review of *Opere Scelte*, by Curzio Malaparte, *L'indice dei libri del mese* 15, 1 (1998): 7. Unexpected similarities

between Malaparte's and Pasolini's polemics are also highlighted by Luigi Baldacci, "Verifiche malapartiane," in *Curzio Malaparte. Il narratore, il politologo, il cittadino di Prato e dell'Europa*, ed. Renato Barilli and Vittoria Baroncelli (Prato: CUEN, 1998), 185; and Sandro Veronesi, "L'Europa Marcia di Malaparte e Pasolini," in *Curzio Malaparte*, ed. Barilli and Baroncelli, 372–79.

5. Stefano Jossa, *L'Italia letteraria* (Bologna: il Mulino, 2006), 63.

6. In a fortunate manual of Italian literature widely used at the university level, Giulio Ferroni dismisses Malaparte with few tendentious lines: "He is an expression of the extreme degradation of the intellectual attention-seeking and vitalism of the early twentieth century: his intellectual dimension manifests itself in grand, excessive gestures, in extremist denials of all rationality [. . .]. His many works constantly reveal frantic incendiary intentions, with results whose vulgarity and bad taste would be difficult to surpass." Giulio Ferroni, *Storia della letteratura italiana. Il Novecento* (Milan: Einaudi Scuola, 1991), 209.

7. "He narcissistically takes center stage even in scenes of carnage, as if genocide were a stage set contrived to set off his own seductive appeal." Dan Hofstaedter, Afterword to Curzio Malaparte, *Kaputt*, trans. Cesare Foligno (New York: NYRB Classics, 2005 [*Kaputt*, 1944]), 434.

8. A typical example of such criticism can be found in Raffaele Liucci's *Spettatori di un naufragio*, which superimposes historical categories a priori on Malaparte's novels, without confirming his claims with actual reference to the texts. Liucci, *Spettatori di un naufragio. Gli intellettuali italiani nella Seconda Guerra Mondiale* (Turin: Einaudi, 2011), 202.

9. Giancarlo Vigorelli, "Malaparte: testimonianza e proposta di revisione," in Curzio Malaparte, *Opere scelte*, ed. Luigi Martellini (Milan: Mondadori, 1997), xxxii.

10. Maurizio Serra, *Malaparte. Vite e leggende* (Venice: Marsilio, 2012); and Maria Pia de Paulis, ed., *Cahier Malaparte* (Paris: Éditions de l'Herne, 2018).

11. Curzio Malaparte, *Mamma Marcia* (Florence: Vallecchi, 1959), 160.

12. Serra, *Malaparte*, 360.

13. For the modern myth of palingenetic war, see George L. Mosse, *Fallen Soldiers: Reshaping the Memory of the World Wars* (Oxford: Oxford University Press, 1990).

14. Leo Bersani, *The Culture of Redemption*. (Cambridge, MA: Harvard University Press, 1990), 122.

15. Giuliana Pieri, "Gabriele d'Annunzio and the Self-Fashioning of a National Icon," *Modern Italy* 21, no. 4 (2016): 328–43.

16. Malaparte, *Mamma Marcia*, 170.

17. See Franco Baldasso, *Curzio Malaparte, la letteratura crudele*. Kaputt, La pelle, e la caduta della civiltà europea (Rome: Carocci, 2019), esp. 21–30. For aestheticism and decadent aesthetics, see Matei Călinescu, *Five Faces of Modernity: Modernism, Avant-Garde, Decadence, Kitsch, Postmodernism* (Durham, NC: Duke University Press, 1987).

258 | Notes to pages 174–78

18. Leone Ginzburg, "A proposito di Malaparte, 'Technique du coup d'état,'" *La Cultura* 9, no. 2 (1932), now in *Scritti*, ed. Domenico Zucàro (Turin: Einaudi, 2000), 86.

19. The book's first edition was published in French translation, on which the available English version is based. Curzio Malaparte, *Coup d'Etat. The Technique of Revolution*, trans. Sylvia Saunders (New York: Dutton, 1932 [*Technique du coup d'état*, 1931]), 178. The Italian text of *Tecnica del colpo di stato*, can be read in Malaparte, *Opere scelte*.

20. Luigi Martellini, *Le "Prospettive" di Malaparte. Una rivista tra cultura fascista, europeismo e letteratura* (Naples: ESI, 2014).

21. Kundera, *Encounter*, 160.

22. Massimo Bontempelli, "La musica," in *Dopo il diluvio. Sommario dell'Italia contemporanea*, ed. Dino Terra (Milan: Garzanti, 1947), 317, 323.

23. Malaparte, *Kaputt*, 3. Changes to the published translation are mine.

24. Malaparte, *Kaputt*, 3.

25. See "The Italian Experience within the Totalitarian Paradigm" and n34 in Chapter 1.

26. Serra, *Malaparte*, 335–36.

27. In his biography, Serra argued that Malaparte showed himself unable, "across the entire post-Fascist period, to deliver a real self-critique, with the result that his position was rendered even more difficult and uncomfortable than it already was." Serra, *Malaparte*, 326.

28. On Malaparte and Surrealism, see the issue dedicated to the relationship Italian literature and art have with Surrealism in his journal *Prospettive*, particularly his introduction: Curzio Malaparte, "Il Surrealismo e l'Italia," *Prospettive* 4, no. 1 (1940): 3–7.

29. See Baldasso, *Curzio Malaparte*, esp. 19–34.

30. Curzio Malaparte, *Das Kapital, pièce en trois actes; précédée de Du côté de chez Proust, impromptu en un acte* (Paris: Denoël, 1951), 91–92.

31. Giovanni Spadolini, review of *La pelle*, by Curzio Malaparte, *Il Messaggero*, February 9, 1950; Guy Tosi, "Curzio Malaparte et 'Kaputt,'" *Paris*, April 19, 1946. Now in Curzio Malaparte, *Malaparte, Vol. 7: 1946–1947*, ed. Edda Ronchi Suckert (Florence: Ponte alle Grazie, 1993), 31.

32. Giorgio Agamben, *Remnants of Auschwitz: The Witness and the Archive* (New York: Zone Books, 1999).

33. Primo Levi, *If This Is a Man*, in *The Complete Works of Primo Levi, Vol. 1*, ed. Ann Goldstein, trans. Stuart Woolf (New York: Liveright, 2015 [*Se questo è un uomo*, 1947]), 85.

34. Jacques Derrida, *Demeure: Fiction and Testimony* (Stanford, CA: Stanford University Press, 2000), 29–38.

35. Tosi, "Curzio Malaparte et 'Kaputt,'" 31.

36. Lucia Re, *Calvino and the Age of Neorealism: Fables of Estrangement* (Stanford, CA: Stanford University Press, 1990), 92.

37. See Italo Calvino, "Preface," in *The Path to the Spiders' Nests*, trans. Archibald Colquhoun (New York: Ecco, 2000 [*Il sentiero dei nidi di ragno*, 1947]), 7–30.

38. Furio Jesi, *Spartakus: The Symbology of Revolt*, trans. Alberto Toscano (London: Seagull Books, 2014), 29–30. Changes in Toscano's translation are mine.

39. See Charles Burdett, "Changing Identities through Memory: Malaparte's Self-Figurations in *Kaputt*," in *European Memories of the Second World War*, ed. Helmut Peitsch, Charles Burdett, and Claire Gorrara (New York: Berghahn, 1999): 110–19.

40. Curzio Malaparte, *The Skin*, trans. David Moore (New York: NYRB Classics, 2013 [*La pelle*, 1949]), 283.

41. See Levi's polemic with Giorgio Manganelli in his article, "About Obscure Writing," in *Other People's Trades*, now in *The Complete Works of Primo Levi, Vol. 3*, trans. Antony Shugaar (New York: Liveright, 2015 [*L'altrui mestiere*, 1985]), 2061–66.

42. Testimonial literature is in contrast with Avant-garde claims of "aesthetic autonomy" but requires instead the authority of a tradition to confirm its credibility. On this specific aspect of testimonial literature and Levi's particular use of literary tradition to support the credibility of his testimony, see Franco Baldasso, *Il cerchio di gesso. Primo Levi narratore e testimone* (Bologna: Pendragon, 2007), esp. 17–45.

43. On Nazi kitsch, see Modris Eksteins, *Rites of Spring: The Great War and the Birth of Modern Age* (Boston: Hougton Mifflin, 1989).

44. Malaparte, *Kaputt*, 60.

45. On September 9, 1943, Malaparte writes in his *Giornale segreto*: "British Airforce's aerial bombing on the Gulf of Salerno. Bellissimo." Now in Malaparte, *Malaparte, Vol. 6: 1942–1945*, 445. Translation here is mine.

46. Günther Anders, *Die Antiquiertheit des Menschen. Band I: Über die Seele im Zeitalter der zweiten industriellen Revolution* (München: Beck, 1956); and *Die Antiquiertheit des Menschen. Band II: Über die Zerstörung des Lebens im Zeitalter der dritten industriellen Revolution* (München: Beck, 1980). For an introduction in English to Anders' anthropology, see Paul Van Dijk, *Anthropology in the Age of Technology: The Philosophical Contribution of Günther Anders* (Amsterdam: Rodopi, 2000). See also Enzo Traverso, *Auschwitz e gli intellettuali. La Shoah nella cultura del dopoguerra* (Bologna: Il Mulino, 2004), 83–108.

47. Curzio Malaparte, "September 22, 1942," *Giornale Segreto 1*. Agenda 1942, Malaparte Archive, Milan, Biblioteca Via del Senato.

48. In a review of the film that appeared in 1951 in *Cahiers du cinéma*, Bazin describes Malaparte's search for a modern tragic aesthetics: "If this universe of stone, of earth, and of men is nevertheless as real as it would be in a documentary, its *time* and its *space* are as unreal and artificial as those of nightmares and tragedies." André Bazin, *André Bazin and Italian Neorealism*, ed. Bert Cardullo (London: Continuum, 2011), 97.

49. Additionally, this contrast is key for the chapter "Blood," the last of *Kaputt,* by describing people's struggle for survival in the poorest quarters of Naples during aerial bombings (938–63). See also the opening scene of *The Forbidden Christ,* with the panoptical view from the plane encompassing the entire Tuscan landscape.

50. Malaparte, *Kaputt,* 729. Foligno's translation omits the whole chapter "The Haywire Rifle." Translation here is by Stephen Twilley.

51. Malaparte, *Kaputt,* 620–24.

52. Malaparte, *Kaputt,* 731.

53. Leonardo Paggi, *Il "popolo dei morti." La repubblica italiana nata dalla guerra (1940–1946)* (Bologna: il Mulino, 2009), 113.

54. W. G. Sebald, *On the Natural History of Destruction* (New York: Random House, 2003), 10.

55. Paggi, *"Popolo dei morti,"* 133. A striking example of this altered shared memory is the case of the massacre of the Duomo di San Miniato, July 22, 1944, examined in James Foot, *Italy's Divided Memory* (New York: Palgrave Macmillian, 2003), 22–29.

56. On these issues, see Gabriella Gribaudi, *Guerra totale. Tra bombe alleate e violenze naziste. Napoli e il fronte meridionale, 1940–1944* (Turin: Bollati Boringhieri, 2005). Malaparte's critical portrayal of Guillaume's Army occupation of Southern Lazio in *The Skin* is examined in Marisa Escolar, *Allied Encounters: The Gendered Redemption of World War II Italy* (New York: Fordham University Press, 2020), esp. 111–31.

57. Malaparte, *Kaputt,* 3.

58. See Robert S. C. Gordon, "The Italian War," in *The Cambridge Companion to the Literature of World War II,* ed. Marina MacKay (Cambridge: Cambridge University Press, 2011); and Philip Cooke, *The Legacy of the Italian Resistance* (New York: Palgrave Macmillan, 2011).

59. Malaparte, *The Skin,* 86–130.

60. Malaparte, *Kaputt,* 242–43.

61. Hannah Arendt, "Nightmare and Flight," in *Essays in Understanding 1930–1954* (New York: Shocken, 2005), 134.

62. See "Specters of a Revolutionary Past: Curzio Malaparte" in Chapter 1.

63. Malaparte, "September 22, 1942," in *Giornale Segreto.*

64. Malaparte, *Kaputt,* 60.

65. As we discussed in the second section of Chapter 1, Malaparte also elaborated his concept of the tragic in modern history with the conflict between justice and charity in *Das Kapital.*

66. George Steiner, *The Death of Tragedy* (New York: Knopf, 1961), 127–35.

67. See, "The 'Political Wrong' of Literature during the Transition" in the Introduction.

68. Malaparte, *The Skin,* 37.

69. Malaparte, *The Skin,* 38.

70. A compelling reading of Malaparte's oeuvre in light of his references to seventeenth-century literature and philosophy can be found in Andrea Orsucci, *Il "giocoliere d'idee." Malaparte e la filosofia* (Pisa: Edizioni della Normale, 2015).

71. The sensational reaction to *The Skin* unleashed in Italy and abroad, which included a political trial and official condemnation by Catholic authorities, is detailed in Serra, *Malaparte*, 376–89. The dozens of articles and reviews of the book, most of them attacking its author for public indecency, are collected in Malaparte, *Malaparte*, Vols. 8–10.

72. Malaparte, *The Skin*, 5.

73. See Malaparte's articles "Risveglio di Belgrado," *Corriere della Sera*, April 22, 1941; and "L'ora che segnò la sorte di Belgrado," *Corriere della Sera*, April 27, 1941; now in *Malaparte, Vol. 5: 1940–1941*, 608–12; 620–24.

74. Malaparte, *The Skin*, 39. A reflection on *The Skin* and Naples's metaphorical corporeality is in Serenella Iovino, *Ecocriticism and Italy: Ecology, Resistance, and Liberation* (London: Bloomsbury Academics, 2016), 27–33.

75. This tradition was codified in the nineteenth century by Francesco De Sanctis with his *History of Italian Literature* (1870). See Jossa, *Italia letteraria*, 61–64.

76. By aligning with Virgil's fate and figuratively following in his footsteps, Malaparte also avoids any direct confrontation with his *own* Fascist past, which remains surreptitiously unresolved.

77. Malaparte, *The Skin*, 40.

78. Benedetto Croce, *Scritti e discorsi politici (1943–1947)*, Vol. 1, ed. Angela Carella (Naples: Bibliopolis, 1993), 101. A long historiographical tradition, now discredited, interpreted the Nazi political aberration as a logical consequence of German people's "special path" (*Sonderweg*) to modernity. This teleological reading of national German history "from Luther to Hitler" has been further popularized in English-speaking countries by journalist William Shirer, author of the greatly influential book *The Rise and Fall of the Third Reich* (1960).

79. Malaparte, *The Skin*, 3.

80. Similar passages elucidate both the distance between Malaparte's populism and the conservative stances of other former ideologues of Fascism, such as Leo Longanesi, and the reasons for his long-standing friendship with Giuseppe Prezzolini. The belief in an anti-bourgeois popular revolution against the conservative elites that suffocate national forces guided Malaparte throughout his life. From his voluntary intervention in WWI to his allegiance to early Fascism, from his 1920s articles for the journal *La conquista dello stato* and the daily *La Stampa* to his reports on the Liberation of Florence for *l'Unità* in 1944, the myth of a popular revolution able to regenerate the nation is a constant presence in his political and polemical output.

81. Spadolini, review, 49.

82. Lorenzo Gigli, "L'ultimo Malaparte," *La Gazzetta del Popolo*, February 10, 1950. Now in Malaparte, *Malaparte, Vol. 9: 1950–1951*, 62.

83. Emilio Cecchi, "La Pelle di Malaparte," *L'Europeo*, February 12, 1950. In Malaparte, *Malaparte, Vol. 9: 1950–1951*, 68.

84. Gigli, "L'ultimo Malaparte," 61–62.

85. Bersani, *Culture of Redemption*, 22.

86. Bersani, *Culture of Redemption*, 22.

87. Malaparte, "Cadaveri squisiti," 6. The author first associates his own writing with cruelty in his 1937 introduction to the collection of short stories entitled *Sangue* (Florence: Vallecchi, 1995), especially 43–44.

88. It is worth mentioning here how even the Risorgimento's heroes were depicted in popular culture and celebrated in public speeches through a Catholic imaginary of sacrifice, as thoroughly analyzed in Alberto Mario Banti, *Nation of the Risorgimento. Kinship, Sanctity, and Honour in the Origins of Unified Italy* (London: Routledge, 2020).

89. For a philosophical inquiry concerning secularization and modernity, see Giacomo Marramao, *Potere e secolarizzazione. Le categorie del tempo* (Turin: Bollati Boringhieri, 2005).

90. Hannah Arendt, *The Origins of Totalitarianism* (New York: Harvest, 1976 [1951]), 457.

91. Malaparte, *The Skin*, 305.

92. Malaparte, *The Skin*, 100.

93. Buonuomo, "Colloquio con Alberto Moravia," 11.

94. About *The Skin*, Guri Schwarz notes the "centrality of sexual references in the definition of a moral order," concluding that "the decline of the myth of the war goes hand in hand with the upheaval of a traditional balance between masculine and feminine." Guri Schwarz, *Tu mi devi seppellir. Riti funebri e culto nazionale alle origini della Repubblica* (Milan: UTET, 2010), 225.

95. Curzio Malaparte, *Viaggi fra i terremoti* (Florence: Vallecchi, 1963); and Serra, *Malaparte*, 462–63. For presence and legacy of Fascism in Argentina, see Federico Finchelstein, *Transatlantic Fascism: Ideology, Violence, and the Sacred in Argentina and Italy, 1919–1945* (Durham, NC: Duke University Press, 2010).

Conclusion: Tearing Down the Monuments

1 Alberto Savinio, *Nuova enciclopedia* (Milan: Adelphi, 2011 [1977]), 109.

2. "A cause of the crisis that distresses and corrupts our time *is this persistent imitation of false models.*" Alberto Savinio, "Lo Stato" (1947), in *Sorte dell'Europa* (Milan: Adelphi, 2005 [1945]), 102.

3. See Ruth Ben-Ghiat, *Fascist Modernities: Italy 1922–1945* (Berkeley: University of California Press, 2001), 4–5.

4. See Claudio Pavone, *A Civil War: A History of the Italian Resistance* (London: Verso, 2014).

5. See Savinio, "Difesa dell'intelligenza," in *Sorte dell'Europa* (Milan: Adelphi, 2005 [1945]), 26–27.

6. Curzio Malaparte, *The Skin*, trans. David Moore (New York: NYRB Classics, 2013 [*La pelle*, 1949]), 287–302.

7. On America's influence in postwar Europe, see Victoria de Grazia, *Irresistible Empire: American Advance through Twentieth Century Europe* (Cambridge, MA: The Belknap Press of Harvard University Press, 2006).

8. "The 'wings of diplomacy' policy [. . .] not only sanctioned the end of Europe's centrality but also inevitably disregarded the scale of values that anti-Fascism had placed at the center of its political agenda." Leonardo Paggi, *Il "popolo dei morti,"* in *La repubblica italiana nata dalla Guerra (1940–1946)* (Bologna: il Mulino, 2009), 30.

9. Tony Judt, *Postwar: A History of Europe since 1945* (New York: Penguin, 2006), 6.

10. Guido Piovene, *Le furie* (Turin: Aragno, 2009 [1963]); Giuseppe Berto, *Incubus*, trans. William Weaver (New York: Knopf, 1966 [*Il male oscuro*, 1964]).

11. Corrado Alvaro, *L'Italia rinunzia?* (Rome: Donzelli, 2011 [1945]), 65.

12. See Domenico Scarpa, "La madre dei racconti. Corrado Alvaro sotto il fascismo," in *Storie avventurose di libri necessari* (Rome: Gaffi, 2010), 33–65.

13. See Siobhan Craig, "Translation and Treachery: Historiography and the Betrayal of Meaning in Anna Banti's *Artemisia*;" *Italica* 87, no. 4 (2010): 602–18.

14. See Percy Allum, "Uniformity Undone: Aspects of Catholic Culture in Postwar Italy," in *Culture and Conflict in Postwar Italy: Essays on Mass and Popular Culture*, ed. Zygmunt G. Baranski and Robert Lumley (London: Macmillian, 1990), 79–96; David Forgacs, "The Italian Communist Party and Culture," in *Culture and Conflict*, ed. Baranski and Lumley; 97–114.

15. Cesare Pavese, *This Business of Living. Diaries 1935–1950*, trans. A. E. Murch (Abingdon, UK: Routledge, 2009 [*Il mestiere di vivere*, 1952]), 341.

16. Italo Calvino, "Preface," in *The Path to the Spiders' Nests*, trans. Archibald Colquhoun (New York: Ecco Press, 2000 [*Il sentiero dei nidi di ragno*, 1947]), 16.

17. Andrea Zanzotto, "Giuseppe Berto tra 'Il cielo è rosso' e 'Il brigante.'" *La provincia di Treviso* 5, no. 2 (1962): 30.

18. Simon Levis Sullam, *I fantasmi del fascismo. Le metamorfosi degli intellettuali italiani nel dopoguerra* (Milan: Feltrinelli, 2021), esp. 52–105.

19. Luigi Meneghello, *Fiori italiani* (Milan: Rizzoli, 1976), 139.

Bibliography

"Recensioni," *Società* 1–2 (1945): 349.
A. A. Review of *Sorte dell'Europa*, by Alberto Savinio. *Mondo Europeo* 1, no. 3 (December 1945).
Adams Sitney, P. *Vital Crises in Italian Cinema: Iconography, Stylistics, Politics.* New York: Oxford University Press, 2013.
Adamson, Walter L. *Avant-Garde Florence: From Modernism to Fascism.* Cambridge, MA: Harvard University Press, 1993.
Agamben, Giorgio. "Attualità di Carlo Levi." In Carlo Levi, *Paura della libertà*, 7–25.
———. "Il congedo della tragedia." In Fofi and Sofri. *Festa per Elsa*, 56–59.
———. *Homo Sacer: Sovereign Power and Bare Life.* Stanford, CA: Stanford University Press, 2020.
———. *Infancy and History: On the Destruction of Experience.* Translated by Liz Heron. New York: Verso, 2007.
———. *Remnants of Auschwitz: The Witness and the Archive.* New York: Zone Books, 1999.
Alatri, Paolo. "Morte apparente del fascismo." *La Nuova Europa* 2, no. 24 (1945): 10.
Alfano, Giancarlo. *Ciò che ritorna. Gli effetti della guerra nella letteratura italiana del Novecento.* Florence: Cesati, 2014.
Alfieri, Vittorio. *The Life of Vittorio Alfieri Written by Himself.* Translated by Sir Henry McAnally. Lawrence: University of Kansas Press, 1953 (*Vita scritta da esso*, 1804).
Alicata, Mario. "Il meridionalismo non si può fermare a Eboli." In *Antropologia culturale e questione meridionale. Ernesto De Martino e il dibattito sul mondo popolare subalterno negli anni 1948–1955.* Edited by Carla Pasquinelli, 175–206. Florence: La Nuova Italia, 1977. Originally published in *Società* 10 (1954): 940–44.
Allum, Percy. "Uniformity Undone: Aspects of Catholic Culture in Postwar Italy." In Baranski and Lumley, *Culture and Conflict in Postwar Italy*, 79–96.
Alvaro, Corrado. *L'Italia rinunzia?* Rome: Donzelli, 2011 (1944).
———. *Il nostro tempo e la speranza. Saggi di vita contemporanea.* Milan: Bompiani, 1952.
Andall, Jaqueline, and Derek Duncan, eds. *Italian Colonialism: Legacy and Memory.* Oxford: Peter Lang, 2005.

a.m. Review of *Sorte dell'Europa*, by Alberto Savinio. *Studium* (June 1945): 179.

Anders, Günther. *Die Antiquiertheit des Menschen. Band I: Über die Seele im Zeitalter der zweiten industriellen Revolution*. München: Beck, 1956.

———. *Die Antiquiertheit des Menschen. Band II: Über die Zerstörung des Lebens im Zeitalter der dritten industriellen Revolution*. München: Beck, 1980.

Anderson, Benedict. *Imagined Communities: Reflections on the Origins and Spread of Nationalism*. New York: Verso, 2006.

Antelme, Robert. *The Human Race*. Translated by Jeffrey Haight and Annie Mahler. Evanston, IL: Marlboro Press, 1998 (*L'éspèce humaine*, 1947).

Arendt, Hannah. *Eichmann in Jerusalem: A Report on the Banality of Evil*. New York: Penguin, 1963.

———. "Nightmare and Flight." In *Essays in Understanding 1930–1954*, 133–35. New York: Shocken, 2005.

———. *The Origins of Totalitarianism*. New York: Harvest, 1976 (1951).

Arthurs, Joshua. "The Eternal Parasite: Anti-Romanism in Italian Politics and Culture since 1860." *Annali d'Italianistica* 28 (2010): 117–36.

———. *Excavating Modernity: The Roman Past in Fascist Italy*. Ithaca, NY: Cornell University Press, 2012.

———. "Settling Accounts: Retribution, Emotion, and Memory during the Fall of Mussolini." *Journal of Modern Italian Studies* 20, no. 5 (2015): 617–39.

Artico, Everardo, and Laura Lepri, eds. *Giuseppe Berto. La sua cultura, il suo tempo*. Venice: Marsilio; Olschki, 1989.

Asor Rosa, Alberto. "Lo Stato democratico e i partiti politici." *Letteratura Italiana*. Vol. 1: *Il letterato e le istituzioni*. Edited by Alberto Asor Rosa, 549–643. Turin: Einaudi, 1982.

Aucor. Review of *A Time to Kill*, by Ennio Flaiano. *La Sicilia*, July 29, 1947.

Auerbach, Erich. "The Knight Sets Forth." In *Mimesis: The Representation of Reality in Western Literature*, 123–42. Princeton, NJ: Princeton University Press, 2013.

Badiou, Alain. *Ethics: An Essay on the Understanding of Evil*. New York: Verso, 2002.

Baglivo, Beatrice, et al., eds., *Curzio Malaparte e la ricerca dell'identità europea (1920–1950)*. Chambéry: Presses de l'Université Savoie Mont Blanc, 2020.

Baldacci, Luigi. "Verifiche malapartiane." In Barilli and Baroncelli, *Curzio Malaparte*, 177–87.

Baldacci, Paolo. *De Chirico: The Metaphysical Period 1888–1919*. Boston: Bulfinch Press, 1997.

Baldasso, Franco. "Alberto Savinio and the Myth of Babel: Homecoming, Genealogies, and Translation in *Hermaphrodito*." *The Italianist* 40, no. 1 (2020): 44–65.

———. *Il cerchio di gesso. Primo Levi narratore e testimone*. Bologna: Pendragon, 2007.

———. "Curzio Malaparte and the Tragic Understanding of Modern History," *Annali d'Italianistica* 35 (2017): 279–303.

———. "Curzio Malaparte e la guerra nei Balcani. Letteratura, propaganda, censura." In Baglivo et al., *Curzio Malaparte e la ricerca dell'identità europea (1920–1950)*, 191–222.

———. *Curzio Malaparte, la letteratura crudele. Kaputt, La pelle, e la caduta della civiltà europea*. Rome: Carocci, 2019.

———. "Diventare stranieri: *Paura della libertà* di Carlo Levi tra storia, redenzione e identità ebraica." *Allegoria* 81, no. 1 (2020): 165–79.

Baldini, Anna. *Il Comunista. Una storia letteraria dalla Resistenza agli anni Settanta*. Turin: UTET, 2008.

———. "Il Neorealismo. Nascita e usi di una categoria letteraria." In *Letteratura italiana e tedesca 1945–1970. Campi, polisistemi, transfer*. Edited by Michele Sisto and Irene Fantappiè, 109–28. Rome: Istituto italiano di studi germanici, 2013.

Ballinger, Pamela. *The World Refugees Made: Decolonization and the Foundation of Postwar Italy*. Ithaca, NY: Cornell University Press, 2021.

Banti, Alberto Mario. *The Nation of the Risorgimento: Kinship, Sanctity, and Honour in the Origins of Unified Italy*. London: Routledge, 2020.

———. *Sublime madre nostra. La nazione italiana dal Risorgimento al fascismo*. Bari-Rome: Laterza, 2011.

Banti, Anna. *Artemisia*. Translated by Shirley D'Ardia Caracciola. London: Serpent's Tail, 2003 (*Artemisia*, 1947).

Baranello, Adriana M. "Giovanni Pascoli's *La grande proletaria si è mossa*: A Translation and Critical Introduction." *California Italian Studies* 2, no. 1 (2011). Accessed January 25, 2022. https://escholarship.org/uc/item/6jh07474.

Baranski, Zygmunt G., and Robert Lumley, eds. *Culture and Conflict in Postwar Italy: Essays on Mass and Popular Culture*. London: Macmillian, 1990.

Barbato, Andrea. "Una finestra sul Danubio." *l'Espresso*, May 20, 1962, 13.

Barbaro, Umberto. *Il cinema e l'uomo moderno*. Milan: Edizioni Sociali, 1950.

Barberi Squarotti, Giorgio. "Quale rosso del cielo." In *Giuseppe Berto vent'anni dopo. Atti del convegno. Padova—Mogliano Veneto 23–24 ottobre 1998*. Edited by Beatrice Bartolomeo and Saveria Chemotti, 15–34. Pisa-Rome: Istituiti Editoriali e Poligrafici Internazionali, 2000.

Barberis, Walter. "Primo Levi e un libro 'fatale.'" In Luzzatto, Pedullà, and Scarpa, *Atlante della letteratura italiana. Vol. 3*, 754–57.

Bardini, Marco. "Dei 'fantastici doppi' ovvero la mimesi narrativa dello spostamento psichico." In *Per Elisa. Studi su "Menzogna e sortilegio."* Edited by Lucio Lugnani et al., 173–299. Pisa: Nistri-Lischi, 1990.

———. *Morante Elsa: italiana: di professione, poeta*. Pisa: Nistri-Lischi, 1999.

Barilli, Renato, and Vittoria Baroncelli, eds. *Curzio Malaparte. Il narratore, il politologo, il cittadino di Prato e dell'Europa*. Prato: CUEN, 1998.

Baring, Edward. "Humanist Pretensions: Catholics, Communists, and Sartre's Struggle for Existentialism in Postwar France." *Modern Intellectual History* 7, no. 3 (2010): 581–609.
Barnabò, Graziella. *La fiaba estrema. Elsa Morante tra vita e scrittura*. Rome: Carocci, 2016.
Battaglia, Roberto. *Un uomo un partigiano*. Rome: Edizioni U, 1946.
Battiati, Daniela, and Immacolata Magnano. *Vitaliano Brancati. Da Via Etnea a Via Veneto*. Rome: Fahrenheit 451, 2001.
Battini, Michele. *The Missing Italian Nuremberg: Cultural Amnesia and Postwar Politics*. New York: Palgrave Macmillan, 2007.
Battistini, Andrea. "La presenza di Vico in *Paura della libertà* di Carlo Levi." In *Encyclopedia Mundi. Studi di letteratura italiana in onore di Giuseppe Mazzotta*. Edited by Ugo Baldassarri and Alessandro Polcri, 3–20. Florence: Le Lettere, 2013.
Bauman, Zygmunt. *Modernity and the Holocaust*. Ithaca, NY: Cornell University Press, 2006.
Bazin, André. *André Bazin and Italian Neorealism*. Edited by Bert Cardullo. New York: Continuum, 2011.
Belardelli, Giovanni. *Il Ventennio degli intellettuali. Cultura, politica, ideologia nell'Italia fascista*. Bari-Rome: Laterza, 2005.
Belau, Linda, and Petar Ramadanovic, eds. *Topologies of Trauma: Essays on the Limits of Knowledge and Memory*. New York: Other Press, 2002.
Bellonci, Goffredo. "Elsa e i suoi critici." *Giornale d'Italia*, March 24, 1949, 3.
Benfante, Filippo. "'Risiede sempre a Firenze.' Quattro anni nella vita di Carlo Levi (1941–1945)." In Brunello and Vivarelli, *Carlo Levi. Gli anni fiorentini 1941–1945*, 11–104.
Ben-Ghiat, Ruth. *Fascist Modernities: Italy 1922–1945*. Berkeley: University of California Press, 2001.
———. "Italian Cinema and the Transition from Dictatorship to Democracy." In Biess and Moeller, *Histories of the Aftermath*, 156–71.
———. *Italian Fascism's Empire Cinema*. Bloomington: Indiana University Press, 2014.
———. "Italian Fascists and National Socialists: The Dynamics of an Uneasy Relationship." In *Art, Culture, and Media under the Third Reich*. Edited by Richard A. Etlin, 257–84. Chicago: University of Chicago Press, 2002.
———. "A Lesser Evil? Italian Fascism in/and the Totalitarian Equation," In Dubiel and Motzkin, *Lesser Evil*, 137–53.
———. "Writing and Memory: The Realist Aesthetic in Italy, 1930–1950." *The Journal of Modern History* 67 (1995): 627–65.
Ben-Ghiat, Ruth, and Mia Fuller, eds. *Italian Colonialism*, New York: Palgrave, 2005.
Ben-Ghiat, Ruth, and Stephanie Malia Hom, eds. *Italian Mobilities*. London: Routledge, 2016.
Benjamin, Walter. *Illuminations: Essays and Reflections*. New York: Schocken, 2007.

———. *Paralipomena to "On the Concept of History."* In *Walter Benjamin: Selected Writings, Vol. 4, 1938–1940.* Edited by Howard Eiland and Michael W. Jennings. Cambridge, MA: The Belknap Press of Harvard University Press, 1996–2003.

———. "The Storyteller: Reflections on the Works of Nikolai Leskov." In *Illuminations*, 83–109.

———. "Thesis on the Philosophy of History." In *Illuminations*, 253–64.

Berardinelli, Alfonso. *Autoritratto Italiano. Un dossier letterario 1945–1998.* Rome: Donzelli, 1998.

Bersani, Leo. *The Culture of Redemption.* Cambridge, MA: Harvard University Press, 1990.

Berto, Giuseppe. *The Brigand.* Translated by Angus Davidson. New York: New American Library, 1953 (*Il brigante*, 1951).

———. *Guerra in camicia nera.* Venice: Marsilio, 1985 (1955).

———. *Incubus.* Translated by William Weaver. New York: Knopf, 1966 (*Il male oscuro*, 1964).

———. "L'inconsapevole approccio" (1965). In *Le opere di Dio.* Milan: Mondadori, 1980.

———. *The Sky Is Red.* Translated by Angus Davidson. New York: New Directions, 1948 (*Il cielo è rosso*, 1947).

———. *Tutti i racconti.* Milan: Rizzoli, 2012.

———. *The Works of God and Other Stories.* Translated by Angus Davidson. New York: New Directions, 1950 (*Le opere di Dio*, 1948).

Biagi, Dario. *Vita scandalosa di Giuseppe Berto.* Turin: Bollati Boringhieri, 1999.

Bianchi Bandinelli, Ranuccio. Review of *L'Orologio*, by Carlo Levi. *Società* 3 (1950): 554.

Biess, Frank. Introduction to *Histories of the Aftermath.* In Biess and Moeller, 1–10.

Biess, Frank, and, Robert G. Moeller, eds. *Histories of the Aftermath: The Legacies of the Second World War in Europe.* New York: Berghahn, 2010.

Biondi, Marino. *Scrittori e miti totalitari. Malaparte Pratolini Silone.* Florence: Polistampa, 2002.

Bistarelli, Agostino. *La storia del ritorno. I reduci italiani del secondo dopoguerra.* Turin: Bollati Boringhieri, 2007.

Bizzarri, Aldo. "Un saggio di Carlo Levi." Review of *Paura della libertà*, by Carlo Levi. *La Fiera letteraria*, February 13, 1947.

Bloch, Ernst. "Nonsynchronism and the Obligation to Its Dialectics." *New German Critique* 11 (1977): 22–38.

Bollati, Giulio. *L'italiano. Il carattere nazionale come storia e come invenzione.* Turin: Einaudi, 1983.

Bondanella, Peter. *The Eternal City: Roman Images in the Modern World.* Chapel Hill: The University of North Carolina Press, 1987.

Bongiovanni, Bruno. "Totalitarianism: The Word and the Thing." *Journal of Modern European History* 3, no. 1 (2005): 5–17.

Bonsaver, Guido. *Censorship and Literature in Fascist Italy*. Toronto: University of Toronto Press, 2007.
Bontempelli, Massimo. "La musica." In Terra, *Dopo il diluvio*, 317–23.
Borsellino, Nino. "Metamorfosi del comico." In Battiati and Magnano, *Vitaliano Brancati*, 27–32.
Bortone, Leone. Review of *Paura della libertà*, by Carlo Levi. *Il Ponte* 6 (1947): 592–93.
Bosworth, Richard J. B. *Whispering City: Modern Rome and Its Histories*. New Haven, CT: Yale University Press, 2011.
Bourdieu, Pierre. *The Field of Cultural Production: Essays on Art and Literature*. New York: Columbia University Press, 1993.
Branca, Vittore. "Lucania magica e desolata." Review of *Cristo si è fermato a Eboli*, by Carlo Levi. *La Nazione del popolo*, March 21, 1946.
———. Review of *La speranza*, by Alberto Moravia. *Il Ponte* 1, no. 2 (1945): 156–60.
Brancati, Vitaliano. *Beautiful Antonio*. Translated by Stanley Hochman. New York: F. Ungar, 1978 (*Il bell'Antonio*, 1949).
———. *Diario romano* (1961). In *Opere 1947–1954*.
———. *I fascisti invecchiano* (1946). In *Opere 1932–1946*.
———. *Il borghese e l'immensità. Scritti 1930/1954*. Edited by Sandro De Feo and G. A. Cibotto. Milan: Bompiani, 1973.
———. *Opere 1932–1946*. Edited by Leonardo Sciascia. Milan: Bompiani, 1987.
———. *Opere 1947–1954*. Edited by Leonardo Sciascia. Milan: Bompiani, 1992.
Braudel, Fernand. *The Mediterranean and the Mediterranean World in the Age of Philip II*. Berkeley, CA: University of California Press, 1995.
Bresciani, Marco. *Quale antifascismo? Storia di Giustizia e Libertà*. Rome: Carocci, 2017.
Brody, Samuel H. *Martin Buber's Theopolitics*. Bloomington: Indiana University Press, 2018.
Brogi, Daniela. *Giovani. Vita e scrittura tra fascismo e dopoguerra*. Palermo: Duepunti, 2012.
Brunello, Piero. "Autonomia e autogoverno negli scritti di Carlo Levi: dalla Torino di 'Rivoluzione liberale' alla Firenze de 'La Nazione del Popolo.'" In Brunello and Vivarelli, *Carlo Levi. Gli anni fiorentini 1941–1945*, 175–94.
Brunello, Piero, and Vivarelli Pia, eds. *Carlo Levi. Gli anni fiorentini 1941–1945*. Rome: Donzelli, 2003.
Brunetta, Gian Piero. *L'Italia sullo schermo. Come il cinema ha raccontato l'identità nazionale*. Rome: Carocci, 2020.
Bucciantini, Massimo. *Esperimento Auschwitz—Auschwitz Experiment*. Turin: Einaudi, 2011.
Buonuomo, Michele. "Un colloquio con Alberto Moravia." In *Malaparte. Una proposta*. Edited by Michele Buonuomo, 11–13. Rome: De Luca, 1982.

Burdett, Charles. "Addressing the Representation of the Italian Empire and Its Afterlife." In *Transnational Italian Studies*. Edited by Charles Burdett and Loredana Polezzi, 249–65. Liverpool: Liverpool University Press, 2020.

———. "Changing Identities through Memory: Malaparte's Self-Figurations in *Kaputt*." In *European Memories of the Second World War*. Edited by Helmut Peitsch, Charles Burdett, and Claire Gorrara, 110–19. New York: Berghahn, 1999.

Buruma, Ian. *Year Zero: A History of 1945*. New York: Penguin, 2013.

Cadel, Francesca. "Umberto Saba, Pierpaolo Pasolini ed Elsa Morante. Scorciatoie anticanoniche nell'Italia del dopoguerra." *Italica* 89, no. 2 (2012): 253–69.

Caillois, Roger. *Man and the Sacred*. Glencoe, IL: Free Press of Glencoe, 1960.

Cairns, John C. "Along the Road Back to France 1940." *American Historical Review* 64, no. 3 (1959): 583–603.

Calamandrei, Piero. *Il fascismo come regime della menzogna*. Bari-Rome: Laterza, 2014 (1944).

———. *Uomini e città della Resistenza. Discorsi, scritti ed epigrafi*. Bari-Rome: Laterza, 1955.

Caldiron, Orio. "La lente smisurata di Vitaliano Brancati." In *Dalla Sicilia all'Europa. L'Italia di Vitaliano Brancati*. Edited by Marco Dondero. Rome: De Luca, 2005.

Călinescu, Matei. *Five Faces of Modernity: Modernism, Avant-Garde, Decadence, Kitsch, Postmodernism*. Durham, NC: Duke University Press, 1987.

Calvino, Italo. "Carlo Levi, *Paura della libertà*." *l'Unità*, Turin Edition, December 15, 1946. In *Saggi: 1945–1985*. Vol. 1, 1114–16.

———. "La compresenza dei tempi." *Galleria* 17, nos. 3–6 (1967): 237–40. In *Saggi: 1945–1985*. Vol. 1, 1122–25.

———. "La letteratura italiana sulla Resistenza." *Movimento di liberazione in Italia* 1 (1949): 40–46.

———. *The Path to the Spiders' Nests*. Translated by Archibald Colquhoun. New York: Ecco, 2000 (*Il sentiero dei nidi di ragno*, 1947).

———. "Preface." In *The Path to the Spiders' Nests*, 7–30.

———. *Una pietra sopra*. Milan: Mondadori, 1995 (1980).

———. "Un romanzo sul serio." *L'Unità*, Turin Edition, August 17, 1948.

———. *Saggi: 1945–1985. Vol. 1*. Edited by Mario Barenghi (Milan: Mondadori, 1995).

Camilletti, Fabio, and Filippo Trentin, eds. *I leoni di Roma. L'orologio di Carlo Levi, la sopravvivenza e la compresenza dei tempi*. Special issue of *Poetiche* 17, no. 42 (1 2015).

Campailla, Sergio. "Malaparte e la cultura ebraica." In Barilli and Baroncelli, *Curzio Malaparte*, 57–75.

Capristo, Annalisa. "'Spettacolo più tetro non vidi mai.' La persecuzione antiebraica nell'Est europeo nei giornali italiani: il 1941." *Rassegna mensile di Israel* 84, no. 1–2 (2018): 179–218.

Carducci, Nicola. *Storia intellettuale di Carlo Levi*. Lecce: Pensa MultiMedia, 1999.
Carrai, Stefano. *Saba*. Naples: Salerno, 2017.
Casanova, Pascale. *The World Republic of Letters*. Cambridge, MA: Harvard University Press, 2007.
Cases, Cesare. "*La Storia*. Un confronto con *Menzogna e sortilegio*." In *Patrie lettere*, 104–25. Turin: Einaudi, 1987.
Casini, Simone. Introduction to *I due amici. Frammenti di una storia fra guerra e dopoguerra* by Alberto Moravia. Edited by Simone Casini, v–lxxiii. Milan: Bompiani, 2007.
———. "Lo scrittore e l'intellettuale." Introduction to *Impegno controvoglia* by Alberto Moravia, v–xxxii.
———. "Moravia e il fascismo. A proposito di alcune lettere a Mussolini e a Ciano." *Studi italiani* 38, no. 2 (2007): 189–237.
Cassin, Barbara et al., eds. *Dictionary of Untranslatables: A Philosophical Lexicon*. Princeton, NJ: Princeton University Press, 2014.
Cattaruzza, Marina. *L'Italia e il confine orientale*. Bologna: il Mulino, 2007.
Cavaglion, Alberto. "Il grembo della Shoah. Il 16 ottobre 1943 di Umberto Saba, Giacomo Debenedetti, Elsa Morante." In *Dopo i testimoni. Memorie, storiografie e narrazioni della deportazione razziale*. Edited by Marta Baiardi and Alberto Cavaglion, 245–61. Rome: Viella, 2014.
———. *Notizie su Argon. Gli antenati di Primo Levi da Francesco Petrarca a Cesare Lombroso*. Turin: Instar, 2006.
Cavazza, Stefano. "La transizione difficile: l'immagine della guerra e della resistenza nell'opinione pubblica dell'immediato dopoguerra." In *La grande cesura. La memoria della guerra e della resistenza nella vita europea del dopoguerra*. Edited by Giovanni Miccoli, Guido Neppi Modona, and Paolo Pombeni, 427–64. Bologna: il Mulino, 2001.
Cecchi, Carlo, and Cesare Garboli. "Cronologia." In Morante, *Opere*. Vol. 1, xvii–xc.
Cecchi, Emilio. "La Pelle di Malaparte." In Malaparte, *Malaparte*. Vol. 9, 66–68. Originally published in *L'Europeo*, February 12, 1950.
Ceserani, Remo. "Italy and Modernity: Peculiarities and Contradictions." In *Italian Modernism: Italian Culture between Decadentism and Avant-Garde*. Edited by Luca Somigli and Mario Moroni, 35–62. Toronto: University of Toronto Press, 2004.
Conti, Davide. *L'occupazione italiana dei Balcani. Crimini di guerra e mito della "brava gente" (1940–1943)*. Rome: Odradek, 2008.
Cooke, Philip. "La Resistenza come 'Secondo Risorgimento.' Un *topos* retorico senza fine?" In *Resistenza e autobiografia della nazione. Uso politico, rappresentazione, memoria*. Edited by Aldo Agosti and Chiara Colombani, 61–79. Turin: SEB, 2012.
———. *The Legacy of the Italian Resistance*. New York: Palgrave Macmillan, 2011.
Ciocchetti, Marcello. *Percorsi paralleli. Moravia e Piovene tra giornali e riviste del dopoguerra*. Pesaro: Metauro, 2010.

Cordelli, Franco. *L'ombra di Piovene*. Florence: Le Lettere, 2011.
Coury, Michèle, and Emmanuel Mattiato, eds. *Curzio Malaparte, témoin et visionnaire*. Special issue of *Cahiers d'études italiennes* 24 (2017).
Craig, Siobhan. "Translation and Treachery: Historiography and the Betrayal of Meaning in Anna Banti's *Artemisia*." *Italica* 87, no. 4 (2010): 602–18.
Crainz, Guido. *Il dolore e l'esilio. L'Istria e le memorie divise d'Europa*. Rome: Donzelli, 2007.
———. *L'ombra della guerra. Il 1945, l'Italia*. Rome: Donzelli, 2007.
Croce, Benedetto. "Il Fascismo come pericolo mondiale." In *Scritti e discorsi politici*, 15–23.
———. "The Fascist Germ Still Lives." *New York Times*, November 28, 1943.
———. *Scritti e discorsi politici (1943–1947)*. Vol. 1. Edited by Angela Carella. Naples: Bibliopolis, 1993.
———. *Storia d'Europa nel secolo decimonono*. Bari: Laterza, 1964 (1932).
Culicelli, Paola. *La coscienza di Berto*. Florence: Le Lettere, 2012.
Cusin, Fabio. *Antistoria d'Italia*. Milan: Mondadori, 1972 (1948).
———. *L'Italiano. Realtà e illusioni*. Rome: Atlantica, 1945.
D'Amico, Silvio. "Vanno in scena a Parigi due commedie di Malaparte." In Malaparte, *Malaparte. Vol. 8*, 229. Originally published in *Il Tempo*. October 25, 1948.
Dainotto, Roberto, and Fredric Jameson, eds. *Gramsci in the World*. Durham, NC: Duke University Press, 2020.
Dal Bianco, Stefano. "Rigurgiti di Arcadia." In Luzzatto, Pedullà, and Scarpa, *Atlante della letteratura italiana. Vol. 3*, 724–28.
David, Michel. "La psicologia nell'opera narrativa di Berto." In Artico and Lepri, *Giuseppe Berto*, 121–46.
De Begnac, Yvon. *Taccuini Mussoliniani*. Bologna: il Mulino, 1990.
Debenedetti, Antonio. *Giacomino*. Venice: Marsilio, 2002.
Debenedetti, Giacomo. *16 ottobre 1943*. Palermo: Sellerio, 1993 (1944).
———. *Intermezzo*. Milan: il Saggiatore, 1972.
———. "Probabile autobiografia di una generazione (Introduzione 1949)." *Saggi critici*. Milan: Mondadori, 1969.
De Ceccatty, René. *Alberto Moravia*. Paris: Flammarion, 2010.
de Céspedes, Alba. *The Best of Husbands*. New York: Macmillan, 1952 (*Dalla parte di lei*, 1949).
———. "Caro lettore." *Mercurio* 4, no. 34 (1948): 5–8.
———. "Lettera a Natalia Ginzburg." *Mercurio* 5, no. 36–39 (1948): 110.
De Donato, Gigliola, ed. *"L'Orologio" di Carlo Levi e la crisi della Repubblica*. Manduria, BA: Piero Lacaita, 1996.
———, ed. *Oltre la paura. Percorsi nella scrittura di Carlo Levi*. Rome: Donzelli, 2008.
De Donato, Gigliola, and Sergio D'Amaro. *Un torinese del Sud: Carlo Levi. Una biografia*. Milan: Baldini and Castoldi, 2001.

de Federicis, Umberto. Review of *Tempo di Uccidere*, by Ennio Flaiano. *l'Avanti!*, Milan edition, July 27, 1947.
De Filippo, Eduardo. *Naples Get Rich (Napoli milionaria!)*. In *Four Plays*. Hanover, NH: Smith and Kraus, 2002 (1945).
Del Boca, Angelo. *Gli Italiani in Africa Orientale, Vol. 1–4*. Rome: Laterza, 1976–1984.
———. *Italiani, brava gente?* Vicenza: Neri Pozza, 2005.
De Grazia, Victoria. *The Culture of Consent: Mass Organization of Leisure in Fascist Italy*. Cambridge: Cambridge University Press, 2002.
———. *Irresistible Empire: American Advance through Twentieth Century Europe*. Cambridge, MA: The Belknap Press of Harvard University Press, 2006.
De Luna, Giovanni. "'L'Orologio' di Carlo Levi e l'Italia del Dopoguerra." In De Donato, *"L'Orologio" di Carlo Levi*, 33–45.
———. *La Repubblica inquieta. L'Italia della Costituzione, 1946–1948*. Milan: Feltrinelli, 2017.
———. *Storia del Partito d'Azione, 1942–1947*. Turin: UTET, 2006.
De Luna, Giovanni, and Marco Revelli. *Fascismo/Antifascismo. Le idee, le identità*. Florence: La Nuova Italia, 1995.
De Paulis, Maria Pia, ed. *Cahier Malaparte*. Paris: Éditions de l'Herne, 2018.
De Paulis-Dalembert, Maria Pia, ed. *Curzio Malaparte. Esperienza e scrittura*. Special issue of *Chronique italiennes* 35, no. 1 (2018).
De Rogatis, Tiziana. "Realismo stregato e genealogia femminile in *Menzogna e sortilegio*." *Allegoria* 31, no. 80 (2019): 97–124.
Derrida, Jacques. *Demeure: Fiction and Testimony*. Stanford, CA: Stanford University Press, 2000.
De Ruggiero, Guido. "Al di là dello storicismo." *La Nuova Europa* 2, no. 4, (January 28, 1945): 9.
———. "Come scrivere la storia per le scuole," *La Nuova Europa* 2, no. 16 (April 22, 1945): 9.
———. "I reduci." *La Nuova Europa* 2, no. 21 (1945): 1–2.
———. *Il ritorno alla ragione*. Bari: Laterza, 1946.
———. "La fase crociana." *La Nuova Europa* 2, no. 3 (January 21, 1945): 9.
———. "Lo storicismo. I precedenti." *La Nuova Europa* 2, no. 2 (January 14, 1945): 10.
De Sanctis, Francesco. *History of Italian Literature*. Translated by Joan Redfern. New York: Harcourt, 1931 (*Storia della letteratura italiana*, 1870).
Diner, Dan. *Beyond the Conceivable. Studies on Germany, Nazism, and the Holocaust*. Berkeley: University of California Press, 2000.
———. *Zivilisationsbruch: Denken nach Auschwitz*. Frankfurt am Mein: Fischer Taschenbuch, 1988.
Di Nicola, Laura. "L'attività giornalistica di Paola Masino negli anni del secondo dopoguerra. L'esperienza di 'Città.'" *Atti della Accademia roveretana degli Agiati* 8, no. 2 (2008): 73–90.

———. "Mercurio." Storia di una rivista 1944–1948. Milan: il Saggiatore/ Fondazione Mondadori, 2012.
Dombroski, Robert S. *Creative Entaglements: Gadda and the Baroque.* Toronto: University of Toronto Press, 1999.
Dondi, Mirco. "The Fascist Mentality after Fascism." In *Italian Fascism: History, Memory, and Representation.* Edited by Richard J. B. Bosworth and Patrizia Dogliani. London: Macmillian, 1990.
Donnarumma, Raffaele. "*Menzogna e sortilegio*. Oltre il bovarismo." *Allegoria* 9, no. 31 (1999): 121–135.
Duggan, Christopher. "Italy in the Cold War Years and the Legacy of Fascism." In Duggan and Wagstaff, *Italy in the Cold War: Politics, Culture, and Society 1948–58*, 1–24.
Duggan, Christopher, and Christopher Wagstaff, eds. *Italy in the Cold War: Politics, Culture, and Society 1948–58.* Oxford: Berg, 1995.
Dubiel, Helmut, and Gabriel Motzkin, eds. *The Lesser Evil: Moral Approaches to Genocide Practices.* London: Routledge, 2004.
Duncan, Derek. "Italian Identity and the Risks of Contamination: The Legacies of Mussolini's Demographic Impulse in the Works of Comisso, Flaiano, and Dell'Oro." In Andall and Duncan, *Italian Colonialism*, 99–124.
Einaudi, Giulio. "Einaudi to Carlo Levi." March 9, 1950, folder 253, Carlo Levi Papers, Archivio Einaudi, Turin, Archivio di Stato.
Eksteins, Modris. *Rites of Spring: The Great War and the Birth of Modern Age.* Boston: Hougton Mifflin, 1989.
Escolar, Marisa. *Allied Encounters: The Gendered Redemption of World War II Italy.* New York: Fordham University Press, 2019.
Esposito, Roberto. *Immunitas: The Protection and Negation of Life.* Cambridge: Polity Press, 2011.
———. *Living Thought: The Origins and Actuality of Italian Philosophy.* Stanford, CA: Stanford University Press, 2012.
Falaschi, Giovanni. "*Cristo si è fermato a Eboli* di Carlo Levi." In *Letteratura italiana. Le Opere. Vol. 4. Il Novecento II: La ricerca letteraria.* Edited by Alberto Asor Rosa, 469–90. Turin: Einaudi, 1996.
———. *Realtà e retorica. La letteratura del neorealismo italiano.* Messina: Casa Editrice D'Anna, 1977.
Faleschini Lerner, Giovanna. *Carlo Levi's Visual Poetics: The Painter as Writer.* New York: Palgrave Macmillan, 2012.
Fantini, Sara. *Notizie dalla Shoah. La stampa italiana nel 1945.* Bologna: Pendragon, 2005.
Farrell, Joseph, ed. *The Voices of Carlo Levi.* Oxford: Peter Lang, 2007.
Fattore, Fabio. "Curzio Malpante, corrispondente di guerra." *Nuova storia contemporanea* 14, no. 3 (2010): 93–108.
Ferrante, Elena. *Frantumaglia.* New York: Europa Editions, 2016 (*Frantumaglia*, 2003).

Ferrari, Chiara. *The Rhetoric of Violence and Sacrifice in Fascist Italy: Mussolini, Gadda, Vittorini*. Toronto: University of Toronto Press, 2013.
Ferrata, Giansiro. "Le scorciatoie di un poeta saggio." *Il Politecnico*. March 30, 1946.
———. "Menzogne di Elsa e canti di Sibilla." *l'Unità*, Milan Edition, August 24, 1948.
Ferroni, Giulio. *Storia della letteratura italiana. Il Novecento*. Milan: Einaudi Scuola, 1991.
Filippi, Antonella, and Lino Ferracin. *Deportati italiani nel campo di Majdanek*. Turin: Zamorani, 2013.
Finchelstein, Federico. *Transatlantic Fascism: Ideology, Violence, and the Sacred in Argentina and Italy, 1919–1945*. Durham, NC: Duke University Press, 2010.
Fiore, Tommaso. "La piccolo borghesia. Voilà l'ennemi." Review of *Cristo si è fermato a Eboli*, by Carlo Levi. *La gazzetta del mezzogiorno*, February 14, 1946.
Flaiano, Ennio. *Aethiopia. Appunti per una canzonetta*. In *Tempo di uccidere*, 289–313. Milan: Rizzoli, 2014.
———. *Diario Notturno*. Milan: Adelphi, 1994.
———. "Flaiano a Tamburi 16. Axum, 11 aprile 1936," Fondo Orfeo Tamburi, Faldone Ennio Flaiano, Archivio Prezzolini, Biblioteca Cantonale di Lugano (Switzerland).
———. "I grandi precursori." In *L'Occhiale indiscreto*, 140–41. Originally published in *Il Secolo XX*, October 16, 1945.
———. *L'Occhiale indiscreto*. Edited by Anna Longoni. Milan: Adelphi, 2019.
———. *A Time to Kill*. Translated by Stuart Hood. London: Quartet, 1992 (*Tempo di uccidere*, 1947).
Focardi, Filippo. "'Bravo italiano' e 'cattivo tedesco': riflessione sulla genesi di due immagini incrociate." *Storia e memoria* 5, no. 1 (1996): 55–83.
———. *La guerra della memoria. La Resistenza nel dibattito politico italiano dal 1945 ad oggi*. Bari-Rome: Laterza, 2005.
Fofi, Goffredo. "Vitaliano Brancati." In Battiati and Magnano, *Vitaliano Brancati*, 107–18.
Fofi, Goffredo, and Adriano Sofri, eds. *Festa per Elsa*. Palermo: Sellerio, 2011.
Fogu, Claudio. *The Historic Imaginary: Politics of History in Fascist Italy*. Toronto: University of Toronto Press, 2003.
———. "*Italiani brava gente*: The Legacy of Fascist Historical Culture on Italian Politics of Memory." In *The Politics of Memory in Postwar Europe*. Edited by Richard Ned Lebow, Wulf Kasteiner, and Claudio Fogu, 147–76. Durham, NC: Duke University Press, 2006.
Folli, Anna. *MoranteMoravia. Storia di un amore*. Vicenza: Neri Pozza, 2018.
Fontana, Benedetto. "Politics and History in Gramsci." *Journal of Modern Italian Studies* 16, no. 2 (2011): 225–38.
Foot, John. *Italy's Divided Memory*. New York: Palgrave Macmillian, 2003.
Forcella, Enzo. *La Resistenza in convento*. Turin: Einaudi, 1999.

———. Review of *Sorte dell'Europa*, by Alberto Savinio. *La città libera*, September 20, 1945.
Forgacs, David. "The Italian Communist Party and Culture." In Baranski and Lumley, *Culture and Conflict in Postwar Italy*, 97–114.
Forgacs, David, et al., eds., *Roberto Rossellini: Magician of the Real*. London: British Film Institute, 2000.
Forlenza, Rosario. *On the Edge of Democracy: Italy, 1943–1948*. Oxford: Oxford University Press, 2019.
———. "The Soviet Myth and the Making of Communist Lives in Italy, 1943–56." *Journal of Contemporary History* 1, no. 24 (2021).
Forlenza, Rosario, and Bjørn Thomassen, *Italian Modernities: Competing Narratives of Nationhood*. New York: Palgrave Macmillan, 2016.
Fortini, Franco. *Agonia di Natale*. Reprinted as *Giovanni e le mani*. Turin: Einaudi, 1972 (1948).
Frandini, Paola. *Il poeta, il cane e la gallina*. Scorciatoie e raccontini *di Umberto Saba tra umorismo ebraico e Shoah*. Florence: Le lettere, 2011.
Frati, Stefano (Giovanni Ansaldo). Review of *Tempo di Uccidere*, by Ennio Flaiano. *Il libraio*, June 15, 1947.
Freud, Sigmund. "Family Romances." In *The Standard Edition of the Complete Psychological Works of Sigmund Freud, Vol. 9 (1906–1908): Jensen's 'Gradiva' and Other Works*, 235–242. London: Hogarth Press, 1959.
Gadda, Carlo Emilio. *Eros e Priapo. Versione integrale*. Edited by Paola Italia and Giorgio Pinotti. Milan: Adelphi, 2016 (1967).
Galli della Loggia, Ernesto. *La morte della patria. La crisi dell'idea di nazione tra Resistenza, antifascismo e Repubblica*. Bari: Laterza, 1996.
Gallo, Niccolò. "La narrativa italiana del dopoguerra." *Società* 6, no. 2 (1951): 324–41.
Garboli, Cesare. *Il gioco segreto. Nove immagini di Elsa Morante*. Milan: Adelphi, 1995.
Garin, Eugenio. *La cultura italiana tra '800 e '900*. Bari: Laterza, 1963.
Gasperina Geroni, Riccardo. *Il custode della soglia. Il sacro e le forme nell'opera di Carlo Levi*. Milan: Mimesis, 2018.
———. "La Sacra Bibbia di Diodati nell'autografo di *Paura della libertà* di Carlo Levi." *Esperienze letterarie* 40, no. 3 (2015): 103–22.
Gatt-Rutter, John. "Liberation and Literature: Naples 1944." *Journal of Modern Italian Studies* 1, no. 2 (1996): 245–72.
Gentile, Emilio. *La Grande Italia: The Myth of the Nation in the Twentieth Century*. Madison: University of Wisconsin Press, 2009.
———. *La via italiana al totalitarismo. Il partito e lo stato nel regime totalitario*. Rome: La Nuova Italia Scientifica, 1995.
———. "The Sacralisation of Politics: Definitions, Interpretations, and Reflections on the Question of Secular Religion and Totalitarianism." *Totalitarian Movements and Political Religions* 1, no. 1 (2000): 18–55.

———. *The Sacralization of Politics in Fascist Italy*. Cambridge, MA: Harvard University Press, 1996.
Gentile, Giovanni. *I profeti del Risorgimento italiano*. Florence: Vallecchi, 1923.
———. "Politica e filosofia." In *Dopo la vittoria*, 138–58. Florence: Le Lettere, 1989 (1918).
Gentili, Sonia. "Personaggio letterario e carattere 'sopraindividuale.' T. Mann, G. A. Borgese, V. Brancati." In *Cultura della razza e cultura letteraria nell'Italia del Novecento*. Edited by Sonia Gentili e Simona Foà, 247–70. Rome: Carocci, 2010.
Gerbi, Sandro. *Tempi di Malafede. Guido Piovene ed Eugenio Colorni. Una storia italiana tra fascismo e dopoguerra*. Milan: Hoepli, 2012.
Ghiazza, Silvana. *Carlo Levi e Umberto Saba. Storia di un'amicizia*. Bari: Dedalo, 2002.
Giacopini, Vittorio. *Scrittori contro la politica*. Turin: Bollati Boringhieri, 1999.
Gigli, Lorenzo. "L'ultimo Malaparte." In Malaparte, *Malaparte. Vol. 9*. Originally published in *La Gazzetta del Popolo*, February 10, 1950.
Gillette, Aaron. *Racial Theories in Fascist Italy*. London: Routledge, 2002.
Ginsborg, Paul. *A History of Contemporary Italy: Society and Politics, 1943–1988*. New York: Palgrave Macmillian, 2003.
Ginzburg, Leone. "A proposito di Malaparte, 'Technique du coup d'état.'" In *Scritti*, 83–86. Originally in *La Cultura*, 9, 2 (1932).
———. *Scritti*. Edited by Domenico Zucàro, Turin: Einaudi, 2000.
———. "La tradizione del Risorgimento." In *Scritti*, 114–26. Originally in *Aretusa* 2, no. 8 (1945): 1–16.
Ginzburg, Natalia. "Discorso sulle donne." *Mercurio* 5, no. 36–39 (1948): 105–10.
———. *The Dry Heart*. Translated by Frances Frenaye. New York: New Directions, 2019 (*È stato così*, 1947).
———. *Family Lexicon*. Translated by Jenny McPhee. New York: NYRB Classics, 2017 (*Lessico famigliare*, 1963).
———. "Menzogna e sortilegio." In Fofi and Sofri, *Festa per Elsa*, 26–28.
———. *La strada che va in città*. Turin: Einaudi, 1945.
Girard, René. *Violence and the Sacred*. Baltimore, MD: Johns Hopkins University Press, 1977.
Glynn, Ruth. "Naples and the Nation in Cultural Representations of the Allied Occupation." *California Italian Studies* 7, no. 2 (2017). Accessed June 5, 2021. https://escholarship.org/uc/item/1vp8t8dz.
Gooch, John. *Mussolini's War: Fascist Italy from Triumph to Collapse: 1935–1943*. New York: Pegasus, 2020.
Gordon, Robert S. C. *The Holocaust in Italian Culture 1944–2010*. Stanford, CA: Stanford University Press, 2012.
———. "The Italian War." In *The Cambridge Companion to the Literature of World War II*. Edited by Marina MacKay, 123–36. Cambridge: Cambridge University Press, 2011.

Gramsci, Antonio. *Letteratura e vita nazionale.* Edited by Felice Platone. Rome: Editori Riuniti, 1996 (1950).
———. *Letters from Prison.* Translated by Raymond Rosenthal. New York: Columbia University Press, 2011 (*Lettere dal carcere,* 1947).
———. *Note sul Machiavelli, sulla politica e sullo Stato moderno.* Edited by Felice Platone. Rome: Editori Riuniti, 1996 (1949).
———. *Prison Notebooks.* Vols. 1–3. Translated by Joseph Buttigieg. New York: Columbia University Press, 2011 (*Quaderni dal carcere,* 1948–51).
Grana, Gianni. *Curzio Malaparte.* Milan: Marzorati, 1961.
Granzotto, Gianni. "La politica a teatro. Parigi decreta il successo a 'Das Kapital' di Curzio Malaparte." In Malaparte, *Malaparte. Vol. 8: 1948–1949,* 338. Originally published in *Il Tempo,* January 30, 1948.
Grassi, Martina, ed. *"La Bourse des idées du monde." Malaparte e la Francia.* Florence: Olschki, 2008.
Greco, Lorenzo. *Censura e scrittura. Vittorini, lo pseudo-Malaparte, Gadda.* Milan: il Saggiatore, 1983.
Gribaudi, Gabriella. *Combattenti, sbandati, prigionieri. Esperienze e memorie dei reduci della seconda guerra mondiale.* Rome: Donzelli, 2016.
———. *Guerra totale. Tra bombe alleate e violenze naziste. Napoli e il fronte meridionale, 1940–1944.* Turin: Bollati Boringhieri, 2005.
Griffin, Roger. *Modernism and Fascism: The Sense of a Beginning under Mussolini and Hitler.* New York: Palgrave Macmillan, 2007.
Guerri, Giordano Bruno. *L'arcitaliano. Vita di Curzio Malaparte.* Milan: Mondadori, 2000.
Gundle, Stephen. "The 'Civic Religion' of the Resistance in Post-War Italy." *Modern Italy* 5, no. 2 (2000): 112–32.
———. "The Legacy of the Prison Notebooks: Gramsci, the PCI, and Italian Culture in the Cold War Period." In Duggan and Wagstaff, *Italy in the Cold War,* 131–47.
Halbwachs, Maurice. *On the Collective Memory.* Chicago: University of Chicago Press, 1992.
Harrowitz, Nancy. "Carlo Levi: Watching the Future of Holocaust Representation." In Farrell, *Voices of Carlo Levi,* 147–58.
Heidegger, Martin. *Letter on "Humanism."* In *Basic Writings: Ten Key Essays, plus the Introduction to Being and Time.* Edited by David Farrel Krell, 213–66. New York: Harper Collins, 1993 (1949).
Heiney, Donald. *America in Modern Italian Literature.* New Brunswick, NJ: Rutgers University Press, 1964.
Hirsch, Marianne. *The Mother/Daughter Plot: Narrative, Psychoanalysis, Feminism.* Bloomington: Indiana University Press, 1989.
Hofstaedter, Dan. Afterword to *Kaputt,* by Curzio Malaparte. Translated by Cesare Foligno, 431–43. New York: NYRB Classics, 2005.

Hollier, Denis. *The College of Sociology*. Minneapolis: University of Minnesota Press, 1988.
Hom, Stephanie Malia. *Empire's Mobius Strip: Historical Echoes in Italy's Crisis of Migration and Detention*. Ithaca, NY: Cornell University Press, 2019.
Horden, Peregrine, and Nicholas Purcell. *The Corrupting Sea: A Study of Mediterranean History*. Oxford: Blackwell, 2000.
Iovino, Serenella. *Ecocriticism and Italy: Ecology, Resistance, and Liberation*. London: Bloomsbury Academics, 2016.
Isnenghi, Mario. "I due occhi di Malaparte giornalista e fotografo." In *Da Malaparte a Malaparte. Malaparte fotografo*. Edited by Sauro Lusini. Prato: Comune di Prato, 1987.
Italia, Paola. *Il pellegrino appassionato. Savinio scrittore (1915–1925)*. Palermo: Sellerio 2004.
Jameson, Fredric. "The Vanishing Mediator; or, Max Weber as Storyteller." In *The Ideologies of Theory, Vol. 2*, 3–34. Minneapolis: University of Minnesota Press, 1988.
Janulardo, Ettore. "Saba: Scorciatoie dopo Majdanek." *Studi e ricerche di storia contemporanea* 64 (2005): 63–67.
Jay, Martin. "Walter Benjamin, Remembrance, and the First World War." *Review of Japanese Culture and Society* 11–12 (1999–2000): 18–31.
Jesi, Furio. *Spartakus: The Symbology of Revolt*. London: Seagull Books, 2014.
Jørgensen, Conni-Kay. *L'eredità Vichiana nel Novecento letterario. Pavese, Savinio, Levi, Gadda*. Naples: Guida, 2008.
Jossa, Stefano. *L'Italia letteraria*. Bologna: il Mulino, 2006.
Judt, Tony. *Postwar: A History of Europe since 1945*. New York: Penguin, 2005.
Kiš, Danilo. "Censorhip/Self-Censorship." In *Homo Poeticus: Essays and Interviews*, 89–94. New York: Farrar, Straus and Giroux, 2003.
Kundera, Milan. "*The Skin*: Malaparte's Arch-Novel." In *Encounter*, 155–79. New York: Harper Collins, 2010.
Labanca, Nicola. *La guerra d'Etiopia. 1935–1941*, Bologna: il Mulino, 2015.
———. *Oltremare: Storia dell'espansione coloniale italiana*. Bologna: il Mulino, 2002.
Laforgia, Enzo. *Malaparte scrittore di guerra*. Florence: Vallecchi, 2011.
Lanaro, Silvio. *Retorica e politica. Alle origini dell'Italia contemporanea*. Rome: Donzelli, 2011.
———. *Storia dell'Italia repubblicana*. Venice: Marsilio, 1992.
Lang, Berel. *Primo Levi: The Matter of a Life*. New Haven, CT: Yale University Press, 2013.
La Penna, Daniela. "*Aretusa*: Continuity, Rupture, and Space for Intervention (1944–46)." *Journal of Modern Italian Studies* 21, no. 1 (2016): 19–34.
———. "The Rise and Fall of Benedetto Croce: Intellectual Positioning in the Italian Cultural Field, 1944–1947." *Modern Italy* 21, 2 (2016): 139–55.

La Porta, Filippo. "Carlo Levi. Liberarsi dalla politica attraverso la politica." In De Donato, *Oltre la paura*, 113–19.

La Rovere, Luca. *L'eredità del fascismo. Gli intellettuali, i giovani e la transizione al postfascismo*. Turin: Bollati Boringhieri, 2008.

Lattarulo, Leonardo. "Il giudizio di Lukàcs su Elsa Morante." In *La stanza di Elsa. Dentro la scrittura di Elsa Morante*. Edited by Giuliana Zagra and Simonetta Buttò, 67–72. Rome: Colombo, 2006.

Leavitt IV, Charles L. "'An Entire New Land'? Italy's Post-War Culture and Its Fascist Past." *Journal of Modern Italian Studies* 21, no. 1 (2016): 4–18.

———. *Italian Neorealism: A Cultural History*. Toronto: University of Toronto Press, 2020.

———. "Probing the Limits of Crocean Historicism." *The Italianist* 37, no. 3 (2017): 387–406.

Levi, Carlo. "Appunti sul 'Dittatore.'" In *Strana idea di battersi*, 71–77.

———. *Christ Stopped at Eboli*. Translated by Frances Frenaye. New York: Farrar, Straus and Giroux, 1998 (*Cristo si è fermato a Eboli*, 1945).

———. "La città." In Terra, *Dopo il diluvio*, 15–21.

———. *Il dovere dei tempi. Prose politiche e civili*. Edited by Luisa Montevecchi. Rome: Donzelli, 2004.

———. *Fear of Freedom*. Translated by Adolphe Gourevitch. New York: Columbia University Press, 2008 (*Paura della Libertà*, 1946).

———. "Malaparte e Bonaparte, ossia l'Italia letteraria." In *Prima e dopo le parole*, 115–22.

———. *Paura della libertà*. Vicenza: Neri Pozza, 2018 (1946).

———. "Prefazione alla prima edizione di *Paura della libertà*" (1946). In *Scritti politici*, 216–19.

———. *Prima e dopo le parole: scritti e discorsi sulla letteratura*. Edited by Gigliola De Donato and Rosalba Galvagno. Rome: Donzelli, 2001.

———. *Roma fuggitiva. Una città e i suoi dintorni*. Edited by Gigliola De Donato. Rome: Donzelli, 2002.

———. *Scritti politici*. Edited by David Bidussa. Turin: Einaudi, 2001.

———. *La strana idea di battersi per la libertà. Dai giornali della Liberazione (1944–1946)*. Edited by Filippo Benfante. Santa Maria Capua Vetere, CE: Spartaco, 2007.

———. *The Watch*. Translated by John Farrar and Marianna Gifford. New York: Farrar, Straus and Young, 1951 (*L'orologio*, 1950).

———. "Un letterato perfetto, Emilio Cecchi." In *Prima e dopo le parole*, 247–48.

Levi, Carlo, and Leone Ginzburg. "Il concetto di autonomia nel programma di G.L." (1932). In *Scritti politici*, 72–80.

Levi, Carlo, and Linuccia Saba. *Carissimo Puck: lettere d'amore e di vita 1945–1969*. Edited by Sergio D'Amaro. Rome: Mancosu, 1994.

Levi, Primo. "About Obscure Writing." In *Other People's Trades*. In *Complete Works*. Vol. 3. Translated by Antony Shugaar (*L'altrui mestiere*, 1985), 2061–66.
———. *The Complete Works of Primo Levi*. Vols. 1–3. Edited by Ann Goldstein. New York: Liveright, 2015.
———. *If This Is a Man*. In *Complete Works*. Vol. 1. Translated by Stuart Woolf (*Se questo è un uomo*, 1947).
———. *Opere I–II*. Edited by Marco Belpoliti. Turin: Einaudi, 1997.
———. *The Periodic Table*. In *Complete Works*. Vol. 2. Translated by Ann Goldstein (*Il sistema periodico*, 1975).
———. "Primo Levi a Umberto Saba. Torino, 10 gennaio 1949." In Bucciantini, *Esperimento Auschwitz*, 161.
Levis Sullam, Simon. *I fantasmi del fascismo. Le metamorfosi degli intellettuali italiani nel dopoguerra*. Milan: Feltrinelli, 2021.
———. *Giuseppe Mazzini and the Origins of Fascism*. New York: Palgrave Macmillan, 2015.
———. "Gli indifferenti 'ebraizzati.'" In Luzzatto, Pedullà, and Scarpa, *Atlante della letteratura italiana*. Vol. 3, 551–58.
Levy, Daniel, and Natan Sznaider. *The Holocaust and Memory in the Global Age*. Translated by Assenka Oksiloff. Philadelphia: Temple University Press, 2006.
Leys, Ruth. *From Guilt to Shame: Auschwitz and After*. Princeton, NJ: Princeton University Press, 2007.
Lijoi, Lucilla. *Il sognatore sveglio. Alberto Savinio 1933–1943*. Milan: Mimesis, 2021.
Liucci, Raffaele. *Spettatori di un naufragio. Gli intellettuali italiani nella Seconda Guerra Mondiale*. Turin: Einaudi, 2011.
Loewel, Pierre. "Romanciers Italiens." In Malaparte, *Malaparte. Vol. 8: 1948–1949*, 232–33. Originally published in *L'Aurore*, October 28, 1948.
Loewenthal, Elena. *Scrivere di sé. Identità ebraiche allo specchio*. Turin: Einaudi, 2007.
Longanesi, Leo. *Parliamo dell'elefante. Frammenti di un diario*. Milan: Longanesi, 1947.
Löwy, Michael. *Fire Alarm: Reading Walter Benjamin's 'On the Concept of History.'* New York: Verso, 2005.
———. *Redemption and Utopia: Jewish Libertarian Thought in Central Europe*. Stanford, CA: Stanford University Press, 1992.
Lucamante, Stefania. *Elsa Morante e l'eredità proustiana*. Fiesole, FI: Cadmo, 1998.
———. *Quella difficile identità. Ebraismo e rappresentazioni letterarie della Shoah*. Rome: Iacobelli, 2012.
Lucamante, Stefania, and Sharon Wood, eds. *Under Arturo's Star: The Cultural Legacies of Elsa Morante*. West Lafayette, IN: Purdue University Press, 2006.

Lugnani, Lucio, et al. eds. *Per Elisa. Studi su "Menzogna e sortilegio."* Pisa: Nistri-Lischi, 1990.
Lukács, György. "L'ottobre e la letteratura." *Rinascita* 42 (October 27, 1967): 23–27.
Luperini, Romano. *Gli intellettuali di sinistra e l'ideologia della ricostruzione nel dopoguerra.* Rome: Edizioni Ideologie, 1971.
———. "Letteratura ed identità nazionale: la parabola novecentesca." In *Letteratura ed identità nazionale nel Novecento.* Edited by Romano Luperini and Daniela Brogi, 7–33. San Cesario di Lecce, LE: Manni, 2004.
Luzzatto, Sergio. *Primo Levi's Resistance: Rebels and Collaborators in Occupied Italy.* New York: Metropolitan Books, 2016.
Luzzatto, Sergio, Gabriele Pedullà, and Domenico Scarpa, eds. *Atlante della letteratura italiana. Vol. 3: Dal Romanticismo a oggi.* Turin: Einaudi, 2012.
Luzzi, Joseph. *A Cinema of Poetry: Aesthetics of the Italian Art Film.* Baltimore, MD: Johns Hopkins University Press, 2014.
Macry, Paolo. *Gli ultimi giorni. Stati che crollano nell'Europa del Novecento.* Bologna: il Mulino, 2009.
Malaparte, Curzio. "Cadaveri squisiti." *Prospettive* 4, no. 6–7 (1940): 3–5.
———. *Coup d'État. The Technique of Revolution.* Translated by Sylvia Saunders. New York: Dutton, 1932 (*Technique du Coup d'état*, 1931).
———. *Il Cristo proibito.* Edited by Luigi Martellini. Naples: ESI, 1992.
———. *Diary of a Foreigner in Paris.* Translated by Stephen Twilley. New York: NYRB Classics, 2020 (*Diario di uno straniero a Parigi*, 1966).
———. *Das Kapital.* Translated and edited by Mario Maranzana. Milan: Mondadori, 1980 (1949).
———. *Das Kapital, pièce en trois actes; précédée de Du côté de chez Proust, impromptu en un acte.* Paris: Denoël, 1951.
———. *Du côté de chez Proust* (1948). In *Das Kapital, pièce en trois actes.*
———. *Kaputt* (1944). In *Opere scelte.*
———. *Kaputt.* Translated by Cesare Foligno. New York: NYRB Classics, 2005 (*Kaputt*, 1944).
———. *The Kremlin Ball.* Translated by Jenny McPhee. New York: NYRB Classics, 2018 (*Il ballo al Kremlino*, 1971).
———. "L'ora che segnò la sorte di Belgrado." *Corriere della Sera*, April 27, 1941. In *Malaparte. Vol. 5: 1940–1941*, 620–24.
———. "La lezione di Firenze. I fiorentini delle 'cronache.'" *l'Unità.* August 23, 1944. In *Malaparte. Vol. 6: 1942–1945*, 513.
———. "Lana Caprina." *Prospettive* 4, no. 5 (1942): 3–4.
———. *Malaparte. Vols. 1–12.* Edited by Edda Ronchi Suckert. Florence: Ponte alle Grazie, Famiglie Ronchi e Suckert, 1991–1996.
———. *Mamma Marcia.* Florence: Vallecchi, 1959.
———. "Nostro peccato." *Prospettive* 4, no. 4 (1940): 3–5.
———. *Opere scelte.* Edited by Luigi Martellini. Milan: Mondadori, 1997.

———. "Risveglio di Belgrado." *Corriere della Sera*, April 22, 1941. In *Malaparte. Vol. 5: 1940–1941*, 608–12.
———. *Sangue*. Florence: Vallecchi, 1995 (1937).
———. "Settembre 9, 1943," In *Giornale Segreto*. In *Malaparte. Vol. 6: 1942–1945*, 445.
———. "Settembre 22, 1942." In *Giornale Segreto 1*. Agenda 1942, Archivio Malaparte, Biblioteca Via del Senato, Milan.
———. *The Skin*. Translated by David Moore. New York: NYRB Classics, 2013 (*La pelle*, 1949).
———. *Storia di domani*. Rome-Milan: Aria d'Italia, 1949.
———. "Il Surrealismo e l'Italia." *Prospettive* 4, no. 1 (1940): 3–7.
———. *Viaggi fra i terremoti*. Florence: Vallecchi, 1963.
———. *Viaggio in Etiopia e altri scritti africani*. Edited by Enzo R. Laforgia. Florence: Vallecchi, 2006.
———. *Viva Caporetto!* (1921). Published as *La rivolta dei santi maledetti* (1923), in *Opere scelte*.
———. *Il Volga nasce in Europa* (Milan: Bompiani, 1943).
———. *The Volga Rises in Europe*. Translated by David Moore. London: Redman, 1957 (*Il Volga nasce in Europa*. Rome, Milan: Aria d'Italia, 1951).
Mangoni, Luisa. "Da *Cristo si è fermato a Eboli* a *L'Orologio*: note su Carlo Levi e la casa editrice Einaudi." In Brunello and Vivarelli, *Carlo Levi. Gli anni fiorentini*, 195–209.
———, ed. *Primato, 1940–1943: Antologia*. Bari: De Donato, 1977.
Marazzi, Martino. "Il Saba di 'Scorciatoie e raccontini' tra Nietzsche e Freud." *Autografo* 7, no. 20 (1990): 27–52.
Marcus, Millicent. *Italian Film in the Shadow of Auschwitz*. Toronto: University of Toronto Press, 2007.
Marelli, Sante. *Scrittori dell'antistoria*. Rimini: Panozzo Editore, 1984.
Marramao, Giacomo. *Potere e secolarizzazione. Le categorie del tempo*. Turin: Bollati Boringhieri, 2005.
Martellini, Luigi. Introduction to *Opere scelte* by Curzio Malaparte, xli–lxvi.
———. "Introduzione. La croce, alcuni segni, un eroe." In Malaparte, *Il Cristo proibito*, 9–65.
———. *Le "Prospettive" di Malaparte. Una rivista tra cultura fascista, europeismo e letteratura*. Naples: ESI, 2014.
Masi, Alessandro. *Idealismo e opportunismo nella cultura italiana 1943–1948*. Milan: Mursia, 2018.
Masino, Paola. *Birth and Death of the Housewife*. Translated by Marella Feltrin-Morris. Albany: State University of New York Press, 2009 (*Nascita e morte della massaia*, 1945).
Mazzantini, Carlo. *In Search of a Glorious Death*. Translated by Simonetta Wenkert. Manchester: Carcanet, 1992 (*A cercar la bella morte*, 1986).
Mazzini, Giuseppe. *Scritti politici*. Turin: UTET, 1972.

Meneghello, Luigi. *Fiori italiani*. Milan: Rizzoli, 1976.

Merola, Nicola. "Al banchetto dei potenti." Review of *Opere Scelte*, by Curzio Malaparte, *L'indice dei libri del mese* 15, 1 (1998): 6–7.

Meuschel, Sigrid. "The Institutional Frame: Totalitarianism, Extermination, and the State." In Dubiel and Motzkin, *Lesser Evil*, 109–24.

Miłosz, Czesław. *The Captive Mind*. New York: Vintage, 1990 (1951).

Moloney, Brian. "*Cristo si è fermato a Eboli* and the problem of the North." In Farrell, *Voices of Carlo Levi*, 99–118.

Monelli, Paolo. *Roma 1943*. Turin: Einaudi, 2012 (1945).

Montale, Eugenio. *Auto da fè. Cronache in due tempi*. Milan: il Saggiatore, 1966.

Montanelli, Indro. *Qui non riposano*. Venice: Marsilio, 1982 (1945).

Morante, Daniele, ed. *L'amata. Lettere di e a Elsa Morante*. Turin: Einaudi, 2012.

Morante, Elsa. *Arturo's Island*. Translated by Ann Goldstein. New York: Liveright, 2019 (*L'isola di Arturo*, 1957).

———. *History: A Novel*. Translated by William Weaver. Hanover, NH: Zolland Books (*La storia*, 1974).

———. *Lies and Sorcery*. Translation by Jenny McPhee. New York: NYRB Classics, forthcoming (*Menzogna e sortilegio*, 1948).

———. *Opere*. Vols. 1–2. Edited by Carlo Cecchi and Cesare Garboli. Milan: Mondadori, 1988.

———. "Pagine autobiografiche postume." In *Opere. Vol. 1*, l–li.

———. *Pro o contro la bomba atomica*. Milan: Adelphi, 1987.

Moravia, Alberto. *Agostino* (1944). In *Opere 2*.

———. "La borghesia." In Terra, *Dopo il diluvio*, 199–215.

———. *Cinema Italiano: recensioni e interventi*. Milan: Bompiani, 2012.

———. *The Conformist*. Translated by Tami Calliope. South Royalton, VT: Steerforth Italia, 1999 (*Il conformista*, 1951).

———. "Diario politico." *Aretusa* 1, no. 2 (1944): 40–50.

———. "Diario politico." *La Nuova Europa* 2, no. 2 (1945): 6.

———. "Diario politico." *La Nuova Europa* 2, no. 6 (1945): 7.

———. "Diario politico." *La Nuova Europa* 2, no. 20 (1945): 9.

———. "Folla e demagoghi." In *Impegno controvoglia*, 3–6. Originally published in *Il Popolo di Roma*, August 25, 1943.

———. *Impegno controvoglia. Saggi, articoli, interviste: Trentacinque anni di scritti politici*. Milan: Bompiani, 2008 (1980).

———. *Man as an End: A Defense of Humanism. Literary, Social, and Political Essays*. Translated by Bernard Wall. New York: Farrar, Straus and Giroux, 1966 (*L'uomo come fine*, 1953).

———. "Man as an End." In *Man as an End*, 13–63.

———. "Nazismo e nazione." *Libera Stampa*, April 11, 1945.

———. *Opere 2. Romanzi e racconti 1941–1949*. Edited by Simone Casini. Milan: Bompiani, 2002.

———. "Quaderno politico." *La città libera*, September 13, 1945.

———. "Questo dopoguerra." *Libera Stampa*, June 5, 1945.
———. "Recalling *Time of Indifference*." In *Man as an End*, 76–81.
———. "La speranza ossia cristianesimo e comunismo" (1944). In *Impegno controvoglia*, 11–29.
———. "Sull'Europa." *La città libera*, June 14, 1945.
———. "Sulle masse." *La città libera*, July 19, 1945.
———. *Two Women*. Translated by Angus Davidson. Hanover, NH: Zolland Books, 2001 (*La ciociara*, 1957).
———. *The Woman of Rome*. Translated by Lydia Holland. Revised by Tami Calliope. Hanover, NH: Zolland Books, 1999 (*La romana*, 1947).
Moravia, Alberto, and Alain Elkann. *Life of Moravia*. Translated by William Weaver. South Royalton, VT: Steerforth Italia, 2000 (*Vita di Moravia*, 1990).
Mosse, George L. *Fallen Soldiers: Reshaping the Memory of the World Wars*. New York: Oxford University Press, 1990.
Muraro, Luisa. *The Symbolic Order of the Mother*. Translated by Francesca Novello. Albany: State University of New York Press, 2018.
Muscetta, Carlo. "Leggenda e verità di Carlo Levi" (1946). In *Realismo neorealismo controrealismo*, 52–67. Milan: Garzanti, 1976.
Mussolini, Benito. *Opera Omnia*. Vols. *1–35*. Edited by Edoardo Susmel and Duilio Susmel. Florence: La Fenice, 1967.
Nogara, Gino. "Galleria delle riedizioni. *Tempo di uccidere*." *La fiera letteraria*, November 28, 1954.
Onofri, Massimo. *Tre scrittori borghesi. Soldati, Moravia, Piovene*. Rome: Gaffi, 2007.
Orlandini, Roberta. "(Anti)colonialismo in *Tempo di uccidere* di Ennio Flaiano." *Italica* 69, no. 4 (1992): 478–88.
Orsucci, Andrea. *Il "giocoliere d'idee." Malaparte e la filosofia*. Pisa: Edizioni della Normale, 2015.
Paggi, Leonardo. *Il "popolo dei morti." La repubblica italiana nata dalla Guerra (1940–1946)*. Bologna: il Mulino, 2009.
Palazzeschi, Aldo. *Tre imperi . . . mancati*. Florence: Vallecchi, 1945.
Papini, Giovanni. "Contro Roma." In *La cultura italiana del '900 attraverso le riviste. Vol. 4: "Lacerba" "La Voce" (1914–1916)*. Edited by Gianni Scalia. Turin: Einaudi, 1961.
Pardini, Giuseppe. *Curzio Malaparte. Biografia Politica*. Milan: Luni, 1998.
———. "Malaparte, Moravia e 'Prospettive.'" *Nuova storia contemporanea* 3, no. 1 (1999): 105–30.
Parigi, Giulio. Review of *Sorte dell'Europa*, by Alberto Savinio. *L'Universo*, March–April 1948.
Patriarca, Silvana. *Italian Vices: Nation and Character from the Risorgimento to the Republic*. Cambridge: Cambridge University Press, 2010.
Pavese, Cesare. *Il compagno*. Turin: Einaudi, 1974 (1947).

———. *The House on the Hill*. Translated by Tim Parks. London: Penguin Classics, 2021 (*La casa in collina*, 1948).
———. *La letteratura americana e altri saggi*. Turin: Einaudi, 1991.
———. "Ritorno all'uomo." In *La letteratura americana e altri saggi*, 197–99. Originally published in *l'Unità*, May 20, 1945.
———. *This Business of Living. Diaries 1935–1950*. Translated by A. E. Murch. Abingdon, UK: Routledge, 2009 (*Il mestiere di vivere*, 1952).
Pavone, Claudio. *A Civil War: A History of the Italian Resistance*. London: Verso, 2014.
———. *Alle origini della Repubblica. Scritti su fascismo, antifascismo e continuità dello stato*. Turin: Bollati Boringhieri, 1995.
Pedullà, Gabriele. "Piero Calamandrei e la Resistenza come narrazione civile." *Contemporanea* 14, no. 2 (2011): 263–88.
Pedullà, Walter. *Alberto Savinio. Scrittore ipocrita e privo di scopo*. Treviso: Anordest, 2011.
Pescosolido, Guido. "Italy Southern Question: Long-Standing Thorny Issues and Current Problems." *Journal of Modern Italian Studies* 23, no. 3 (2019): 441–55.
Piazzesi, Gianfranco. Review of *Cristo si è fermato a Eboli*, by Carlo Levi. *Società* 5 (1946): 260.
———. "Review of *Pietà contro pietà*, by Guido Piovene." *Il Ponte* 2, no. 7–8 (1946): 873.
Pieri, Giuliana. "Gabriele d'Annunzio and the Self-Fashioning of a National Icon." *Modern Italy* 21, no. 4 (2016): 328–43.
Pigro, il [Alberto Moravia]. "Rivoluzione e pessimismo." *Città*, November 23, 1944.
Pintor, Giaime. "L'ora del riscatto." In *Il sangue d'Europa (1939–43)*. Edited by Valentino Gerratana. Turin: Einaudi, 1950.
Piovene, Guido. "Gli amanti della malafede." *Città*, November 11, 1944.
———. "La chiesa." In Terra, *Dopo il diluvio*, 25–40.
———. "Est, est: non, non." *La città libera*, May 31, 1945.
———. *I falsi redentori* (1949). In *Opere Narrative*.
———. *Le furie*. Turin: Aragno, 2009 (1963).
———. "Gli interprovinciali." *Città*, November 23, 1944.
———. "Non furono tetri." *Mercurio* 1, no. 4 (1944): 286–90.
———. *Opere Narrative*. Vols. *1–2*. Edited by Clelia Martignoni. Milan: Mondadori, 1976.
———. *Pietà contro pietà* (1946). In *Opere Narrative*.
———. "Scorciatoie di Saba." *Corriere della Sera*, November 3, 1946.
———. "Sinistra e destra nell'arte." *Il Tempo*, July 11, 1944.
Piperno, Martina. "Con Vico ne *L'Orologio*." *Poetiche* 17, no. 42 (1 2015): 53–74.
Ponzanesi, Sandra. "Beyond the Black Venus: Colonial Sexual Politics and Contemporary Visual Practices." In Andall and Duncan, *Italian Colonialism*, 165–89.

Ponzani, Michela. "Il mito del Secondo Risorgimento nazionale. Retorica e legittimità della Resistenza nel linguaggio politico istituzionale." *Annali della Fondazione Luigi Einaudi* 37 (2003): 199–258.
Pratolini, Vasco. *A Tale of Poor Lovers*. New York: Viking, 1949 (*Cronache di poveri amanti*, 1946).
———. *Two Brothers*. Translated by Barbara Kennedy. New York: Orion, 1962 (*Cronaca familiare*, 1947).
Pugliese, Stanislao. *Carlo Rosselli: Social Heretic and Antifascist Exile*. Cambridge, MA: Harvard University Press, 1999.
Pullini, Giorgio. "Dialettica di due forme terapeutiche: l'afflato cristiano e l'autonomia." In Artico and Lepri, *Giuseppe Berto. La sua opera, il suo tempo*, 29–70.
———. *Giuseppe Berto: da "Il cielo è rosso" a "Il male oscuro."* Modena: Mucchi, 1991.
Quasimodo, Salvatore. "Carlo Marx resuscitato da Malaparte." In Malaparte, *Malaparte. Vol. 8: 1948–1949*, 375. Originally published in *Tempo*, February 5–12, 1949.
Rancière, Jacques. *Disagreement: Politics and Philosophy*. Minneapolis: University of Minnesota Press, 1999.
———. *The Names of History: On the Poetics of Knowledge*. Minneapolis: University of Minnesota Press, 1994.
———. *The Politics of Literature*. Cambridge: Polity, 2011.
Raimondi, Ezio. *Letteratura e identità nazionale*. Milan: Bruno Mondadori, 1998.
Re, Lucia. *Calvino and the Age of Neorealism: Fables of Estrangement*. Stanford, CA: Stanford University Press, 1990.
———. "Italy's First Postcolonial Novel and the End of (Neo)realism." *The Italianist* 37, no. 3 (2017): 416–35.
Rea, Domenico. *Spaccanapoli*. Milan: Rusconi, 1995 (1947).
Ricciardi, Alessia. "The Italian Redemption of Cinema: Neorealism from Bazin to Godard." *Romanic Review* 97, nos. 3–4 (2006): 483–500.
Righi, Andrea. *Italian Reactionary Thought and Critical Theory: An Inquiry into Savage Modernities*. New York: Palgrave Macmillan, 2015.
Rizi, Fabio Fernando. *Benedetto Croce and the Birth of the Italian Republic, 1943–1952*. Toronto: University of Toronto Press, 2019.
Rodogno, Davide. *Fascism's European Empire: Italian Occupation during the Second World War*. Cambridge: Cambridge University Press, 2006.
Romani, Bruno. "A Parigi si leggono opere di scrittori italiani." In Malaparte, *Malaparte. Vol. 8: 1948–1949*, 104–6. Originally published in *Il Tempo*, April 1948.
Rondini, Andrea. "Da Umberto Saba a Primo Levi," *Rivista di letteratura italiana* 26, nos. 2–3 (2008): 45–53.
Rosselli, Carlo. *Liberal Socialism*. Translated by William McCuaig. Princeton, NJ: Princeton University Press, 2017 (*Socialismo liberale*, 1930).

Rossi-Doria, Manlio. "La crisi del governo Parri nel racconto di Carlo Levi." In De Donato, *"L'Orologio" di Carlo Levi*.
Rothberg, Michael. *Multidirectional Memory: Remembering the Holocaust in the Age of Decolonization*. Stanford, CA: Stanford University Press, 2009.
———. *Traumatic Realism: The Demands of Holocaust Representation*. Minneapolis: University of Minnesota Press, 2000.
Rousset, David. *The Other Kingdom*. Translated by Ramon Guthrie. New York: Reynal and Hitchcock, 1947 (*L'Univers concentrationnaire*, 1946).
Ruozzi, Gino. *Ennio Flaiano, una verità personale*. Rome: Carocci, 2016.
Rusconi, Gian Enrico. *Possiamo fare a meno di una religione civile?* Bari-Rome: Laterza, 1999.
Saba, Umberto. "From *Shortcuts and Very Short Stories*." In *Stories and Recollections of Umberto Saba*. 163–92.
———. "Gratitudine." In *Il Canzoniere*, 523. Turin: Einaudi, 2014 (1961).
———. *Lettere sulla psicanalisi. Carteggio con Joachim Flescher 1946–1949*. Milan: SE, 2007.
———. "Poesia, filosofia, psicanalisi." In *Tutte le prose*, 964–73.
———. *Scorciatoie e raccontini* (1946). In *Tutte le prose*.
———. *Songbook. The Selected Poems of Umberto Saba*. Translated by George Hochfield and Leoanrd Nathan. New Haven, CT: Yale University Press, 2008 (*Il Canzoniere*, 1961).
———. *La spada d'amore. Lettere scelte 1902–1957*. Edited by Aldo Marcovecchio. Milan: Mondadori, 1983.
———. *The Stories and Recollections of Umberto Saba*. Translated by Estelle Gibson. Riverdale-on-Hudson, NY: Sheep Meadow Press, 1993.
———. *Tutte le Prose*. Edited by Arrigo Stara. Milan: Mondadori, 2001.
———. "Umberto Saba a Primo Levi. Trieste, 3 Novembre 1948." In Bucciantini, *Esperimento Auschwitz*, 159.
Sacerdoti, Guido. "I transeunti Dei del nostro tempo." In De Donato, *Oltre la paura*, 41–58.
Sacco, Leonardo. "Contadini e luigini." In De Donato, *"L'Orologio" di Carlo Levi*, 97–106.
———. *L'Orologio della Repubblica. Carlo Levi e il caso Italia*. Lecce: Argo, 1996.
Salvati, Mariuccia. *Passaggi. Italiani dal fascismo alla Repubblica*. Rome: Carocci, 2016.
Salvemini, Gaetano. "Salvemini a Rossi e a Valiani." In *Lettere dall'America. Vol. 1, 1944–1946*. Edited by Alberto Merola, 356–57. Bari: Laterza, 1967.
Salvemini, Gaetano, and Giorgio La Piana. *La sorte dell'Italia*. Rome: Edizioni U, 1945.
Santner, Eric. *On Creaturely Life: Rilke, Benjamin, Sebald*. Chicago: University of Chicago Press, 2006.
———. *Stranded Objects: Mourning, Memory, and Film in Postwar Germany*. Ithaca, NY: Cornell University Press, 1990.

Sapegno, Natalino. "Marxismo, cultura, poesia." *Rinascita* 2, nos. 7–8 (1945): 182–84.
Sarfatti, Michele. *The Jews in Mussolini's Italy: From Equality to Persecution.* Madison: University of Wisconsin Press, 2006.
Sartre, Jean-Paul. *Existentialism Is a Humanism.* New Haven, CT: Yale University Press, 2007 (1946).
Sassoon, Donald. "Italy after Fascism: The Predicament of Dominant Narratives." In *Life after Death: Approaches to a Cultural and Social History of Europe During the 1940s and 1950s.* Edited by Richard Bessel and Dirk Schumann, 259–90. Cambridge: Cambridge University Press, 2003.
Satta, Salvatore. *De Profundis.* Milan: Adelphi, 2003 (1948).
Savinio, Alberto. "Conclusione." Archivio contemporaneo Gabinetto G. P. Vieusseux, Carte A. Savinio, AS II. 20.49.
———. "Illusione del definitivo." In *Scritti dispersi*, 154–60.
———. "Inquieti adolescenti." In *Scritti dispersi*, 169–72.
———. *Maupassant e "l'Altro."* Milan: Adelphi, 1975 (1960).
———. *Nuova Enciclopedia.* Milan: Adelphi, 2011 (1977).
———. *Opere: Scritti dispersi tra guerra e dopoguerra (1943–1952).* Edited by Leonardo Sciascia and Franco De Maria. Milan: Bompiani, 1989.
———. *Scritti dispersi 1943–1952.* Edited by Paola Italia. Milan: Adelphi, 2004.
———. "Senza titolo." Archivio contemporaneo Gabinetto G. P. Vieusseux, Carte A. Savinio, Ad. II. 52. 61.
———. *Sorte dell'Europa.* Milan: Adelphi, 2005 (1945).
———. "Tommaso Moro e l'utopia." In *Scritti dispersi*, 85–102.
———. "Voltaire e Federico II." In *Scritti dispersi*, 188–212.
Scapolo, Andrea. "Scattered Ashes: The Reception of the Gramscian Legacy in Postwar Italy." In *Gramsci in the World.* Edited by Roberto Dainotto and Fredric Jameson, 93–112. Durham, NC: Duke University Press, 2020.
Scarano, Emanuella. "La 'fatua veste' del vero." In Lugnani et al., *Per Elisa*, 95–171.
Scarpa, Domenico. "Chiaro/oscuro." *Primo Levi.* Edited by Marco Belpoliti. *Riga* 13 (1997): 230–53.
———. "La madre dei racconti. Corrado Alvaro sotto il fascismo." In *Storie avventurose di libri necessari*, 33–65. Rome: Gaffi, 2010.
———. "Prefazione. Un volontario sincero." In Giuseppe Berto. *Il cielo è rosso*, ix–xxvi. Turin: UTET, 2007.
Schivelbusch, Wolfgang. *The Culture of Defeat: On National Trauma, Mourning, and Recovery.* New York: Metropolitan, 2001.
Schlemmer, Thomas. *Invasori, non vittime. La campagna italiana di Russia 1941–1943.* Bari-Rome: Laterza, 2009.
Schneider, Jane, ed. *Italy's "Southern Question": Orientalism in One Country.* London: Routledge, 1998.

Schoonover, Karl. *Brutal Vision: The Neorealist Body in Postwar Italian Cinema*. Minneapolis: University of Minnesota Press, 2012.
Schwarz, Guri. *Tu mi devi seppellir. Riti funebri e culto nazionale alle origini della Repubblica*. Milan: UTET, 2010.
Scianna, Bastian Matteo. *The Italian War on the Eastern Front, 1941–1943: Operations, Myths, and Memories*. New York: Palgrave Macmillan, 2019.
Sciascia, Leonardo. "Del dormire con un occhio solo." In Brancati, *Opere 1932–1946*, vii–xxii.
Sebastiani, Gioia. "Editori a Roma dopo la Liberazione: *Le Edizioni Documento*." In *Gli archivi degli editori, studi e prospettive di ricerca*. Edited by Gianfranco Tortorelli, 157–81. Bologna: Patron, 1998.
Sereni, Vittorio. *Algerian Diary*. Translated by Paul Vangelisti and Ippolita Rostagno. San Francisco: Red Hill Press, 1985 (*Diario d'Algeria*, 1947).
———. *La tentazione della prosa*. Edited by Giulia Raboni. Milan: Mondadori, 1998.
Serra, Maurizio. *Malaparte. Vite e leggende*. Venice: Marsilio, 2012.
Serri, Mirella. *I Redenti. Gli intellettuali che vissero due volte, 1938–1948*. Milan: Corbaccio, 2005.
Sebald, W. G. *On the Natural History of Destruction*. New York: Random House, 2003.
Sforza, Carlo. *L'Italia dal 1914 al 1944 quale io la vidi*. Milan: Mondadori, 1946.
———. *The Real Italians: A Study in European Psychology*. New York: Columbia University Press, 1942.
Sgorlon, Edda, and Carlo. "Profilo di Elsa Morante." In *Cahiers Elsa Morante*. Edited by Jean-Noel Schifano and Tjuna Notarbartolo, 19–20. Naples: ESI, 1993.
Sheehan, James J. *Where Have All the Soldiers Gone? The Transformation of Modern Europe*. Boston: Mariner, 2009.
Shirer, William L. *The Rise and Fall of the Third Reich: A History of Nazi Germany*. New York: Simon and Schuster, 1960.
Soldati, Mario. *Corrispondenti di Guerra*. Edited by Emiliano Morreale. Palermo: Sellerio, 2009.
———. *Fuga in Italia*. Edited by Salvatore Silvano Nigro. Palermo: Sellerio, 2004 (1947).
Sòrgoni, Barbara. *Parole e corpi: antropologia, discorso giuridico e politiche sessuali interrazziali nella colonia Eritrea (1890–1941)*. Naples: Liguori Editori, 1998.
Spadolini, Giovanni. Review of *La pelle*, by Curzio Malaparte. *Il Messaggero*. February 9, 1950.
Spinelli, Altiero. *Il Manifesto di Ventotene*. Bologna: il Mulino, 1991 (1943).
Steimatsky, Noa. *Italian Locations: Reinhabiting the Past in Postwar Cinema*. Minneapolis: University of Minnesota Press, 2005.

Steiner, George. *The Death of Tragedy*. New York: Knopf, 1961.
Suckert, Eric Curt [Curzio Malaparte]. "Gli eroi capovolti." *La Rivoluzione liberale* 1, no. 23 (1922): 85–86.
Sullam Calimani, Anna-Vera. *I nomi dello sterminio. Definizioni di una tragedia*. Bologna: Marietti, 2019.
Svevo, Italo. *Zeno's Conscience*. Translated by William Weaver. London: Penguin, 2019 (*La coscienza di Zeno*, 1923).
Taylor, Charles. *A Secular Age*. Cambridge, MA: The Belknap Press of Harvard University Press, 2007.
Tecchi, Bonaventura. "I vantaggi della sconfitta." *La Nuova Europa* 2, no. 41 (1945), 5.
Terra, Dino, ed. *Dopo il diluvio. Sommario dell'Italia contemporanea*. Milan: Garzanti, 1947.
Tesio, Giovanni. "*L'Orologio* di Carlo Levi tra Giona e Narciso." In Farrell, *Voices of Carlo Levi*, 55–66.
Thomson, Ian. *Primo Levi: A Life*. London: Hutchinson, 2002.
Tomasello, Giovanna. "Flaiano e gli incubi della coscienza." In *L'Africa tra mito e realtà. Storia della letteratura coloniale italiana*, 208–15. Palermo: Sellerio, 2004.
Torriglia, Anna Maria. *Broken Time, Fragmented Space: A Cultural Map for Postwar Italy*. Toronto: University of Toronto Press, 2002.
Tosi, Giuseppe. "*Morte della patria* and Mourning Elaboration: Memoirs and State of Consciousness after 8 Settembre's Italy." In *Italy and the Bourgeoisie: The Re-Thinking of a Class*. Edited by Stefania Lucamante, 63–75. Madison, NJ: Fairleigh Dickinson University Press, 2009.
Tosi, Guy. "Curzio Malaparte et 'Kaputt.'" In Malaparte, *Malaparte. Vol. 7: 1946–1947*, 31. Originally in *Paris*, April 19, 1946.
Traverso, Enzo. *Auschwitz e gli intellettuali. La Shoah nella cultura del dopoguerra*. Bologna: Il Mulino, 2004.
———. *Il secolo armato. Interpretare le violenze del Novecento*. Milan: Feltrinelli, 2012.
———. *Il totalitarismo. Storia di un dibattito*. Milan: Bruno Mondadori, 2002.
Trebbi, Giuseppe. "Italia ed Europa nel pensiero di Fabio Cusin." In *Attilio Tamaro e Fabio Cusin nella storiografia triestina. Atti del Convegno in ricordo di Arduino Agnelli, Trieste 15-16 ottobre 2005*. Edited by Silvano Cavazza e Giuseppe Trebbi, 213–47. Trieste: Deputazione di Storia Patria per la Venezia Giulia, 2007.
Trouillot, Michel-Rolph. *Silencing the Past: Power and the Production of History*. Boston: Beacon Press, 1995.
Trubiano, Marisa. *Ennio Flaiano and His Italy*. Madison, NJ: Fairleigh Dickinson University Press, 2010.
Tumiati, Corrado. Review of *Cristo si è fermato a Eboli*, by Carlo Levi. *Il Ponte* 2 (1946): 182–83.

Vacca, Giuseppe. "Gramsci Studies since 1989." *Journal of Modern Italian Studies* 16, no. 2 (2011): 179–04.
Van Dijk, Paul. *Anthropology in the Age of Technology: The Philosophical Contribution of Günther Anders*. Amsterdam: Rodopi, 2000.
Ventresca, Robert. *From Fascism to Democracy: Culture and Politics in the Italian Election of 1948*. Toronto: University of Toronto Press, 2004.
Veronesi, Sandro. "L'Europa Marcia di Malaparte e Pasolini." In Barilli and Baroncelli, *Curzio Malaparte*, 371–79.
Viganò, Renata. *L'Agnese va a morire*. Turin: Einaudi, 2005 (1949).
Vigorelli, Giancarlo. "Diario di un romantico." *Oggi*, February 18, 1947.
———. "Malaparte: testimonianza e proposta di revisione." In Malaparte, *Opere scelte*, ix–xxxix.
———. Review of *Il cielo è rosso*, by Giuseppe Berto. *Oggi*, February 11, 1947.
———. Review of *Paura della libertà*, by Carlo Levi. *Oggi*, February 2, 1947.
Violo, Evaldo. "La fortuna editoriale e il pubblico di Berto." In Artico and Lepri, *Giuseppe Berto*, 285–96.
Visconti, Luchino. "Cinema antropomorfico." *Cinema* 8 (1943): 108–9.
Visser, Romke. "Fascist Doctrine and the Cult of Romanità." *Journal of Contemporary History* 27 (1992): 5–21.
Vittorini, Elio. "Fascisti i giovani?" *Il Politecnico* 15 (1946): 69–73.
———. *Men and Not Men*. Translated by Sarah Henry. Marlboro, VT: Marlboro Press, 1985 (*Uomini e no*, 1945).
———. "Una nuova cultura." In *Letteratura arte società. Vol. 2: Articoli e interventi 1938–1965*. Edited by Raffaella Rodondi, 234–237. Turin: Einaudi, 2008. Originally in *Il Politecnico* 1, 1 (1945).
Ward, David. *Antifascisms: Cultural Politics in Italy, 1943–46*. Madison, NJ: Fairleigh Dickinson University Press, 1996.
———. *Carlo Levi. Gli italiani e la paura della libertà*. Florence: La Nuova Italia, 2002.
Weidlich, Martin. *Tramonti e aurore di Alberto Savinio. Percorso meandrico di un intellettuale europeo del '900*. Milan: Scalpendi, 2017.
Wieviorka, Annette. *The Era of the Witness*. Ithaca, NY: Cornell University Press, 2006.
Wood, Sharon. "Models of Narrative in *Menzogna e sortilegio*." In Lucamante and Wood, *Under Arturo's Star*, 94–111.
Wydra, Harald. *Politics and the Sacred*. Cambridge: Cambridge University Press, 2015.
Young-Bruehl, Elisabeth. *Hannah Arendt: For the Love of the World*. New Haven, CT: Yale University Press, 1982.
Zangrandi, Ruggero. *Il lungo viaggio attraverso il fascismo. Contributo alla storia di una generazione*. Milan: Feltrinelli, 1962.
———. *Il lungo viaggio. Contributo alla storia di una generazione*. Turin: Einaudi, 1948.

Zanzotto, Andrea. "Giuseppe Berto tra 'Il cielo è rosso' e 'Il brigante.'" *La provincia di Treviso* 5, no. 2 (1962): 29–31.
Zincone, Vittorio. "Quello che manca alla Costituzione." *Mercurio* 3, no. 25–26 (1946): 14–18.
———. *Lo stato totalitario*. Rome: Ideazione, 1999 (1947).
Ziolkowski, Saskia. *Kafka's Italian Progeny*. Toronto: University of Toronto Press, 2020.
Zunino, Pier Giorgio. *La Repubblica e il suo passato*. Bologna: il Mulino, 2003.

Index

8½ (Fellini), 120

absolution, 68, 85, 91, 202, 204
Accademia dell'Arcadia, 96
Actionists, 8, 100, 145, 157
Action Party, 96–97, 100–101, 140–147, 168, 215n56, 235n2
Adorno, Theodor, 170
"Advantages of the Defeat, The" (Tecchi), 68–69
Aeschylus, 189
aestheticism, 37–39, 84–85, 145, 151, 174
aesthetics: of Croce, 97; Fascist, 70; historicist, 122; of C. Levi, 152–153, 164; of Malaparte, 178–179; Neorealist, 4; redemptive, 86; of Savinio, 103
Agamben, Giorgio, 149, 154, 160, 177–178
Agamemnon (Aeschylus), 189
Alatri, Paolo, 28, 33
Alfano, Giancarlo, 232n26
Algerian Diary (Sereni), 66
Alicata, Mario, 159, 213n39, 253n79
Alvaro, Corrado, 6–7, 202–203
anarchism, 6, 41, 145, 149–160, 163, 179, 188, 194
Anders, Günther, 182
Animal Farm (Orwell), 30
Ansaldo, Giovanni, 120
Antelme, Robert, 115
Antihistory of Italy (Cusin), 97, 101–102
anti-Semitism, 28, 69, 81–82, 98, 106–107, 114, 117, 151, 159, 225n51
"Arcadia and Eighteenth-Century Poetry" (Croce), 96

Arendt, Hannah, 29, 81, 107, 155, 187, 194, 222n17
Aretusa (journal), 6, 56
Ariosto, Ludovico, 162
art, 84, 86, 163, 174, 178, 193
Artemisia (Banti), 203, 247n152
Arthurs, Joshua, 255n98
Asor Rosa, Alberto, 24, 27, 30–31
atonement, 19, 46, 68, 75, 196
Attlee, Clement, 8
Auschwitz, 54, 82, 109–111, 169–170
autonomy, 24–26, 32–35, 38–40, 93, 98, 122, 141, 146–160, 177

Badiou, Alain, 58
Balbo, Italo, 33
Banti, Alberto, 19, 247n152
Barberi Squarotti, Giorgio, 74
Barberis, Walter, 210n12, 241n68
Bataille, Georges, 12, 110
Battaglia, Roberto, 13
Beautiful Antonio (Bolognini), 87
Beautiful Antonio (Brancati), 25, 70, 87, 93–95, 133
Belardelli, Giovanni, 255n97
Bellonci, Goffredo, 136, 236n5
Ben-Ghiat, Ruth, 28, 210n9
Benjamin, Walter, 42, 80–81, 84–85, 152, 160–161, 164, 187
Bergson, Henri, 88
Bernard, Jacques, 117
Bersani, Leo, 86, 174, 193
Berto, Giuseppe, 6, 9, 16, 24–25, 65–68, 71–82, 95, 185, 204, 231n21, 232n25
Best of Husbands, The (de Céspedes), 247n152
Bianchi Bandinelli, Ranuccio, 143
Bicycle Thieves (De Sica), 210n16

296 | Index

Biess, Frank, 14
Big Deal on Madonna Street (Monicelli), 133
Bizzarri, Aldo, 251n43
Black Gazette, The (Piovene), 83
Bloch, Ernst, 152, 156, 162–163, 251n47
Blum, Léon, 18
Bolognini, Mauro, 87
Bolshevism, 35–36, 41, 225n42
Bompiani, Valentino, 35
Bonhomme Lénine, Le (Malaparte), 33, 36, 41
Bontempelli, Massimo, 175, 236n5
Bortone, Leone, 251n43
Bosworth, Richard, 166
Bottai, Giuseppe, 38–39, 69, 165, 213n39
bourgeoisie, 67–68
Bragaglia, Carlo Lodovico, 125
Branca, Vittore, 58, 145–146
Brancati, Vitaliano, 5, 7, 9, 12, 14–16, 24–25, 65, 87–95, 133, 200, 212n26, 235n93
Braudel, Fernand, 143, 158, 253n77
Brigand, The (Berto), 16
Buber, Martin, 151–152, 155–156
Buchenwald, 54, 169
Business of Living, The (Pavese), 203
Butler, Judith, 246n147

Cabiria (Pastrone), 123
Cahier Malaparte (de Paulis), 173
Caillois, Roger, 12, 154
Calamandrei, Piero, 50–51, 91, 143
Calvino, Italo, 9, 17, 21, 136, 151, 178, 203
Campanella, Tommaso, 104
Camp de la mort lente, Le (Bernard), 117
Cancogni, Manlio, 169
"Can Youth Be Fascist?" (Vittorini), 46
"Capital, The" (Brancati), 89–90
Captive Mind, The (Miłosz), 40
Carducci, Nicola, 67, 166, 249n14, 251n47
Casini, Simone, 52
Catholic Church, 48, 89, 109, 128, 145, 195, 255n98

Cattaneo, Carlo, 147
Cavaglion, Alberto, 117
Cecchi, Emilio, 192–193, 195, 246n135
"Censorship/Self-Censorship" (Kiš), 40
Cervantes, Miguel de, 162
Ceserani, Remo, 214n48
Chaplin, Charlie, 153, 157
"Characters" (column) (Piovene), 86
Christian Democrats (DC), 2, 6, 46, 203; "excess of speech" and, 97; Gentile and, 255n98; Italian Communist Party *vs.*, 19; lost generation and, 66; Mussolini and, 69; Saba and, 109, 115–116, 141–142; totalitarianism and, 49, 220n119; transnational policies and, 23
Christmas Agony (Fortini), 79–80
Christological figures, 44, 187–188, 193–195
Christ Stopped at Eboli (C. Levi), 10, 26, 31, 66, 140–151, 155–160, 163, 166, 168
"Church, The" (Piovene), 86–87
"Cities, The" (C. Levi), 147–148
Città (journal), 97, 236n5
City of the Sun, The (Campanella), 104
civil war, 19, 28, 61, 91, 97, 210n12, 212n32
Civil War, A: A History of the Italian Resistance (Pavone), 20
Cold Stars, The (Piovene), 83
Cold War, 3–4, 14, 22, 30, 45, 62, 69, 118, 144
Collège de sociologie, 12
Colletti, Duilio, 171
Comisso, Giovanni, 230n3
Communism. *See* Italian Communist Party (PCI); Marxism
Communist Manifesto (Marx and Engels), 104
concentration camps, 54, 81, 109–111, 153, 170, 177–178
"Concept of Autonomy in the Program of G. L., The" (C. Levi and Ginzburg), 147
Confessions of an Italian (Nievo), 178
Conformist, The (Moravia), 52, 58, 202
"Conscientious Objection" (Malaparte), 39–40

Cooke, Philip, 17–18
Copernicus, 103, 105, 237n24
Corriere della Sera, 34, 36–37, 39, 82, 89, 183–184, 190, 225n51
Croce, Benedetto, 2–3, 23, 102, 149, 154, 161, 177, 191, 235n3, 236n12, 237n15; Fascism and, 8; freedom and, 12–13, 90; historicism and, 98, 108, 211n20; moral authority of, 96–97; as moral leader, 99–100; Saba and, 101–102, 105; World War II and, 29
"Crocean Phase, The" (De Ruggiero), 100–101
Culture of Redemption, The (Bersani), 174
Cummings, Henry, 192
Cusin, Fabio, 97, 101–102, 108

Dante Alighieri, 75, 102, 133–134
D'Annunzio, Gabriele, 123, 166, 174
Darwin, Charles, 105
Das Kapital (Malaparte). See *Kapital, Das* (Malaparte)
David, Michel, 81
DC. See Christian Democrats (DC)
Death in Venice (Mann), 80
Death of the Fatherland, The (Galli della Loggia), 66
Death of Tragedy, The (Steiner), 188–189
Debenedetti, Giacomo, 13, 116, 125, 214n48
De Céspedes, Alba, 10–11, 82, 97, 215n53, 247n151
De Federicis, Umberto, 121
"Defense of Intelligence" (Savinio), 164–165
De Filippo, Eduardo, 80
Del Boca, Angelo, 123
De Luna, Giovanni, 10, 141, 212n30, 220n119
De Martino, Ernesto, 13, 143
democracy, 3–7, 9, 11, 19, 21, 23, 47, 62, 101, 106, 137, 148, 185, 204
De Paulis, Maria Pia, 173
De Profundis (Satta), 15
De Robertis, Giuseppe, 114, 117
De Ruggiero, Guido, 25, 97, 99–100, 102, 105, 219n104, 237n13

De Sanctis, Francesco, 102
De Sica, Vittorio, 210n16
Dianeo, Eudoro, 96
Diner, Dan, 110
Di Nicola, Laura, 215n53
Divine Comedy (Dante), 75
Divini Redemptoris (Pius XII), 19–20
Divorce, Italian Style (Germi), 133
Dolce vita, La (Fellini), 120
Don Quixote (Cervantes), 162, 254n86
Dry Heart, The (Ginzburg), 247n152
Du côté de chez Proust (Malaparte), 177
Duncan, Derek, 243n102
Durkheim, Émile, 154

Earth Cries Out, The (Colletti), 171
Earth Trembles, The (Visconti), 3
"Eight Jews" (Debenedetti), 117
Einaudi, Luigi, 8, 125, 143–144, 214n51
Engels, Friedrich, 104
Ernesto (Saba), 118
Eros and Priapus (Gadda), 10, 22–23, 237n24
Ethiopia, 19, 71, 80, 99, 118–119, 122–123
"Eucalyptuses Will Grow" (Berto), 81
Europe's Fate (Savinio), 97, 103–106
evil, 42, 72, 75, 111, 145, 158, 187, 189
"excess of speech," 10–11
"Exquisite Corpses" (Malaparte), 37–38, 176, 193

Falaschi, Giovanni, 209n8
Faleschini Lerner, Giovanna, 252n49
False Redeemers, The (Piovene), 15, 83, 85
Family Lexicon (Ginzburg), 9–10
Fascism: aesthetics of, 70; in Brancati, 87–93; in Calamandrei, 50–51; in Croce, 99; in Cusin, 101; ending of, 28; in Gentile, 33; history and, 100–101; imperialism and, 94; in C. Levi, 159–160; in Malaparte, 35–36; masculinity and, 87, 93, 95; as personal failure, 65–71; in Piovene, 82–87; propaganda in, 2, 7, 101; rhetoric of, 82–87; rise of, 29–30; *Romanità* and, 29, 95, 164–166, 255nn97–98; in Saba, 116

"Fascist Germ Still Lives, The" (Croce), 29
Fascists Grow Old, The (Brancati), 88
Fear of Freedom (C. Levi), 12, 26, 31, 140, 149–158, 253n69
Fellini, Federico, 120, 124
feminism, 246n147
Ferrante, Elena, 247n149
Fiore, Tommaso, 145, 157
Flaiano, Ennio, 5, 9, 12, 24–25, 99, 118–125, 202, 244nn109,118
Florence, 164–165
Foà, Vittorio, 143
Focardi, Filippo, 28
Fofi, Goffredo, 234n72
Fogu, Claudio, 7, 12, 18
Forbidden Christ, The (Malaparte), 45, 171, 182, 188
Forcella, Enzo, 4, 9, 19, 200, 238n32
Forlenza, Rosario, 4–5
Fortini, Franco, 79–80
Fosse Ardeatine massacre, 117
Frati, Stefano, 120
freedom, 12–13, 21, 34–35, 40, 48, 55–57, 59–62, 88–90, 92–94, 97, 106, 113, 139, 148
French Surrealism, 39, 176
Freud, Sigmund, 12, 98, 102, 105, 113, 118, 127–128, 136
"Fronte dell'uomo qualunque" ("Common Man's Front"), 90
Furies, The (Piovene), 83, 202
Futurism, 148, 165

Gadda, Carlo Emilio, 6, 10, 22–23, 33, 237n24
Galli della Loggia, Ernesto, 66–67
Garboli, Cesare, 129, 137
Gatt-Rutter, John, 41
Gentile, Giovanni, 5, 19, 33, 88, 211n20, 255n98
George, Stefan, 174
Gerbi, Sandro, 69
Germany, Year Zero (Rossellini), 74, 185
Germi, Pietro, 133
Giacopini, Vittorio, 153, 156
Giannini, Guglielmo, 32, 90
Gigli, Lorenzo, 192

Ginzburg, Leone, 8–10, 143, 147, 150, 174, 250n39
Ginzburg, Natalia, 125, 247nn151–152
Girard, René, 149
"Giustizia e Libertà" ("Justice and Freedom"), 142–143, 146, 150
Gobetti, Ada, 91
Gobetti, Piero, 31, 41, 101, 147, 250n25
Goethe, Wolfgang, 239n44
Gordon, Robert S. C., 20–21, 116
Gramsci, Antonio, 13, 59, 68–69, 176, 216n65, 255n108
"Gratitude" (Saba), 107
Great Dictator, The (Chaplin), 153, 157
"Great Forerunners, The" (Flaiano), 123
guilt, 22, 70, 72, 80, 88, 93, 119, 123, 130–131, 202, 219n101
Guttuso, Renato, 213n39

Hegel, Georg, 101, 105, 237n13
Here They Do Not Rest (Montanelli), 17
Herodotus, 199
historical materialism, 102, 156, 160–161, 168
historicism, 7, 12–13, 19, 23, 25, 96–103, 105, 107–108, 120, 138
history, 90, 100, 156–157, 165, 239n44
Hitler, Adolf, 97, 103, 143, 153, 163, 189
Holocaust, 5, 29, 54, 80, 110, 118, 170–171, 178, 240nn53,57
Homer, 80
homosexuality, 86, 106, 239n41
Hope: Christianity and Communism (Moravia), 25, 57–58, 60
Horden, Peregrine, 158–159
House by the Medlar Tree, The (Verga), 76
humanism, 53, 66, 140–149, 172

"I do not love my age" (Brancati), 90
If This Is a Man (P. Levi), 10, 80, 108–110, 217n75
Iliad (Homer), 80
imperialism, 21, 25, 65, 70, 94, 98, 120–121, 123–124, 200, 243n102
Incubus (Berto), 72
"Instinct and Intuition" (Brancati), 87–88

Italia Libera (journal), 6
Italian Communist Party (PCI), 6, 8–9, 12–13, 59, 66, 69, 89, 97, 102, 116, 143, 166, 213n39, 236n12, 255n98; historicism and, 23; C. Levi and, 141–142; Malaparte and, 220n119; Moravia and, 30; Piovene and, 83; redemption and, 19
Italian Liberal Party, 46
Italo-Ethiopian War, 122
Italo-Turkish War, 19
Italy's Renunciation? (Alvaro), 202–203

Jesi, Furio, 178
Jørgensen, Conni-Kay, 251n46
Jossa, Stefano, 13
Judaism, 43–45, 118, 150, 156. See also anti-Semitism; Holocaust
Judt, Tony, 14, 202

Kafka, Franz, 53, 187, 194
Kant, Immanuel, 105
Kapital, Das (Malaparte), 24, 32, 41–42, 44–45
Kaputt (Malaparte), 2, 14–15, 26, 31–32, 39, 172–177, 180–187, 193
Kiš, Danilo, 40
Kundera, Milan, 26, 45, 172

Lacan, Jacques, 246n147
Lanaro, Silvio, 10
La Penna, Daniela, 6, 102, 216n65, 236n12
La Rovere, Luca, 9, 17, 19, 46–48, 214n48
Late Mattia Pascal, The (Pirandello), 110–111
Leavitt, Charles L. IV, 3, 237n15
Leopard, The (Tomasi di Lampedusa), 133
Leopardi, Giacomo, 53, 90
Let's Talk about the Elephant: Fragments of a Diary (Longanesi), 91
Letters of a Novice, The (Piovene), 83
Levi, Carlo, 5–7, 10–12, 14, 26, 31, 66, 118, 140–171, 200–201, 249n20, 250n25, 251n47, 252n55
Levi, Primo, 6, 10, 53, 82, 106, 108–110, 177, 180, 213n41, 217n75, 239n43

Lies and Sorcery (Morante), 10, 25, 98–99, 125–139, 200, 204, 232n30, 247n149
"Likely Autobiography of a Generation" (Debenedetti), 13
Lilli, Virgilio, 36
Liucci, Raffaele, 249n14, 257n8
Loewenthal, Elena, 109
Longanesi, Leo, 24, 32, 91, 120, 125, 230n3
Long Journey, The (Zangrandi), 17, 46
Loren, Sophia, 244n121
Löwy, Michael, 156, 161
Lucian of Samosata, 104
Luftkriegsliteratur, 74, 184
Lukàcs, György, 125, 156, 160
Luperini, Romano, 4, 13
Lussu, Emilio, 143

"Magical and Desolate Lucania" (Branca), 145–146
Magical World, The (De Martino), 13
Magic Mountain, The (Mann), 186
Malaparte, Curzio, 2, 4, 6, 14–17, 24, 26, 31–45, 68, 92–93, 107, 170–197, 220n119, 232n30, 257n8
Malaparte: Lives and Legends (Serra), 173
Man and Partisan (Battaglia), 13
Man as An End (Moravia), 25, 30–31, 52–53
Mangoni, Luisa, 142–143, 214n51
"Manifesto of Anti-Fascist Intellectuals" (Croce), 100
Manifesto of the Communist Party (Marx and Engels), 104
Mann, Thomas, 80, 186
March on Rome, 7, 29, 45
Marx, Karl, 41–42, 45, 101, 104, 160
Marxism, 45, 105, 149, 156, 167, 177, 187, 240n49; Benjamin and, 160; Brancati and, 90; Croce and, 102, 108; history and, 100, 154; imperialism and, 94; C. Levi and, 11, 141, 151; Muscetta and, 169; realist poetics and, 176; utopia and, 104
"Marxism, Culture, and Poetry" (Sapegno), 13
masculinity, 87, 93, 95, 173, 196, 262n94

Maselli, Ercole, 236n5
Masino, Paola, 97, 236n5, 247n152
materialism, historical, 102, 156, 160–161, 168
Mazzini, Giuseppe, 13, 165
Men and Not Men (Vittorini), 66, 115
Meneghello, Luigi, 204
Mercurio (journal), 6, 10–11, 49, 82–83, 97, 116, 215n53, 247n151
messianic redemption, 152–153
Milan, 164
Miłosz, Czesław, 40
modernism, 84, 162, 182
Molotov-Ribbentrop Pact, 30
Monelli, Paolo, 1
Monicelli, Mario, 133
Montale, Eugenio, 148–149
Montanelli, Indro, 17, 24, 32, 36, 38
"Moot Points" (Malaparte), 39
moral regeneration, 66–67
Morante, Elsa, 1–5, 10, 14, 25, 64, 98–99, 108, 118, 125–139, 200, 204, 232n30, 245n127, 246n139, 247nn149,152, 248n161
Moravia, Alberto, 2, 5, 7, 14, 23–25, 30–31, 39–40, 51–63, 67–68, 97, 202, 236n5, 244n121
More, Thomas, 104
Muscetta, Carlo, 143–144, 167–170, 213n39, 249n20, 253n74
Muselmann, 177–178
Mussolini, Benito, 1, 7, 27, 55, 63–64, 67–68, 86, 91, 96–97, 101, 120, 126, 166, 174, 200

Napolitano, Giorgio, 32–33
nationalism, 7, 9, 12, 25, 47, 60–62, 67–68, 70, 90, 98, 103–104, 108, 151–152
Neorealism, 203, 209n8; Berto and, 64; Fascist propaganda and, 2; global reach of, 14; imaginary of, 3–4; impact of, 3; C. Levi and, 11; memoirists and, 13; Morante and, 126–127; Verga and, 76; *The Watch* and, 11
Neue Sachlichkeit, 176
New Encyclopedia (Savinio), 199

Nietzsche, Friedrich, 12, 86, 88, 98, 102, 104–105, 107, 118, 165–166
Nievo, Ippolito, 178
Nocturnal Diary (Flaiano), 244n109
Nogara, Gino, 120
"Notes from a Dream" (Sereni), 70
"Notes on *The Great Dictator*" (C. Levi), 153
Nuova Europa, La (journal), 6, 11, 61, 97–98, 100, 105, 237n13

"On Masses" (Moravia), 63
On the Concept of History (Benjamin), 160–161
On the Genealogy of Morals (Nietzsche), 104
On the Natural History of Destruction (Sebald), 184
On the Uses and Disadvantages of History for Life (Nietzsche), 105
Oresteia (Aeschylus), 189
Orientalism, 122–123
Origins of Totalitarianism, The (Arendt), 155
Orlandini, Roberta, 120–121
Orlando Furioso (Ariosto), 162
Ortega y Gasset, José, 154
Orwell, George, 30
"Our Sin" (Malaparte), 33–34
OVRA operation, 142

Paggi, Leonardo, 21, 184–185, 263n8
Pardini, Giuseppe, 40
Parigi, Giulio, 238n32
Parri, Ferruccio, 8, 55, 62, 96–97, 145, 163
Pascoli, Giovanni, 19, 118
Pastrone, Giovanni, 123
Path to the Spiders' Nests, The (Calvino), 9, 178, 203
Pavese, Cesare, 21, 142–144, 201, 203
Pavone, Claudio, 20
PCI. *See* Italian Communist Party (PCI)
Pedullà, Gabriele, 51
Pedullà, Walter, 106
Periodic Table, The (P. Levi), 106
Piazzesi, Gianfranco, 143
Pintor, Giaime, 8

Piovene, Guido, 6, 15, 23–25, 40, 65, 70, 82–89, 202, 236n5
Pirandello, Luigi, 33, 110–111
Pity against Pity (Piovene), 83, 85–86
Pius XII, Pope, 19–20
Plato, 106
pluralism, 6, 144, 147–148
"Poetry, Philosophy, Psychoanalysis" (Saba), 105
Politecnico, Il (journal), 4, 13, 46, 213n39
"Political Diary" (Moravia), 55–57, 60–64, 97
Ponte, Il (journal), 6, 58
populism, 13, 32, 41, 90, 117, 216n66, 227n76, 261n80
Pratolini, Vasco, 66
Prezzolini, Giuseppe, 2, 15
Primato (journal), 38
Prison Notebooks (Gramsci), 13, 69
Promethean shame, 182
propaganda, Fascist, 2, 6–7, 84, 101. *See also* rhetoric
Prospettive (journal), 33, 37–38, 40–41, 51, 175
psychoanalysis, 105
Ptolemy, 103, 237n24
Purcell, Nicholas, 158–159
Pure Anti-Fascism, 7

racial campaigns, 28
racism, 21, 36, 52, 94, 98, 124, 154–155, 202
"Racism and Idolatry of the State" (C. Levi), 155
Rancière, Jacques, 10–11, 14, 159, 216n67
rationalism, 61, 151
Real Italians, The: A Study in European Psychology (Sforza), 29
reason, 50, 56–57, 59, 89, 187, 190, 192
redemption: collective, 3, 9, 19–20, 49, 188–189, 204; culture of, 193; descent of Christ and, 158; men and, 173; messianic, 152–153; narratives of, 2; political, 66; questioning possibility of, 191
redemptive aesthetics, 86

relativism, 84
religious crisis, national defeat as, 71–82
Remnants of Auschwitz: The Archive and the Witness (Agamben), 177–178
responsibility: ethical, of writing, 68; personal, 20, 65–66, 87–95
Restitutio ad Integrum, 156
"Restless Adolescents" (Savinio), 103–104
"Revolution and Pessimism" (Moravia), 58–60
rhetoric, 82–87, 90, 99, 107, 117, 121, 166, 174–175, 203. *See also* propaganda, Fascist
Ricciardi, Alessia, 209n8
Rinascita (journal), 13, 213n39
riscatto, 3, 8, 128
ritual self-mutilation, 154
Rivoluzione Liberale, 147
Rivoluzione liberale, La (journal), 41
Roman Diary (Brancati), 12, 70, 89, 91–92
Romani, Bruno, 16
Romanità, 29, 95, 164–166, 255nn97–98
Rome, 164–167
Rome 1943 (Monelli), 1
Rome Open City (Rossellini), 3, 16
Rosselli, Carlo, 142, 147
Rosselli, Nello, 142
Rossellini, Roberto, 3, 74, 185, 210n16
Roth, Philip, 109
Rotten Mother (Malaparte), 196–197
Ruozzi, Gino, 236n7, 244n109
Rusconi, Gian Enrico, 219n101
Russian Revolution, 174
Russo, Luigi, 215n60

Saba, Umberto, 5, 7, 9, 12, 25, 98, 101–102, 105–118, 202, 240n57, 241n68, 242n84
sacrifice, 7, 75, 77, 79, 115, 153–154, 173–174, 187–197
Salvati, Mariuccia, 215n53
Salvatorelli, Luigi, 11, 97, 143
Salvemini, Gaetano, 30
Santner, Eric, 22

Sapegno, Natalino, 13, 215n60, 239n49, 240n49, 250n25
Sartre, Jean-Paul, 66, 68, 160, 176
Satta, Salvatore, 15, 251n45
Savinio, Alberto, 6, 40, 97, 102–108, 164, 166, 199, 201–202, 236n5, 238n32, 239nn41,44
Schivelbusch, Wolfgang, 21
Schmitt, Carl, 187
Scholem, Gershom, 156
Schwarz, Guri, 18
Sciascia, Leonardo, 88, 239n45
Sebald, W. G., 74, 184–185
Secondo Risorgimento, 2, 8, 12, 19, 140–141, 189, 212n32
Secret Journal (Malaparte), 182, 187–188
self-mutilation, 153–154, 157
Sereni, Vittorio, 66, 70, 230n4
Serra, Maurizio, 41, 173, 176, 178, 258n27
Serri, Mirella, 69
Sforza, Carlo, 29
Sgorlon, Carlo, 136–137
Sgorlon, Edda, 136–137
Sheehan, James J., 80
Shortcuts and Very Short Stories (Saba), 12, 25, 98, 102, 106, 108–118
Skin, The (Malaparte), 17, 26, 35, 44–45, 92–93, 170–179, 184–197, 200–201, 232n30
Sky Is Red, The (Berto), 16, 24–25, 66, 71–81, 185, 204, 232nn25,30
Smith, William Robertson, 154
socialist realism, 92, 178
Società (journal), 6, 13, 213n39
Society of Jesus, 48
Soldati, Mario, 68, 91, 199
Sorel, Georges, 88
Soviet Union, 30–31, 35–37, 47, 110, 181, 189
Spadolini, Giovanni, 177
Spengler, Oswald, 154
Spinella, Mario, 117
Spinelli, Altiero, 143
Stalin, Joseph, 30
Stampa, La, 33
Steiner, George, 188–189
Stendhal, 71, 166

"Story of a Manuscript" (Malaparte), 175–176
Strozzi, Gianni, 40
subjectivity, 57, 148
Surrealism, 39, 176
Symposium (Plato), 106

Tamburi, Orfeo, 122–123
Tecchi, Bonaventura, 68–69
Technique de coup d'état (Malaparte), 33, 174
Tempo, Il, 16, 42, 46, 89, 164
temporality, 162–164
theocracy, 48, 103, 145
theology, 5, 31, 60, 128, 186–187, 195, 197
Tikkun, 156
Time of Indifference, The (Moravia), 52, 58
Time to Kill, A (Flaiano), 12, 25, 99, 118–125, 133, 202, 204, 244n118
Togliatti, Palmiro, 23, 32, 69, 220n119
Tomasi di Lampedusa, Giuseppe, 133
Tosi, Guy, 177–178
totalitarianism: in Asor Rosa, 27; Christian Democrats and, 220n119; exclusion and, 154; history and, 7; human nature and, 81; Italian experience within, 27–33; in C. Levi, 147, 149–154, 201; in Malaparte, 33–45, 68, 177, 181, 195–196; in Morante, 139; in Moravia, 31, 51–63, 202; origin of term, 27; propaganda and, 6; racism and, 154; in Saba, 115; theocratic, 103; writing and, 69; in Zincone, 32, 45–51. *See also* Fascism
Totalitarian State, The (Zincone), 24, 32, 46–48
tragic genre, 188–189
translations, 178, 232n30, 258n23
Traverso, Enzo, 30
Trouillot, Michel-Rolph, 17
Truce, The (P. Levi), 82
Tumiati, Corrado, 145, 157
Turkey, 19
Two Women (Moravia), 244n121

"Unintential Approach, An" (Berto), 72–73

Unita, l', 40, 151, 220n119
Utopia (More), 104

Valéry, Paul, 189
Verga, Giovanni, 76
Vigorelli, Giancarlo, 66, 151–152, 173
virility, 70, 87, 93, 95, 196. *See also* masculinity
Visconti, Luchino, 3
Vittorini, Elio, 4, 33, 46, 66, 115, 201, 213n39
Viva Caporetto! (Malaparte), 174
Volga Rises in Europe, The (Malaparte), 24, 35–37, 41
Volpe, Gioacchino, 5, 211n20
Voltaire, 107, 166, 239n45
vulgarity, 93–94

Ward, David, 9, 141, 157
War of a Black Shirt, The (Berto), 72
Watch, The (C. Levi), 11, 26, 31, 140, 143, 160–171, 200, 254n86, 255n108
"What the Constitution Lacks" (Zincone), 49–50
Woman of Rome, The (Moravia), 52, 202
Wood, Sharon, 127, 132, 137
Works of God, The (Berto), 71, 75–81, 95
Wydra, Harald, 211n23

Zangrandi, Ruggero, 17, 19, 46
Zanzotto, Andrea, 24, 73, 79, 204
"Zinc" (P. Levi), 239n43
Zincone, Vittorio, 6, 24, 32–33, 45–51
Zunino, Pier Giorgio, 236n3, 251n44

Franco Baldasso is Assistant Professor of Italian and Director of the Italian Program at Bard College. He is Fellow of the American Academy in Rome and co-Director of the Summer School "The Cultural Heritage and Memory of Totalitarianism" at Sapienza University in Rome. His main research interests are twentieth-century literature, art, and intellectual history. His work focuses on the complex relations between Fascism and Modernism, the legacy and memory of political violence in Italy, and the idea of the Mediterranean in modern aesthetics. He has written two books: *Il cerchio di gesso. Primo Levi narratore e testimone* (2007), and *Curzio Malaparte, la letteratura crudele. Kaputt, La pelle e la caduta della civiltà europea* (2019).

World War II: The Global, Human, and Ethical Dimension
G. Kurt Piehler, *series editor*

Lawrence Cane, David E. Cane, Judy Barrett Litoff, and David C. Smith, eds., *Fighting Fascism in Europe: The World War II Letters of an American Veteran of the Spanish Civil War*

Angelo M. Spinelli and Lewis H. Carlson, *Life behind Barbed Wire: The Secret World War II Photographs of Prisoner of War Angelo M. Spinelli*

Don Whitehead and John B. Romeiser, *"Beachhead Don": Reporting the War from the European Theater, 1942–1945*

Scott H. Bennett, ed., *Army GI, Pacifist CO: The World War II Letters of Frank and Albert Dietrich*

Alexander Jefferson with Lewis H. Carlson, *Red Tail Captured, Red Tail Free: Memoirs of a Tuskegee Airman and POW*

Jonathan G. Utley, *Going to War with Japan, 1937–1941*

Grant K. Goodman, *America's Japan: The First Year, 1945–1946*

Patricia Kollander with John O'Sullivan, *"I Must Be a Part of This War": One Man's Fight against Hitler and Nazism*

Judy Barrett Litoff, *An American Heroine in the French Resistance: The Diary and Memoir of Virginia d'Albert-Lake*

Thomas R. Christofferson and Michael S. Christofferson, *France during World War II: From Defeat to Liberation*

Don Whitehead, *Combat Reporter: Don Whitehead's World War II Diary and Memoirs*, edited by John B. Romeiser

James M. Gavin, *The General and His Daughter: The Wartime Letters of General James M. Gavin to His Daughter Barbara*, edited by Barbara Gavin Fauntleroy et al.

Carol Adele Kelly, ed., *Voices of My Comrades: America's Reserve Officers Remember World War II*, foreword by Senators Ted Stevens and Daniel K. Inouye

John J. Toffey IV, *Jack Toffey's War: A Son's Memoir*

Lt. General James V. Edmundson, *Letters to Lee: From Pearl Harbor to the War's Final Mission*, edited by Dr. Celia Edmundson

John K. Stutterheim, *The Diary of Prisoner 17326: A Boy's Life in a Japanese Labor Camp*, foreword by Mark Parillo

G. Kurt Piehler and Sidney Pash, eds., *The United States and the Second World War: New Perspectives on Diplomacy, War, and the Home Front*

Susan E. Wiant, *Between the Bylines: A Father's Legacy*, Foreword by Walter Cronkite

Deborah S. Cornelius, *Hungary in World War II: Caught in the Cauldron*

Gilya Gerda Schmidt, *Süssen Is Now Free of Jews: World War II, The Holocaust, and Rural Judaism*

Emanuel Rota, *A Pact with Vichy: Angelo Tasca from Italian Socialism to French Collaboration*
Panteleymon Anastasakis, *The Church of Greece under Axis Occupation*
Louise DeSalvo, *Chasing Ghosts: A Memoir of a Father, Gone to War*
Alexander Jefferson with Lewis H. Carlson, *Red Tail Captured, Red Tail Free: Memoirs of a Tuskegee Airman and POW, Revised Edition*
Kent Puckett, *War Pictures: Cinema, Violence, and Style in Britain, 1939–1945*
Marisa Escolar, *Allied Encounters: The Gendered Redemption of World War II Italy*
Courtney A. Short, *The Most Vital Question: Race and Identity in the U.S. Occupation of Okinawa, 1945–1946*
James Cassidy, *NBC Goes to War: The Diary of Radio Correspondent James Cassidy from London to the Bulge*, edited by Michael S. Sweeney
Rebecca Schwartz Greene, *Breaking Point: The Ironic Evolution of Psychiatry in World War II*
Franco Baldasso, *Against Redemption: Democracy, Memory, and Literature in Post-Fascist Italy*

www.ingramcontent.com/pod-product-compliance
Lightning Source LLC
Chambersburg PA
CBHW020355080526
44584CB00014B/1019